Organisations,
Competition and the

CENTRE

IVERSI

Pearson Education

We work with leading authors to develop the
strongest educational materials in business and finance,
bringing cutting edge thinking and best learning
practice to a global market.

Under a range of well-known imprints, including
Financial Times Prentice Hall, we craft high quality
print and electronic publications which help
readers to understand and apply their content,
whether studying or at work.

To find out more about the complete range of our
publishing please visit us on the World Wide Web at:
www.pearsoneduc.com

Organisations, Competition and the Business Environment

ANDRÉ CLARK

FINANCIAL TIMES
Prentice Hall

An imprint of **Pearson Education**

Harlow, England · London · New York · Reading, Massachusetts · San Francisco · Toronto · Don Mills, Ontario · Sydney
Tokyo · Singapore · Hong Kong · Seoul · Taipei · Cape Town · Madrid · Mexico City · Amsterdam · Munich · Paris · Milan

Pearson Education Limited
Edinburgh Gate
Harlow
Essex CM20 2JE
England

and Associated Companies throughout the world

Visit us on the World Wide Web at:
http://www.pearsoneduc.com

First published 2000

Many of the designations used by manufacturers and sellers to distinguish their products
are claimed as trademarks. Pearson Education Limited has made every attempt to supply
trademark information about manufacturers and their products mentioned in this book.
A list of trademark designations and their owners appears on this page.

ISBN 0-201-61908-3

British Library Cataloguing-in-Publication Data
A catalogue record for this book is available from the British Library

Library of Congress Cataloging-in-Publication Data
Clark, André.
    Organisation, competition, and the business environment / André
Clark.
        p.   cm.
    Includes bibliographical references and index.
    ISBN 0-201-61908-3
    1. Industrial management—Great Britain.   I. Title.
HD70.G7C55 1999
658'.00941—dc21   99-36577
                                                                        CIP

10 9 8 7 6 5 4 3
06 05 04 03 02

Trademark Notice
BMW is a trademark of BMW AG; Burger King is a trademark of Burger King Corporation,
Creme Egg and Dairy Milk are trademarks of Cadbury Schweppes plc; Jaguar is a trademark
of Jaguar Cars Ltd; Kelloggs is a trademark of Kellogg Company, Kenco is a trademark of
Kraft Jacobs Suchard Ltd; Levi is a trademark of Levi Strauss & Co; Marmite is a trademark
of CPC (UK) Ltd; Mars Bar and Mars Egg are trademarks of Mars, Inc; McDonald's is a
trademark of McDonald's Corporation; Mercedes is a trademark of of Daimler Chrysler AG;
Motorola is a trademark of Motorola, Inc; Nescafé is a trademark of Nestlé; Pentium is a
trademark of Intel Corporation; Rolls-Royce is a trademark of Rolls Royce plc; Rover is a
trademark of Rover Group Limited; Vegemite is a trademark of Kraft Foods Ltd.

Text design by Claire Brodman
Typeset by 35 in 10/12 Plantin Light
Produced by Pearson Education Asia Pte Ltd
Printed in Singapore (MPM)

CONTENTS

PREFACE

Those of us engaged in learning about the business environment, either as educators or as students, face a daunting task. Unlike most other fields of study, we are not asked to look at one dimension of a problem or to cover one approach to dealing with it. Rather, we are expected to consider all the various dimensions of the business environment using a range of approaches. Little wonder then that, despite our best intentions, what we often end up with is descriptive rather than analytical educational outcomes. Ultimately, however, this does not satisfy the requirements of employers who, in increasingly turbulent times, require analytical rather than descriptive skills.

The solution is to develop analytical tools that can be used to investigate the components of the business environment and its effect on firms. In this sense the solution adopted in this text; of using supply and demand analysis, is doubly integrative since the same tool does both. This does not, however, mean that an economic approach is adopted uncritically; refinements, extensions, reductions and indeed criticisms are made where necessary to suit our needs.

The aim of this book is threefold. In the first part it is to develop an understanding of the context in which firms operate and to show how we can predict the effect of changes in that context on firms, using supply and demand analysis. In the second part, the aim is to build a stock of knowledge about the different components of the business environment with particular reference to the UK. In the third part, the aim is to understand how firms analyse their environments and to consider how this should be done in light of what has been learnt in the first two parts.

In Parts 1 and 2 this text covers the whole of the new EdExcel BTEC 'Organisations, competition, and environment' syllabus, which from 2000 will replace existing HND/C 'business environment' courses. It is also suitable as a substitute for standard introductory economics texts for those doing Business Studies at degree level. In addition, Part 3 develops certain themes and ideas that may be used at a higher level and makes the whole package suitable for second and subsequent years of study and for those doing an MBA.

A set of slides to accompany the text is available on request.

Note that throughout this text the term 'firm' is used as shorthand for 'organisation involved in the business world' and as such encompasses a number of organisational forms, including government-run, 'public sector' ones (although, in parts, the peculiarities of the public sector have necessitated additional comments). A list of the different forms is included at the back of the book.

PART 1

Organisations and competition

The aim of this part is to develop an understanding of the context in which firms operate and to show how we can predict the effect of changes in that context on firms. To do this we will utilise the tool of supply and demand analysis:

A NOTE ON METHOD

Before we proceed it is worth noting the distinction between statements of opinion (normative statements) and statements of fact (positive statements), since disagreements on the former might not be resolved by appeal to any data. Economists are very keen on making this distinction, although most would also recognise that facts never speak for themselves but need interpreting by people with opinions on what data is important and why. Nonetheless, it is worth being able to spot the difference as it is only through positive statements that ideas are tested and debates moved on. See if you can spot whether the following statement is a positive or a normative one:

In 1998 there was no one registered as unemployed in the UK.

You might look at that and decide that it is simply wrong, but the fact that you can come to that conclusion is proof that it is a positive statement, for being able to prove it right or wrong is the hallmark of a positive statement. You should not conclude from this discussion that opinions are unimportant, just that statements of opinion cannot be relied on to settle disagreements or move a debate forward.

CHAPTER 1

Introduction

After studying this chapter, you should be able to:

- define the business environment;
- appreciate the role of markets in the business environment, and the advantages of trade;
- appreciate the role of organisations within the business environment;
- appreciate the implications of the coexistence of organisations and markets;
- comprehend the nature of the link between organisations and markets and the significance of this for the analysis of the relationship between organisations and their environments;
- understand that the relationship between organisations and environments is a reciprocal one.

1.1 INTRODUCTION

In looking at the **business environment**, we are concerned with those things that affect a firm but are not a part of the firm. In effect, we are looking at the business jungle in which firms live. One of the keys to survival in this, as in any other type of jungle, is to learn what threats and opportunities exist within it, which is why as a business leader of the future you are asked to read this text. In this sense, it is a pest, not only for you but for businesses too, since life would be simpler without it. It is a pest in another sense too: since it has Political, Economic, Social and Technological dimensions, we often refer to it as the PEST environment. This is, however, not to suggest that these four are the only dimensions of the business environment, and if you prefer a longer acronym, try CONTEXTUALISE. This is harder to remember but it is appropriate since the aim of this book is to put organisations in context; in other words, our purpose *is* to contextualise.

3

C. Competition. All firms face competition of some sort for both customers and resources.

O. Oligarchy. The UK, Europe and much of the world are political oligarchies, which means that there is 'rule by a few'. Organisations are subject to the rules thus made, but can also influence them by bringing pressure to bear on the ruling few.

N. Natural. All resources are ultimately derived from nature and such things as weather and climate can determine the fate of whole industries. In addition, there is a growing concern for environmental destruction in terms of both what is taken out and what we throw back into the ecosphere.

T. Technology. All organisations are influenced by technological changes. Where, for example, would the mighty Microsoft Corporation be without the invention of the computer? And what did that invention do to the manufacturers of typewriters?

E. Economic. The state of the economy, interest rates, exchange rates, and a whole host of environmental influences can be lumped under this heading.

X. Traditionally 'x' indicates the unknown and it is worth remembering that no list can be expected to provide a complete coverage of all the environmental factors that may influence a firm.

T. Training. The amount and type of education and training that an employee has acquired has a direct impact on their productivity. Changes in the provision of education and training provided by governments will therefore affect the productivity of firms, as well as changing the training burden that is placed upon them. Technological and legislative changes also affect the kinds of training that firms have to provide.

U. Unions. Employee legislation, and the power of unions and organised workers have to be taken into account since this affects the price and availability of labour and the nature of work, and even the nature of the firm. The extent of their power and the legislative framework that surrounds them is subject to change depending on the political hue of the government and the prevailing attitude towards their activities.

A. Attitudes and tastes refer to the patterns of likes and dislikes which, while not always explicable, are important and are subject to change.

L. Laws. Traditionally we think of laws as the result of the national political process. However, increasingly in the UK laws affecting firms are the result of a European process that is essentially bureaucratic rather than political, since as yet the European Parliament has a relatively minor role in it.

i. Internet environment. This is an emerging new type of business environment, with its own set of rules and ways of operating, that will have an effect on all firms.

S. Society. Firms are embedded in society; everything they do must be legitimised by society, including their very existence. All kinds of social attitudes, conventions and arrangements affect firms and all are subject to change.

E. Europe. The UK's international trade is now predominately with Europe. In addition, many of our laws come from Europe in the form of 'directives' and there is the possibility that we will join the European single currency in the near future. This would mean that much of the running of the UK economy would be done within Europe too.

We can also visualise the way that the business environment operates in respect of a particular firm by considering the links involved (Figure 1.1).

Figure 1.1 An ice-cream manufacturer's business environment.

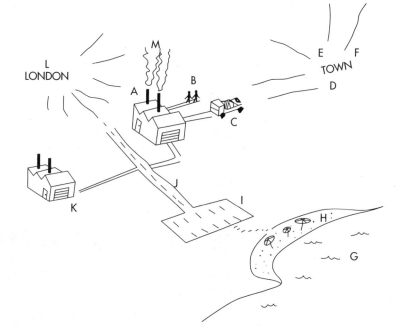

In this illustration a number of links are highlighted:

A. The interest payment on the loan needed to buy the factory is influenced by economic and political factors.

B. Employment laws and a country's culture determine who can work and in what conditions.

C. Suppliers of raw materials (in this case milk, cream, electricity and so on) can, by putting their prices up or down, affect the firm's costs.

D. The local planning authority can veto the firm's plans for expansion of its premises.

E. The local health inspector has the power to close the factory down if it is in serious breach of health and safety regulations.

F. The firm sells its ice-cream to local shops, pubs and restaurants.

G. Sales abroad depend on the exchange rate between currencies and international politics. There is also now a growing tide of legislation originating from the European Union that directly affects firms.

H. Ice-cream sales depend on the weather, and additional sales can be made from the firm's beach-side hut in the summer. Sales are also affected by demography, that is, trends in the size or composition of the population; in this case the biggest consumers tend to be youngsters.

I. The building of a car park by the council near the beach may increase summer trade.

J. Technological infrastructure and laws relating to transportation and communications affect how the firm operates, and its choice of location.

K. The number and behaviour of competitors will affect the firm and what our firm does will affect them.

L. Much of the legislature that affects firms originates in parliament in London.

M. The amount of pollution permitted is governed by legislation and is influenced by cultural attitudes regarding the exploitation of the natural environment.

The fact that this firm, like every other firm, has many links to its environment has two implications. Firstly, that it is open to a number of external influences. Secondly, that what the firm does impinges on a variety of groups outside the firm as well as those within it. This means that people both inside the firm and outside the firm have a stake in what it does.

1.2 STAKEHOLDERS

The different groups within the firm that we count as **internal stakeholders** include the managers and the workers. These groups have a big stake since for most of them, working for the firm will be their primary source of income. We also count owners as internal stakeholders, since in the private sector the firm generates income for them in the profits that it makes. In the public sector, we also include the government since in this case it acts as the owner, taking any income generated and financing any deficits that arise from the activities of organisations in that sector. Other groups in the business environment can be categorised as **external stakeholders**. These include the customers and suppliers who have a stake in the success of the firm since they benefit from selling to it, or buying from it. The general public can also be seen as a stakeholder in the firm since the firm's activities can impact upon the community in all manner of indirect ways. If, for example, the firm generates pollution then people in the community will be adversely affected by its activities even if they have never worked for it, sold to it, or bought from it. Finally, we should include the government as an 'external stakeholder' for private sector firms as well as an 'internal stakeholder' for public sector ones. It is an 'external stakeholder' for private sector firms as it acts as a customer, regulator, and in some cases subsidiser, to many of them.

Having looked at the relationship between a firm and its environment in terms of who is involved, we will now look at it in terms of what is involved. In other words, we will look at the role of firms within the business environment.

1.3   THE ROLE OF FIRMS IN THE BUSINESS ENVIRONMENT

In a modern consumer society, like the UK, the resources used to produce things, the **factors of production** as they are called, are insufficient to provide us with all the things we want. These factors of production encompass all forms of labour effort, land and other natural resources, capital resources such as machines, factories and offices, and knowledge. Often this last one is omitted, but as Alfred Marshall, (1842–1924), the man perhaps above all others responsible for defining the scope and method of modern economics, wrote in 1890, 'capital consists in a great part of knowledge and organisation'. He goes on to conclude that we should therefore count organisation, or knowledge, 'as a distinct agent of production' (1956, p. 115). Indeed for Marshall: 'Knowledge is our most powerful engine of production; it enables us to subdue nature and force her to satisfy our wants.' (op. cit.) We tend to think of the entrepreneur as the person whose knowledge and effort are used to combine the other factors and create the things we want, but more generally it is organisations that do this, so in that sense all organisations are entrepreneurial to one degree or another. But, however these factors are combined, a fundamental problem remains; there simply is not enough land, labour, capital and knowledge to go around. For although there are vast amounts of each in the world, they are scarce when set against all the things we desire, such as goods (like cars and TVs) and services (like entertainment and education), that they can be used to create (Figure 1.2).

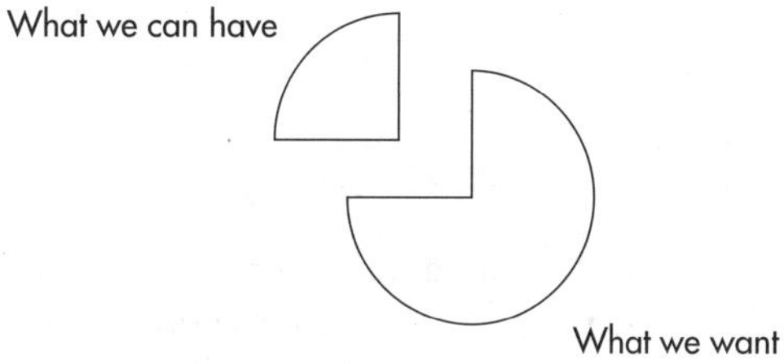

Figure 1.2 Resources are scarce relative to our wants.

What we can have

What we want

If we cannot have all the things that we want then we have to decide upon three things. Firstly, we have to decide what to produce, for if we cannot produce everything some things must be given priority. Secondly, we have to decide how to produce the things we want, bearing in mind that wasting resources will mean fewer of our wants being met. Thirdly, it means deciding who will get the things we make. Making these decisions is, in practice, a mammoth task; in terms of the first decision alone, the complexity involved is enormous since everyone has their own list of things they want, both for themselves and for society, and in addition, these things are subject to daily revision as priorities change. The task of coordinating all these decisions has been approached in different ways in different societies. In the Soviet Union, choices were expressed in detailed plans drawn up by bureaucrats (civil servants), working for the state. In such 'centrally planned' or 'command' economies the sheer volume of work creates a problem, so that in practice the list of priorities becomes too few and too rigidly set to satisfy the vast majority. Leon Trotsky, one of the founders of the Soviet system, anticipated the problem when he wrote that 'only a universal mind . . . could draw up a faultless economic plan'. In contrast, a **free market** economy is one in which no central planning occurs and choices are made in a decentralised way by millions of participants making their views known on a daily basis through the price mechanism of 'markets'. A market being any arrangement whereby the price of something is agreed and a trade occurs, which can vary from a street market in which the trading is done face to face, to types of international automated trading that are done without any human intervention at all. The one feature that all markets have in common is that there are both buyers and suppliers, as without both of them being present a market cannot form.

The major coordinating agent in a market system is the privately owned firm, rather than bureaucrats, since firms act as the link between markets, and thus ultimately between wants and resources. Firms do this by acting as buyers to forge **factor markets** with the capitalists, workers and landowners, who supply the inputs to the firm. At the same time, firms create markets for goods and services by supplying their output to meet the demands of consumers (Figure 1.3).

Figure 1.3 The role of firms in the business environment.

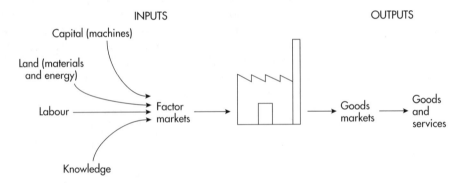

If there are a lot of firms actively competing for resources and customers, three benefits of free markets come about. The first of these is that consumers determine what is produced simply by buying products, since if there is competition for customers firms will respond to this signal by producing more, which is often referred to as **consumer sovereignty** as it means that firms obey the wishes of consumers. This is beneficial to society insofar as the public get to decide on the 'What to Produce?' issue. A second benefit is that with competition the market process ensures that firms that produce the same product cheaper than their rivals, or for the same price produce something better, win the custom. In effect, therefore, the firms that are most efficient at turning inputs into outputs win. This is a benefit to society as it means that those firms with the best answer to the 'How to Produce' question get to answer it. Thirdly, and more controversially, it can be argued that markets answer the question of 'Who to Produce For' in a way that benefits society insofar as it encourages productive effort. With markets the question of who gets the output is determined by how much money a consumer has, with those that own most getting most say in this. This is clearly inequitable, but if markets work perfectly the wealth of a consumer is determined by the value of their labour (or other factor that they own), which means that wealth reflects the value of someone's contribution to the productive process. This is controversial because it suggests that someone's contribution to society can be measured solely by his or her contribution to production and it ignores the role of inheritance in determining the distribution of wealth. In addition, markets, even highly competitive ones, seldom work perfectly and their shortcomings in practice are one of the reasons why most countries, including the UK, have large government-run public sectors. This gives rise to the expression **a mixed economy**, since both free markets and central planning are present.

Although different societies have answered the 'what', 'how' and 'who' questions in different ways, there has, in recent decades, been a marked decline in the popularity of central planning. This has been apparent both in the collapse of central planning in Russia and Eastern Europe and in the increasing use of markets in the public sectors of mixed economies, including the UK. This means that we can utilise the analysis of how markets work (which we shall examine in the first part of this book) to investigate the environments of public sector organisations as well as private sector ones. The main difference is that the indicators of performance in the public sector will tend to be based on things other than profits, which is the key indicator in the private sector. However, as we shall see, all indicators point to essentially the same thing – efficiency.

Whether the choices made reflect the wishes of planners or consumers, it is the fact that resources are relatively scarce that makes choosing necessary. The implication of this is that every time we decide to have more of one thing we are simultaneously making a decision to have less of something else, since using resources for the purpose selected means that fewer resources are available for other purposes. Indeed this is the real cost to society of economic decisions. The value of the next best alternative, the one that is not chosen, is called the **opportunity cost**, as it is the cost of an opportunity forgone. Valuing this for a firm's activities is complicated and is seldom done by a firm's accountants; however, economists have to consider it since it reflects the true costs of business decisions, with which economists are concerned. Even decisions in your own daily life may reflect this hidden cost. For example, your choice about whether to attend an early morning lecture or not may involve weighing the benefits of the knowledge gained against the costs of attending. These costs may include lost earnings if you have a job, in which case an actual cost can be calculated, or it may simply be the cost of staying in bed, which does not entail any actual payment but nonetheless has a value to you. Indeed, if you go to a party the previous night the value of this may increase to such an extent that the opportunity cost of it exceeds the benefit of the lecture and you decide not to go.

1.4 THE ADVANTAGES OF TRADE

In the modern world people have to engage in trade because everyone has such specialised jobs and few of us have enough land to provide sufficient food to ensure our own survival if we decide not to trade. However, even in cases where we could survive without it there are still advantages to trade. In fact specialisation reflects the extensive benefits of trade rather than any conspiracy to channel people into narrowly defined roles, as we would all be considerably poorer without it. Indeed, even if someone is better at everything than anyone else it is still worth their specialising in what they do best and engaging in trade to acquire the rest of what they need. Consider, for example, a newly married couple, David and Victoria, who find that Victoria is better at both washing up and cooking as indicated by the following timings:

	David	Victoria
Washing up	*35 mins*	*10 mins*
Cooking	*25 mins*	*20 mins*
Total:	*1 hour*	*30 mins*

Victoria's superiority means that if she cooks and washes up her own stuff she can be sat in front of the TV or out clubbing, while David is still doing his washing up. She will nonetheless benefit from trading with David despite her 'absolute advantage' in both activities. To see why, we need to look at the relative opportunity costs of the tasks (as measured by time) for the activities:

	David	Victoria
Washing up	*35/25 (1.4)*	*10/20 (0.5)*
Cooking	*25/35 (0.7)*	*20/10 (2)*

For Victoria, since cooking takes twice as long as washing up, it has double the opportunity cost. However, although David is not as good at either, he is relatively better at cooking than washing up, so for him the opportunity cost is only 0.7, which is less than Victoria's opportunity cost of 2. In other words, David has a 'comparative advantage' in cooking. This means that if they trade by swapping chores, with David doing the cooking for both of them and Victoria the washing up, they will both gain. If David does all the cooking, he will spend 50 minutes in total, rather than 1 hour, and if Victoria does all the washing up, she will only spend 20 minutes in total rather than 30 minutes. Both will therefore gain 10 minutes from trading chores. If money needs to be used to facilitate the exchange then the fair price will reflect the opportunity cost, and as we shall see in Chapter 5, if there is completely open access to resources and markets work perfectly, prices will equate to opportunity cost.

In this light, we can see that trade is a form of mutually beneficial collaboration. This is of course a very simplified example; in reality, cooking for two is not twice as time consuming as cooking for one, for reasons that we shall look at in Chapter 3. In addition, even in considering such a mundane example we should not ignore the effect of the environmental context of these economic decisions. In this case, we find that in many marriages it is expected that women will do more of the chores even if both partners work full time. This means that when we look at the division of household chores, what we observe is not necessarily evidence of mutually beneficial exchange but evidence of the use of power.

1.5   WHY ORGANISATIONS AND MARKETS COEXIST

The workings of the price mechanism mean that in effect markets organise exchange without the intervention of bureaucratic hierarchies and other trappings of formal organisations, so why are they necessary at all?

For many sociologists and political scientists, firms arise because of unequal access to resources that occur from the political and social process of a society, in our case of Capitalism (so named because traditionally those who owned capital took charge of the organisation of production in return for profit, although increasingly it is organised by firm's managers). To understand how this happens means investigating the unfolding of power relationships through history. However, not everyone accepts that firms need to be explained in terms of politics, power, or relationships between people as political and social theorists picture it. For some, such as Alchian and Demsetz (1972) and a number of other economists, the distinction between firms and markets is a false one. They argue that, for example: 'Telling an employee to type this letter rather than to file that document is like my telling a grocer to sell me this brand of tuna rather than that brand of bread' (1972, p. 777). As you might imagine, this is a more popular view with economists than with sociologists and political theorists engaged in the study of firms, since it suggests that they need not bother because economists have already explained it in their analysis of markets. For people like Alchian and Demsetz the only difference between firms and other forms of markets is that firms tend to have longer-term exchange arrangements, in particular employment contracts. But even in respect of labour this difference is not significant because the exchange is as equal as buying bread, as the employer can no more be seen as exerting power over the worker to type a letter than the employee can be seen to be coercing the employer into paying their wage. Similarly, while the firm can dismiss the worker, the worker can dismiss the firm too; indeed it is more common for workers to leave than to be sacked.

On the other hand, many economists accept that there is a fundamental difference between markets and firms, but believe that as well as historical, social and political reasons, there is also a logical reason why firms exist, because they do something that markets do not do well. In this approach, firms are a logical response to a market failure. As Coase (1937) argued, the reason a trader needs 'to establish a firm would seem to be that there is a cost of using the price mechanism' (1937, p. 390). In other words, that there is a cost involved in actually using markets, that is, in actually doing the transacting. Coase (1960) points to a number of these **transaction costs**, including the costs of gathering information on who to trade with and on what basis to deal, as well as the legal costs of drawing up contracts and the like. In addition, there are the costs of policing the contract, that is, of ensuring that all parties to the trade get what they thought they were going to get. In this approach firms are more efficient than markets when the cost of using a hierarchical organisation is less than the cost of doing the same thing using markets. Several factors are likely to favour this. Firstly, if there are lots of steps in the production process, the multitude of exchanges needed will incur costs in excess of a planning and contracts-based formal organisation. For example, putting a burger in a bun may seem a relatively simple operation, but when you consider the number of transactions needed to achieve it, even just the bun bit, it becomes clearer why we need firms: to create the simple bun without firms would involve the purchase of wheat from the wheat market, yeast from the yeast market, salt from the salt mines, and so on. So, even for the small amount of buns each individual requires in a day, it would be a virtually impossible daily task, and there are then further transaction costs in actually baking them, involving the creation of electricity and heat and so on. A second factor likely to make the market approach more costly is if the market is too 'thin', that is, if too few trades occur for the price mechanism to work, in which case formal organisation is called for. Thirdly, if the market is turbulent then firms may have advantages insofar as formal organisation will establish boundaries between the relatively volatile and uncertain market and the stable and predictable world of personal obligations, loyalty, duty, careers, teamwork, and shared cultures. Whether, however, all these bulwarks against the vagaries of the market can be conceptualised as a type of cost remains to be seen. This matters, because if they cannot then we must look to the historical unfolding of power, to the very history of capitalist society itself, to explain the existence of firms.

1.6 OVERVIEW OF MAJOR HISTORICAL PATTERNS IN THE UK BUSINESS ENVIRONMENT

Advances in communications and information technology coupled with the increasing globalisation of competition mean that some of the most advanced economies are specialising more and more in the production of intangibles; in the production, for example, of information, and new technologies and new products that relate to this. Indeed, already in the UK the output of the financial sector, which is essentially intangible, exceeds that of the manufacture of tangible goods. Increasingly people talk of the emergence of the 'weightless' economy, or simply a 'knowledge-driven economy', as the next stage of specialisation of production for us. Broad 'sectoral shifts' of this sort imply a change in the basis of competitive advantage and some suggested implications are shown in Figure 1.4 for the general pattern in the UK.

Figure 1.4 Main engines of production in the UK over the past three centuries.

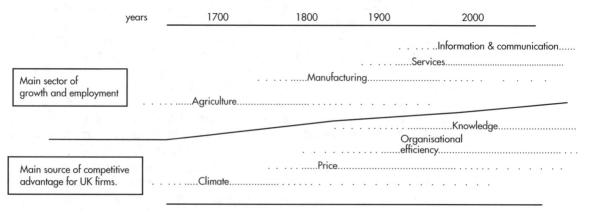

To talk of sectoral shifts and single sources of competitive advantage is very crude, of course, but certain broad-brush implications do arise which are worth at least considering as pointers to the changes that are afoot.

Firstly, as the pace of change accelerates, whole new ranges of products are emerging; the mobile phone for example has in a decade become the biggest selling consumer durable of all time. An accelerated rate of change is likely to mean that innovation will prove to be an ever more important engine of growth, and key to business success across all sectors rather than just a few as at present. Secondly, the skill of the entrepreneur is likely to become more important; as more threats and opportunities arise, those firms with the ability to turn them into wealth-creating activities will have the greatest competitive advantage. Thirdly, the need to retain, develop and exploit knowledge assets will become more important; this may be good for workers since they may be one of the most crucial of such assets. However, workers will remain in competition with each other both nationally and internationally so no predictions of a golden age for UK workers in general can reasonably be made. Fourthly, national success will continue to depend on governments providing firms with macroeconomic stability, an educated workforce, assistance in general training and in supplying 'blue sky' research and ensuring a low, and stable, cost of capital for investment purposes.

1.7   THE ECONOMICS OF THE INFORMATION AGE

Given that we may be entering a new era, it is worth reflecting on whether the tools we are going to discuss in this book, the tools of the economist, are up to the task of analysing the new order. Current models of management and economics were developed in the era of heavy industry to describe that world. In the opinion of some, that makes them singularly inappropriate today since we are at the dawn of the post-industrial society, of the information age, when the key to success will be the use of information to create knowledge. In this world, those with the best knowledge acquisition and knowledge management skills will have the competitive advantage over those efficient merely in the use of land, labour and capital. The problem for economists is that information is not scarce in the same way that land, labour and capital are. This is a problem since economics is about scarcity, because it is the fact that something is not freely available that makes the economic activities of production, distribution and exchange necessary. None of these are necessary for a free good like air (although pollution may change that); we do not have to make it or take it to the consumer, and we cannot exchange it for money. This means that no firms need be involved in it and no one makes any money out of it. Traditionally it has been hard to think of examples, since as a society we tend to use everything (indeed, even air can be bought). It would be somewhat ironic, t herefore, if the future of our economy becomes dominated by the kind of resources that economists have for so long found it difficult to find examples of, and about which they have little to say. Fortunately for economists, while knowledge is qualitatively different from other resources, it is scarce, since even if we were to acknowledge that raw facts must exist out there in infinite abundance, nothing is obvious; everything is processed. So while knowledge may be a resource it is also undeniably a product too and as such it must be scarce in the economists' definition of the word. Indeed, not only is there a production process involved in making the world meaningful, but also once created, knowledge has to be distributed and exchanged. Nonetheless, knowledge becomes the ascendant resource then that is a big enough change in the business environment in itself. However, in addition, we have to acknowledge that it is different: firstly we have to recognise that it has some of the properties of what economists refer to as a public good, which makes it a 'mixed' good, being neither purely a private good nor an entirely public good. The key difference between information and other goods or services is that it can be sold without reducing the seller's stock of it. In other words it can be both kept and given away. This is one of the characteristics of a public good that we shall look at in Chapter 8, where we will find that as a result the good in question becomes undervalued. In this case, it means that firms will tend to undervalue the stock of knowledge that they own. They may also undervalue it in exchange since buying it does not guarantee any advantage. In addition, where it does produce an advantage, since exclusive rights over knowledge are not guaranteed, the advantage may be easily imitated and lost. This applies equally to knowledge kept within the firm since this is still exchanged if not sold as such. Secondly, it is in the nature of it that it will be of radically different value to different people, (this is true of everything, of course, but at least when we produce cars we have an idea of what kind of people will like what kind of car.) This means that producing knowledge out of information can be somewhat hit and miss; this is where theories come into play to point us in the direction of the 'right' information. The final major difference is that knowledge can be distributed at very low cost. This means that in terms of distribution, issues of 'how' and 'why' will dominate over issues of cost economies.

These differences between knowledge and other factors of production mean, for example, that the emerging Internet environment, being information based, represents a new type of business environment with new rules and practices. In the Internet environment the distinction between firms is much less clearly defined than elsewhere, with firms sharing sites, having links within pages to other sites, even those of rivals. Indeed the idea of a firm as a network of relationships is most clearly observed in this environment. The distinction between products and services is also harder to observe in this environment, since a lot of the searching involves a sale to an advertiser using the searched pages to promote their products. For example, not so long ago finding a book that was not available from the few hundred kept at the local book shop often involved the use of a specialist service to search for the book. Thereafter, numerous phone calls and possibly a trip to the library to enlist their help may also have been needed, and finally, if you were lucky the purchase of the book would occur, but not from anyone with whom you had thus far dealt. In contrast, the whole process can now be done from one Web page on the Internet. The searching of a database of several million books, the payment by credit card number and the delivery arrangements can all now be arranged in moments, from the comfort of your own keyboard. Delivery is still done by post, rather than electronically, because people like the feel and portability of books and because of the difficulty of holding on to, and thus earning money from, the text, if it becomes computer code. In the future, of course, suppliers will find new ways of making money from stories (as with all information on the net), as books cannot ultimately escape encoding any more than records and films can.

1.8 MANAGING THE ENVIRONMENT

The business environment is by definition outside of the day-to-day control of the firm. This is not to say, however, that firms have no influence upon it; in the modern world firms are a powerful force within society, and as such are in a reciprocal relationship with their environment. In other words, it influences them, and they influence it. The simplest way in which a firm can attempt to influence its environment is to publicise and advertise its products, but it can be done in more subtle and pervasive ways than that. Firms can, for example, make entirely new markets by making new products and creating the need in consumers to have whatever it is. At the extreme, firms can take charge of a part of the business environment and thereby make it a part of the firm. In the Third World, firms can take over the running of the entire state, but even in the First World firms can internalise parts of their environment by acquiring suppliers, or taking over rival firms. Firms can also 'capture' those who are appointed to oversee their activities, such as government-appointed regulators, by wining and dining them until they see things the firm's way. Firms can even affect broad social attitudes; at its least subtle, they can do this simply by the use of advertising and product placement. Firms can also influence the political and legal environments through all manner of formal and informal links with politicians; in the case of insurance, for example, firms have played a part in making governments pass laws that make it illegal not to use their products. How exactly a firm gets its case across in the political arena depends on the firm and the constitutional arrangements of the country concerned and on the political hue of the government. Currently in the UK, the main links are through politicians who act as advisors to particular firms and through lobbyists who utilise their political contacts for firms in return for a fee. The influence of any one firm or industry may be limited but collectively firms form an important lobby. For example, drinks manufacturers played a part in the lengthening of pub opening hours and the big retailers were influential in changing the rules on Sunday trading. Even academics, who, as a group, stress their impartiality, are not exempt from the persuasive powers of firms. Some scientists, for example, were paid to do research into the effect of smoking by tobacco firms and found less harmful effects than other researchers, while in the early 1980s there were considerable funds available from house-builders to show the strength of the desire for private property ownership amongst the public. One of the reports funded in this way found that people who moved from renting to owning tended to become more likely to vote Conservative; this report was unsurprisingly taken up as further proof of the desirability of home ownership by the Conservative government of the day. The suppliers of private housing thereby encouraged the policy of home ownership and ultimately the demand for their own product in a round about way. This is not to imply any organised conspiracy, simply to show that firms, while often having to accept some things as beyond their control and work within them, nonetheless seek to control their environments and influence their stakeholders too.

Managing the business environment case study

THE POWER OF TOBACCO FIRMS

In the 1930s, 1940s and 1950s, tobacco manufacturers cultivated links with major film stars and this undoubtedly contributed to the widespread perception of smoking as glamorous. Ultimately, however, this attitude changed as medical reports, beyond tobacco firms' control, showed the link between smoking and cancer. However, although the link between smoking and cancer is a biological one and therefore as such entirely beyond the control of the tobacco firms, they have nonetheless played a major part in delaying the dissemination of this finding and are currently being sued by cancer sufferers for their part in that concealment. Ultimately the facts have become well known and, although industry revenues in the UK alone top £10bn per annum, the major tobacco firms are feeling the effects of a change in attitude to their product. In Europe and the USA, there has been a significant decline in smoking amongst adults, particularly men, over the past 20 years. This decline has three aspects: firstly, fewer people are smoking, secondly, those who smoke are smoking less, and thirdly, those who smoke are smoking lower tar brands. The decline is largely associated with health fears. The publication of research showing a link between smoking and cancer was ultimately fairly conclusive and has led to a decline in smoking in many countries. There is also an increasingly antagonistic reaction against smoking because of fears over 'passive smoking' as there is growing evidence that there are health risks associated with being near smokers too. Currently in the UK this has led to the division of restaurants into smoking and non-smoking and changes of that ilk, but in the USA it has gone further, with the banning of smoking in public places even if there is no fire risk and it is outdoors. On the other hand, there is growth in sales in areas of the world where restrictions on tobacco are less than in the West, such as

Africa, South America, parts of the Far East, and the former Soviet bloc. There is also continued targeting of youth in the West by the major producers. This takes a number of forms. Formal advertising is banned but product placement is not, so tobacco firms are keen to get top stars to smoke their products both on and off screen. Manufacturers are also aware of the fact that smoking acts as an appetite suppressant and that young girls, in particular, may see this as one reason to take it up. To keep this association in their mind, many manufacturers have done deals with the waif-like supermodels who adorn the glossy women's magazines and the catwalks of the world to smoke their brand exclusively (and publicly). Indeed, it now seems to be commonly accepted within the industry that, in the West at least, young girls are an easier target than young men. Youngsters in general are particularly important for growth in this industry; because of the addictive nature of the product, a considerable, if not life long, habit can be established at an early age. Firms have also been keen to sponsor sporting events, particularly those that appeal to the young, although they have been banned from many aspects of football and there have been moves to ban their involvement elsewhere. There have recently, for example, been attempts to ban their involvement in Formula 1 motor racing. However, these attempts seem to be floundering and it has been suggested that this may in part be due to a financial contribution from the head of Formula 1 to the Labour Party, although this has been vigorously denied and the money returned. In addition, the power of the firms means that while there are threats that all advertising by tobacco firms will be outlawed within Europe, the EU also provides massive subsidies for the growing of tobacco in the southern European states.

1.9 SUMMARY

- We can break up the context of organisations into elements and give them common-sense labels, such as the 'political environment', while recognising that all these elements interact to form a complex multidimensional web.

- Trade has advantages, which means that all organisations interact with each other and with the wider community that constitutes their business environment.

- The major form of trade is through markets, which means that markets are the link between the business world and the individual organisation, and as such are crucial to our analysis.

- Organisations have different stakeholders to whom they are responsible and so not only are they a part of the social and economic collective, they also have a degree of responsibility to that collective.

- Firms are in a reciprocal relationship with the business environment, as it influences them and they influence it.

1.10 QUESTIONS

1. Why do we need firms?

2. What do you understand by the term the 'business environment'?

3. (a) What opportunity cost do you incur by deciding to do this course?
   (b) What is the link between opportunity cost and business decisions?

   nists make a distinction between normative and positive statements?

   term 'mixed economy' refer to?

   estions of what to produce, for whom to produce, and how to pro-
   d in a free market economy?

CHAPTER 2

Demand

After studying this chapter, you should be able to:

- define demand and be able to represent it in terms of a demand curve;
- understand how and why demand curves shift;
- appreciate why economists are attached to neo-classical consumer theory;
- appreciate the link between demand and a firm's revenue;
- understand the concept of price elasticity of demand, its determinants, and its implications for running a firm;
- understand the concept of cross price elasticity of demand, its determinants, and its implications for running a firm;
- understand the concept of income elasticity of demand, its determinants, and its implications for running a firm.

2.1 INTRODUCTION TO THE ANALYSIS OF MARKETS

There are two sides to any market. On one side we have the buyers who want the good or service, or who want to use the factor. On the other side, there are the suppliers who have made the good or service, or who own the factors and are willing to sell them. These days the trading is facilitated by the use of money, as without money people would have to barter things directly; with people doing very specialised tasks these days, this would be disastrous because most of us have very little to swap. A lecturer, for example, would be hard pressed to find a farmer willing to swap food for lectures. The relative inefficiency of barter became apparent in Germany in the 1920s, when the monetary system broke down and people began to starve because so little trade occurred. Money enables people to swap their factors of production for goods and services in an indirect way, with workers, for example, trading their labour for money, which they then trade for goods and services.

A sale occurs when a price is agreed, so when we look at how markets work we will focus on the mechanism by which prices are agreed. This entails looking at how much would be sold at different prices from both the buyer's and supplier's perspective. Looking at the relationship between prices and sales will also allow us to build a picture of the effect of changes in the business environment on firms' prospects for survival insofar as such changes affect a firm's profits. This is because the price and quantities of a firm's inputs determine its costs, and the price and quantities of a firm's output determine its revenues, and profit is simply revenue minus cost (Figure 2.1).

Figure 2.1 Revenues, costs and profits.

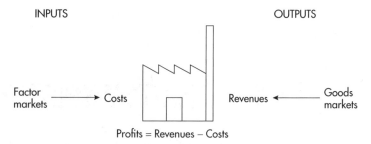

We will begin by looking at demand, in particular at the demand for firms' output.

2.2 DEMAND

We will begin our investigation of the determination of how much will be sold at different prices by looking at the relationship between price and the quantity that buyers are willing and able to buy, which is termed 'demand'. This means that we are ignoring all the desires that people have that are not backed by money, and pushing to the back of our minds any consideration of the social and psychological determinants of those desires. In looking at the relationship between price and demand, one clear pattern emerges: buyers are willing to buy more when prices are low, as long as we are talking about the same product (with no changes in its characteristics or quality). There are two reasons for this. Firstly, there is an obvious **substitution effect**, which is that our preference for a good that has gone down in price will rise, as it comes to represent more value for money than goods whose prices remain unchanged. The second effect, the **income effect**, is not so obvious. This relates to the fact that when the price of a good falls, buying the same amount of it will effectively make the buyer richer, by leaving them more income for other things. One of those other things that they can then afford more of is the good in question, so more may be bought (although not always, as we shall see later in this chapter). In fact, the tendency for more to be bought when the price is low is called the **law of demand** because exceptions are so rare. We can represent this idea in a graph (Figure 2.2), with higher prices producing a relatively low level of demand like point A, and a lower price producing a higher level of demand like point B. (The dotted lines are simply to draw your eye to the relevant parts of the graph).

Figure 2.2 The relationship between demand and price.

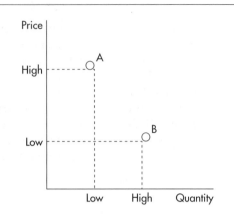

2.3   DEMAND CURVES

The same rule applies for any number of points between and beyond A and B, and ultimately we can envisage filling in all the gaps to produce a line that we call a demand curve, which shows what would be bought at different prices. (Although in practice such neatness is seldom found, unless you know the details of the pattern straight lines are preferred for the sake of simplicity).

The demand curve (Figure 2.3) shows us what buyers will do when suppliers lower or raise the price at which they are willing to supply the good. In looking at demand, we have to be clear about the time frame involved, that is, whether we are looking at demand in a week, a month or a year, as clearly the quantities involved will be different for each. We therefore formally define a demand curve as a 'series of points representing the amount that would be bought at different prices within a given period'.

Figure 2.3 The demand curve.

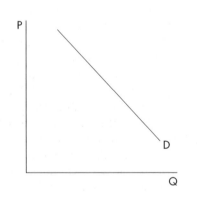

We can add individual demands together to get the **market demand curve**, as this is simply the sum of the individual ones. This means that the market demand curve will look like the individual ones from which it is constructed, except that it will involve bigger numbers on the Q axis, as shown in Table 2.1.

Table 2.1

Price	At this price customer x said they would buy in a week	At this price customer y said they would buy in a week	Total that would be bought at that price
£4	0	0	0
£3	1	1	2
£2	2	2	4
£1	3	3	6

Graphically this gives a market demand curve that looks similar to the individual ones; indeed, in practice market demand curves may be smoother than individual ones since idiosyncrasies tend to cancel out (Figure 2.4).

Figure 2.4 Deriving the market demand curve.

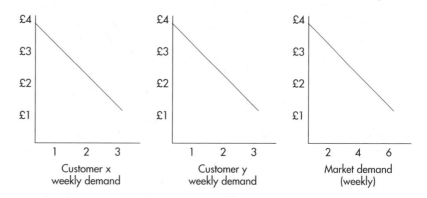

This principle of similarity allows us to use essentially the same diagram regardless of whether we are referring to individuals or to markets involving millions of individuals, which is very convenient.

2.4   SHIFTING THE DEMAND CURVE

Figure 2.5 shows that when a company lowered the price of their packet tea from £1.95 per 250g packet to £1.49 per pkt, sales increased from 13,000 pkts a week to 25,000 a week. The act of cutting the price revealed the demand curve and, as expected, more people wanted to buy more of their tea when the price was low. In this case, rather than use market research and ask people what they would buy if prices were lower, the supplier actually lowered prices and in this way revealed a part of the demand curve.

However, we cannot be sure that this is a demand curve because something else could have helped increase demand between the two weeks to which the figures relate. Suppose, for example, that when they lowered their prices it was announced that drinking tea slows the rate of hair loss in men then more tea would be demanded. The law of demand would still apply; if prices fell, even more would be demanded, so the demand curve is still downward sloping but

Figure 2.5 A demand
curve revealed?

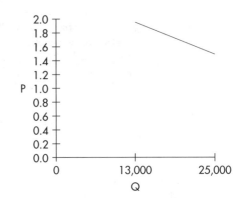

demand would be greater at each and every price. In effect, the demand curve
would have shifted to the right and what we observe in Figure 2.5 would therefore be a mish-mash of a movement down the demand curve and a shift in it.

In fact, anything that changes demand other than a change in price gives
us a new demand curve. This means that whenever we draw a demand curve
we must assume that other things are remaining equal (often denoted by the
Latin term *ceteris paribus*). Whether this is a sensible assumption is a matter
of judgement. This judgement can be based on one of three things. Firstly,
the firm can apply some common sense. Everyone in an ice-cream firm, for
example, may know that ice-cream sales go up in summer and therefore that
cutting prices in early summer would be a bad way of trying to find the demand
curve as at that time it would be a moving target. The problem with common
sense is that it provides only rough guides and can be based on unwarranted
assumptions. Secondly, firms can employ the statistical techniques discussed
in Chapter 15 to identify the position of the demand curves for its products;
the problem with this is that it is difficult to do well. Finally, the firm can use
market research. The problem with finding the demand curve from sales data
is that the data is collected over time, and over time circumstances change, and
the longer the time frame, the more they are likely to change. Market research
can get around this simply by asking people what they would do in response
to a price change taken in unchanged circumstances. The problem with this
approach is that people seldom do what they say they will, not necessarily because
they are lying but simply because it is hypothetical. Since each approach has
its limitations, we find that in practice many firms use common sense born
of experience in combination with statistical analysis of past sales data and
market research to estimate demand.

Once we have found the demand curve we can then include all the other
things in the world that affect demand in our analysis by seeing how they shift it.
A shift in the demand curve to the left means less would be demanded at each
price and a shift to the right means more demand at each price. For example,
at a price of £1.50 a pub finds that it can sell about 100 pints of lager on
a Friday night; this rises to 150 when United are playing at home, and falls to
only 50 when United are playing away. The reason is that demand shifts in
response to the fans either being in town or away, as shown in Figure 2.6.

Figure 2.6 Sales of lager in one pub on a Friday night.

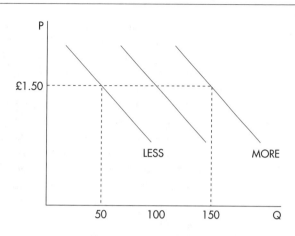

Many things will cause demand to shift; the only thing that definitely cannot is a change in price, since that moves us up or down the line. Because there are so many possibilities, we need to group them together:

1. Tastes: A change in tastes or fashion can produce a rightward shift if the change is a favourable one. An unfavourable change will result in a leftward shift.

2. Persuasion: Advertising and other marketing efforts should produce a rightward shift. This is one way in which suppliers try to influence demand, to, in effect, 'manage' their customer environment. Bad publicity or even occasionally duff advertising can produce a leftward shift.

3. Substitutes: A rise in the price of a substitute, that is, something that could be used instead of the good or factor in question, will produce a rightward shift. For example, a rise in the price of Tetley tea will shift the demand for PG tea to the right. A fall in the price of a substitute has the opposite effect.

4. Complements: A complement is something that tends to be purchased to go along with the good, services or factors under consideration, such as tools for a worker, or milk for tea. A fall in the price of the complement will produce a rightward shift; a fall in the price of tea, for example, will shift the demand for milk to the right and more milk will be demanded even though its price has remained the same. A rise in the price of a complement will shift demand to the left.

5. Facilitators: This is a catch-all term for anything that makes buying something easier. A new car park, for example, may boost demand for a store insofar as it makes it easier to shop at the store, as might a new bus route, or longer opening hours.

6. Incomes: If a rise in consumers' incomes shifts demand to the right then the good is called a normal good, and as the name implies, this is what you would normally expect. There are, however, some goods that are demanded less when incomes rise, and more when incomes fall. These are **inferior goods**, but although the name implies it, inferior goods are

not necessarily low quality goods, or badly made, and neither are they a bad thing for a business to be involved with. For example, potatoes are an inferior good but they are not badly made in any sense or a bad business to be in; McDonald's, for example, make more profits out of potato chips than anything else they sell. In fact, firms often have inferior products in their portfolio (collection) of products to keep the company afloat in times of recession when many peoples' incomes fall. The fact that a rise in income can lead to more or less demand will affect the buyers' response to a price change too, as each price change has both a substitution and an income effect. For inferior goods the income effect will work in the opposite direction to the substitution effect and can in extreme cases lead to an upward-sloping demand curve (as discussed below).

7. Expectations: If buyers expect prices to rise they will buy now to avoid paying more later and demand will shift right. In fact, their action will help to make the rise happen and can even be the main cause of a rise. For example, in the late 1980s a major cause of the boom in house prices was that everyone thought they were going to rise and acted accordingly. If, on the other hand, people expect prices to fall they may reduce their demand now in anticipation and thereby shift demand to the left.

8. Quality: People will pay more for a better quality product, so an improvement in quality will shift demand to the right. On the other hand, a lowering of quality will produce a leftward shift. It is important to note that although lower quality goods are usually cheaper than higher quality goods, when we envisage a firm lowering its prices we are not implying that it reduces the quality too, since that would reduce demand rather than increase it.

9. Several of the mechanisms listed above apply to PEST factors; a change in the price of a substitute is clearly a change in the competitive environment of the firm, for example, but some PEST changes cannot be classified with reference to the list above and must be considered individually.

2.5 UNUSUAL DEMAND CURVES

Upward-sloping demand curves are rarer than people think. Often people buy in anticipation of price rises and, in shifting demand to the right, create the impression that demand is upward sloping when in reality, if asked the question would they like to pay more or less for the same product, they would always say less. There are, however, occasions where for the same quality product we would choose the more expensive one; where, in other words, we would deliberately choose the worst value for money option. Robert Giffen (1837–1910) believed that he had discovered such a case amongst the urban poor of his day, since many of them bought more bread when its price was high than when it was low. He related this to the fact that the Victorian poor had to spend so much of their income on bread. This meant that when the price of bread fell they were made sufficiently wealthier to be able to afford more of other foods and were able, therefore, to use less bread. In effect, the change in the price of bread had such a large impact on their effective income that it outweighed the natural tendency for them to substitute a good that had fallen in price with one that had not. In other words, the negative income effect of this inferior good was so large that it completely outweighed the substitution effect. A more commonly encountered reason for upward-sloping demand curves in the West today stems from our desire to show off. As Thorstein Veblen (1857–1929) argued, if a major part of the reason for demanding a good is to indicate how wealthy we are to others, then this 'conspicuous consumption' could mean that if its price falls, less will be demanded. However, while there are many goods that have an element of conspicuous consumption, only for a few is it significant enough to ensure that their demand curves are actually upward sloping.

2.6 NEO-CLASSICAL CONSUMER THEORY

The study of the behaviour of firms, individuals and markets that forms the basis of the branch of economics known as Microeconomics is dominated by the neo-classical approach, developed over 100 years ago with contributions by W.S. Jevons (1835–82), C. Menger (1840–1921), L. Walras (1834–1910) and Marshall. The term **neo-classical** refers to the type of economics in which matters are simplified by assuming that agents (firms or individuals) seek to maximise their utility (satisfaction), subject to certain constraints, and that their behaviour is consistent with this, that in other words they are **rational maximisers**. So, for example, a woman's purchases of dresses are seen in this approach to reflect her desire to enjoy the buying and wearing of dresses, within the limits imposed by her income and how much time she has to go shopping, and so on. What gives people satisfaction is not an issue in this approach; if someone enjoys watching synchronised swimming and buys a ticket to see some, then they are a rational maximiser, despite the fact that the rest of us may see the desire itself as irrational. Where people's desires come from is also not an issue in this approach; therefore whether production and consumption should be the predominant goals of a society or not is completely ignored. However, the fact that such big issues are left out does not bother neo-classical economists since they pride themselves on looking at things as they are, rather than pontificate on the way they think things should be. The big advantage of this approach is that with relatively few assumptions, powerful predictions about consumers' behaviour emerge. Consider my simple choice over what to have for lunch, for example. I would like some sandwiches and some beer for my lunch. However, I only have £2.80 to spend on lunch; this is my 'budget constraint'. If sandwiches cost £1.40 a pack and beer is 70p a glass, then I can afford four glasses of beer and no sandwiches (option A), or two beers and a sandwich (option B), or two sandwiches and no beer (option C). I could, of course, have less to eat or drink and hang on to some of my money. But assume I am a maximiser; I have decided to maximise my utility (satisfaction level) by spending £2.80 on lunch. This means I must choose only options 'a', 'b' or 'c' in Figure 2.7. It is my preference to like both beer and sandwiches for lunch. Given my preferences and constraint, you can work out that I will consume 'b' if I am a 'rational maximiser' as 'b' is consistent with maximising my utility. Without this assumption, you cannot predict what I will buy. Using the same approach we can explain the thinking that lies behind the demand curve and develop predictions of what consumers will do when their budgets change or the prices of goods change.

Figure 2.7
Maximisation subject
to constraint.

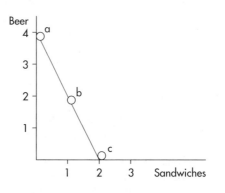

We can also refine this approach to look at what attributes of a good are being demanded, for as Lancaster (1971) argued, most goods are demanded not for themselves but for their characteristics. So, for example, the demand for a house is not for what it is – a load of bricks, mortar and slates. The demand is for its attributes – rooms to sleep in, relax in, cook in, space for the children to play in, peace and quiet, accessibility to school, shops, work and so on.

2.7 REVENUE

The effect of demand on revenues can be looked at in terms of totals, averages and marginals.

2.7.1 Total revenue (TR)

This is all the money a firm makes from selling its produce. In other words, it is the price of its products multiplied by how many it sells, that is, $P \times Q$. For a downward-sloping demand curve we find that the total amount of revenue that the firm would receive if prices were cut always goes up and then down. The firm is selling more as we do this; Q is going up, but $P \times Q$ begins to fall because eventually the loss from cutting P exceeds the gains from increasing Q. We can see how this works by looking at the revenue that would be made at different prices using the market demand curve in Figure 2.4.

$P \times Q = TR$
$4 \times 0 = 0$
$3 \times 2 = 6$ *At a price of £3 sales would be 2, the firm therefore earns £6.*
$2 \times 4 = 8$ *When P = £2 demand = 4, consumers would spend £8 and so TR = £8.*
$1 \times 6 = 6$ *When P = £1 sales go up to 6, but total spending, and thus TR too, is only £6.*

Graphically this gives a TR curve that goes up and then down in the manner shown in Figure 2.8.

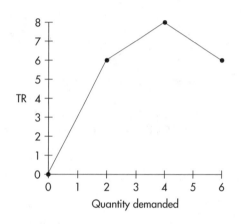

Figure 2.8 Total revenue curve.

Figure 2.9 The relationship between TR and shifts in demand.

Shifts in the demand curve also entail different levels of revenue for the firm; a shift to the right means more revenue since Q is bigger, while a shift to the left means less revenue since Q is smaller, as shown in Figure 2.9.

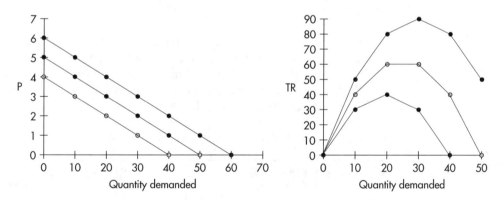

As both movements along the demand curve and shifts in the demand curve change firms' revenues, it is important to be clear about which is occurring, and it is not always obvious since sometimes firms try to fool us. A firm can, for example, effectively raise prices by reducing a product's value for money in some hidden way. Few people, for example, notice if the weight of a packet of crisps, sweets or nuts is reduced by a few grams, since the manufacturers do not advertise the fact. It is also important to be aware of the difference between a movement and a shift in the demand curve when investigating a firm's strategic options. In recent years, for example, some newspapers have cut their prices to encourage sales, whereas the *Daily Mail* has taken a different approach, that of improving quality by hiring more journalists. In both cases it worked, sales were increased, but one strategy involved shifting the demand curve and the other involved moving along it, and hence the effects on revenues were by no means similar. In fact, the price-cutting strategy led to a fall in revenues rather than a rise, as the price cuts were taking the firm down the other side of the TR hill. This has led to the accusations that the price-cutting strategy is in this case an example of the unfair practice of 'predatory pricing', where a firm is willing to lose money on a venture simply to push rivals who cannot follow suit out of business.

2.7.2 Average revenue (AR)

Average revenue is simply TR divided by Q. However, as the revenue on average is simply the price, AR is simply the demand curve by another name.

2.7.3 Marginal revenue

The term marginal means 'the next one'. Marginal revenue is the gain in revenue from each extra unit sold, which is the change in TR divided by the change in Q. Often the term 'change in' is replaced by the Greek letter Δ, which means we can write MR as:

$$MR = \frac{\Delta TR}{\Delta Q}$$

If the change in Q is one then we have been lucky; often in practical applications we find that sales change by an untidy number. In the example below, using the data for the demand curve from Figure 2.4 again, the change in Q is two. Since the marginal unit arises in going from one case to the next, it is common practice to put it between the other values on both tables and graphs (if possible).

For our tie case, the result is shown in Table 2.2.

Table 2.2

TR	Change in TR	Q	Change in Q	MR
0	0	0	0	3
6	6	2	2	1
8	2	4	2	−1
6	−2	6	2	−

Each extra sale (or two in this case) raises some revenue. However, as firms need to lower prices to sell more, all the goods that would have been sold at the higher price now have to be sold at the lower price, so each extra sale also loses some revenue too. This latter effect eventually dominates and causes TR to fall and the MR to become negative, since MR in effect tells us what is happening to TR. In fact, MR is the slope of the TR curve, which means that its graphical shape is entirely predictable given the shape of TR, which in turn is entirely predictable given the shape of the demand curve. As can be seen from Figure 2.10, the main features of the MR function are that it is twice as steep as AR and cuts the x-axis when TR is at its peak (because at that point the slope of TR is zero).

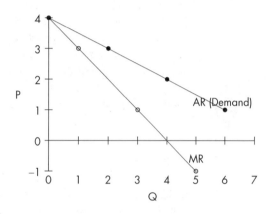

Figure 2.10 Average revenue and marginal revenue curves.

These diagrams show that revenues depend on the relationship between price and quantity but they do not show the exact nature of this relationship. For that, we need to turn to the concept of 'price elasticity of demand' developed by Alfred Marshall. This concept enables us to express the relationship between price changes and quantity changes in such a way that we can tell at a glance exactly what is implied for revenue.

2.8 PRICE ELASTICITY OF DEMAND

If someone told you that sales in one industry had today risen by 1000, you might think that was good. If on the other hand the news was that sales had increased by one, you might assume that this was not so good. However, if the first case relates to ball bearings and the second to contracts for oil tankers, you would be wrong since the oil tanker contract would be front-page news, while the rise in ball bearing sales would be negligible. The problem is that numbers mean different things in different industries. Fortunately, we can make limitless comparisons without having to be an expert in limitless different industries by using percentage changes, as a 10% increase in demand is bigger than a 5% increase, regardless of the units commonly used in the industries being compared. This advantage of percentages led Marshall to apply them to the question of the relationship between price changes and quantity demanded in constructing his price elasticity of demand formula as shown below:

$$\text{PeD} = \frac{\%\ \text{change in Quantity demanded}}{\%\ \text{change in P}}\ \text{or PeD} = \frac{\%\ \Delta \text{Qd}}{\%\ \Delta \text{P}}$$

To see how we can use this formula to predict the effect of price changes on revenue, we will look at what happens when we cut prices by X%. For a downward-sloping demand curve, quantity demanded will go up, but there are three possibilities, which have different implications for revenue. Firstly, the rise in Qd could be less than X%, in which case we have an **inelastic** demand and a PeD between 0 and 1. Secondly, it could be exactly X%, in which case we have a **unit elastic** demand and a PeD of 1. Thirdly, it could be more than X%, in which case we have an **elastic** demand and a PeD in excess of 1. When we do this calculation in practice, the numbers for a downward-sloping demand curve will be negative, since Qd goes up as P goes down, which means we can restate the possibilities as shown in Table 2.3.

Table 2.3

Calculated figure	PeD
0 to −1	Inelastic
−1	Unit elastic
−1 to −infinity	Elastic

Using the demand curve in Figure 2.11 we find that if we lower prices by 1p from 99p to 98p, Qd goes up from 1 to 2. In this case a small percentage reduction in P (just over 1% in fact) produces a large percentage increase in Qd, 2 being 100% bigger than 1, so PeD = 100 / −1.01 = −99. This means that for this demand curve, demand is elastic for a price cut from 99p to 98p; it does not mean we have an elastic demand curve for reasons that will become apparent below.

Figure 2.11 A very straight demand curve to illustrate the concept of PeD.

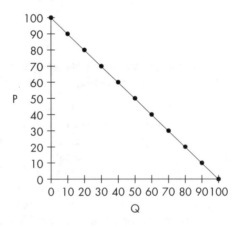

Halfway along the line a price cut from 50p to 49p would produce an elasticity of −1, which means that in this case the demand is unit elastic. Still further along we find that a price cut from 20p to 19p would produce a figure of −0.25, which indicates that at this point it is inelastic. So, although our line has the same slope all the way along it, the elasticities along it vary. In fact for this unusually straight and regular demand curve, the elasticities go uniformly from infinity at the top through −1 in the middle to zero at the bottom. The elasticities tell us about revenue since when the PeD is elastic, price cuts will take us down the demand curve but up the TR hill. On the other hand, if PeD is inelastic then we are on the other side of the TR hill, and the only way to get more TR is to go back up the demand curve by raising prices, as shown in Figure 2.12.

Figure 2.12 The AR, MR and TR curves associated with the demand curve in Figure 2.9.

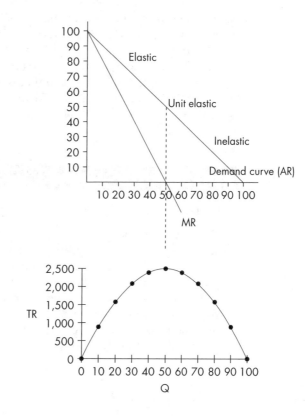

The link between PeD and TR is summarised in Table 2.4.

Table 2.4 The link between PeD and TR.

Calculated figure	PeD	TR
0 to −1	Inelastic	P down = TR down, and vice versa
−1	Unit elastic	TR unaffected by change in P
−1 to −infinity	Elastic	P down = TR up, and vice versa

Firms do not know the exact nature of the demand curves that their products face, and, particularly when large price changes are envisaged, all PeD figures should be treated as approximate. Nonetheless, given the different implications for revenue it is important for firms to have an idea of whether a product faces an elastic or inelastic demand. The importance of the distinction can be gauged by considering how Gerald Ratner turned a small family jewellers into Europe's largest by finding an unexploited elastic demand for cheap cosmetic gold jewellery, which he was able to meet by mass producing hollow gold products. Ratner also calculated that demand for the high-class jewellers, Zales, would be inelastic, and within days of taking them over was able to boost revenues and profits simply by putting their prices up.[1]

The need for firms to decide if something has an inelastic or an elastic demand when setting their prices means that firms have to do a lot of market research or statistical estimation to establish the exact nature of the demand curves they face. Alternatively, they can consider the following four determinants of PeD as a rough, but simple, guide. There is one caveat to bear in mind whichever approach is adopted, however, and that is that people may react differently to price rises and price falls, so that a demand curve might be elastic for a price rise and inelastic for a price fall.

2.9   DETERMINANTS OF PeD

PeD is largely determined by the following four factors:

1. Substitutes: If there are plenty of substitutes PeDs will be higher than if there are few since the presence of a lot of alternatives means that consumers may find it easy to switch between goods. If the price of one good goes down they will switch to it, and if its price goes up they will tend to switch away from it. If, on the other hand, consumers were forced to pay for air they would pay whatever was necessary since there is no substitute and the PeD would be very low! In fact, give or take a few gulps, it will be 'perfectly' (totally) inelastic, as shown in Figure 2.13.

Figure 2.13 A perfectly elastic demand curve.

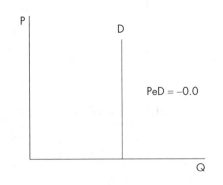

$$PeD = -0.0$$

---

[1] Turning the industry on its head made him unpopular, however, and when subsequently he made a joke about the naffness of one of his products it somehow became front-page news.

Generally, the number of substitutes for an industry is less than for individual products; for example, there are several substitutes for Brutus jeans, but few substitutes for 'clothes'. So if Brutus lower their prices for men's jeans and trousers they will steal custom from their rivals who do not, and their demand will therefore go up a lot. On the other hand, if everyone in this industry cuts their prices they can only steal custom from the kilt industry, and demand for each firm will therefore go up only a little. This means that the individual firm or product may face an elastic demand while the market demand curve taken as a whole is inelastic. One important implication of this is that while firms in an industry would lose out if any one of them raised their prices, if all of them do they will all gain. As we shall see in Chapter 5, this is a big incentive for firms to collaborate rather than compete in setting prices. This is not to suggest that brands will always have relatively high elasticities, since effective branding and advertising can be used to increase brand loyalty and sometimes result in brands with very low elasticities. For example, while for many people there are lots of alternatives to Levi jeans, from some people's perspectives there are none.

2. The nature of the need for the product: If a good is considered to be a discretionary (optional) form of spending, it is likely to have a higher PeD than if it is thought to be a necessity, since this is likely to mean that it has no substitutes yet must be bought. Again, firms can try to persuade people that something is more essential than they would otherwise have thought, through advertising.

3. Time: If we are considering the effect on demand over a long time period, PeDs will be higher than if we are considering a short time period as people will have longer to look for substitutes.

4. Proportion of income spent on the good: If the expenditure on the good takes a large proportion of people's incomes, PeDs will tend to be higher. For price rises, the reason is simply that they are more likely to be noticed and acted upon. So, while few people notice or care much if the price of salt doubles since it accounts for so little of their income, an increase in the mortgage rate is a major political issue because it accounts for so much of their income. For price falls it is a little more complicated: a price fall has more effect for goods that take a large part of people's incomes because it means that a sizeable chunk of income is freed, which effectively makes people richer. This income effect encourages demand in addition to the natural substitution effect of switching expenditure towards goods that have become cheaper.

2.10   DRAWING PeD

The demand curve in Figure 2.10 has elasticities falling as we go down the line, so clearly elasticity is not the same thing as the slope of a line (which for a straight line does not vary as we go along it). However, we can get an idea of relative elasticities by drawing flatter lines to mean more elastic, since the flatness implies a bigger response in terms of quantities. This means that for convenience we can indicate our views on the elasticity of a demand curve by drawing them steep to imply an inelastic response and shallow to imply an elastic one (Figure 2.14).

Figure 2.14 Indicating PeD in a diagram.

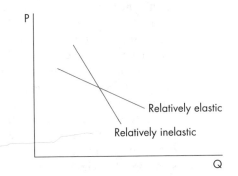

2.11 **PRICE DISCRIMINATION**

Firms can try to extract more revenue from a demand curve by charging different people different prices, as some people will be willing to pay more than others. This way of segmenting the market is called **price discrimination**; the difficulty with it is that the segments must be kept apart otherwise there will be a customer revolt. Nonetheless, most firms manage some price discrimination, even if it amounts to no more than better deals for regular customers, students or pensioners.

2.12 **HOW FIRMS CAN USE ESTIMATES OF PeD**

2.12.1 Pricing

Generally, when pricing a product it makes sense to move towards the point of maximum revenue, where PeD = −1; at its simplest the firm can pick a price based on its estimate of what the response will be. It can then move closer to maximising total revenue by trial and error. So, for example, if a firm were to produce a new cola drink that was not selling well at 70p a bottle, it could try a lower price, say 65p. If TR goes up this would vindicate the decision and suggest scope for further cuts until TR falls, in which case the firm knows that it has gone too far. In this way, the firm can price high for inelastic products and low for elastic ones without having to work out any elasticities, as such. For some firms the main objective seems to be to maximise revenue; however, for many it is more complicated than this since they seek to maximise profit rather than revenue, which means they must include a consideration of both PeD and costs, as we shall see in Chapter 3.

2.12.2   New product pricing

We can also use elasticity to guide the pricing of a new product. If demand is thought to be inelastic the firm could charge a high **market skimming** price, particularly if, like this year's Christmas fad, it is unlikely to remain in demand for very long. This strategy allows the firm to extract as much value from the market as quickly as possible, but it does not tend to encourage new custom. If, on the other hand, it is felt that the new product is likely to face an elastic demand, a low **penetration** price can be used, which will tend to encourage future growth in demand.

2.12.3   Cross-price elasticity of demand

Firms can evaluate the amount of competition that their products face by looking at **cross-price elasticity of demand**, XeD, which measures the effect of a change in the price of one product on the demand for some other product.

$$XeD = \frac{\%\ \Delta Qd \text{ of one good}}{\%\ \Delta P \text{ of some other good}}$$

If this comes out as a positive number then we are dealing with substitutes. If, for example, the two goods are Nescafé Coffee and Kenco Coffee and the price of Nescafé Coffee goes up, we would expect the demand for Kenco Coffee to go up in response. On the other hand, with complements like fish and chips a rise in the price of chips should mean a fall in the demand for fish; this means that for complements we get a negative XeD figure. Firms are not just interested in whether their products are competing with or complementing their own products or the products of other firms, but want to know the strengths of these relationships, which is what the size of the XeD figure will tell them. Calculating XeDs will therefore enable the firm to predict exactly how badly it will be hit by a cut in the price of a substitute, or by the rise in the price of a complement. Equally, of course, it will tell it how much of a rise in revenue it can expect if the price of a complement falls, or if its competitors raise their prices. This is not to imply, however, that a firm's competitors are the only source of such changes, as some substitutes and complements will be supplied by firms in more distant parts of the business environment. For example, a rise in the price of potatoes can affect the demand for fish, as fish and chips are complements, despite the fact that the fishing and agricultural industries are in all other respects separate. Substitutes can also come from other industries, so that, for example, to encompass all the substitutes for its products a car firm may need to monitor other car producers' prices, and the price of public transport.

Firms can also monitor XeDs year by year to see which are getting bigger and which are getting smaller. If a positive XeD is getting bigger then the products are becoming stronger substitutes. On the other hand, if a positive XeD is falling it indicates that the products are competing less. In both cases, the change could reflect a deliberate policy by firms, since at times they may want to compete more fiercely, while at others they may want to increase the distance between their products and those of their rivals. Monitoring XeDs will also alert firms to any new threats that appear, so that their marketing strategies can be directed to where they are most needed. Firms can also use XeDs to check the degree to which their own products compete with each other. Sometimes firms plan for new brands to replace their own products, and sometimes firms allow products to overlap each other to discourage any newcomers from seeing a gap in their portfolios as an invitation to invade. In both cases, some degree of competition as well as complementarity between the firm's own products can be tolerated, but sometimes firms simply miscalculate how close their products are likely to be. Mars Eggs, for example, were introduced to compete with Cadbury's Creme Eggs but in fact competed mainly with Mars Bars.

2.12.4 Income elasticity of demand (YeD)

Elasticity is a general concept to describe the extent of the relationship between two things, so in principle you can do it for anything. There is, however, one more type worth singling out and that is **income elasticity of demand**, or YeD for short:

$$YeD = \frac{\% \Delta Qd}{\% \Delta Income}$$

(The reason Y is often used is that I is mainly used to mean investment.) Calculating YeD can help firms to predict what will happen to their business if the incomes of their customers go up or down. If the calculated figure is negative then the product is an inferior good since a rise in incomes reduces the demand for it. If the figure is positive then we are dealing with a **normal** good. We can also make a further distinction based on the size of the elasticity: if the figure is less than 1 it may be thought of as a **necessity**, if greater than 1 the term **luxury** or **superior** good may be used to reflect the fact that the boost to income has made customers buy a lot more.

2.13 SUMMARY

- Economists define demand in terms of prices and quantities to produce 'demand curves'.
- Prices and quantities are used to define demand for two reasons: firstly because prices are an important determinant of the amount of demand, and secondly because it allows us to look at all the other determinants systematically by giving us a starting point.
- Other determinants of demand such as tastes and the level of buyers' incomes can be investigated systematically because they act to shift the demand curve.
- The economists' analysis of demand allows us to see how changes in the business environment that shift demand might impact on a firm's revenues, since revenues are simply prices multiplied by quantities.

- The economists' analysis of demand also allows us to see how changes in the business environment that do not shift demand but move us up or down the demand curve will also affect revenues, using the summary measure of price elasticity of demand.

- Price elasticity of demand is important since it tells us whether a price rise or a price cut will make a firm's revenues go up.

- Cross-price elasticity of demand can also be calculated. This shows the empirical relationship between products and can be used by firms to gauge which products are substitutes, and which are complements, for those they produce.

- Income elasticity of demand can also be calculated to show the relationship between changes in income and demand.

2.14   QUESTIONS

1. Pick a product that you buy. Then, by asking yourself what you would buy if the prices went up by some amount, or down by some amount, construct your demand curve for it. Then think of three things that will shift the demand curve that you have drawn.

2. You have been asked for advice on how to increase total revenue in the following cases. The only option is a change in price as in each case there is no money to spend on advertising or improving the quality of the product. There are no figures available to help you.
   (a) Mains water.
   (b) The beer in the Rovers Return, on Coronation Street.
   (c) Your dentist's private work.
   (d) A building society's variable rate mortgage product (in this case the interest rate charged to borrowers is the price).
   (e) Rail journeys between London and its suburbs.

3. An ice-cream manufacturer finds that demand for its ice-cream increases as it cut its prices over a six-week period starting in the middle of May. Can the firm be sure that it has uncovered its demand curve?

4. Can you think of any products that do not obey the law of demand?

5. A company reduces the price of its tea from £1.95 to £1.49 and demand goes up from 13,000 to 25,000 packets. What is the PeD?

6. Comment on the PeDs shown below:

Water	*−0.2*
Bread	*−0.3*
Petrol	*−0.4*
Tobacco	*−0.5*
Wine	*−0.5*
New cars	*−1.2*
Spirits	*−2.6*

7. Are the demands for the following likely to be elastic or inelastic?
   (a) Toothpaste
   (b) Heroin
   (c) Chocolate

8. Which of the following goods would you expect to be 'normal' and which would you expect to be 'inferior'?
    (a) Cars
    (b) Black and white TVs
    (c) Skiing holidays
    (d) Mark II Ford Cortina car

9. Calculate some PeDs for the demand curve you constructed in answer to Question 1, above.

10. At what price should the following company sell its spring water? Both brands are the same, but they are marketed differently.

Price in £	Product A: 'Poncier Isotonic Spring Water' Sales per month	Product B: 'Mountain Spring' Sales per month
1.75	1,700	700
1.50	2,000	1,100
1.25	2,100	1,500
1.00	2,300	2,000
0.75	2,700	2,900
0.50	3,000	3,800

(Price is per 2ltr bottle.)

11. The demand curve shown in Figure 2.15 has an elasticity of –1 all the way along its length. What price should the firm charge for the product?

Figure 2.15 A unit elastic demand curve.

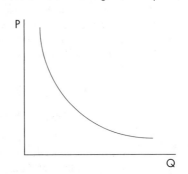

12. Give an example of a complementary product to Marmite, which is currently the most popular of the spreads that are made from the yeast that is a by-product of the fermentation of beer.

13. A few years ago, the makers of Marmite began estimating the cross-price elasticity of demand between their product and Vegemite. Initially they found no evidence of a relationship but have since found one that is positive and getting bigger. What does this imply?

14. A study some years ago revealed that the price elasticity of demand for Marmite was less than 1.
    (a) Give reasons to explain this finding and discuss the implications for the pricing of the product.
    (b) Do you think that a similar study would find the same thing today?

15. (a) Name one substitute and one complement for lager.

(b) A brewer estimates the following elasticity figures. Comment on their findings.

	Income elasticity of demand	Price elasticity of demand
Standard 3.3% alcohol lager	+0.8	−1.0
Premium 5% alcohol lager	+2.2	−0.7
Supermarket branded tinned lagers (2.4% alcohol)	−1.5	−1.8

16. The Ship Inn public house has a happy-hour between 6 p.m. and 7 p.m. when all prices are temporarily lowered by a considerable amount. This increases revenue, so why does the owner not lower prices permanently?

CHAPTER 3

Supply

After studying this chapter, you should be able to:

- define supply, and be able to represent it in terms of a supply curve;
- appreciate the distinction between the short run and the long run;
- understand the law of diminishing marginal returns and appreciate its implication for costs and supply;
- appreciate the difference between fixed and variable cost;
- understand the principle of the short run profit maximising supply curve;
- understand the concept of price elasticity of supply;
- comprehend the nature of supply shifts and identify their causes;
- appreciate the determinants of long run supply, and understand the factors that give rise to economies of scale;
- understand the effects that the passage of time has on production.

3.1   INTRODUCTION TO SUPPLY

Having looked at the demand for goods and services in terms of P and Q, it makes sense to look at supply in terms of P and Q too, as this will enable us to look at what buyers and suppliers do using one graph. We therefore define firms' **supply** as the amount of a good or service made available for sale at different prices within a given time period. We can view supply as representing what suppliers do when demand changes, in the same way that we saw demand as representing what buyers do when supply changes. However, before we express firms' output in terms of a graph, it is important to build a picture of what firms do to achieve the transformation of inputs into outputs, and what the constraints are on this process are.

We can represent the firm as the organisation through which the inputs of land, labour, capital and knowledge are converted into the outputs that people demand. We can represent this in terms of a diagram as shown in Figure 3.1, or algebraically as: $Q = f(L, Lb, Ca, K)$, which is to say that the quantity of output is a function of the inputs, namely land, labour, capital (using Ca rather than C, which is used to denote consumption), and knowledge.

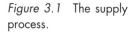 *Figure 3.1* The supply process.

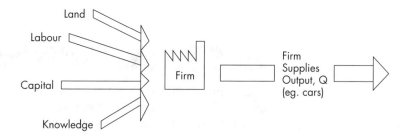

As Marshall noted, there are three possibilities regarding the availability of inputs. The first possibility is that none of them can be increased, the second is that some can, and the third is that they all can. The first case, where no more inputs can be used, he termed the **immediate run** (the term 'run' simply refers to a production run, or sequence). The second case, where some inputs can be increased while others are fixed, he called the **short run**. The final case, where all inputs can be varied, he dubbed the **long run**. Since all three involve different constraints on the use of inputs, they have different implications for a firm's supply.

3.2   THE IMMEDIATE RUN

In the immediate run all factors are fixed; no more are forthcoming and therefore output must be fixed too. We can use a bar to mean fixed and write this as:

$$\bar{Q} = f(\bar{L}, \bar{Lb}, \bar{Ca}, \bar{K})$$

The resulting perfectly inelastic supply curve can be graphed in terms of P and Q as in Figure 3.2.

Figure 3.2 Supply in the immediate run.

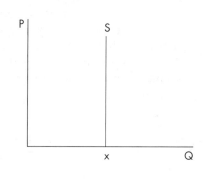

Taken on any one day, this is likely to be the case for most goods and many services. We can use the same example as Alfred Marshall to illustrate this – fishing. Once the trawlers have returned, no price rise can call forth any more fish from their holds; the amount that can be supplied is therefore fixed at some amount 'x' representing the day's catch. The price might go up if lots of people at the quayside want fresh fish, but supply remains the same until the next catch is brought home.

3.3 THE SHORT RUN

The short run is when there is at least one factor of production that cannot be increased, when others can. The fixed factor is usually the 'scale of production', such as the size of the factory or office block, or field in the case of farming. In the short run more goods or services can be produced by increasing the use of the variable factors – by hiring more labour, by using more fuel, by using more raw materials, or whatever. This is the situation most firms are in most of the time, as firms increase the scale of their production relatively infrequently. In the short run, we find that more is supplied at higher prices, which means that the supply curve is upward sloping, as shown in Figure 3.3.

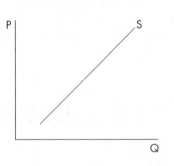

Figure 3.3 Supply in the short run.

It may seem rather obvious that if firms observe prices rising they will want to supply more, as higher prices mean more revenue. However, that does not explain why the prices rise, for if a firm can get more revenue by supplying more without raising prices then competition will ensure that they will. It must therefore be the case that they cannot increase supply unless they get a higher price. The reason for this is that the costs of supplying more go up in the short run, which means firms must receive a higher price if they are to supply more (once they have used up any stock reserves). Costs go up because production in the short run is constrained by the fact that marginal returns diminish.

3.4   THE LAW OF DIMINISHING MARGINAL RETURNS

This law states that the output that the firm gets in return for using each extra unit of a variable factor (the marginal returns to that input) eventually fall if the variable factor is being applied to a fixed factor. There is therefore an optimum amount of inputs to add to a fixed factor, which means that it is counterproductive simply to add more and more. For example, a hotel that has to cater for a rush of guests can hire more chefs to cope, but unless it can make its kitchen facilities bigger it will find that its output does not rise one for one with the number of chefs employed but exhibits the pattern shown in Figure 3.4.

Figure 3.4 The effect on output of adding more inputs in the short run.

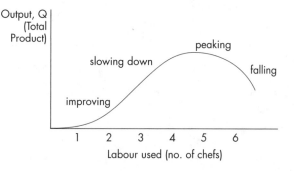

Although something of a smoothed stylisation, this graph nonetheless gives an idea of what typically happens. The shape of the line shows that as we add more labour we get more output Q (total product), but that the first chef adds very little as in his case there is simply too much to do. The next two chefs add a lot. However, the next two add less and the last worker actually reduces the output of the whole firm, since at this stage the chefs are beginning to get in each other's way. The same pattern emerges whether we are talking in terms of extra labour employed or extra hours worked, unless the extra hours involve using the fixed factor when it would otherwise be idle, such as adding a night shift. The reason for this pattern is to do with the fact that the labour is being applied to a fixed factor, and it will always appear as long as the law of diminishing marginal returns operates. The details of course will vary depending on the nature of the production process, and the size and organisational arrangements of the firm. The fact that it will happen is no reflection on the individual worker; chefs 2 and 3 do not work any harder than chef 6, it is just bad luck on number 6 that he is the sixth chef to be hired.

3.5   THE SHORT-RUN PROFIT-MAXIMISING SUPPLY

Before we proceed to examine the effect of the law of diminishing marginal returns on a firm's supply, we need to establish the basis on which the firm is offering its output. To begin with, we will assume that the firm supplies the amount that maximises its profits. As profits are revenues minus costs, this means that the firm must look at both its costs and the likely demand for its products in deciding how much to supply. We will look at this in some detail for a small firm that produces kayaks.

The firm has found that lowering prices can increase sales, as shown in Table 3.1.

Table 3.1
Lowering prices can
increase sales.

Price per kayak in £	Orders (demand) per week
750	0
700	1
650	2
600	3
550	4
500	5
450	6

Drawn on a graph, this gives the demand curve shown in Figure 3.5.

Figure 3.5 Demand
for one firm's kayaks
in a week.

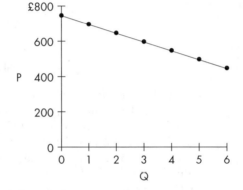

This creates a TR curve like the one shown in Figure 3.6.

Figure 3.6 The kayak
firm's TR curve for
different levels of
demand.

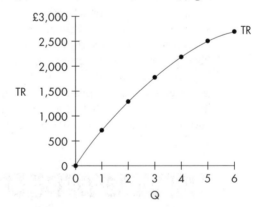

From this we might assume that the firm should keep cutting its price beyond £450 as it clearly faces an elastic demand and could continue to increase revenues by cutting prices still further. However, at a price of £450 the firm will actually make a loss, its profits at this point being minus £1,100 per week, and if it lowers its price further it will make even bigger losses. To understand why we have to look at the cost side too.

The firm could meet any level of demand shown above but it would need to use more workers (worker hours) to do so, as detailed in Figure 3.7.

Figure 3.7 How the law of diminishing returns affects the kayak firm.

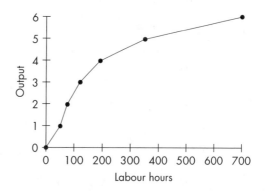

Given that the workers will be using a fixed amount of certain inputs such as moulding equipment and factory space, the law of diminishing marginal returns has come into play. However, unlike the stylised diagram in Figure 3.7, we do not see a fall in output since this firm is sensible enough to stop before it gets to that point. We can look at what happens in terms of averages and marginals as well as totals: the contribution to output of each extra hour worked, the marginal product (MP), is simply the change in total product resulting from the change in the factor used. (In this case, labour.)

$$MP = \Delta TP/\Delta L$$

This is the extra output associated with each extra hour, but we have increased hours in lumps, so as is often the case, the margin is not one extra but several extra. We can also look at the average productivity of the hours worked, which is simply:

$$AP = TP/L$$

The figures that resulted for the kayak company are shown in Table 3.2.

Table 3.2

Output	Number of worker hours needed	Average product (kayaks per hr)	Marginal product
0	0	0	
			0.02
1	50	0.02	
			0.04
2	75	0.027	
			0.022
3	120	0.025	
			0.0143
4	190	0.021	
			0.006
5	350	0.014	
			0.003
6	700	0.003	

Plotting these on a graph gives a typical rise and then falls for each of MP and AP that results from the operation of the law of diminishing marginal returns (Figure 3.8).

Figure 3.8 Marginal and average product at the kayak firm.

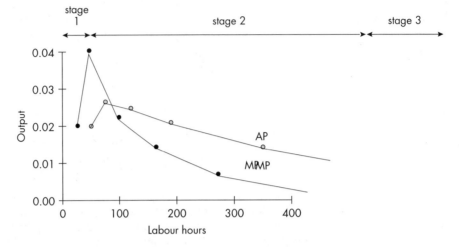

There are three stages to short-run production. In stage 1, the firm can improve productivity by increasing its use of labour. In stage 2, each extra worker adds less to production than the previous one, but although MP and AP are falling they are nonetheless positive; the extra workers are adding something to production. This means that although worker productivity is maximised when the firm supplies two kayaks and uses around 75hrs of labour, this firm, like most firms, actually maximises profits when in stage 2. In stage 3, the MP becomes negative; this is the point at which total output falls and extra workers just make things worse. However, as was noted earlier, our firm is not that daft, so we do not enter stage 3 in this case. A firm in stage 3 can increase both productivity and profitability by cutting back.

The law of diminishing marginal returns sets in after we reach an output of two, since thereafter output goes up but an increasing number of hours are needed to provide each extra kayak. This has implications for the firm's costs and therefore how much it will supply. Since workers are paid for the hours they work, the cost of providing each extra kayak goes up as productivity declines. It might be possible to adjust pay to reflect individual productivity in some way, but generally this can only be done where there is a clear output per person so that workers can be paid per piece produced (piece work); in this case, like most others, this is not possible.

3.6 COSTS

A firm's cost of production depends on two things, firstly the cost of its inputs which in turn depends on their unit costs and how many are used, and secondly the productivity of the factors.

3.6.1   Fixed costs

In the short run, some factors are fixed in supply and the associated costs are therefore termed fixed costs, as they are fixed in respect of the firm's output, although they can of course vary for other reasons. For example, a mortgage on a factory goes up when interest rates go up, but it does not go up because the firm is producing more, hence it is described as a fixed cost. For many firms, much of the labour they use is a fixed cost since the staff get their pay each month for doing the job, regardless of what the monthly output for the firm is. Similarly, the costs associated with many types of machines and other forms of capital do not change with output.

3.6.2   Variable costs

In the short run, if a firm wishes to produce more, it needs to use more variable factors. In the case of the kayak firm, more labour is used, which means more wages have to be paid, so in this case the labour cost is a variable cost, since it varies with output. In addition, the firm will need to use more raw materials and so these costs are likely to rise too, which makes them variable costs as well.

3.6.3   Opportunity costs

The costs for the kayak manufacturer are easily calculated by the firm's accountants, except for the opportunity costs, which the firm must include if it is to make an accurate estimate of the real costs involved in creating its output. There is however a simple principle that we can apply to help us do this: if the firm has something and makes no explicit payments to use it, then the opportunity cost is what could be earned from it if it were put to another use. (Although calculating such 'implicit costs' may involve guesswork ignoring them is worse, since that means giving them an improbably low value of zero.) On the other hand, some costs are 'explicit' insofar as they involve a direct payment to someone; in such cases the price the firm pays is the opportunity cost. If, for example, the firm pays £200 for a worker, it loses the opportunity to spend that £200 on something else, so the opportunity cost is simply £200 and no additional opportunity cost calculation need be made. In general, therefore, it is in respect of resources that the firm owns that we have to add (or subtract) some numbers from those provided by accountants to incorporate opportunity costs, as shown in the economic accounting case study later in this chapter.

3.6.4   Costs for the kayak firm

Capital and land

Any contribution of funds either from retained profits or from owners' pockets would be counted as having both an explicit value equal to the size of the investment and an implicit value equal to what the investment could have earned elsewhere. If, for example, it had been put in the bank, the interest rate paid by the bank could be used to calculate an opportunity cost for the investment in the firm, which would then be added to our cost figures. However, in this case there are no such costs.

Taking each component of the firm in turn:

1. The factory (fixed cost): The firm pays £100 a week on rent and rates for the factory; these are explicit and therefore no adjustment needs to be made to include opportunity cost.

2. The equipment (fixed cost): The firm owns the equipment that it uses so no explicit costs are incurred; in addition, as the equipment is rather old or of use only to this firm, it has no opportunity cost. This means there are no equipment costs to include in our calculations. This may seem odd, but where an investment in an asset cannot be recovered because the asset cannot be leased, lent or sold, its costs are **sunk costs** and they play no part in determining the costs of production today or tomorrow. The money spent on the sign on the factory and the machine that embosses the kayak firm's logo on the kayaks are examples of such lost costs. The historic cost – what the firm paid for them – is irrelevant (unless of course it is still paying for them), since to anyone else they are worthless.

3. Raw materials (variable cost): Including resin and electricity, the raw material costs are about £100 per kayak. These are explicit costs so no adjustment for opportunity cost needs to be made.

4. Staff (fixed cost): For many firms a lot of the labour is a fixed cost, with people getting paid for the job regardless of the output of the firm, but in this case that does not apply as the owner does all the managing and office work. All hired labour will therefore be treated as a variable cost. There is, however, an adjustment to be made here to include the opportunity cost of the owner's time as she believes she could make £300 a week working for a rival firm as a manager. The additional opportunity cost for the firm is therefore only the fixed amount of £300 per week that the owner could get working elsewhere, which if added to the £100 that the firm pays in rent, gives total fixed costs of £400 per week.

5. Staff (variable cost): The main variable cost for the kayak firm is labour, which is an average £4 per hour once we include National Insurance payments and so on. We do not have to add any opportunity costs to these figures, as they are all explicit costs. The pattern in the variable costs tabulated in Table 3.3 is dominated by the effect of the law of diminishing returns on the cost of labour for this firm.

Table 3.3 Variable
costs for the kayak firm.

Output (Kayaks)	Labour hours	Cost of labour at £4 per hr	Cost of raw materials	Variable costs
1	50	£200	£100	£300
2	75	£300	£200	£500
3	120	£480	£300	£780
4	190	£760	£400	£1,160
5	350	£1,400	£500	£1,900
6	700	£2,800	£600	£3,400

Adding the fixed costs of £400 per week to these figures gives us total costs as shown in Table 3.4.

Table 3.4 Total costs
for the kayak firm.

Output (Kayaks)	FC	VC	Total Costs
0	£400	£0	£400
1	£400	£300	£700
2	£400	£500	£900
3	£400	£780	£1,180
4	£400	£1,160	£1,560
5	£400	£1,900	£2,300
6	£400	£3,400	£3,800

If we put the numbers from Table 3.4 into a graph, the rise in total costs, that comes from the increase in labour costs, that results from the fall in productivity, that results from the operation of the law of diminishing marginal returns, can be seen (Figure 3.9).

Figure 3.9 Total cost
curve for the kayak
firm.

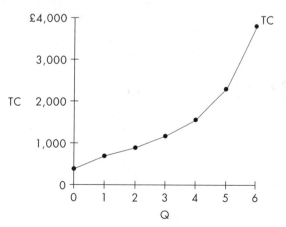

3.7 SUPPLYING TO MAXIMISE PROFIT

From the figures we have, we are now in a position to determine the profit-maximising output for the kayak firm. We can do this graphically as shown in Figure 3.10, simply by putting its total revenue curve and total cost curve on the same graph.

Figure 3.10 Revenues, costs, and profit for the kayak firm at different levels of output.

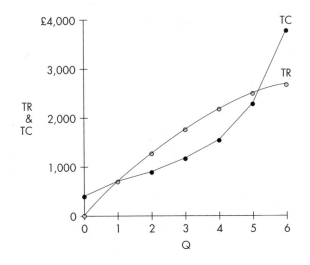

We can see the amount of profit made at each output level since this is simply the gap between the two lines. However, because we include opportunity cost in our cost figures, a firm that makes no apparent profit will nonetheless stay in business as it will be creating a sufficient return to cover the opportunity costs of owners' investments. For this reason, breaking-even using economists' cost figures actually means making some minimum amount of profit that ensures survival, which is termed **normal profit**. To fit with this term, profits above zero are referred to as **super** (above) **normal profit** (SNP), although given that this is something of a mouthful the term profit remains in use, particularly where the distinction between normal and super normal profits is obvious or unimportant.

In terms of our figures this is as shown in Table 3.5.

Table 3.5 Profit for the kayak firm.

Q	TR	TC	Profit = TR − TC
0	£0	£400	£−400
1	£700	£700	£0 'Normal Profit' output.
2	£1,300	£900	£400
3	£1,800	£1,180	£620
4	£2,200	£1,560	£640 Profit maximising output.
5	£2,500	£2,300	£200
6	£2,700	£3,800	£−1,100

These figures relate to how much can be produced in a week, and in any one week, the firm can choose only one price–output combination. From these figures, we can see that the firm maximises profits when output is 4, and the price is £550. This is the amount the firm should supply to maximise profits. We can arrive at the same results using our marginal data. **Marginal cost** (MC) is the cost of supplying each extra kayak (or put another way, is the change in TC divided by the change in Q). **Marginal revenue** (MR) is the revenue earned by each extra kayak (in other words the change in TR divided by the change in Q). This is shown in Table 3.6.

Table 3.6 Profits for the kayak firm calculated using marginal data.

Q	MR	MC
0		
	£700	£300
1		
	£600	£200
2		
	£500	£280
3		
	£400	£380
4		
	£300	£740
5		
	£200	£1,500
6		

If we plot MC and MR on a graph, we find that they meet at the point where profits are maximised, as shown in Figure 3.11.

Figure 3.11 Profit maximisation using MC and MR curves.

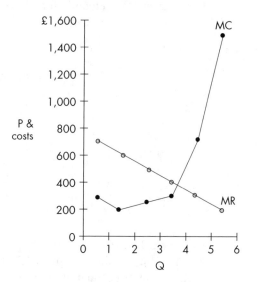

In fact, we can see that profits are maximised at an output of 3.7, for which the corresponding price is £564. We need to be careful here, however, because when using graphs we join up the dots with lines, and we may therefore input a degree of accuracy in the figures that is not there. This is not to say that we should not be accurate but that we need to be careful about how we communicate our findings. Given the data that we have in this case, it is perhaps more realistic to talk of the profit-maximising output for this firm being about 4.

3.7.1 The Golden Rule of profit maximisation

That profits are maximised when MR = MC is termed the '**Golden Rule of profit maximisation**'; it suggests that a supplier should stop when the revenue made on the last item produced is no more than it cost to provide. Beyond this point, profits decline inexorably, as the law of diminishing returns dictates that the costs involved in producing an extra unit of output go up, while the law of downward-sloping demand curves dictates that the revenues from each extra unit sold goes down. The Golden Rule does not explain how businesses arrive at their supply decisions, as each firm's decision-making process will be the result of a complex interplay of personalities, strategies and 'office' politics. However, insofar as shareholders' funds gravitate towards profit maximisers, as profits are the rewards for the owners, there is a tendency for those firms that get closest to maximising profits to survive, which means that there is an incentive for firms to search for the point at which MR = MC.

3.7.2 The profit maximisers' supply curve

If the demand curve were to shift left, or right, the MR would shift with it and thus the point at which MR = MC would also move up or down the MC line. If, for example, demand shifted right in the way shown in Figure 3.12, the profit-maximising output for the firm would change from 'a', to 'b', to 'c'.

Figure 3.12 The effect of shifting demand on the profit-maximising output.

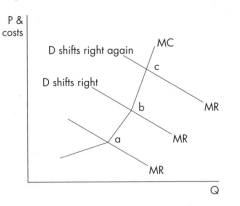

However, the price corresponding to the amount supplied is not given by the MR line but by the demand (AR) line which, as we have seen, is above the MR. So the price–quantity combination that constitutes the supply curve will reflect the shape of the MC curve, although it will lie somewhere above it, as shown in Figure 3.13, (for an output of four kayaks per week, rather than 3.7).

Figure 3.13 The price charged by the profit-maximising firm.

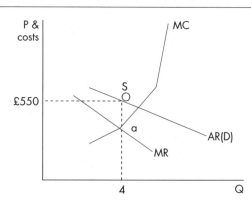

The same is true for other levels of output too, as shown in Figure 3.14, and as before we can join up the dots to show, in this case, the kayak firm's supply curve.

Figure 3.14 The kayak firm's supply curve.

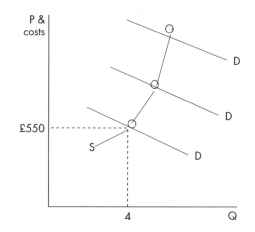

That the amount supplied is determined by the amount demanded lies at the heart of our analysis, for, if you recall, the amount demanded depends on the amount supplied, which means that each depends on the other. Although we shall look at how this interdependency works in more detail in the next chapter, at this stage we simply note the fact that the prices and quantities that actually get bought and sold are determined jointly by the interaction of both supply and demand.

3.7.3 Some caveats

There are some caveats about this analysis.

1. The Golden Rule only applies if the MC is cutting the MR from below. So, for example, point 'x' on Figure 3.15 is the profit-maximising point, not 'z'. At 'z' it is possible to increase profit by increasing output since to the right of 'z' MR exceeds MC.

Figure 3.15 MC must
cut MR from below.

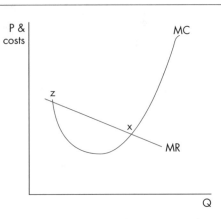

2. If a firm has costs that exceed revenue at all levels of output, perhaps, for example, because demand has fallen due to a recession, then rather than maximise profits the best a firm can do is minimise its losses (Figure 3.16).

Figure 3.16
Loss-minimising output.

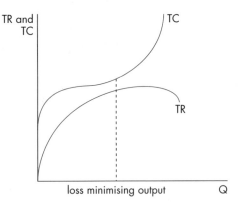

3. When demand is inelastic, MR is a negative number, which means it goes below the x-axis on the graph. However, if a firm faces an inelastic demand the profit-maximising solution is always to produce less and charge a higher price, since that will both raise revenue and allow costs to be reduced. Therefore, the profit-maximising point cannot be below the x-axis.

4. Firms may have difficulty identifying MR and MC, and may not aim to maximise profit. These issues are discussed in detail in Chapter 6.

3.8   VARIETIES OF SHORT-RUN COST CURVES

Firms that operate with a fixed carrying capacity, such as a hotel, a theatre or football ground, are able to supply extra seats at little or no extra cost until all the seats are filled, at which point it becomes impossible to supply more, regardless of price. For example, the marginal cost of filling an empty seat on an aeroplane is virtually zero, since filling it involves only a tiny extra amount of fuel and food. Therefore, in order to ensure that all seats are taken price discrimination will be used, involving lower fares for some types of passenger. On the other hand, if the plane is full, offering to pay more will not get you a seat. The MC curve, and thus the supply curve, will look something like Figure 3.17.

Figure 3.17 A supply curve for a theatre; football ground or aeroplane.

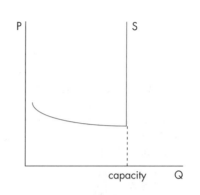

In addition to the possibility of odd shapes occurring, there is also the possibility that a firm will supply more at lower prices, and thereby exhibit a downward-sloping supply curve. Firms can do this as although there are forces pushing them towards profit maximisation, they can be evaded, at least for a while. If a firm does this in the short run it would, given a rising MC curve, meaning making losses. Firms may, however, be willing to do this in order to steal market share in the hope of recouping their losses at a later date by putting their prices back up, if they can force their rivals out of business. Such predatory pricing is open to legal challenge, however.

3.9   SHUTTING DOWN

We now turn to the issue of how little can be supplied before the firm calls a halt to production. The firm should stay in production even if it is making losses if producing an output is helping to pay off its fixed costs, as these have to be paid anyway for as long as the firm stays in business. (The point at which it should decide to close down in the long run and therefore quit the business altogether is discussed in the next section.) In the short run, it means it should shut down when price no longer exceeds **average variable cost** (AVC). This is shown by a in Figure 3.18 using an AVC curve that is consistent with the pattern of costs discussed above, (and examined in more detail below).

Figure 3.18 The shirt-run shut-down point.

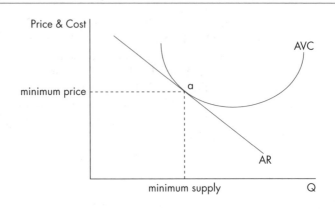

3.9.1 Price elasticity of short-run supply

We can calculate elasticities of supply in a similar way to PeD, except that with PeS we look at the relationship between price and the quantity offered for sale, which gives:

$$PeS = \frac{\% \, \Delta Qs}{\% \, \Delta P}$$

For upward-sloping supply curves, the calculated figures will be positive. In the case of supply, the distinction between elastic and inelastic curves is not important *per se*, although of course PeS is important in itself as it indicates the scale of the response of firms to changes in demand. If the supply curve is going to intercept the x-axis, as in Figure 3.19 on the left (using straight lines for convenience), then the PeS although varying is nonetheless inelastic all the way along the line. In this case, firms respond to a change in demand by changing prices rather than output. If, on the other hand, the supply intercepts with the y-axis then the firm responds to a change in demand by supplying more or less rather than changing prices, and we have an elastic supply, as shown on the right, although again the actual figure will vary along the line.

Figure 3.19 Price elasticity of supply.

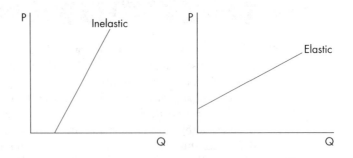

One final case is where the line is a ray that comes from the origin (Figure 3.20). In such a case, the PeS is 1 regardless of where along the line we take the measurements.

Figure 3.20 Unit
elastic supply.

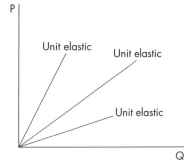

Supply curves will be more elastic if any of the following conditions obtains:

- Producing more does not add much to costs. If, for example, a firm uses raw materials that are easy and cheap to obtain and has a ready supply of cheap labour then it will be able to supply more if demand goes up without having to raise prices very much; it will, in other words, have an elastic supply.

- If the firm can switch production to the product if demand goes up, this flexibility will allow them to supply more without raising prices much.

- A product can easily be moved from one market to another. If, for example, a shirt manufacturer finds that demand for their shirts is greater in Newcastle than in London it can simply shift supply from London to Newcastle without incurring many extra costs and without therefore needing to raise prices very much.

- If the decision makers within the firm see the change in demand as permanent they may decide to invest in new capacity, increase the scale of their production, and, for a while at least, supply under the condition that we have labelled the 'long run', which we shall consider below. This will allow a greater degree of elasticity, and may even allow costs to fall sufficiently for them to lower prices rather than raise them.

- If we are considering a longer period of time, rather than a short one, then suppliers will have more scope to increase scale as discussed above. But they will also have time to switch production, reorganise, and learn more about the growth market, which should mean that costs rise less than they do initially (or, as before, costs may even fall).

- PeS also depends on the aims of firms, how much competition there is, and how firms expect their rivals to react, all topics that we shall cover in detail later in this text. For now, we can note that if a firm is powerful it will have scope to do what it wants rather than what its cost curves dictate.

3.9.2   Adding averages to our graphs

We will now add averages to our graphs. These are not important for making the supply decision; however, they do enable us to see the profit-maximising price and quantity combination as well as how much profit is being made on one graph. This makes the graph popular with teachers as it encompasses so much; it is, however, unpopular with students since encompassing so much makes it visually complex.

As we have seen, total costs can be broken down into total fixed costs and total variable costs, algebraically:

TC = TFC + TVC

From these totals, we can calculate the following averages, averages being calculated by simply dividing the various totals by output:

Average total costs, ATC (or simply AC) = TC/Q

This is simply the cost on average of producing the output and is often referred to simply as unit costs. On a graph it is bowl shaped given the typical pattern of costs discussed above. In addition, MC always cuts it at its minimum point for algebraic rather than economic reasons. The fall and rise of average and marginal costs reflect the rise and fall in productivity discussed earlier, and the average and marginal product curves in Figure 3.9 show the same pattern, though of course inverted.

For **average fixed costs** we have:

AFC = TFC/Q

AFC declines as we increase output because we are dividing a fixed amount by an increasing amount of output.

For **average variable costs** we have:

AVC = TVC/Q

All the cost curves are shown in Figure 3.21.

Figure 3.21
Cost curves for the kayak firm.

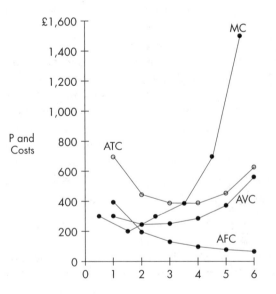

3.9.3 Adding MR and AR to the graph

We can calculate the total profit using averages since the profit made on average is given by average revenue minus average cost, and if we multiply this average profit by the number of sales, we get total profit. This gives the shaded area in Figure 3.22, which equals the total profit. We can, therefore, include in one diagram the marginal curves to indicate the basis of the profit-maximising decision, the average revenue showing the price associated with that decision, and the total profit that results from that decision. (To keep things as simple as possible the separate AVC and AFC curves are omitted from this diagram.)

Figure 3.22 Cost and revenue curves for the kayak firm.

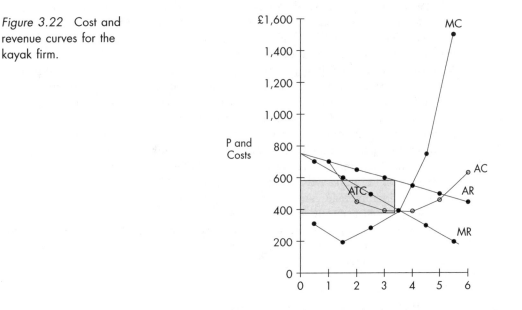

In practice, many firms operate with spare capacity built into their facilities, since designers know that demand fluctuates. The result of this is that in practice many firms' costs look a bit like the one shown in Figure 3.23, with a range of capacity in which the firm feels it can safely operate (over which MC = AVC).

Figure 3.23 Operating with spare capacity.

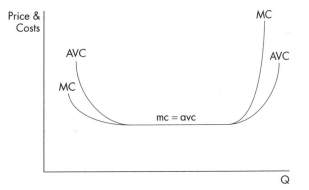

3.9.4 Are firms able to do the graphs?

Many small firms and larger firms with several products find it difficult to identify MR and MC. It is difficult for small firms insofar as most of them are run by people with an expertise in some trade, and are unlikely and disinclined to invest time and effort in conceptualising their firm. Bigger firms are more interested but they often find it difficult because they generally have so many products that correctly identifying the costs attaching to each product, let alone identifying a sensible marginal cost for each, is a mammoth task. On the other hand, finding averages is relatively straightforward and so, as Hall and Hitch (1939) found, firms tend to base their decisions not on MC but on average costs. In fact Hall and Hitch found that firms set their prices (and thus their quantities too) by simply adding a profit mark-up over costs. If, for example, it cost £10 to make a product on average then if we add a profit mark-up of 50% it would mean selling the product at £15. This is called **cost plus pricing**. This seems to rule out considerations of demand altogether; however, subsequent studies have found that firms do consider demand when setting prices. For example, a recent study by the Bank of England (1996) of 654 firms found that most base their prices on both costs and a consideration of the factors that determine price elasticity of demand. Indeed, although firms have difficulty isolating MR, most have an idea of the PeDs that apply to their products. However, PeD and MR are related, since PeD tells us what happens to AR. In addition, average variable costs and MC are related too; if the AVC is flat over a range of output, as in Figure 3.23, then it will be equal to MC. Because of these two links it can be shown that, armed with just PeD and AVC, a firm can find the profit-maximising price and output combination, as the following illustration shows:

Link 1
PeD and MR are related in the following way:

$$MR = P\left(1 + \frac{1}{PeD}\right)$$

And profits are maximised when MR = MC.
So we can substitute MC for MR in the equation above, so

$$MC = P\left(1 + \frac{1}{PeD}\right)$$

Link 2
MC will be the same as AVC over a range of output, so we can substitute AVC for MC in the equation above, which gives:

$$AVC = P\left(1 + \frac{1}{PeD}\right)$$

which rearranges to a rule for pricing:

$$P = AVC\left(\frac{PeD}{1 + PeD}\right)$$

This pricing rule allows the firm to set a price that equates MR and MC using just AVC and PeD.

For example, if a firm estimates that the PeD for its product is −2 and AVC = £10, applying the formula gives:

P = £10(−2/−1) = £20

In this case, the profit-maximising price is £20. The mark-up is 100%. If the PeD were −4 it would be P = £10(−4/−3) = £13. We can see from this that the higher the PeD, the smaller the profit-maximising mark-up. (If the demand is inelastic then this does not work since, as we have seen, the profit-maximising solution in such cases is always to raise price because that increases revenue and reduces costs.) Table 3.7 shows some profit-maximising prices based on an AVC of £10 and various PeDs, which shows this inverse relationship.

Table 3.7

PeD	Price	Mark-up % $\left(\frac{P - AVC}{AVC}\right)$
−2	£20.00p	100
−3	£15.00p	50
−4	£13.33p	33
−5	£12.50p	25
−6	£12.00p	20
−7	£11.67p	17

It is clear, therefore, that the pricing practices of the majority of firms based on mark-ups on costs and elasticities can be seen as a way of establishing profit-maximising prices and quantities when information on MR and MC is limited.

3.10 THE LONG RUN

In the long run, all factors are variable, including the scale of production. In this case, we have no bars to increased production:

Q = f(L, La, Ca, K)

3.10.1 Long-run costs

When a firm has experienced a prolonged expansion in demand for its products, or when a firm is launching a major new product, it may decide to expand its capacity; when it does, there are three possible outcomes. Firstly, the firm may experience **constant returns to scale**, where a given percentage increase in scale leads to the same increase in output, so that, for example, a doubling of scale leads to a doubling of output. Secondly, the firm may experience **decreasing returns to scale**, where the increase in output is less than the increase in scale. Finally, the firm may experience **increasing returns to scale**, where the increase in output exceeds the increase in scale, so that, for example, a doubling of scale leads to a trebling of output. In such a case, unit costs will fall, as happens in Figure 3.24 when a firm builds a bigger factory. If the firm wants to produce Q1 it will choose to stay at its old scale and will be happy to stay in factory A. If, however, it wishes to produce Q2, then if it stays with factory A it will experience a rise in costs from 'a' to 'b'. If, on the other hand, it moves to a bigger scale, it can produce Q2 at lower costs as shown by 'c', as instead of going up the short-run average cost curve of factory A it will go down the AC curve of factory B. So, in effect, as scale is increased the long-run AC (LRAC) curve envelops the short-run AC curves.

Figure 3.24 The effect of increasing returns to scale on costs.

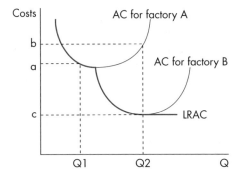

If we add successively larger scales of production, we can see more clearly a downward-sloping LRAC emerging (Figure 3.25).

Figure 3.25 The envelope curve.

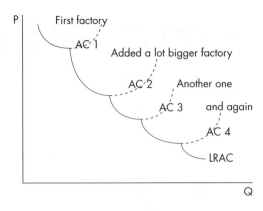

In fact we can envisage the associated long-run marginal cost curves as well, with LRMC eventually exceeding LRAC when (and if) the firm gets so big that it experiences constant returns to scale and then decreasing returns to scale as shown in Figure 3.26.

Figure 3.26 The effect on costs of increasing, constant, and decreasing returns to scale.

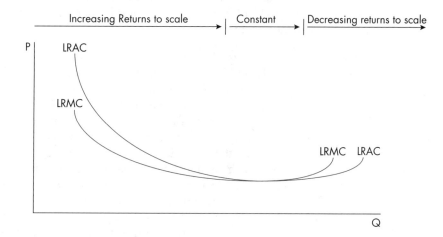

The LRMC curve determines the long-run profit-maximising supply, in the same way that the short-run one determines the short-run supply (Figure 3.27). This means that as increasing returns to scale are generally found to apply (for reasons that we shall consider in the next section), firms in the long run can often supply more at lower prices rather than less.

Figure 3.27 The typical long-run supply curve.

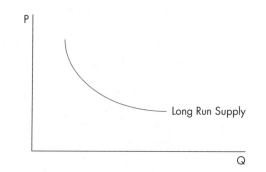

One of the implications of this is that while initially a rise in demand is likely to be met by firms operating in the short run putting prices up, a sustained rise in demand may lead to lower prices, as producers respond by moving to the long run by increasing scale. If, for example, more consumers demand organic food, the price of producing organic food will fall as organic producers get bigger. Once each firm has finished expanding it will find itself back in the short run, but subsequent price rises will start from a lower base.

We now turn to the issue of why increasing returns and decreasing costs tend to be the commonest outcome of an increase in scale.

3.11 ECONOMIES OF SCALE

There are several reasons why costs fall as we increase the scale of production, which are collectively termed **economies of scale**. These are usually presented as simply a function of scale but it is important to recognise the role of management in achieving these:

1. The division of labour: That a greater division of labour into smaller specialist tasks increases output and reduces costs has been recognised for some time. Adam Smith (1776), for example, discussed the importance of this in detail in his discussion of the pin-making industry. He observed that by dividing the job of pin making into a number of separate, simple, repetitive tasks productivity could increase dramatically. While an individual working through the whole process could, in Smith's estimation, not make 20 in a day, with the job divided 10 men could produce 48 thousand pins in a day. The division of labour increases productivity by allowing workers to specialise in what they do best and by making tasks simpler and easier to do. For example, in the production of cars the number of separate skills include design, engineering, marketing, management and many more, while the assembly of the vehicles itself involves hundreds of separate, simple operations. Smith also noted the importance of learning in fully capitalising on the benefits of the division of labour when he found that cost economies tend to increase over time as firms' employees learn from experience the best ways to do individual tasks and managers learn how best to organise the doing of them. This is rather grandly termed 'dynamic economies of learning' today, whereas in Smith's day it was simply called 'learning by doing'. Bigger scale also allows more specialisation in the use of capital and land with further gains in productivity a possibility.

2. Indivisibilities: Some cost-reducing inputs cannot be used in part, or operate inefficiently if not fully utilised, and therefore only come into play when scale is increased. Combine harvesters, for example, come in one size, big, which means that they work relatively inefficiently, if at all, in a small field. Even people can be indivisible, for although someone may be paid hourly they may not be forthcoming if the firm cannot offer them enough work to employ them at least on a part-time basis. So, for example, a small firm might have enough work for a quarter of a marketer, but not for a whole one; therefore, either the general managers do the marketing relatively inefficiently, or they hire a consultancy at great cost.

3. Managerial economies of scale: There are economies of scale associated with particular management functions. For example, there may be marketing economies since advertising is cheaper if you book it in bulk. Bigness may also be an advantage for the sales staff since bigger firms can develop bigger product ranges, which will enable sales staff to tailor a sale to a customer's precise needs. Greater product diversity will also spread the risks associated with environmental uncertainty, so that if one market is in decline the whole firm is not put at risk.

4. Dimensional economies of scale. These are often encountered in transportation and storage; they result from the fact that surface area to volume ratios decline with size. This means that, for example, doubling the length of a boat's storage hold will more than double its holding capacity. This means that it is much more efficient to transport half a million tons of oil in one big oil tanker than in half a million smaller vessels.

5. Power: Because bigger firms are likely to be more significant customers for their suppliers than smaller firms, they are likely to be able to exert more power over them to get bulk discounts and preferential treatment.

6. Economies of pooled resources: Most of the economies of scale mentioned above relate to a firm getting bigger by adding capacity, but firms can also grow in other ways by merging with, or acquiring, other firms. This creates another kind of economy of scale since pooling resources reduces average fixed costs, through the de-duplication of staff functions and so on.

7. External economies of scale: There can also be economies of scale that relate to changes outside the firm, so, for example, a firm can benefit from improved infrastructure and support services because the industry they are in has grown. So, for example, an individual hotel may not need to advertise if the hotel industry in a town grows big enough to warrant support from the local council in advertising the whole resort.

3.11.1 Diseconomies of scale

There may also be diseconomies of scale, where unit costs go up as scale is increased. These may stem from coordination problems, since lines of communication become longer and more complex the bigger the organisation becomes. There may also be motivational problems associated with a greater division of labour, particularly when this leads to workers doing increasingly simple and repetitive tasks, as on assembly lines. Demotivation in such cases results both from boredom and from a sense of alienation from any creative process, and may become manifest in any number of ways that result in management having to devote more time and effort to the control and motivation of the workforce. Indeed, if we were to include job satisfaction as part of the output of a firm, we might view small-scale production in a very different light, as Schumacher (1973) argued in his book *Small is Beautiful: A reconsideration of Economics as if people mattered*. There may in addition be external diseconomies when firms in an industry experiencing high rates of growth find that shortages of skills and specific inputs put their costs up.

3.11.2 The evidence

The empirical evidence suggests that in most industries there are economies of scale, and that in many industries there are significant economies of scale still to be had. This means that if firms were even bigger than they currently are (and most industries are already dominated by a few big firms), efficiency could be increased. We can gauge the scope for economies of scale in different industries by estimating the point at which no extra economies of scale are possible (given the current state of technology), which is called the **minimum efficient scale** and is indicated by 'x' in Figure 3.28. This means that at output levels below 'x' cheaper goods can be produced if firms are allowed to get bigger.

Figure 3.28 Minimum efficient scale (MES).

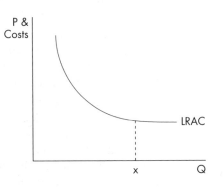

We can compare estimates of this 'x' figure for different industries, either taking the firm as a whole or for each production facility (factory or whatever), and compare it with the size of the market. This will indicate how many firms would remain in business if maximum cost efficiency were to be achieved, so, for example, if we find that the two figures are the same (MES = 100% of the market), then this means that only one firm could get to 'x'. This has two implications: firstly, that having more than one firm in such a case is inefficient, and secondly, that the biggest firm can always undercut everyone else until there is only one firm left. For some people this suggests the need for state intervention to ensure that this does not happen, for others it suggests that in the interest of efficiency winners should be allowed to emerge so that UK-based firms are better able to compete on a world stage. It is not until MES falls to 50% of the size of the market that there is room for another firm. So expressing MES as a percentage of the total output in a market gives us an impression of how much competition is consistent with efficiency, or likely to occur if the market is left to its own devices and winners allowed to emerge. In the case of brick production, for example, economies of scale are exhausted in supplying only a fraction of the market, so the existence of many firms all producing at lowest possible costs is possible. The reason for this is that in the case of bricks they are baked in underground ovens, the size of which is largely fixed by the nature of the process, which means that building bigger ones has few advantages. However, in some industries we find less scope for competition; car producers, for example, cannot achieve full economies of scale by just supplying the UK market, although they can if we look at the bigger European Union (EU) market, as Table 3.8 shows.

	MES as % of total UK production	Implied no. of production facilities	MES as % of total EU production	Implied no. of production facilities
(a) Individual production facilities				
Cellulose fibres	125%	Less than 1	16%	6
Refrigerators	85%	1	11%	9
Steel	72%	1	10%	10
Washing machines	57%	1	10%	10
TVs	40%	2	9%	11
Cigarettes	24%	4	6%	17
Beer	12%	8	3%	33
Bricks	1%	100	0.2%	500
(b) Firms		*Implied no. of firms*		*Implied no. of firms*
Cars	200%	Less than 1	20%	5
Lorries	102%	1	21%	4
Tractors	98%	1	19%	5

Table 3.8 Some examples of MES as % of production, adapted from Pratten (1988).

The implied number of firms is simply the inverse of the MES. Although these figures relate to the 1980s and some differences can be expected to have occurred between then and now, the overall conclusion that there is both scope and incentive for firms to increase scale beyond current levels remains valid.

3.12   SHUTTING DOWN IN THE LONG RUN

To conclude our analysis of the long run we shall look at the circumstances in which the firm should shut down, which in the long run means shutting down permanently. As the long run refers to production runs in which everything is variable, there are no fixed costs. So, unlike the short-run case shown in Figure 3.19, no distinction needs to be made between fixed and variable average costs and the shut-down point is therefore given by the tangency of demand and average costs taken as a whole, in other words between AR and LRAC.

3.13   SHIFTING THE SUPPLY CURVE

As with demand, we can generalise about the kinds of things that will shift supply without being an expert in every industry. In looking at this we will draw short-run supply curves, as in any one week, or month, most firms will not be experiencing an increase in scale. We can represent shifts, as before, by simply drawing new lines to the right or left of the initial one, with a shift to the left indicating less and a shift to the right indicating more, as shown in Figure 3.29, using straight lines for convenience.

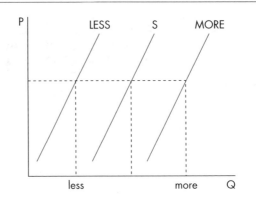

Figure 3.29 Shifting the short-run supply curve.

3.13.1   Time

Thus far we have been looking at output as a function of inputs; when none can be varied we have the immediate run, when some can we have the short-run case, and when all can we have the long run. Time scales were not the issue, but in reality all production occurs in time and so we need to consider the effect of this.

Over time supply curves shift back and forth, but generally they drift to the right. The result is that for many goods more is provided for less today than in the past. So, for example, despite what our grandparents might say, bread is, in 'real' terms (after inflation of prices and incomes is stripped out), cheaper in the UK today than it has ever been. The rightward shift of most supply curves over time is largely due to:

- Economies of scale: Although the long run is not defined in terms of time, nonetheless, over time, we observe more and more firms taking advantage of economies of scale by expanding capacity. This is made possible by the fact that the demand is there, as demand is greater at lower prices and because over the long term people in the West have become materially wealthier. However, some of this expansion has come at the expense of other firms. Indeed, as winners emerge markets tend to become dominated by fewer and fewer firms, although this 'concentration' of industry is not uniform and government policies in both Europe and the USA may have, in some cases at least, put a limit on this.

- Technological advance: Improvements in technology and other inputs increase supply as firms will tend to adopt technologies that improve their efficiency. We shall return to this issue in Chapter 14.

- Learning: This is a process that takes time, so if there are any benefits to it, then these must accumulate over time to some extent.

- De-bugging: A part of the learning process, but worth mentioning separately, is the learning that is associated with getting to know how new inputs or processes or technologies work best for the firm, since even the best-laid plans cannot anticipate exactly how things will pan out.

We can see how the effect of some of these have worked over a relatively short period to bring down costs and prices in the Pentium computer chip market, as shown in Figure 3.30.

Figure 3.30 The market for Pentium-type computer chips.

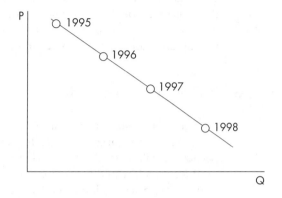

In this market the costs of production have fallen significantly over the past few years as firms gained experience in producing these chips, as the technology involved improved, and as economies of scale were exploited as firms switched from producing a few to producing many. The effect is to shift supply to the right. What we observe over time can be interpreted as the intersection of supply and demand curves in motion, which we shall look at in more detail in the next chapter, but which at this stage we can nonetheless envisage by looking at Figure 3.31. In this case, in order to reflect some knowledge of costs in this industry I have drawn curves, albeit stylised ones, rather than straight lines.

Figure 3.31 The shifts in supply of Pentium-type computer chips.

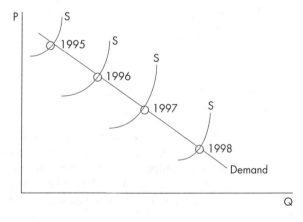

In practice, it is often difficult to identify the source of a fall in costs since economies of scale, changes in technology, and experience all come into play over time. It is important, therefore, not to think of the fall in costs that typically occurs after a firm enters a new market, or introduces a new product, process or technology, as simply an 'experience curve' since other factors may be at work too.

3.13.2 Entry

If firms enter an industry, then supply will shift right, since this has the same effect as an increase in scale by incumbent firms. However, it inevitably means that the incumbent firms have to share the market with the newcomers (the implications of which are discussed in more detail in the next chapter). Firms leaving an industry will reduce supply.

3.13.3 A change in costs

A change in costs that is not caused by increasing output will shift supply. A reduction in variable costs, for example, will shift supply to the right because it will shift MC to the right; in effect it makes each piece cheaper to produce than it would otherwise have been. This enables a firm to supply more at the same price, as indicated by moving from 'a' to 'b' in Figure 3.32, or to supply a bit more at a lower price like 'c'; or if the full reduction in costs were to be passed on by the firm, the firm could supply the same but cut prices from 'a' to 'd'. However, although firms' options are given by the new supply curve, which combination of P and Q gets chosen depends on demand too (as we shall see in the next chapter).

Figure 3.32 The effect of a reduction in cost on supply.

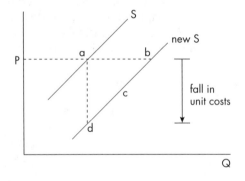

A reduction in fixed costs will also shift market supply to the right, for although it does not affect MC it does make it cheaper to enter the industry, so more firms will enter the market and therefore more will be supplied. A rise in either type of costs will shift market supply to the left.

Costs might fall for a number of reasons:

- A change in wages: A cut in wages makes each piece cheaper to produce and therefore means that, unless it results in an offsetting fall in productivity, supply will shift right. A cut in productivity is, however, a distinct possibility since a cut in wages, or even just a cut in real wages (if wages fail to keep up with inflation), can have a strong demotivating effect on staff. Any rise in wages not matched by a rise in productivity will put unit costs up and thereby shift supply to the left.

- Indirect tax: A reduction in tax on the good will shift supply to the right. Taxes on products are called **indirect** taxes to distinguish them from direct taxes that are taken directly from incomes, like income tax. An increase in indirect tax will effectively add to firms' costs so that supply will shift left, while a reduction in indirect tax will have the opposite effect. There are two main types of indirect tax, 'specific' and '*ad valorem*'. The defining characteristic of an ***ad valorem*** tax is that a percentage is levied on the price, so for example value added tax (VAT) of 17.5% is levied on the sale of computers in the UK, so that the more expensive the computer the more tax is paid. Diagrammatically this means that the supply curve is swivelled rather than shifted by changes in this type of tax (Figure 3.33).

Figure 3.33 The effect of an *ad valorem* tax.

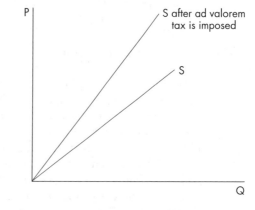

In the case of **specific** taxes a fixed amount is added per unit sold; examples include petrol where so many pence per litre is levied. In this case, the tax per unit does not rise as more is sold, so the shift is a parallel one. The diagram below shows the effect of the rise in the tax on petrol that usually comes each year when the government announces its plans for spending and taxation on 'Budget day'.

Figure 3.34 The effect of an increase in specific tax.

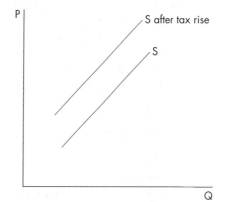

There are also products to which both types of indirect tax apply, such as tobacco. With tobacco, for each packet sold the government takes both an amount per packet and a percentage too (which in combination account for more than half the price of the product).

- Subsidies: A government subsidy will shift supply to the right as it effectively reduces the firm's costs. The removal of a subsidy will add to costs and shift supply left.

- Innovations: Although we have already considered the effect of new processes, procedures or technologies, it is important to count this separately as an important influence in costs, since a cost-reducing innovation can cover any change from an organisational rearrangement to the invention of an entirely new production technique. While an innovation in production will normally reduce costs and shift supply right, innovations that raise costs and shift supply left may occasionally be taken up if they improve quality.

3.13.4 Complements in supply

If in producing one good it becomes easier to produce another, then a movement along the supply curve of one may shift the supply of the other. For example, beef and leather are perfect complements in supply since both result simultaneously from the same production process. If, therefore, the price of beef goes up, more beef and more leather will be supplied, which, since the price of leather did not change, is a shift. Similarly, if a production process has a by-product then more supply of one will shift the supply of the other. So, for example, sawmills produce wood shavings as a by-product; therefore, if their output goes up the supply of wood shavings for pub floors and potpourris shifts right.

3.13.5 Substitutes in production

If a firm can produce more than one product with its existing production process then an increase in the price of a substitute in production will shift supply of the original product to the left, as production is switched, while a rightward shift would result from a price fall in the substitute. So, for example, farmers can produce cabbages or potatoes from the same type of field; therefore, if the price of potatoes goes up the supply of cabbages will shift left as fewer farmers will grow cabbages.

3.13.6 Expectations

Suppliers can act in anticipation of changes in prices if there are substitutes in production. If, for example, a farmer expects potato prices to rise next season, she can plant seed-potatoes this year rather than cabbages. The result is that the supply of potatoes will shift right in anticipation of extra demand. This can, however, cause a problem since in this case demand is relatively stable and the price depends largely on how much is supplied, which means that the price of potatoes is likely to fall, not rise. If subsequently farmers respond by cutting back production for next season, then next season's supply will fall and the price of potatoes will shoot back up again. In fact this volatility in supply and prices is common in industries with long time lags between the start and end of the production run, which is one reason for government interference in these types of markets, which we will discuss in Chapter 8.

3.13.7 Nature

Many production processes, particularly agricultural ones, are affected by natural forces like the amount of sunshine or rain. Adverse weather will shift supply left, while favourable weather will shift supply to the right. The way other PEST factors cause supply to shift, usually through one of the mechanisms listed above, will be considered in more detail in the relevant chapters.

Economic accounting case study

To estimate the real costs facing a firm is not easy, but there are some principles that we can follow in comparing economic (opportunity) costs with the figures provided by accountants. Accountants' figures for all limited companies are recorded for public inspection in their 'Report and Accounts', logged at Companies House, Cardiff. Fortunately, some of the figures do not need adjusting to reveal the opportunity cost; in addition, some firms provide an idea of their 'added value' which approximates to an economist's version of real profits.

To assess the economic costs we need to make a distinction between explicit and implicit costs. Explicit costs are paid-for factors not owned by the firm and are an exact measure of the opportunity cost.

Some examples of explicit costs for a small shoe manufacturer, 'Salvatorie's Shoes', are as shown in Table 3.9:

Table 3.9 Costs for Salvatorie's Shoes.

£ per annum Cost	Accounting statement	Economic statement
Raw materials (leather, glue, nails)	£50k	Same
Labour	£100k	Same
Electricity	£20k	Same
Rental of retail outlet (shop)	£10k	Same
Hire of photocopier and other equipment	£2k	Same
Total explicit costs	£182k	£182k

Implicit costs relate to factors that are owned by the firm and involve no explicit payments to other parties outside the firm. If, for example, the firm is owner managed, then the opportunity cost of this is the salary that the owner could get working somewhere else. Suppose, for example, Mr Salvatorie pays himself £30k but could earn £40k elsewhere. His salary will then understate the real cost to the firm of using him in this way by £10k. Consider next the buildings, or other physical assets such as machinery, owned by the firm. If any of these could be rented out or hired out to other firms, the amount that could be made from doing this is the opportunity cost. If, for example, the shoe factory was owned outright and could be rented out for £15k a year, then the opportunity cost of not renting it out is £15k. Similarly, if the firm owns machinery that could be hired out, for say £10k a year, then the opportunity cost of not doing this is £10k. The same argument can be applied to any financial assets owned and used by the firm, as these could be lent to other firms. This applies to any finance provided by the owner and any retained profits. Mr Salvatorie, for example, put £20k of his own money into the firm this year, and, in addition, the firm used £10k of retained profits. For these, the opportunity cost is the value that the £30k could have earned if it had been invested elsewhere, which with interest rates around 10% at the time would have been around £3k. We therefore count £3k as the opportunity cost to the shoe firm of keeping and using the money itself. For similar reasons, we should also consider the opportunity cost of money invested by the firm. Suppose, for example, the shoe firm buys a machine for £50k that embosses the word 'Salvatorie' on the shoes; this will be included as a cost by the accountant but the economist would add the alternative use of the money to the accountant's figure. Supposing again that an interest rate of around 10% could have been earned by putting the money to another use, we have an additional opportunity cost of about £5k.

Although at every point thus far we have added more costs, there are some cases where accountants' conventional costing practices overstate the true costs, particularly in respect of depreciation. Suppose, for example, that the embossing machine was expected to last 10 years; conventional accounting practice would discount the machine at, perhaps, £5k a year, and this £5k would appear each year as the cost of the service provided by the machine. This would overstate the opportunity cost insofar as the machine does not have an alternative use; as there is no other shoe firm with the name 'Salvatorie', there is no opportunity cost in owning and using the machine. The £5k calculation might serve to remind the firm that the machine is wearing out, and that it should consider the costs of replacing it in future. However, since it does not relate to any current cost it should not therefore count in assessing the profitability of the firm or in making decisions about the level of production. Once the £50k was spent on the machine, it became a sunk cost. The differences between accountants' and economists' calculations for implicit costs are shown in Table 3.10:

Table 3.10
Accountants'
and economists'
calculations for
implicit costs.

£ per annum Cost	Accounting statement	Economic statement
Owner's earnings	£30k	£40k
Factory use	None	£15k
Machines use	None	£10k
Use of financial assets	None	£3k
Purchase of embossing machine (explicit cost)	£50k	£50k
Use of money to buy embossing machine	None	£5k
Depreciation on embossing machine	£5k	None
Total costs	£85k	£123k

If we add these costs to the firm's explicit costs and subtract these from the firm's total revenues of £300k, we get total profits as shown in Table 3.11.

Whereas the accountant's report would indicate that this firm is making a profit of £33k, in truth the owner would be better off working for somebody else, closing

Table 3.11 Total profits.			
	Total explicit costs	£182k	£182k
	Total implicit costs	£85k	£123k
	Total costs	£267k	£305k
	Total revenue	£300k	£300k
	Total profits	£33k	£–5k

the firm down, putting his money in the bank, and renting out the factory and machines. This is not to say that he must do that; as an owner manager he might like to keep things going, as long as accounting losses are not too large, in the hope that better days lie ahead for his firm. He may also be emotionally attached to running his own business. The same cannot be said for firms owned by shareholders, as they tend to be in it for the return they can get. Whatever the decision, the consideration of opportunity cost will play a part, either explicitly or implicitly, and this is why economists include them in their cost curves since they are drawn to explain the decisions that business people make.

3.14 SUMMARY

- Economists define supply in terms of price and quantities; this allows us to put a supply curve on the same graph as a demand curve.

- Supply curves tend to be upward sloping in the short run, but may be downward sloping in the long run.

- The short run is when at least one input factor is fixed; this constraint means that the costs associated with adding more of the variable factors (the variable costs) will eventually rise as output is increased. This is the basis of the law of diminishing marginal returns.

- The law of diminishing returns means that a profit-maximising firm will supply more at higher prices to compensate for rising marginal costs, producing an upward-sloping supply curve.

- The long run is when no fixed factors are applied; when, for example, a firm builds another factory, in which case the law of diminishing returns is temporarily side-stepped.

- Building another factory or increasing the scale of production in any other way often results in much lower unit costs, which means that in the long run the supply curve can be downward sloping.

- We often focus on the short run since most of the time it will apply. A number of factors will cause the short-run supply curve to shift, including lower or higher wages, taxes and subsidies, and innovations.

- Although the difference between short-run and long-run production is not one of time *per se*, time will have an effect on supply, which to avoid confusion we consider as a separate factor.

3.15 **QUESTIONS**

1. Which of the following might be a fixed cost for an ice-cream firm?
    (a) A variable rate mortgage on the factory
    (b) Petrol
    (c) Milk
    (d) Business rates (local tax)

2. Which one of the following could cause supply to shift left?
    (a) The imposition of an indirect tax on the good
    (b) A subsidy
    (c) A rise in incomes
    (d) A fall in wage costs

3. Which one of the following could cause the supply of bread to shift right?
    (a) Good growing weather
    (b) The invention of microwave baking
    (c) The entry of new firms into the market
    (d) A tax on bread

4. There is some evidence that in the UK we invest less in capital than some other countries.
    (a) What are the implications of this for the relative productivity of UK labour?
    (b) What does this imply for the UK's overall economic performance?

5. Bestfoods, who own the Marmite yeast spread brand, initiated a significant reorganisation of their European production facilities in 1997. They closed many smaller production facilities and expanded the scale of the remaining ones. What do you think they hope to achieve by doing this? Illustrate your answer with a diagram.

CHAPTER 4

Supply and demand analysis

After studying this chapter, you should be able to:

● understand how prices and the quantity of goods sold is determined by the inter-action of supply and demand;

● appreciate why it is necessary to depict the interaction of firms and consumers, or firms and their suppliers, using a diagram rather than with words alone;

● define what is meant by the equilibrium price and quantity, and appreciate how market forces work;

● explain how changes or trends in the business environment through their impact on supply or demand can change the equilibrium price and quantity prevailing in a market;

● explain how the effects of changes or trends in the business environment entail threats and opportunities for firms that are revealed by considering their likely impact on the equilibrium price and quantity prevailing in a market;

● appreciate that while environmental contingencies help to determine strategic opportunities and threats they do not dictate firms courses of action;

● understand that managing the environment by manipulating markets remains a strategic option for many firms.

4.1 SUPPLY AND DEMAND

The market represented in Figure 4.1 is an estimate of the weekly market for kayaks in the UK, based on multiplying the figures for the kayak firm discussed in Chapter 3 by 10. This number was chosen because the firm's owner estimates that her firm's sales account for 10% of the UK market. There are better ways of estimating supply and demand curves, but we leave the discussion of those until Chapter 16.

Figure 4.1 The UK
market for kayaks.
Weekly figures.

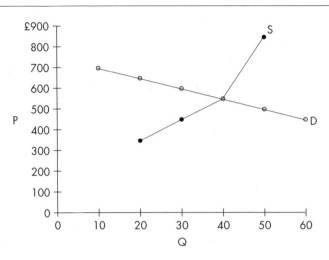

If the price in this market was on average £850 per kayak, suppliers would
be willing to supply 50 a week, but demand would be zero, and hence none
would be sold. At this price, there is therefore an excess supply, in other words
a surplus. In this case, the surplus would be 50 unsold kayaks (per week).
However, as long as there is competition one firm could undercut this price
and corner the market (that is, take all the customers). If, for example, our
firm offered kayaks for sale at £700 it could sell 10. This would be great news
for our kayak firm as its profit-maximising output is 4 in the short run; it would
mean it could open another factory and, at £700 a kayak, make significant
super normal profits. However, any firm can do this and, unfortunately for
our firm, they will. Therefore, everyone does and thus the market is shared
rather than cornered by one firm, but as this happens the price is forced down
until we get to the point where the lines cross. If a firm lowers its price below
this, it would not be able to meet the demand this would generate and customers would be disappointed. For example, at a price of £450 there is an
excess demand, or shortage, since suppliers can supply 30 but consumers want
60, which means that any firm can sell their kayaks at a higher price and still
find buyers. As before, all firms will try to do this, which will force prices back
up to the point at which the shortage is zero where the two lines cross. All that
is required for these forces to operate is that there is some competition; if there
is no competition the firm might be quite happy to see surpluses or shortages,
or in short, do whatever it likes. The more competition there is, the greater
these 'market forces' will be. The strength of market forces also depends on
the nature of the production process; in mining, for example, output cannot
be adjusted quickly and, if a surplus results, suppliers will often carry large
stocks for months before they lower prices. On the other hand, in baking, any
surplus generally gets sold the next day at half price.

The way competition creates market forces that guide traders to the mutually agreeable price, inspired Adam Smith (1723–90) to call it the 'invisible
hand', although in his day the description of it was verbal rather than graphical. The advantage of graphs is that it is easy to see to where the invisible

hand is pushing traders, as it is the place where the lines cross. This point is called the **equilibrium** or **market clearing** point: equilibrium because it is a point of rest, since everywhere else there are forces pushing traders towards it, which, once reached, stop; market clearing because at this price there are no unplanned surpluses or shortages as every supplier who wants to sell at that price can find a buyer, and every buyer who wants to buy at that price can find a supplier, so the market is cleared out (except for deliberately held stocks on shelves). That it is the point at which both sides of a market are brought into agreement does not mean that trades outside of equilibrium cannot happen. However, in most markets the forces are sufficient to ensure that looking at what happens to the equilibrium will tell us where the market is headed. This means that insofar as any change in the business environment shifts supply or demand we can, by looking at the effect of these changes on the equilibrium point, assess the implications for prices, quantities, costs, revenues and profits for firms. So, although complicated to build, supply and demand analysis is a very simple tool to use for analysing the impact of changes in the external environment on firms. It is simple to use since any environmental change will normally affect only one of the curves, which means that to get our answers we move one line and read off the result. If, on reflection, we decide that the change, or indeed trend, in the business environment will not affect supply or demand then we can ignore it, since that implies that it has no effect on prices, quantities, revenues, costs or profits.

To do this analysis correctly all we have to do is answer two questions:

Question 1   *Does the change shift supply or demand?*

Question 2   *Which way? Right (more) or left (less)?*

We can then draw this and read off the results for prices and quantities transacted (sales) in the market. To do this we simply draw a cross to represent the starting position of supply and demand, and then move a line to see in which direction the equilibrium goes. It can only go in one of four general directions, of course, as Figure 4.2 shows.

Figure 4.2 The four general directions in which the equilibrium can go.

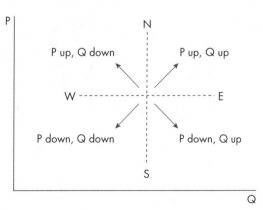

EXAMPLE 1

Market: Cornish ice-cream   Environmental change: Fall in wages

Result: Supply shifts right, leading to lower prices and more sales as the equilibrium moves from 'e' to 'e1' (Figure 4.3). In this case there is more demand as we go down the demand curve in response to the lowering of the supply price. We often refer to this as an **extension** of demand (or **contraction** if going the other way) simply to differentiate this increase in demand from an increase in demand caused by a shift.

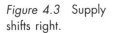
Figure 4.3 Supply shifts right.

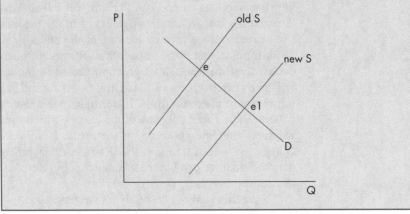

EXAMPLE 2

Market: Cider   Environmental change: Price of lager rises significantly

Result: An increase in the price of a substitute will shift demand to the right, more cider will be sold, and cider prices will rise as the equilibrium moves from 'e' to 'e1' (Figure 4.4). As before, we can refer to this increase in supply in response to the increased demand as an extension of supply (or contraction if going the other way) to differentiate it from an increase caused by a shift in supply.

Figure 4.4 Demand shifts right.

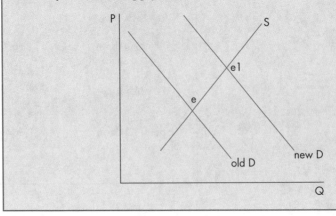

Although the idea of looking at things in terms of supply and demand has been around for a long time, the simple diagrammatic analysis with the two lines that cross was largely developed by Alfred Marshall (1842–1924) in the 1890s. It is often called **partial equilibrium analysis** because it entails looking at part of the economy at a time, for example at one market, or even at one firm. It is also often called **comparative statics** since it involves comparing one static position with another, in contrast to dynamics which involves looking at the path by which we move from one situation to another.

In applying this analysis it is important to resist the temptation to move both lines as in most cases any change will mainly affect one line not both. Consider, for example, the market for new cars in the UK. If there is a recession then, as cars are normal goods (taken as a whole), the demand curve will shift left and sales will fall. The temptation is to think that suppliers will see the recession coming and cut prices. We can represent this by shifting the supply curve to the right in anticipation of the fall in demand as shown in Figure 4.5.

Figure 4.5 Moving both lines.

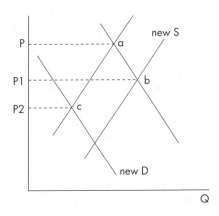

This shows the firms cutting prices from 'P' to 'P1', moving the equilibrium from 'a' to 'b'. However, firms do not respond to recession by increasing supply, which means that moving both lines is a mistake. If, instead, we let the model speak for itself and simply shift the demand curve and leave it at that, we can see that firms do in fact cut prices from 'P' to 'P2' as a response to the decline in demand, moving the equilibrium from 'a' to 'c'. We do not need to move supply as well because the supply curve shows what suppliers do when demand changes, as indicated in Figure 4.6.

We could draw the supply curve steeper if we want to imply that the price cutting is extensive, or flatter if we wish to imply less price cutting and more loss of sales. But generally we should only move another line if we want to consider another environmental change, in which case it is better to have another diagram too. We could even consider another aspect of recession, perhaps that by pushing unemployment up it results in lower wages and a rightward shift in supply. In this case, we have another cause–effect sequence; this time the cause is unemployment. The fact that the term 'recession' encompasses a number of causes and effects simply encourages us to be clear about what aspect of recession we are considering, rather than move lines willy-nilly. The alternative is to look at all the knock-on effects simultaneously which is the

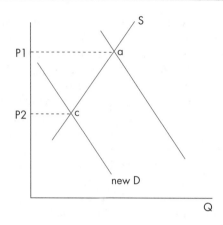

Figure 4.6 Not moving both lines.

general equilibrium approach. However, research suggests that knock-on effects tend to be relatively minor and that the direction of a price–quantity change is unaffected; therefore, although any quantitative approach will be affected by the fact that everything affects everything else, our 'qualitative' diagrams are not. Even in the case of workers' wages, which are an important factor in both demand and supply, one effect normally dominates at the level of the firm. A cut in wages, for example, means more supply but less demand, which for the whole economy can mean that a cut in all wages makes firms poorer. However, at the level of the individual firm this interdependency between supply and demand is negligible, as its workers will not be its only customers or even a significant part of the total.

This is not, however, to say that we should never move both lines; in some cases, both sides are affected by an environmental change. Take oil, for example; this affects supply as it is an input into the production processes of firms using or making plastics or using electricity, or diesel power for transportation and it affects demand because petrol takes such a large chunk of consumer's incomes that changes in its price affect everyone's spending power. This means that if oil prices go up significantly consumers are effectively made poorer, and the demand for many products will fall, while at the same time many firms' costs go up too, so we might find that we go from 'a' to 'c' in Figure 4.7 rather than from 'a' to 'b'.

Figure 4.7 Oil prices affect both supply and demand.

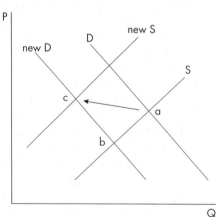

Firms' power also affects the separability of supply and demand. Take advertising, for example. This is an attempt by firms to manipulate demand, in other words, to manage that part of their environment, but doing so involves adding to their costs. So again, both supply and demand are affected. In this case, we might go from 'a' to 'c' in Figure 4.8 rather than 'a' to 'b'.

Figure 4.8 Managing the environment can have implications for both supply and demand.

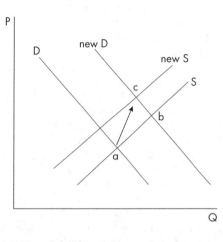

Case study

THE CAR INDUSTRY

The increase in supply in the car industry in recent years comes from both traditional multinationals such as Ford and from the entry of newcomers such as Hyundai and Daewoo.

Figure 4.9 World supply and demand for cars.

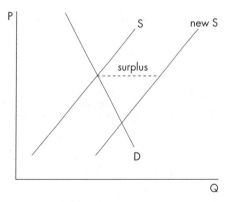

Combined, this means that worldwide it is estimated that at 1998 prices supply now exceeds demand by as much as 40%. This situation is pictured in Figure 4.9.

Prices have already fallen in both real and nominal terms, but could fall a lot further. The lower prices represent a threat to all firms in this industry. Firstly, firms that are either too small to compete on price or unable to command a premium price by virtue of their distinctive qualities may go bust. Indeed Kia, the third-biggest South Korean car manufacturer, was on the brink of collapse before it was 'rescued' by being taken over by Hyundai, the biggest South

Korean producer. Secondly, taken as a whole, the demand for cars is likely to be inelastic, which means that lower prices will mean lower revenues for the whole industry.

To deal with this problem, the biggest firms in this industry are engaging in a programme of take-overs and mergers to eliminate the 'over-capacity' and increase their economies of scale. Hyundai, as mentioned above, has already moved on its ailing rival Kia; BMW has acquired the Rover group and Chrysler has merged with Daimler. In addition, Ford, which has already swallowed minnows like Jaguar, has a $25bn 'war chest' for some bigger moves, with possible candidates including Honda, Nissan, Volvo and BMW. Ford is also looking to make some 'strategic alliances' with its biggest rivals that would eliminate competition by allowing the collaborative production of some cars and yet by-pass existing monopolies and merger regulations. As Jac Nasser CEO of Ford says in discussing the nature of rivalry in this industry 'We are always talking. In this business anything is possible.'

National interest is another card that some manufacturers are playing. For example, in South Korea the car industry accounts for 10% of its national output and is a major export earner for a country whose success is built on its ability to penetrate foreign markets. This means that the current in-fighting within the Korean car market has become a threat to the whole economy. The solution according to Hyundai is that the Korean authorities agree to support rather than discourage collaboration between itself and Daewoo, its biggest rival.

The situation in the UK

Since the early 1980s, British governments have encouraged car manufacturers to set up production in the UK. In particular, non-European producers were encouraged to set up plant here through all manner of grants and subsidies as a way of getting a foothold into the European market. This was seen as a way of mopping up the unemployment that had resulted from the collapse of our own manufacturing base. In that respect it has certainly helped; actual vehicles produced have rocketed from less than 900,000 in 1982 to over 1.7 million in 1998, while nearly 350,000 people are now directly employed in car manufacturing in the UK. Indeed, it is over double that if we include support industries such as car retailing and so on. However, we have the capacity to produce perhaps in excess of 5 million, since producers are running at around a quarter of capacity, because of lack of demand. We might expect that, with supply exceeding demand by this amount, prices would tumble. This need not be disastrous for the producers; if demand is elastic, revenues will go up and if production levels are increased more economies of scale would come into play. This would mean that the price cuts would no more lead to lower profits for today's producers than the price cuts initiated by Henry Ford in the 1920s led to lower profits for Ford. However, many industry watchers are worried that demand overall is inelastic and that plant closures and layoffs will play a big part in the story of how this industry adjusts to this excess capacity.

4.1.1 Summary table of demand and supply shifters

Table 4.1   A summary of demand and supply shifters is given in Table 4.1.

Cause	Direction of change	Effect	Effect on prices and quantity sold
Demand shifters Consumer tastes (fashion) – the subjective preferences that are not influenced by price.	Increase (in total, consumers decide they wish to have more of this good).	Demand shifts to the right.	P up, Q up.
	Decrease (in total, consumers have gone off this good).	Demand shifts to the left.	P down, Q down.
Substitute good or service (a good which can be used instead of the good in question, e.g. Vegimite and Marmite).	Fall in value for money, i.e. an increase in price (e.g. price of Marmite goes up) or a fall in quality of Marmite.	Demand shifts right (demand for Vegimite goes up).	P up, Q up.

Table 4.1   (cont'd)

Cause	Direction of change	Effect	Effect on prices and quantity sold
	Rise in VFM: decrease in price (price of Marmite goes down) or improved quality at the same price.	Demand shifts left (demand for Vegimite falls).	P down, Q down.
Complementary good or service (a good which is consumed along with the good in question, e.g. film and cameras)	Fall in VFM due to increased price (price of cameras rises) or reduction in quality.	Demand shifts to the left (less demand for film).	P down, Q down.
	Rise in VFM: decrease in price (fall in price of cameras) or improved quality.	Demand shifts to the right (more demand for film).	P up, Q up.
Income	Increase	Demand shifts right for normal goods.	P up, Q up.
		Demand shifts left for inferior goods.	P down, Q down.
	Decrease	Demand shifts left for normal goods.	P down, Q down.
		Demand shifts right for inferior goods.	P up, Q up.
Advertising and marketing in general	Increased information or persuasion.	Demand usually shifts right.	P up, Q up.
	Decreased information or persuasion.	Demand usually shifts left.	P down, Q down.
Expectations	Expected rise in price in future.	Demand shifts right in advance.	P up, Q up.
	Expected fall in price in future.	Demand shifts left in advance.	P down, Q down.
Supply shifters Land	Land prices fall.	Supply shifts right (when firm needs more land).	P down, Q up.
	Land prices rise.	Supply shifts left (if firm uses land).	P down, Q up.
Labour	Works better or cheaper (real wages fall).	Supply shifts right (depending, as above, on how much is used).	P down, Q up.
	Productivity falls or real wages rise.	Supply shifts left.	P up, Q down.
Fixed capital	Production machinery gets cheaper or better as technology advances.	Supply shifts right.	P down, Q up.
	Production machinery becomes more expensive or deteriorates in quality.	Supply shifts left.	P up, Q down.

Table 4.1   (cont'd)

Cause	Direction of change	Effect	Effect on prices and quantity sold
Raw materials	Raw material prices fall.	Supply shifts right.	P down, Q up.
	Raw material prices rise.	Supply shifts left.	P up, Q down.
Indirect *Ad valorem* tax (a % of the price)	Increase (e.g. VAT up).	Supply swivels to the left.	P up, Q down.
	Decrease (e.g. VAT down).	Supply swivels to the right.	P down, Q up.
Indirect Specific tax (fixed amount is taxed on each unit sold, e.g. 10p)	Increase (e.g. excise duty on petrol up).	Supply shifts left.	P up, Q down.
	Decrease (e.g. excise duty on petrol down).	Supply shifts right.	P down, Q up.
Subsidy	Increase.	Supply shifts left.	P up, Q down.
	Decrease.	Supply shifts right.	P down, Q up.

4.2   OPPORTUNITIES AND THREATS

All aspects of the business environment can be seen as affecting the firm's ability to supply an output, or as affecting consumers' demand for that output. Through the analysis of supply and demand we can therefore characterise the kinds of effects that trends and changes in the business environment will have on firms, which we can categorise as opportunities or threats, for each of the four directions in which a market may be headed.

4.2.1   Demand shifts left

This might be due to a change in any of the PEST factors; for example, for a normal good a recession will lead to a fall in demand, as shown in Figure 4.10.

Figure 4.10 A shift in demand to the left.

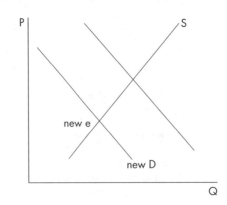

Threats and opportunities

This shift contains a clear threat to profitability as total revenue has fallen. The lower prices may have an uneven effect, however; low cost providers, for example, may get a bigger slice of the cake, even though the whole cake is smaller. Those without a cost advantage may therefore face a double squeeze on their profits; they may in response seek to increase the degree of differentiation between their product and those of their rivals. Perhaps they can improve quality in some way, or perhaps they can cut costs by reducing quality, which may be particularly useful if the cause of the fall in demand is recession, or perhaps they can alter some of the other characteristics of the product in some way. Alternatively, they may put considerable effort into pushing demand back up; indeed, some of the biggest advertising campaigns ever mounted have been undertaken by firms with their backs against the wall in this way.

4.2.2 Demand shifts right

This might be due to a change in any of the PEST factors; for example, for a normal good a rise in incomes will have the effect shown in Figure 4.11.

Figure 4.11 A shift in demand to the right.

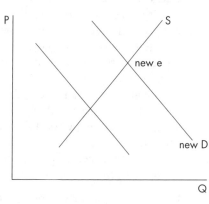

Threats and opportunities

In this case, we have a market in which there is an increase in total revenue and profitability, although with that comes an increased threat of entry, as profits act as a magnet to other firms. In addition, rises in prices mean that a higher spend is involved for each purchase and therefore consumers may spend longer considering their purchasing decisions, which could lead to a search for quality or for alternatives. With these possibilities in mind, incumbent firms (firms already in the market) should not take a rise in demand as an opportunity to rest on their laurels.

4.2.3 Supply shifts left

Any PEST factor causing a reduction in productivity, or a rise in costs, can do this (Figure 4.12).

Figure 4.12 Supply shifts left.

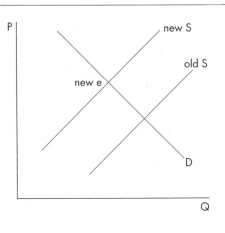

Threats and opportunities

In general, if supply shifts to the left firms will get less profit as revenues fall, unless they face an inelastic demand, in which case revenues will rise. However if the reason for the supply shift is a rise in costs then this will exceed any such rise in revenue, since only if the demand is perfectly inelastic will they be able to pass the full cost rise on to their customers. This means that for a cost rise all firms are likely to lose out, but the more elastic the demand, the more they lose.

The ability of firms facing inelastic demands to pass some of the burden of adjustment of a cost rise on to their customers is why governments put taxes on goods such as petrol, tobacco and alcohol. For these goods, governments know that a rise in tax will raise revenue for the exchequer without forcing firms out of business. Generally the burden of any increase in cost (or the benefits of any fall) are shared by buyers in the following way:

1. Producer power will be low and their share of the burden higher the more elastic the demand and the less elastic the supply, as shown in Figure 4.13.

Figure 4.13 The burden of adjustment falls mainly to firms.

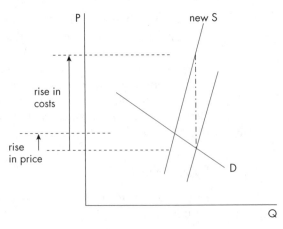

2. Consumer power will be less, and they will pay more the more inelastic is their demand and the more elastic the supply, as shown in Figure 4.14.

Figure 4.14 The burden of adjustment falls mainly to consumers.

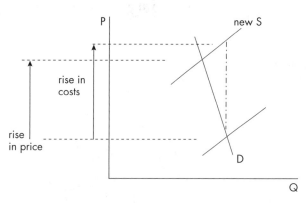

We can see the effect that differences in elasticity have on the burden of adjustment by looking at what happened when the government introduced VAT on take-away food in the budget of 1984. Within a few months traditional fish and chip shops were reporting reduced sales and profitability, so much so that a newsworthy number went bust, while more expensive take-away outlets such as Indian restaurants and hamburger chains reported little change in sales or profitability. It was the same change in the business environment that applied to both sectors but the effect of it was very different because fish and chip shops faced more elastic demand curves. The difference this makes can be seen by comparing 'a' and 'b' in Figure 4.15.

Figure 4.15 Two different markets within the same industry.

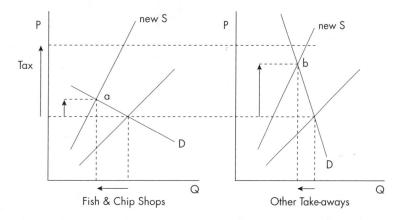

For fish and chip shops, sales fell considerably and little of the rise in costs could be passed on in terms of higher prices, which led to a significant fall in profits. For other take-away outlets, sales fell less and more of the rise in costs could be passed on to consumers, so that profits fell little.

The effect on a firm of a rightward shift depends on whether it entails the exit of competitors; indeed, if it is entirely due to the exit of rivals the remaining firms would benefit unequivocally. In such a case, for the remaining firms the only effect is more demand, which means that although for the market it is a supply shift, as far as the remaining firms are concerned it is a demand shift, as shown in Figure 4.16.

Figure 4.16 The effect of firms leaving a market on those that remain.

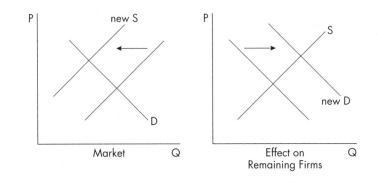

4.2.4 Supply shifts right

This can be due to any change in the PEST factors that improves productivity or reduces costs (Figure 4.17).

Figure 4.17 Supply shifts right.

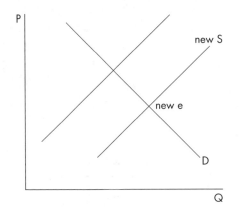

Threats and opportunities

If the increase is due to lower costs, suppliers will benefit from the change by expanding production and grabbing more customers, which for an elastic demand means both lower costs and more revenue. Industry demand curves are, however, often inelastic, which means that as costs fall, revenues will also fall. The net effect depends on the size of the cost fall and the degree of inelasticity (as discussed in Section 4.2.3 above), but will always be positive; that is, firms will always make more profit, unless the demand is perfectly inelastic. If demand is perfectly inelastic, any fall in unit costs will be totally passed on in lower prices, and firms will gain nothing except happier customers, as shown in Figure 4.18.

Figure 4.18 Only with a perfectly inelastic demand does a firm gain nothing from a fall in costs.

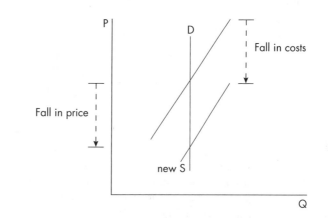

If the reason for the shift is an increase in capacity or new entry then any benefits are likely to be taken by those who are doing the expanding or entering, and even if the market demand is elastic it is rarely elastic enough to allow more revenue for both old and new firms alike (if it was, incumbents would probably have increased output themselves). If the market demand is inelastic then the total market revenue will fall; it can still be profitable for the new entrants but the cake will have shrunk. In addition, the incumbent firms will get a smaller slice of the cake since it is now being shared, so the demand for their products will shift to the left. One obvious way around these problems is to collaborate with the newcomers to keep prices and profitability up in return for an unchallenged slice of the market, possibly (if they represent a big enough threat) even to the extent of merging with them. Alternatively, incumbent firms may price low to keep newcomers out, in the hope that if it is a costly market to enter this may help to put them off, and in the knowledge that they probably have lower production costs than newcomers. They may also start an advertising campaign in order to strengthen brand loyalty and again put newcomers off. However, while both of these may work to deter newcomers they would have little effect if the increase in supply is due to an existing rival simply increasing their scale.

4.3   FROM QUALITATIVE TO QUANTITATIVE

Our diagrams represent a qualitative approach, insofar as they allow us to make predictions on the directions but not the magnitudes of changes. We can, however, see that there is a link between what we have drawn and the numbers involved by comparing the scale of the changes in TC and TR implied by any change. For example, if demand shifts left we have a fall in profits equal to the shaded area shown in Figure 4.19.

Figure 4.19
Quantifying the effect on profits of a shift in demand.

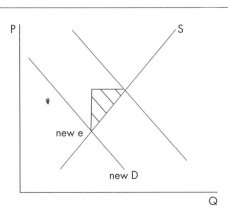

In this industry profits fall by the amount indicated by the shaded triangle because this triangle shows the scale of the change in TR minus the change in TC, since TR is given by P × Q and TC is the area under the supply curve, as shown in Figure 4.20.

Figure 4.20
Calculating the change in profit.

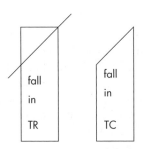

This, of course, assumes that the effect on the firm under consideration mirrors what happens to the whole market and that we know how far to shift the lines, and if we did know the numbers we would not need to do the drawing. The point, however, is simply to illustrate the link between our qualitative analysis and quantitative results, for in practice we have better ways of dealing with quantification which we shall look at in Chapter 15.

4.4   IMPACT ASSESSMENT GRID

So using supply and demand analysis, we can categorise the effects on firms of changes and trends in the business environment. However, a prerequisite of this is that we decide what changes or trends to look at. To help us make such decisions we can use some form of impact assessment grid. This is based on the idea that there are two considerations to bear in mind when deciding what to look at: firstly, whether the change will occur (or if we are looking at trends, whether the trend will continue); secondly, whether it will have a big impact on the firm or not. If the firm's decision makers can agree that something is both likely to happen and likely to have a big impact on the firm then further investigation is warranted (Table 4.2). Supply and demand analysis can then be used to articulate the nature of the threat or opportunity and an estimation of the effects on the firm using statistics may be carried out (as discussed in Chapter 15).

Table 4.2

		Effect on firm	
		HIGH	**LOW**
Likelihood of change occurring or trend continuing	HIGH	Evaluate and include in your plans	Keep an eye on it
	LOW	Draw up a contingency plan in case it happens	Ignore

Of course, the trends or changes that we choose to ignore today might be important next time we look, so no such assessment can be thought of as set in concrete. Having decided what PEST factors to focus on, the firm may input the expectations about environmental patterns of its own experts, or of senior managers, or it may turn to the expertise of others.

4.5 SOURCES OF INFORMATION ABOUT ENVIRONMENTAL PATTERNS

There is, in fact, a multi-million pound forecasting industry from which a firm can extract the best guesses about likely patterns in the external environment. There are, for example, a number of sources of economic forecasts, including the government itself, the London Business School and the National Institute for Social and Economic Research. There are other groups, such as the Henley Centre, that provide forecasts of a range of social as well as economic factors and the government also provides demographic (population) forecasts. There are also many 'futurologists' looking at very long-term trends relating to all sorts of things. On political proposals, we can refer to manifesto documents and regular statements from political parties. In addition, we should not overlook the fact that there is a lot of information published in the press, and discussed on the TV and radio, which can be accessed at very low cost.

4.6 SWOT ANALYSIS

Having decided what to look at, collected our data and done our analysis we can assess individual firms' characteristics, in short their strengths and weaknesses, in order to determine how well placed they are to deal with the environmental changes we envisage. In doing this, it is important not to see the firm's strengths and weaknesses in isolation but as contingent upon the threats and opportunities that we foresee. So, for example, while we might acknowledge that a firm is strong in quality, if the market values low price above quality then this may be a weakness since it is likely to entail higher costs. One device that forces us to think simultaneously of strengths, weaknesses, opportunities and threats, is the SWOT matrix, since by virtue of being a matrix, it forces us to cross-reference SW with OT. Even if we cannot attach payoffs to a SWOT matrix we can use it to assist in formulating strategy, since it shows for each environmental trend or change under review what is likely to be involved in maximising strengths, minimising weaknesses, and taking advantage of the opportunities and avoiding the threats that it contains. What to do to achieve this is covered in more detail in texts on corporate strategy, of course.

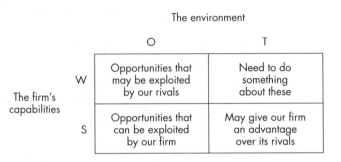

4.7 | MANAGING THE ENVIRONMENT

We should also remember that we cannot rule out the strategic option of reversing a change in the business environment that looks like it will hurt the firm, or of intervening in the operation of the business environment to the firm's advantage. Indeed, every time we consider an environmental change and investigate what firms might do in response to it, we must remember that managing the environment is one of the strategic options (for some of the bigger firms at least). When, for example, in the early 1980s everyone started wearing light cotton trousers rather than jeans, some firms responded by lowering prices, as shown in Figure 4.21.

Figure 4.21
The market for denim jeans in the early 1980s.

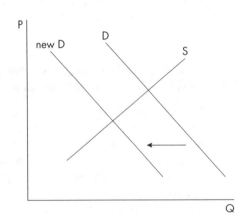

But the Levi-Strauss Corporation did not; reluctant to lower prices, it instead initiated the largest advertising campaign ever involving, in one memorable case, Nick Kamen undressing in a launderette, which was so successful that sales of jeans were restored, as shown in Figure 4.22.

Figure 4.22 The market for denim jeans in the mid 1980s, after the Levi advertising campaign.

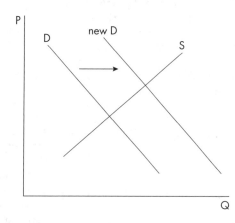

This was very successful for Levi. However, it should be noted that managing the environment, in this or indeed any other way, is not an easy option; there are no guarantees any more than there are with any other strategy. The Levi Corporation is, for example, in difficulty now because of the popularity of substitute clothing, but the prospect of reversing the trend as they did in the 80s now seems remote, since with the likes of Tony Blair, Bill Clinton and Jeremy Clarkson wearing Levi's today, it would be harder than it was in the past to persuade youngsters that they were the in-thing, although, of course, advertising is only one of a number of things a firm can do to manage its environment.

Case study of supply and demand in action

THE UK HOUSING MARKET FROM BOOM TO BUST 1985-90

Over 75% of people own their own homes, so the biggest part of the housing market is the market for private house purchase, on which we shall focus here. Several types of firms are directly involved in this:

- estate agent who markets the property and arranges for buyers and sellers to meet;
- solicitors who arrange the transfer of ownership of the property;

- surveyors who inspect the property;
- building societies and banks who provide the mortgage loans to purchase the property;
- insurance companies, building societies and banks who provide the investment vehicle that will pay off the mortgage in due course, such as an endowment policy;
- insurance companies who insure the property and cover the risk of default on the loans;

- removals firms;
- house builders who supply new houses (although most sales are, of course, re-sales).

There are also firms that, while not directly involved, are nonetheless significantly affected by house purchase, such as the DIY and furnishing companies, because people tend to make major purchases of this sort when they move. Beyond this, changes in this market have repercussions for a host of other industries and ultimately the whole economy because buying a house is such a major purchase.

We begin this case study in the mid-1980s. At this time there seemed to be a lot of changes in the external environment that suggested a rightward shift in housing demand, including:

- rising incomes;
- a bulge in the population of 'marrying' (and buying their first house) age;
- falling interest rates (for most people the main cost of a mortgage is the interest payments);
- government encouragement for home ownership;

- deregulation of the mortgage market increased competition and made it easier to get a loan;
- a green-belt area around London that restricts the building of housing in the area of greatest demand.

The first three of these could be quantified as they had occurred many times before. It was estimated that the income elasticity of demand for private housing at the time was between one and two. In other words, a rise in incomes of 1% increased housing demand by between 1% and 2%. The remainder could be assessed only by surveys of people's intentions and these seemed to show that the government's message was getting through, with more and more people polled saying they would like to own their own homes.

On the supply side, we know that the supply of properties is upward sloping, so the result of a rightward-shifting demand curve was a rise in house prices. In fact, the supply is inelastic, especially for new houses, and particularly around London, so the rise in prices for each shift in demand is large, as indicated in Figure 4.23.

Figure 4.23 The housing boom of the late 1980s.

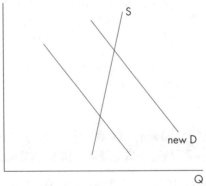

In light of this, most commentators predicted a significant rise in house price, which occurred; in fact, on average they more than doubled between 1985 and 1989. The expectation of further rises led to something of a band-wagon effect that pushed demand even higher. All the firms involved in this market benefited greatly from the rise in revenues that this created, although not all firms

benefited equally; building societies, for example, did well but temporarily lost their dominance of the mortgage market because of the entry of other firms.

In late 1988 this bubble burst, and demand shifted to the left over the next few years as the economy went into recession and house prices fell. The main shifters were again on the demand side:

- Incomes fell in real terms.
- Interest rates went up.
- The demographic bulge passed its peak.
- The government did little to keep this market afloat, despite its earlier rhetoric.
- People began to expect house prices to fall.

The result for the firms involved was widespread decline in total revenues and profits. Those that anticipated the decline are likely to have suffered least, but to the extent that they were locked into this market could only 'manage the damage' rather than escape it.

You may think that this example is getting rather dated; there is, however, a danger in assuming that we have learnt from our mistakes, simply because something has not happened for a while. This was exactly the kind of thinking that characterised this period. At the time it was widely believed that the house price boom of the early 1970s was a one-off, and that Conservative reforms had liberated the economy from its tendency to go from boom to slump and back again, so that any rise in house prices would be sustained. Today we are certain that, with the Bank of England determined to beat inflation, we will never again go on a house price roller-coaster ride, and many commentators have said as much. However, as long as the housing market works in the way that it does, with an inelastic supply coupled with a potentially volatile demand, large swings in house prices remain a possibility.

4.8 SUMMARY

- Because we have defined what both buyers and sellers do in terms of prices and quantities, we can put them together in a single graph.
- The interaction of supply and demand generates 'market forces' that push traders towards the 'equilibrium' point at which supply and demand meet.
- Looking at the market equilibrium point shows us what price will prevail and how much will be sold when trade takes place, whether between firms and consumers, or between firms and those that supply them (such as other firms and workers).
- This means that changes or trends in the business environment through their ability to shift supply or demand can be investigated in terms of the effect they have on the equilibrium price and quantity prevailing in a market.
- This in turn means that changes or trends in the business environment entail threats and opportunities for firms that are revealed by considering their likely impact on the equilibrium price and quantity prevailing in a market.
- This, however, does not mean that we can predict exactly what all firms will do in any given circumstance, merely that contextualising firms in this way will enable us to see which strategic paths open up and which close down when the business environment changes.

4.9 QUESTIONS

1. Use comparative static supply and demand analysis to predict the effects of the following events on the equilibrium price and quantity transacted in the market for cars:
   (a) People's incomes rise.
   (b) The price of petrol falls significantly.
   (c) The price of metals including steel falls.
   (d) Investment in the railways goes up.
   (e) Car workers' wages are cut.

2. Use comparative static supply and demand analysis to predict the effects of the following events on the equilibrium price, and quantity transacted, in the market for cross-channel ferry tickets:
   (a) Consumers realise that they can get their alcoholic drinks a lot cheaper in France.
   (b) Ferry operators cut their prices.
   (c) The number of bank holidays goes up as the UK is brought in line with the rest of Europe regarding official days off.

3. Use comparative static supply and demand analysis to predict the effects of the following events on the equilibrium price and quantity transacted in the market for denim jeans if:
   (a) people's incomes rise;
   (b) the price of cotton shirts falls significantly;
   (c) the price of cotton trousers falls significantly;
   (d) bad weather severely reduces the cotton crop.
   Discuss the implications of each of these for a firm of your choice that manufactures denim jeans.

4. If you look at the total market for kayaks at the start of this chapter, you will note that although it is simply the kayak firm's figures multiplied by 10, the elasticity of demand is lower. The simple act of increasing the numbers has reduced the elasticity. Explain why.

5. European interest rates are half those of the UK at present. Examine the possible effects on the UK housing market of our joining the European single currency and thereby having to have interest rates equivalent to those of Europe.

6. Using partial equilibrium 'supply and demand' diagrams, show the effect of the following events on the equilibrium price and sales in the UK market for yeast spreads:
   (a) the introduction of the yeast spread Vegemite into the UK;
   (b) the introduction of a range of recipes using Marmite by popular TV chef Gary Rhodes;
   (c) an increase in beer drinking;
   (d) a rise in concern regarding the amount of salt in people's diets (yeast spreads have high salt content).

7. The demand for coffee worldwide actually fell during the 1980s but seemed to have stabilised in the 1990s. Production peaked in 1991 at over 5 million tons, with wholesale coffee prices at only 40 cents per lb. Unhappy at this low price, the Association of Coffee Producing Countries decided to withhold a large percentage of the coffee crop to force prices up. By 1994, production was down to 4 million tons and the price

had reached $1 per lb. Using a partial equilibrium supply and demand diagram, explain what happened in this market during this period.

8. In 1979 and 1980 bad weather severely affected the sugar crop and sugar prices shot up to 40 cents per lb. In the following two years, good growing weather, and some entry into the market, meant that prices fell to below 6 cents per lb., as shown in Figure 4.24.

   Use a partial equilibrium supply and demand diagram to show what happened.

Figure 4.24 Sugar prices.

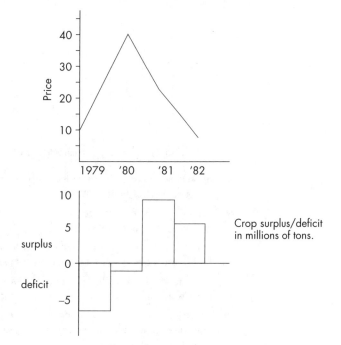

Crop surplus/deficit in millions of tons.

CHAPTER 5

The competitive environment

After studying this chapter, you should be able to:

- appreciate the importance of the number of competitors in a market in determining the behaviour of firms in that market;
- define the key market structures of perfect competition, monopolistic competition, oligopoly and monopoly;
- appreciate how, in the perfectly competitive environment, firms make only normal profits and have no strategic options, other than to compete on price;
- understand why, in an environment characterised by monopolistic competition, competitive advantage comes from differentiation, as well as price;
- understand how, in an environment characterised by oligopoly, competitive advantage comes from collusion, non-price competition, and ability to predict strategic move and countermove;
- understand how, in a monopoly environment, competitive advantage comes from keeping competitors out and keeping regulators at bay;
- understand how the prevalence of market power increases profits and the scope for strategic choice by firms.
- be able to apply, and discuss the strategic implications of applying, a 'five forces' analysis to a firm, SBU, strategic group, or industry.

5.1   MARKET STRUCTURE

One important factor in the firm's environment is competition, the amount and nature of which is likely to be related to the number of other firms in a market, which we can divide into broad categories or 'market structures', as shown in Table 5.1.

Table 5.1 Market structures.

No. of firms	Name	Number of substitutes for a firm's products	Implied PeDs for firm's products
Infinite number	Perfect competition	Infinite	Infinitely elastic
Lots	Imperfect competition	Many	High
A few	Oligopoly	A few	It depends on what they do
No competitors	Monopoly	None	Low

It may seem silly to investigate the implications of the market structure called monopoly where there is no competition and no substitutes, when in fact there are nearly always alternatives, and even worse to look at the case where there is an infinite number of competitors and substitutes, which is more than unlikely – it is impossible! However, although in reality most of the markets in the world will fall somewhere between these two extremes, they are worth considering as benchmarks. Looking at the extremes will reveal how the behaviour of firms is affected by the amount of competition at all points in between, in the same way that all the shades of grey on a black and white TV can be explained by the amounts of the two extremes (black and white) that are present.

5.1.1 Perfect competition

Where there are many firms supplying the same product we approach a state of total competition or, as it is usually known, **perfect competition**. In reality, competition is never perfect but some markets may approach this at times.

Under perfect competition we are envisaging a world in which there are so many goods in each market that there is nothing to choose between them. This is difficult to imagine because we are used to a world in which the better the quality of the good, the fewer the substitutes. In contrast, in this imaginary world there are always many substitutes, even for top-quality goods. So many, in fact, that a buyer really does not care which of the competitors they choose to buy from. To get so many substitutes we must assume an infinite number of suppliers and a free movement of firms into the market, so that anywhere there are profits to be made many suppliers will come along and meet the demand.

Sources of competitive advantage in a perfectly competitive environment

If there is infinite competition and therefore an infinite number of substitutes for each product, then there is literally nothing to choose between them in terms of quality, or any other characteristic, except price. This means that the only source of competitive advantage in this environment is price, with firms that have lower costs per unit of output than their rivals being able to price below them and steal all the custom, while firms with higher costs and prices find no buyers whatsoever. If, for example, one firm has more expensive carpets and decor than its rivals, that is, in Leibenstein's (1966) terms, it is **X-inefficient**, then because such luxuries will add to its costs but not improve productivity, it will have to price a fraction higher than its rivals and consequently go out of business. This is not to say that prices cannot be different temporarily, but since any firm that does not minimise costs will fail to survive, environmental pressure ensures that in the long run at least, all remaining firms are **productively efficient**. This means firms supply the amount of goods where the average cost of each item produced is at its lowest, which graphically is the lowest point of the average total cost curve, as shown in Figure 5.1.

Figure 5.1 Productive efficiency.

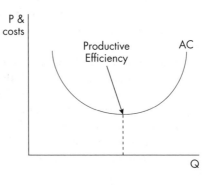

This happens because the assumption of infinite substitutes produces a flat demand curve for the firm's output since each firm will be able to sell any, or all, of its output if it matches the market price. Whereas, if it asks for a price above the prevailing market price, demand will fall to zero as customers can go elsewhere for any one of an infinite number of identical products; in effect, the firm is a **price taker**, as shown in Figure 5.2.

Figure 5.2 In a perfectly competitive environment, each firm faces a perfectly elastic demand curve.

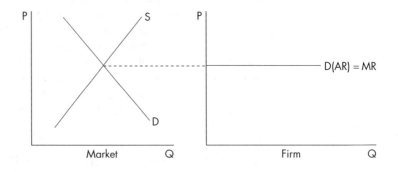

If the demand curve is flat then AR = MR, as selling one more at the same price gains the value of that sale and loses nothing. If we add a firm's cost curves to Figure 5.2, we can see how productive efficiency results from the flat demand curve. It also means that only profit maximisers will survive, since in this environment profit maximisation and cost minimisation amount to the same thing. In the case shown in Figure 5.3, the firm supplies S1 where MC = MR and where AC is at a minimum.

Figure 5.3 Producer equilibrium in a perfectly competitive environment.

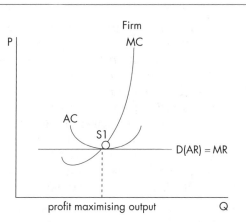

If there is a rise in demand under perfect competition from D1 to D2, in Figure 5.4, supply will increase from S1 to S2 along the MC curve. In this case, because of the flat demand curve, the MC curve exactly defines the supply curve and the market supply curve is simply the sum of all firms' MC curves.

Figure 5.4 The MC curve is the supply curve in a perfectly competitive environment.

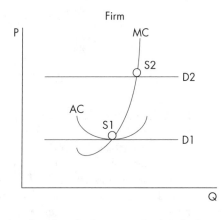

However, the rise in the demand curve depicted above has caused a gap between AR and AC, which means that super normal profits are being made, as indicated by the shaded area in Figure 5.5.

Figure 5.5 Super normal profits result from a change in the environment.

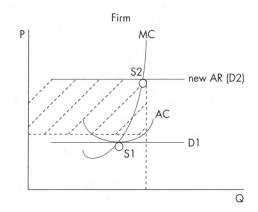

However, in this environment super normal profits can only be made in the short run; in the long run they are competed away, as the super normal profits act as an incentive for firms to enter the market. This will increase supply as shown in Figure 5.6, until the super normal profits have been competed away and the incentive to enter the market vanishes, at which point the demand for each firm's output is back to the D1 level (ignoring my tendency for costs to be lower in the long run). Something like this happened in the market for farmed salmon. The first firms to produce farmed salmon did very well, but subsequently suffered from a fall in prices and reduced demand as other firms entered the arena, which in this case is easy as the set-up cost are low and brand loyalty is almost non-existent.

Figure 5.6 Super normal profits do not last in a perfectly competitive environment.

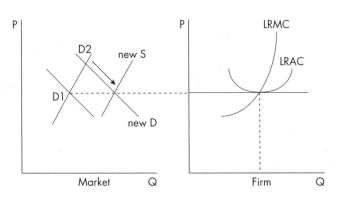

Since in the long run, when all adjustments have taken place, all firms can only be making normal profits, all firms are offering products to the market at the price it costs to produce them (MC). The consumer is therefore paying exactly what it costs to create the good (P = MC), including the opportunity cost (normal profit); indeed, a penny less and it would not be feasible to produce the good at all. If no firm is making excess profits and society's resources are being efficiently used, and if, as in this case, these are being used to produce what consumers want, then there is no possibility of improving consumer welfare. We say therefore that resources are being allocated efficiently and that there is **consumer sovereignty** because if consumers want more of something they get it. If, for example, consumers decide to demand more organic farm produce, farmers will see this as a signal to grow more organic products and ultimately more organic produce will be supplied.

We can summarise this result in terms of supply and demand, with 'allocative efficiency' (where P = MC) being achieved when supply equals demand (Figure 5.7).

Although there are no markets that are perfectly competitive, the more competition there is, the more we get productive and allocative efficiency and the lower the level of profit for each firm. In addition, we can achieve some of the efficiencies mentioned above as long as markets are open enough to allow rivals to enter or exit if they so wish. If they are then we have a 'contestable market', in which, according to Baumol et al. (1982), the threat of competition makes firms behave as if there were perfect competition, even if, in fact, there are relatively few firms. In recent decades, Conservative governments,

Figure 5.7 Allocative efficiency.

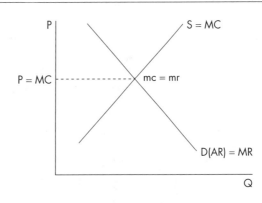

impressed with the apparent benefits to society of competition, have introduced a range of measures to encourage it. However, because the existence of many firms in a market means that the benefits of economies of scale cannot also be achieved, this has not meant much breaking up of markets found to be dominated by a few firms.

5.1.2 Monopoly

We consider monopoly, the other end of our spectrum, before looking at the middle, in order to compare and contrast the two extremes of perfect competition and no competition. A **monopoly** exists if there is no competition, so that one firm supplies the whole market and consumers have no choice – they either buy it from the monopolist or they do not have it. Graphically, this means that the firm faces the market demand curve and we do not, therefore, have two separate diagrams for the firm and the market. Defining what a monopoly is depends on how we define the market. For example, the government has a legal monopoly on the production of legal tender (notes and coins) in the UK, so much so that 'firms' who set up in competition end up in prison. Nonetheless, consumers can buy goods using cheque-books, debit cards, luncheon vouchers, IOUs and so on. In addition, what is a monopoly for some is not for others; water companies have regional monopolies on supplying water, but I get mine from a spring. Our task, however, is not to try to pigeon-hole all companies into one of four categories but to look at the implications of different degrees of competition, and in this case the implication is clear: monopoly means power.

In Figure 5.8 the monopolist faces the market demand curve and could choose to sell the amount where P = MC, which is where we would end up under perfect competition. However, doing that means earning only normal profits, and why should a monopoly choose this unless the government tells it to? Left to its own devices the monopolist can choose a higher price. To keep our analysis simple we shall assume that the monopolist sets prices to maximise profits. In this case that means supplying only the amount 'Qm' in Figure 5.8: supplying that quantity allows them to charge a price of 'Pm', at which AR is considerably above AC, creating super normal profits on a scale indicated by the shaded area.

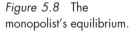

Figure 5.8 The monopolist's equilibrium.

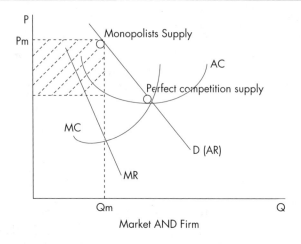

This is the most profit that this market can possibly provide as long as only one price is charged for all consumers. However, the fact that the demand curve is downward sloping means that some people will pay more than others for the same product; a monopolist can therefore make even more profit if it can charge different consumers different prices. Although 'price discrimination' of this sort is practised by monopolists, it is relatively limited in scope. Generally it amounts to things like special deals for those willing to pay least, such as pensioners and students, and higher prices in more affluent regions, or at peak times, and so on, rather than everyone being charged the maximum that he or she would pay.

Sources of competitive advantage in a monopoly environment

The monopolist does not take the price given by the market. It is a **price maker** rather than a price taker; it has **market power**, and as long as there are **barriers to entry**, like patents, brand loyalty, and laws that keep other firms out, it will retain that power. This means that it can make super normal profits in the short run and in the long run too, and hence we do not need to draw another diagram to show what happens in the long run since the answer may be that nothing changes. For a monopolist the primary aim must therefore be to maintain the barriers and keep its privileged position in the business environment. It can at the same time use the profits it makes to finance expansion in new directions, for as Penrose (1958) argued, the business environment does not dictate an optimum equilibrium size for firms since they can always move into different markets. We cannot say, for example, that a regional water monopoly cannot grow faster than the growth of water demand in its region, since it can use its super normal profits to expand into electricity and gas supply, indeed into anything it wants.

Looking again at Figure 5.8, we can see that 'PmQm' is not as good for buyers as the P and Q that would occur under perfect competition. This means that, in effect, customers are being exploited as the price they pay exceeds the cost of providing it. There is, in addition, no incentive for monopolists to minimise costs, and firms with a lot of market power are notorious for their x-inefficiency; their lavish buildings and generally lax attitude to cost control. Clearly perfect competition has certain benefits for consumers since they are not exploited and costs are minimised (allocative and productive efficiency). This is one of the reasons why competition is thought to be desirable by a broad spectrum of political opinion. We can see the differences by looking again at Figure 5.8; the supply for the monopolist is, *ceteris paribus*, less than we would get under perfect competition. In fact, the discretion over price that a monopolist has makes it more appropriate to think of their supply as a range of possibilities, as shown in Figure 5.9.

Figure 5.9 Monopoly and perfect competition compared.

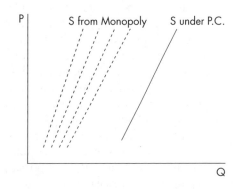

However, as we have already discovered, there can be benefits to being big if there are economies of scale to be had; in such cases even the most exploitative of monopolists could make super normal profits and still supply more at lower prices than perfectly competitive firms. Supermarkets, for example, have more market power than a corner shop, but sell food cheaper than the corner shops they replace and yet still make super normal profits, because they benefit from economies of scale such as the ability to buy in bulk. Indeed, some products may not be supplied at all unless produced by big firms. For example, jumbo jets would be uneconomic to produce if the market consisted of many, relatively small, suppliers. In fact, capital costs can be such a significant factor that, in some cases, if a market is shared between even as few as two firms it becomes unprofitable for both parties. For example, the costs of providing two rival sets of plumbing to each house might make it impossible for two companies to make any profits in supplying water. This industry might then be classified as a 'natural monopoly'.

The fact that economies of scale are desirable but exploitation by monopolists is not has led many to argue for public ownership ('nationalisation') of natural monopolies, and this is what happened in the past, in the coal, steel, telecommunications, train, water and electricity industries. In recent years, however, these nationalised industries have been 'privatised', that is, sold to the share-owning public, often as monopolies, but also with minor but ongoing introduction of some forms of competition wherever possible. In addition, where the monopoly power remains largely intact, such as in the domestic water supply industry, the government has established a watchdog regulator to constrain the supplier's power. In some cases, this has led to a constant battle between the regulators and the respective industries. On the other hand, there are also cases where the regulators have been accused of taking the firm's side rather than that of the consumer. In such cases people often talk of the regulators being 'captured' by the industry. Firms clearly have an incentive to wine and dine the regulators, as this will internalise a part of the external environment that is a potential source of instability to the firm. So while regulatory capture is hard to prove and while acknowledging that firms that have been privatised have improved their efficiency, largely by reducing staffing levels, suspicions are aroused by the fact that many have also managed to increase their prices. In the case of the water industry, for example, suppliers have increased prices significantly in real terms. The regulator has allowed this to enable the firms to have enough cash to invest in reducing waste and increasing holding capacity, although as yet, very little of the profits they make have found their way into such investments.

To summarise, under perfect competition firms have little power over their environments and have no strategic options; competitive advantage comes only from minimising costs. In contrast, under monopoly the firm has great power over its environment; it can set the price, its strategic options are many, and competitive advantage is based on maintaining its privileged position and using its power to enter other markets. Between these two extremes, we have a range of different environments that imply different constraints and sources of competitive advantage. We group this vast range into two broad types – imperfect competition and oligopoly. Although there is a global long-term trend towards fewer but bigger firms, these two still encompass most of the firms in existence today and account for most of what is produced in the world today.

5.1.3   Imperfect (monopolistic) competition

Two different names apply in this case because a similar set of ideas were published simultaneously (in 1933), with one author, Joan Robinson, calling it **imperfect competition**, and the other, Edward Chamberlin, calling it **monopolistic competition**.

Under imperfect competition, there are many firms, so each has a small share of the market, but they produce goods that are slightly different to each other, which gives them some market power, because as they are imperfect substitutes the demand for each is not perfectly elastic. They can, therefore, charge slightly more than perfectly competitive firms and thereby make some super normal profits. It is not just the case that the profit in the market is being shared amongst fewer firms; it is that the profit level for the whole market is higher too because prices are higher. The extent of their power to put prices above perfectly competitive levels and, therefore, the extent to which they can make super normal profits, depends on the elasticity of demand that each imperfectly competitive firm faces. There may, for example, be many pubs in a district, but if a pub is the only one in town it would expect to make more profit than if it was one of half a dozen. Graphically, this produces the same result as monopoly but the super normal profits may not last (as there are fewer barriers to entry), and the demand curve is very much more elastic, because of the greater number of substitutes for each firm's products. A comparison with perfect competition is shown in Figure 5.10, with imperfectly competitive firms being able to charge price 'P(ic)' and make super normal profits equal to the shaded rectangle.

Figure 5.10
Comparing perfect and imperfect competition.

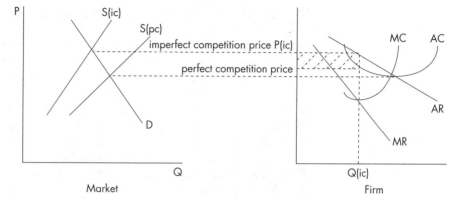

We can compare imperfect competition with perfect competition in the long run too if we assume that firms can enter the market. This will eliminate the super normal profits but there will still be higher prices P(ic) and less supply Q(ic) with imperfect competition since the products are still differentiated and therefore imperfect substitutes, as shown in Figure 5.11.

Figure 5.11
Comparing perfect and imperfect competition in the long run.

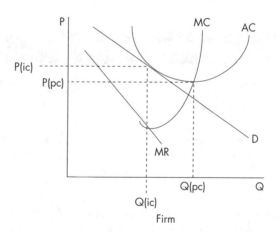

The diagram also shows that with imperfect competition, profit maximisation is not consistent with productive efficiency, as at Q(ic) we are not at the bottom of the AC curve. In other words, imperfect competition results in excess capacity since there is scope for an expansion of output and a lowering of costs if competition is increased. In addition, consumers are charged more than it cost to make the goods, since P is above MC, so we do not have allocative efficiency either. We should, however, avoid drawing too many conclusions from comparing something that does exist (imperfect competition) with something that does not (perfect competition).

Sources of competitive advantage in an imperfectly competitive environment

Anything less than perfect competition means that, in addition to price competition, altering the qualitative dimensions of a product such as its performance, styling, or location becomes a strategic option capable of creating competitive advantage. The great variety of slightly different products we see around us is testimony to this. This differentiation can take a number of forms. A product might be differentiable on the basis of some objectively definable characteristic. Some customers might, for example, prefer a big car while others like small ones, which means that in the car market there is scope for a range of differently sized cars. In the UK, for example, we prefer small and medium sizes, whereas in the USA they prefer bigger ones; this means that not only is there scope for a range of different products by size in both markets, but that in each market the range is different too. Other differences might be harder to define; the difference between a nutty beer and a fruity beer is a distinction that eludes most people, but as long as some beer drinkers can tell the difference it is worth a brewery including either characteristic in its products. In addition, some differences may have little objective reality at all; a marketer may through effective advertising or stylish packaging convince us that some product is better than another even though no discernible objective difference can be found.

Case study in product differentiation

IF YOU WANT A DIFFERENT PRICE, GET A DIFFERENT PRODUCT

W.K. Kellogg invented cornflakes in 1894; the firm Kellogg's that he founded has won awards for its advertising of cornflakes, and everyone recognises the Kellogg's Cornflakes box. Although Kellogg's is a big firm and as such would generally be classed under the heading oligopoly, the increasing amount of competition that their cornflakes face is pushing it into the realm of monopolistic competition, in which advantage comes not from size and power but mainly from product differentiation. The question for Kellogg's cornflakes is increasingly whether it is intrinsically different enough to command a premium price: whether advertising and effective branding alone are enough to differentiate this brand sufficiently to combat the cheaper own-brand rivals that have come onto the market. The question can be simply put in terms of whether there is any difference

between Kellogg's and any other brand of cornflakes, once the advert has been watched, the box admired, the packet opened, and the contents tipped into a bowl and covered in milk. Increasingly, consumers are switching to cheaper brands as more and more they realise that the answer to this question is that there is no intrinsic difference. If products are homogeneous, pretending that they are not does not seem ultimately to work. Generally it seems to be easier to command a premium price if there is something tangibly better (or at least different) about the product that distinguishes it from its rivals; in other words, if the advertising and branding clearly do point to some unique characteristics than if they do not. There are exceptions, of course, for in the case of Veblen goods people buy the product for the name itself.

5.1.4 Oligopoly

Oligopoly is Greek for 'few sellers', so in this case we are looking at markets dominated by a few big players. Industries that are classed as oligopolies include the toiletries, soap powder, chemicals, brewing, retailing and newspaper industries, in which a few firms do most, but not all, of the business. Why each of these is dominated in this way depends on the specifics of the industry, but there is a general tendency over time for markets to become dominated by fewer and fewer firms since this increases the profits of those that remain. It can be achieved simply by being better than rivals, but more usually it involves either the merging of firms or the buying of rivals in a take-over. In some cases, it occurs when a firm invents a new product or devises a new line of business that others cannot imitate, either because it is hard to do, or because the original firm has a patent or copyright on it.

Sources of competitive advantage in an oligopolistic environment

The domination of an industry by a few firms means that one firm's loss tends to be another firm's gain, and therefore that competition can be particularly damaging, and that decisions become interdependent. This interdependency means that a lot of strategic effort by oligopolists revolves around the assessment of moves and countermove, which we will look at in detail below. The damage to firms that competition does and the advantages of not competing have been documented since the time of Adam Smith (1723–90), who wrote that: 'People of the same trade seldom meet together, even for merriment or diversion, but the conversation ends in a conspiracy against the public or in some contrivance to raise prices.' For oligopolists the benefits of such a conspiracy are that together they form, in effect, a monopoly and can set prices at monopoly levels to maximise the amount of profits extracted from any market. When erstwhile competitors work together, without formally joining their organisations in a merger or a take-over, we have **collusion**. This is not confined to oligopoly, of course; two hairdressers in a village may collude and we would probably characterise that as imperfect competition. However, with oligopoly the amount of daily contact between individuals within the firms is limited, and so the form, and extent, of collusion differs enormously, yet because of the interdependence, getting collusion right and knowing what to do when it goes wrong are major sources of competitive advantage when we have competition amongst the few.

Forms of collusion

1. Cartel: A **cartel** is a highly organised formal arrangement to fix prices. Cartels are generally illegal in the UK, Europe and the USA, but are accepted, even encouraged, in some countries. The problem that cartels face is that once everyone agrees on the price, any one firm can make even more money by secretly selling the product slightly cheaper. So, while the firms welcome

the high prices, the restricted supply necessary to keep the prices up means that each firm has an incentive to cheat. This means that the cartel has to be well organised and have sanctions to deter firms from breaking the agreement, otherwise they tend to break down into price wars, until every firm remembers how damaging that is and the cartel re-forms. Although cartels are largely outlawed today in the UK, there are nonetheless arrangements that are permitted that are akin to cartel behaviour. For example, there is a system of **recommended retail prices** that electrical goods manufacturers set for their products, which, if undercut by a retailer, will lead to their being blacklisted by all the manufacturers. Certain similar 'arrangements' are also common in the car manufacturing business.

2. Tacit (hidden) collusion: Firms can collude without formal arrangement simply by copying rather than competing. If, for example, a rival raises its prices to monopoly levels, a tacit colluder, instead of undercutting them and starting a price war, will put their prices up too. This follow-the-leader behaviour, **price leadership** as it is called, can take many forms. Sometimes it is simply a case of following the biggest firm; while in other industries everyone follows a sensible firm that acts as a good barometer of market conditions. It can also be quite subtle. For example, after the breakdown of their cartel in the 1980s, the building societies kept up a dialogue on their strategic intentions in thinly disguised articles on house prices in the newspapers and on TV. The importance of having a leader when engaging in this kind of collusion is evidenced by the fact that in emerging markets agreements on how to avoid competition are harder to establish because clear leaders may not have emerged and as a result price competition dominates, as Stinchcombe (1965) found.

3. Rules of thumb: The loosest form of collusion is simply to have easily understood strategies. Since their actions impact significantly on each other, insofar as one firm's gain is often largely another firm's loss, oligopolists face a lot of strategic uncertainty. One way to reduce this is to follow simple rules. One example is that of always re-pricing to a set of commonly agreed prices that act as 'benchmarks'. Prices 5p below the nearest pound or a penny below the nearest half-pound are popular ones. If then costs rise or fall by some untidy amount (which is likely to be slightly different for each firm and may therefore lead to different price changes), all firms go up or down to the next benchmark. The chance of inadvertently starting a damaging price war by coming in at a price which is below that set by rivals is thereby greatly reduced.

In general, with collusion oligopolists are able to reduce price competition and replace it with **non-price competition**, based on branding, styling, quality and advertising. This has two main advantages. Firstly, branding and advertising coupled with the economies of scale that bigness creates all add up to significant barriers to entry, so that any new firm hoping to enter an oligopolistic market has the costs of setting up, brand loyalty, and extensive advertising to combat as well. Secondly, it is relatively safe; prices are the major determinant of revenue, and therefore a price war will tend to create winners and losers, and it is impossible to predict who will win. A big company might think it could beat a smaller company, but the potential rewards for winners of eliminating a rival are so great that all kinds of financial backers can come to the aid of either side. In contrast, the worst that can normally happen with non-price competition is a temporary loss of market share if the branding or advertising fails to do its job. This is not to say that price wars between oligopolists never happen (we have recently seen outbreaks in the baked bean and newspaper industries, for example), but the extent of price competition in oligopolistic markets can be something of an illusion. One form of non-price competition is to create a new brand with slightly different characteristics from existing brands; this leads to a plethora of brands being produced by each oligopolist, which can create the impression that there are many firms competing on price. You might think, for example, that there are a lot of firms producing washing powder, when in fact the market is dominated by two firms (Lever Brothers and Procter & Gamble), who have lots of brands with different characteristics. You might also think that there is a lot of price competition because the brands have different prices. However, the price range reflects the different characteristics and quality (or degree of loyalty) of the different brands, in other words their PeDs. In fact, the firms have similar prices for similar products; in effect, similar brands are paired up price for price with those of their rivals, and price competition is thereby usually avoided. However, this creates the impression of price competition, when in fact it results from the drive to have different brands and indicates non-price competition, which is consistent with maintaining super normal profits, rather than price competition, which is not.

Non-collusive oligopoly

Non-price competition is the dominant form of behaviour even when oligopolists are not trying to collude. One reason is that when one firm's loss is another's gain, rival firms have an incentive to respond to price changes in a destructive way. If, for example, a firm raises its prices, its rivals will benefit most if they do not raise theirs, since that will mean that they will gain customers at the expense of the firm that raises its prices. Any firm initiating a price rise will, therefore, lose market share and face a highly elastic demand curve, and a fall in TR. If a firm lowers its price its rivals can only benefit by following suit, which means that for price cuts everyone acts together and we move down the market demand curve. Sales are likely to rise, as demand curves tend to be downward sloping, but the TR of all firms, including the initiating firm, may fall, as the market demand curve will tend to be relatively inelastic. No one will necessarily gain a bigger share of the market and no one will necessarily lose market share either, but all may end up poorer (if the PeD is less than 1 then all firms will end up poorer unless a clear winner emerges from the price war). In effect, therefore, individual firms contemplating significant (big enough to warrant a response from rivals) price changes face a **kinked demand curve**, since for price rises they face a much more elastic demand curve than for price cuts (Figure 5.12).

Figure 5.12 A kinked demand curve.

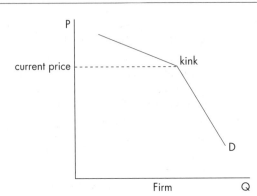

This means that the best strategy on price is to do nothing. This means that even if firms are not intent on colluding they will tend to exhibit sticky prices and a strategic preference for non-price competition. Indeed, even if costs rise or fall, the firm will keep to the current price. For example, in Figure 5.13, even if costs rise by the distance 'a' to 'b', because the kink results in a perfectly vertical portion of MR at any point along which profits are maximised, the firm will not change the price. Only if the cost change takes us above 'b' or below 'a' is it worth the firm changing its price.

Figure 5.13 Only a significant change in costs warrants a price change when a firm faces a kinked demand curve.

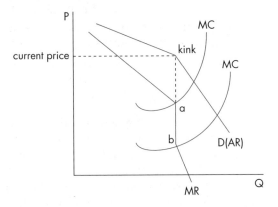

Price stickiness has an implication for our supply and demand analysis as firms would rather not pass on cost changes that affect them alone because that would put their prices out of line with everyone else's. In other words, they do not shift their supply curves left if there is a small increase in their costs, or move them right for a small reduction in costs. For example, if Maxwell House workers get a better pay deal than people working for Nescafé, then Maxwell House might decide not to alter the basis of their supply, and not to put prices up. This would mean less profits, but up to a point they might consider that preferable to risking a price rise that no one else follows and thereby losing a lot of their share of the market. We should bear this in mind whenever we are looking at cost changes for specific oligopolists, although of course when looking at the whole market we do not find a kinked demand curve or the same degree of price stickiness.

The power of supermarkets

The first supermarket in the UK was opened by the Co-op in 1948, but it was not until certain environmental changes in the 1960s and 1970s that they began to spread to every town. The first development was the rapid rise in car ownership, the second the rapid rise in the number of households who owned a fridge. This made bigger, less frequent, trips to the shops possible. Complementing this was the rise in the number of women taking jobs outside the home, which meant that few would welcome the daily trip to the shops that their mothers were used to.

The prices and the profit margins of British supermarkets exceed that of their major European and American counterparts, and for the first time people are publicly questioning the deal they get from UK supermarkets. In addition, the Office of Fair Trading is investigating the matter. Below is a list of reasons why the big British supermarkets do well, in addition of course to the fact that they are well run enough to equate supply with demand (in other words to give us what we want):

- They are oligopolists; collectively they account for the vast majority of food sales, and within that the top four account for 70% of all supermarket sales.

- Although people criticise the size of their margins, the real source of their power is their size and associated high turnovers that come from being oligopolists. Margins do vary, however; the biggest operate on margins of around 6% or 7%, while Kwik Save manages on less than 4%, as do many European and American retailers.

- They collude to deter entry by foreign rivals, and thereby maintain their oligopolistic power. Their size and the economies of scale this creates, as well as the high fixed capital involved in building enough stores to compete with the biggest, and the amounts of advertising they do, are some of the obvious barriers to entry which only the biggest and bravest foreign rivals can overcome. In addition, there is some evidence of less obvious barriers involving collusion and political lobbying, and many supermarket chiefs take senior government posts while running their firms and after they retire.

- They are big enough to exert considerable influence over those that supply them (including their employees), and their huge economies of scale allow them to price lower than smaller rivals while avoiding head-on price competition.

- They use special offers and loss leaders to create the impression of overall price competitiveness.

- Their own brands are cheaper than the brands they imitate, but could be even cheaper since all the hard work and expense of developing the original brand are avoided.

- They eliminate local competition; indeed, they have been found guilty of acting to undermine even insignificant local rivals.

- They locate to avoid unnecessary overlap with any other major supermarket, and will often enlist local council support in this. This means that, given the main reason we use them is convenience, for many there is only one convenient store, which gives the firm some monopoly power over their customers.

- They use loyalty cards to promote loyalty and in return they collect information through the cards on people's shopping habits.

The power of supermarkets and their reluctance to spark price wars have been noticed recently in connection with the beef crisis, since they failed to pass on the bulk of the fall in the price of beef. Indeed, the same is happening again with lamb, for recently farmers have been getting as little as £2 a head for lamb while supermarkets continued to sell it at more than £2 a pound. More generally, while supermarket prices are rising (albeit not by much), world commodity prices have actually been falling.

This is not to say that occasional price wars, or rather skirmishes, never occur. In 1996, for example, there was a price war, not over the full range of many thousands of products that a typical supermarket sells, but just one: tins of baked beans in tomato sauce. This product is virtually unheard of in much of Europe, but average sales in the UK exceed 3 million tins a day. The war started with new entrants into the supermarket business, such as Aldi, and the lower-cost incumbents such as Kwik Save. Prices in 1996 went as low as 4p, but because of the economies of scale involved, this is actually no lower than they cost to make. However, this sort of price spells trouble for firms like Heinz, who claim that they use more expensive, better quality, ingredients and cannot produce their typical beans at such low prices (although they can and do produce lower quality beans too). Neither can Heinz take succour from the extra demand that lower prices bring, as it seems that, even for large

Game theory

The fact that oligopolists are independent and must therefore take each other's reactions into account means that move and countermove, as might occur in a game, characterise many of the strategic choices in this environment, with competitive advantage being achieved by playing the game well. There are two ways of looking at such strategic interaction: deterministic and non-deterministic. By **deterministic** we mean that the outcome of the interaction is predetermined by the nature of the interaction, whereas with **non-deterministic** interaction it is not. We can model deterministic interaction in terms of three things: firstly, the motives of the players; secondly, the rewards for different strategies (the payoffs); and thirdly, the type of choices that can be made (the rules of the game). Knowing these will allow us to establish what will happen, using 'game theory'. For non-deterministic interaction the nature of the game is contingent on the choices made by the firms or individuals involved, which means that the payoffs are not knowable at the start and understanding the game means understanding individual players and contexts. This is the subject of business historians, political scientists and organisational sociologists who investigate the nitty-gritty of firms' interactions and use of power, without being obliged to trace how any given circumstances lead to a given outcome. However, economists desire to trace outcomes in this way means that they have focused more heavily on the deterministic approach despite its limited scope, and it is on this approach that we will focus here.

Formal 'game theory' as developed by John von Neumann and Oskar Morgenstern (1944) is a theory of how rational choices can be made when the costs and benefits for each player depend on what other players do. Games can be classified in a number of ways, firstly by whether they are a **cooperative** game, in which all players discuss the problem and work out an agreed solution, or **uncooperative**, where they do not. They can also be classified according to whether the pay-off sum for the whole game is positive, negative or zero. A **positive-sum game** is where all players benefit from playing the game. A **negative-sum game** is where all players lose by playing the game, and a **zero-sum game** is where one player's gain is another player's loss, which means that there is no gain in total, just a reallocation. We shall now look at an example of a game. In this game we have two car manufacturers, one Italian and one French, contemplating whether to focus the advertising of their new 'hatchback' in the press and on radio, or on TV. The matrix below shows the pay-offs in extra profit, in millions of £ earned in a year, for both players, with the actions of each affecting the pay-off for the other. The Italian firm's pay-offs are in italics:

	Italians choose either	
	TV *or*	*Press and radio*
French choose either:		
TV	8	10
	7	*3*
Press and radio	3	4
	10	*4*

The matrix shows that if the French firm chooses TV it will gain 8 if the Italian follows suit, or 10 if the Italians choose the press option, whereas if the French firm chooses the press instead it will only gain 3 if the Italians choose TV or 4 if the Italians choose press too. Given these pay-offs we can calculate the rational choice. There are several ways of doing this. The **maximax** strategy is to pick the strategy with the highest pay-off. If the French choose TV and the Italians do too they will only get 8, but if the Italians choose to advertise in the press, the gains to the French are 10. On the other hand, if the French choose to advertise in the press the best they can hope for is that the Italians choose press too, but this still only gets them 4. Therefore, TV is the preferred maximax choice (in the hope that the Italians choose press). If the French are worried that the Italians might act in the least helpful way, they might consider a different decision criterion that focuses on the worst that can happen, which is what the **maximin** strategy is based upon. In the maximin strategy, the aim is to maximise the minimum possible profit. In this case, if we consider the options for the French, the minimum pay-off for the TV option is 8, whereas if the French choose the press option the worst that can happen is that the Italians pick TV and the French end up with only 3. The best of these is the first option – that the French firm chooses TV. This means that with both decision criteria, the French choose TV; for them it is a dominant strategy as under different criteria it outperforms the press option. For the Italians the situation is similar, because their gain is largely at the expense of the French since the market for hatchbacks will not grow enough in a single year to absorb both firms' extra output. The maximax strategy for the Italians is also therefore TV; if the French choose press the Italians will gain 10, which is better than the maximum 4 if they choose press. The maximin strategy for the Italians is again also TV, since the worst that can happen is that the French also choose TV and the Italians only gain 7, whereas choosing press could mean gains as low as 3. The TV option is therefore the dominant strategy for both players and we would expect both to choose this option, producing the pay-offs of £8m for the French and £7m for the Italians. In looking at this matrix we might conclude that there is nothing to be gained by collusion; acting together, the firms are likely to go for the same option since the total pay-off is greatest if both choose TV (8 plus 7). However, collusion is a bigger game and can encompass options such as, in this case, the staggering of launch dates, and consultation to ensure that both cars have different characteristics (some '**unique selling points**' as they are sometimes called). Both will ensure that the cars are not in head-to-head competition, which means that the pay-offs above will not apply. Collusion might even extend to co-production agreements, in which case not only do the pay-offs above no longer apply but the game itself no longer applies as only one type of car will be produced.

Game theory and strategy

Although we can use game theory in considering firms' strategies, it should be borne in mind that it is not a comprehensive theory of strategy as it focuses on only one aspect of strategy – that of rivals' reactions. In reality, a lot of the strategic decisions that firms take relate to other issues, such as how to improve the efficiency of their operation. In addition, many concern innovations – such as diversification, integration or re-engineering – where no two games are ever quite the same and the rules, players and pay-offs are unknowable. Indeed, even in the simple games outlined above, sensible strategies emerge as a result of the pay-offs as written in by the author, when in reality these are likely to be little more than guesses, with different firms likely to have different guesses. Finally, we need to recognise that in many real-world situations players have different access to resources, have different strengths and weaknesses and are different in terms of size and market power, so that one player's moves are partly independent of its rivals, even for oligopolists.

5.1.5 Managing the business environment

You may have noticed that when we looked at perfect competition the environment dictated that firms maximise profits and supply the amount indicated by their MC curve. This in turn depends on the scarcity of the resources being used and the impersonal law of diminishing returns. In this environment, we can see that firms have no strategic choices as there is only one path to survival, and managing the environment is impossible. We can visualise this lack of scope for managing the environment and demand by drawing flat demand curves, which dictate to the firm that there is only one price and that the only way to survive is to match that price. We can also visualise it on the demand side by not allowing the firm to be able to manipulate that demand in any way. This means that in the case of perfect competition, even the brute force of advertising is ruled out, let alone the subtle manipulation of the political and social environments.

We can also visualise the constraints on choice regarding the amount supplied in a perfectly competitive environment by showing how survivability is very much lower either side of the profit-maximising supply curve as shown in Figure 5.14.

Figure 5.14 A supply curve in an environment that gives little room for strategic choice.

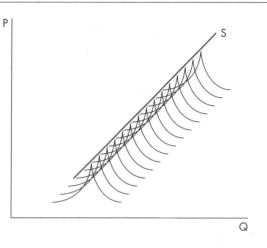

But, as we have seen, when we move away from the infinitely perfect world and into the real world the scope for choice increases, as different ways to increased profit are revealed, such as product differentiation, advertising and branding. We might also add a raft of social and political interventions that firms can use, as mentioned in Chapters 1 and 4 and to which we shall return, but we can summarise all this in one word – power. Outside of the perfectly competitive environment we acknowledge that firms have power, and the more power they have the more profits they can make. On the demand side, we can show this by a steepening of the demand curve and we can add the possibility of shifting it too; indeed, we might even see its very existence as dependent on what firms do since they can both make and destroy markets. We can also see how this affects supply as, outside of perfect competition, even profit-orientated firms do not have to supply the amount that corresponds to MC. So, although costs will affect the elasticity of supply in these environments, there is an element of choice. In such cases, supply should be seen more as what firms choose to do in reaction to changes in demand rather than as the offshoot of some impersonal law of diminishing returns. Indeed, in the case of monopoly, although we stuck with the assumption of profit maximisation in the discussion above, the impossibility of defining a supply curve from costs was mentioned, and a fuzzy line was drawn in Figure 5.9. In addition, different paths to survival other than profit maximisation also come into play as we move away from perfect competition, as we shall see in Chapter 6. The oligopolist, for example, can choose to maximise total revenue whereas the perfectly competitive firm cannot. With monopoly the options are even greater; indeed, with monopoly the success of the firm depends largely on its ability to deal with government regulators and ensure social support for its continued privileged position; in other words, to manage its business environment.

Generally therefore, outside of perfect competition it is best to think of supply as a reaction curve, showing what firms will choose to do at different levels of demand, rather than treat it simply as an offshoot of their cost curves. To contrast this with the perfect competition case, consider Figure 5.15 which shows that the range of survivability for the previous supply curve is in this case much greater.

Figure 5.15 A supply curve in the real world.

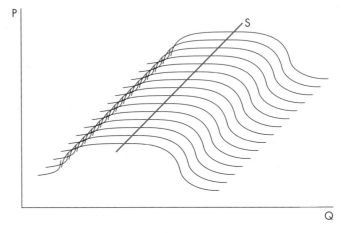

Table 5.2 Comparison of market structures.

We can summarise these findings by amending our market structures comparison table as shown in Table 5.2.

	Sources of competitive advantage	Degree of strategic choice	Extent to which firm can manage its business environment
Perfect competition	Cost and price	None	Zero
Monopolistic (imperfect) competition	As above, plus product differentiation	Some	A little
Oligopoly	As above, plus advertising, strategic gamesmanship, degree of collusion and barriers to entry and exit	Extensive, but depends on nature of rivalry in the industry	Collectively very high. Individually depends on bargaining power in each case
Monopoly	As above, plus always has considerable bargaining power over buyers and suppliers. Main advantage comes from keeping others out	Extensive	Huge; its whole position depends on its ability to do this

5.2   MARKET STRUCTURE AND PROFITABILITY

As we have seen, the more competitive a market, the greater the number of firms and substitute products and the lower the profits for each firm, as summarised in Figure 5.16.

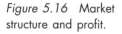

Figure 5.16 Market structure and profit.

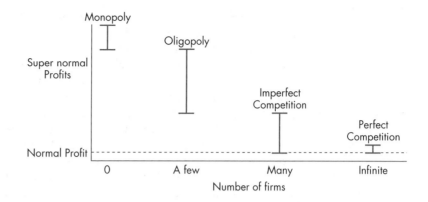

It is important, in looking at this graph, to realise that the number of firms is not the same as the number of brands, since producing many brands is a feature of oligopoly. Note also that the band of profits for oligopoly (and, to a lesser extent, for imperfect competition) are drawn longer than the others. This is to indicate that with oligopoly the level of profit depends on how firms play the game, with price wars pushing prices and profits down towards perfect competition levels and collusion pushing them up to monopoly levels.

Large profits act as an incentive for firms to enter a market and so, if there are no barriers to entry and exit, markets would become increasingly competitive. However, in the real world, the drift is the other way; industries are becoming more rather than less concentrated, and oligopolists and monopolists continue to make huge profits by maintaining barriers to entry. Indeed, the mere fact that existing firms in a market are big acts as a barrier, as they benefit from economies of scale that newcomers would find hard to match. Advertising and brand loyalty act as a barrier too, and these can be actively manipulated by incumbent firms to reduce the threat of entry. Firms can also set their prices to deter new entry; this 'entry preventing pricing' means that the firm sets prices below the profit maximising amount, which has two effects. Firstly, it makes the prices harder for newcomers to match, and secondly, it makes the industry less profitable in the short run and therefore less attractive to potential entrants. The sacrifice of lower profits today is, however, rewarded by the lack of entry of new firms, so that super normal profits, albeit lower than the maximum, continue to be enjoyed by incumbent firms in the long run.

The number of competitors in a market is a major influence on the profits that each firm makes since more competition in a market means that the custom has to be shared out amongst a greater number. Profits are also reduced by the presence of many firms insofar as this leads to price competition, which is good for consumers but reduces the total profit haul from a market. Price competition occurs because the more a market is shared, the more elastic the demand curve for each firm becomes, and this necessitates lower prices, as we have seen. In addition, more competition reduces the options for achieving competitive advantage. At the extreme, under perfect competition, firms have only one way to maintain a share of the market, let alone gain any advantage over their rivals, and that is to be cost and price minimisers. This is not to say that prices in a perfectly competitive market will necessarily be lower to the customer, since bigger firms will benefit from economies of scale and can therefore simultaneously provide goods more cheaply and make more profits. Firms with market power have more strategic options, and will make more profit. This is why the Competition Commission allows firms to merge even if it looks like the amalgamated firm will have considerable market power. But are also punished less by their environments if they are inefficient, which means they can be 'X inefficient' and their 'organisational slack' may lead to them ignoring profitable opportunities. Profitability also reflects the power of the individuals or firms with which the firm deals. A firm may, for example, be a monopolist but may nonetheless have high costs if the supplier of its inputs is a monopolist too. Likewise, if it sells to only one buyer (a **monopsony**), then its power to put prices up will be countered by the monopsonist's power to push them down, with the result depending on the relative power and therefore the market structure (amongst other things) of each side. Therefore, a more comprehensive approach to profitability, that will allow us to assess the profit potential of the environment of individual industries and firms, rather than of four broad market structures, is to look at firms' market power in terms of all the markets that they are involved in as both suppliers and buyers. This is a mammoth task, since most firms are involved in hundreds of markets, but according to Michael Porter we can, by focusing on only five links, encompass most of the determinants of an individual firm's profitability.

Case study in managing the environment and market structure

WHAT'S SCARCITY GOT TO DO WITH IT?

The reason that diamonds originally commanded a high price was that they were both desirable and scarce. Today they still command high prices, not because they are scarce but because their supply is controlled by a cartel. At the heart of the cartel is De Beers, whose mines produce half the world's diamonds and who control 70% of the world's supply of top-quality diamonds. De Beers spends around $200m a year on advertising to remind people of the desirability and exclusivity of their products. There are producers who, while benefiting from the high price in this industry, would nonetheless like to sell more at slightly lower prices. However, they tend to be kept in check by the knowledge that not only does De Beers control over half the mines, but those that it controls include the least-cost ones, which puts De Beers in a position to win any price wars. In addition, De Beers is actively acquiring other suppliers and wooing African nations to capture their diamond-producing facilities. This is not to say that its position is inviolate, however; new mines with lower extraction costs no doubt await discovery, and world supply exceeds world demand so that unsold stocks are growing. In addition, the expected slowdown in world growth as we enter the new millennium could reduce demand and margins further.

In response to the fact that the abundance of diamonds will one day undermine all attempts to keep its prices up, De Beers is attempting to differentiate its product in an attempt to corner the top-quality end of the market. It hopes to achieve this by laser-etching the De Beers logo on to each and every diamond it sells and giving each an individual serial number. This means that even if both the first reason for the high price of diamonds (scarcity) and the second reason (collusion and monopoly power) are gone, a third reason why some diamonds at least will command a higher price will remain (the quality of a leading brand name).

5.3   PORTER'S FIVE-FORCES APPROACH

Since Porter tends to envisage the environment as acting upon firms, rather than the reverse, these linkages can be seen as representing five forces acting upon firms as shown in Figure 5.17. Most of the ideas discussed in respect of these five forces are based on neo-classical textbook economics, so in that sense there is nothing new here. Indeed, we shall add some comments based on text-book economics that are omitted in Porter's approach. It is nonetheless worth following the framework as set out by Porter, because this limits the number of avenues down which we will pursue our search of the environment and because Porter's research suggests that his five forces encompass much of what we need to know as: 'the collective strength of these forces determines the ultimate profit potential in the industry' (Porter 1980, p. 5).

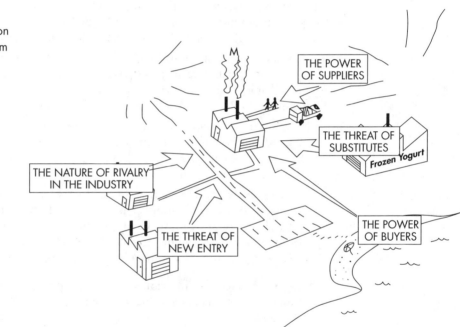

Figure 5.17 Porter's five forces, acting upon our ice-cream firm from Chapter 1.

We need to consider each of these in turn, but in doing so we need to recognise that they are interrelated. To clarify the discussion the firm being described will be referred to as 'our firm'.

5.3.1   Supplier power

Supplies include raw materials and semi-finished goods that our firm uses as well as inputs of financial capital, land, labour, and knowledge.

The importance of individual suppliers

Their importance to us depends on the extent to which we need them and they need us.

Whether we need them depends on:

- The structure of the industry: If our firm can get the same supplies from elsewhere then we have more bargaining power. This depends on how many suppliers there are to choose from. If, for example, our firm is supplied by a monopoly, it will extract a high price from us, as we cannot go elsewhere. As a result, our costs will be higher than if perfectly competitive firms supply us. In other words, it depends on the structure of the suppliers' industry. This also applies in looking at labour supply; if we need to use workers in short supply we will have to pay more. On the other hand, if our suppliers benefit from economies of scale then the price they charge us may fall when we demand more. This means that sometimes more competition amongst suppliers would be bad for us if it means that none of them can fully exploit the cost economies that come from being big.

- Collaboration (collusion) by suppliers: Even if our suppliers are numerous they may collaborate to push prices up; workers, for example, can form trades unions and professional associations that can push wages above the equilibrium, in other words above that warranted by their relative scarcity.

- Product differentiation within the suppliers' industry: Supplier power also depends on how well differentiated the supplier's products are since if the alternatives are not quite as good in some way then we will be less keen to switch to any other supplier.

- Ease of switching: Even if we wish to switch supplier we will tend to stick with our current supplier if it is difficult or costly to change. If, for example, there are contracts tying us to a supplier, these may be difficult to undo or we may incur a financial loss or loss of reputation (which will cost us in one way or another), if we break them.

All the above determine individual firms' power over us, that is, how much we need them. Counterbalancing this is how much they need us, which depends on whether our custom is important to them. If we are the only customer for any of our suppliers then as a monopsonist we would expect to be charged less than if we are one of many. In other words, whether they need us depends on the structure of the industry that we are in when it comes to buying inputs (rather than in terms of the market that we sell to).

Take-over threat

The threat that a supplier could buy our firm may sometimes act as a deterrent to our exploitation of them. On the other hand, the threat of our taking them over can deter them from exploiting us.

Collectively these factors determine the ability of our suppliers to restrict supply and push our input prices up and the ability of our firm to restrict demand for their output and push those input prices down. This battle determines the price we pay for our inputs: if we are weak relative to them then the price will be high and our costs will be high, as shown in Figure 5.18, on the left. If, on the other hand, we are powerful relative to them then our costs will be low, as on the right. (For more on this see Chapter 7).

Figure 5.18 Power of suppliers.

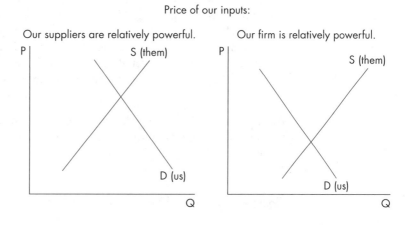

5.3.2 Buyer power

Here we are concerned with the demand for our firm's products, so now we are the supplier. This means that some of the arguments are repeats of those presented above except that now the boot is on the other foot. In this case, if we are powerful relative to our customers we can push revenue up. The constraints on us doing this are as follows.

The importance of individual customers

This depends on:

- Number of buyers: Buyer power will tend to be high when there are few of them. Sainsbury's gets its fruit and vegetables cheaper than a corner shop, since, as a big powerful customer, it can insist on low prices. Therefore, if our firm supplies Sainsbury's our margin will be low (although volumes are likely to be high). If we sell to a monopsonist, it could dictate terms to us and push our prices and profit margins right down, although again this would not be a disaster if volumes are high.

- Collaboration by our customers: Even if there are many consumers, they may act in concert to force our prices down. Some consumer groups have effectively lobbied firms to lower prices or change the basis on which they operate. A recent case involving a foreign supplier's use of slave labour to produce sporting goods led to an immediate response from the UK-based retailer when it was exposed in the media.

- Ease of switching: Our price will tend to be forced down if finding a substitute is easy (because there are many alternatives and people know about them), if buyers have an incentive to switch (perhaps because the purchase is a major one for them), and if the costs of switching are low.

- Differentiation: If we can make our product unique or more attractive in some way, then we will reduce people's desire to switch. This might involve changing the product so that it has a different mix of characteristics from those of its rivals, perhaps by altering the quality in some way to make it more attractive, durable or useful. We can, in addition, differentiate our product through marketing efforts to delineate it as a clear brand, rather than one of many similar alternatives, without necessarily changing it at all.

All the factors above help determine the amount of demand for our output; in other words, they determine the position of the demand curve we face and its elasticity.

Competition within the industry

Although considered separately below, it is worth considering this factor here too as the structure of our industry is an important determinant of buyer power since a lot of firms fighting for the same custom will increase the relative power of each customer. Collaboration with our erstwhile rivals can reduce this problem, whereas collaboration amongst our customers will exacerbate it.

Take-over threat

If we consider the case where the buyer is another firm, then there is always some risk of its taking our firm over. Such a threat may encourage us to keep our prices down.

5.3.3 Threat of entry

If firms can enter our market, profits for incumbent firms will generally fall (as discussed in Chapter 4). To determine the size of this threat the firm must answer the following questions:

Do other firms want to enter our market?

This depends on whether newcomers think that:

- they can do what we do: If consumers perceive that the entrant cannot match the incumbent in some way, that in some respect the existing product is better than that of the newcomer, then entry is deterred. In this case, we will have differentiated our product to such an extent that it cannot be imitated, or looked at another way, we have some competency, or expertise, that they cannot match.

- it will be worth doing: Firms will want to enter our market if they see us making significant super normal profits. This desire can be reduced by disguising the profitability of our markets through 'entry-preventing pricing' and the like.

Can we keep them out even if they want to come in?

In other words, are there 'barriers to entry' into our niche?

Barriers to entry include the following:

- Legal restrictions are the obvious and most impenetrable barrier. They remain in some industries, particularly in service industries dominated by the professions; for example, only doctors can perform certain medical functions. Deregulation in the 1980s has eliminated many traditional barriers in the UK, while similar reforms have been initiated across Europe. One legal barrier to competition that remains intact is the patent system which acts to protect innovators and thereby encourage innovation.

- Cost economies for existing firms:
  - It is often found that incumbent firms in an industry can do things cheaper than new entrants, simply because they have been doing it for longer. These learning economies can be significant (as discussed in Chapter 3), and therefore lack of experience can act as a major barrier to entry.
  - If there are high set-up costs, existing firms have an advantage insofar as they have already paid them, whereas newcomers will have to invest heavily if they are to compete on price. For example, in the production of steel, large capital investment is required since a steel-mill needs to be built.
  - If there are large cost savings to be made from producing a lot, then new firms being forced to start on a smaller scale will have higher costs by missing out on some economies of scale.

- Existing arrangements: The existence of networks of relationships between incumbent firms and their suppliers, customers and regulators can put newcomers off. A special arrangement with suppliers, for example, may put newcomers off if they cannot make the same arrangements. Wall's, the ice-cream producer (a subsidiary of Lever Brothers Ltd), has two-thirds of the UK ice-cream market and yet faces major international competition from the American firm Mars and the Swiss firm Nestlé. How then does it manage to hang on to such a large market share? One reason is that most small shops in the UK use freezers to store ice-cream that are lent – free of charge – by Lever Brothers.

- Distribution: Another example of the value of existing relationships, which is worth considering separately, is the availability of distribution channels, since access to distribution does not come simply from entering the industry. Producing a newspaper, for example, is not the same as getting it into every shop in Britain, nor does leasing a few aeroplanes entitle you to flight slots at major airports, without which entry into the mainstream airline business is impossible.

- Location: Geographical proximity alone can confer benefits on incumbent firms since closeness to markets and suppliers lowers costs.

- Retaliation: If incumbent firms expect entry to reduce profitability then they will resist it. How incumbents react and what lengths they will go to depends on how much of a threat the entrant is. Retaliation is likely if:
  - incumbents have the resources to win a fight; this might mean power over suppliers, buyers, or financial resources;
  - there is excess capacity in the industry; for many production processes it becomes very costly to operate at reduced outputs, in which case incumbent firms will strive to maintain output levels even if that means cutting prices;
  - the industry concerned is not growing, since in such a case a new entrant's profits are more likely to come at the expense of incumbent firms;
  - there is cross-subsidisation. If an incumbent firm can subsidise one part of its business with funds from another part then it can charge prices that cannot be matched by a firm that cannot cross-subsidise. For example, in the newspaper business there are occasional price wars where prices fall below costs, which are made possible only by cross-subsidisation from other parts of the media empires that own them.

- Collusion: Competition reduces margins so firms have an incentive not to compete and, although open collusion is often illegal, tacit collusion continues. Collusion is made easier when there is a clear leader in the market and when the players are known to each other, are relatively few in number, and are well established. Firms can of course collude to enter a market as well as to stop entry.

- Incumbent firms can deliberately build barriers to entry: Heavy advertising, for example, deters entry since incumbent firms become well known and brand loyalty is thereby encouraged. The industry can also collaborate to emphasise its benefits relative to other industries, so, for example, the milk marketing board emphasises the fact that the calcium and protein in milk make it different from other drinks. Trade associations also have a marketing and public relations side, often putting the case for the industry in the news. There are also barriers to exit that stop firms exiting an industry. These are important since if the potential entrant will 'lose their shirt' if their entry fails, then they may be less keen to enter than if they can pull out without too much damage. The cost of exit largely depends on 'asset specificity'; that is, if the assets invested can be used for something else then if the entry ultimately fails the value of the asset is not lost. If, on the other hand, the assets invested in are specific to that industry and cannot be used for anything else then it will be difficult to sell them or use them if entry fails, and the costs will become sunk costs. Adding entry and exit considerations together tells us how 'contestable' a market is and, as Baumol et al. (1982) argue, a 'contestable market' (characterised by free entry and exit) will be subject to hit-and-run competition and will have profit levels as low as those of perfect competition.

5.3.4 Threat of substitutes

Treating substitutes as a separate force may seem odd since it is mentioned when discussing all the other forces; however, it is important to do this since rivals in the same industry do not supply all of the alternatives for our firm's products. It is important, therefore, to treat substitutes as a separate factor rather than count it purely as a function of competition within the industry. The degree of substitutability of a firm's products is important insofar as having many substitutes increases elasticity of demand and thereby reduces the product's profit potential.

Substitutes can be divided into three types:

- Products that meet the same need: All products compete for consumers' money, so substitution is a question of degree. Ferries and the Chunnel both meet the same need to get to and from the continent and are therefore strong substitutes. On the other hand, holidays abroad and CDs both compete for the money we spend on leisure but are weak substitutes. Where firms draw the line in their analysis is partly a matter of experience, but calculating cross-price elasticities can help.

- Products that eliminate the need for our product: In other words, a product that removes the need for our product; for example, no one needs typewriters or slide rules, now that we have computers.

- Not bothering: Unless the product is an absolute necessity, then to one degree or another, not fulfilling the need that the product satisfies is a substitute. For example, smokers trying to quit were expected to take this option and leave their desire for nicotine unanswered before nicotine patches and gum became widely available as substitutes.

Buyers' propensity to use substitutes depends on the relative price and quality of the alternative, the ease with which customers can switch if they want to, and the aggressiveness with which the suppliers of substitutes promote their products. If the price of a substitute goes up (or performance or availability falls), this will increase the demand for our product; this is largely beyond the control of our firm but our firm can reduce the degree of substitutability of its products. This can be approached in three ways. Firstly, since substitutability is partly subjective, our firm can try to reduce it for our product by altering people's perceptions by marketing and branding. Secondly, we can increase the objective benefits of our product by making it better in some way. Thirdly, we can make it harder for people to switch; we can, for example, reward loyalty as supermarkets have done. Alternatively, we can make it costly for people to switch, as building societies have done with penalty clauses for product switching.

Complements do not feature so prominently in the Porter approach but are an essential feature of neoclassical economic analysis. They are important insofar as a cut in the price of complements shifts the demand for our products to the right. Complements are often supplied by firms in industries that are otherwise unconnected, so, for example, with cars and petrol, what happens to petrol prices is largely beyond the control of car manufacturers. In this sense, complements can often be a very external part of the business environment. Our firm can internalise this part of the environment to the extent that it can make the complements for its products itself, if it is economical to do so.

5.3.5   Competition within the industry

(Or competitive rivalry as Porter calls it): Although this has been mentioned in reference to the other four forces (especially with regard to collaboration to deal with external threats), there are nonetheless elements of this worth considering separately.

- Market structure: The number of firms doing what we do will affect the level of profit, for reasons discussed earlier in this chapter.

- Product differentiation: Even if there are many competitors, if our product is in some way separated from the pack then rivalry and the PeD for our product will be reduced.

- Switching costs: If it is difficult or costly to switch brands then the effect of competition on profits will be reduced.

- Leadership: The relative size of firms is important insofar as a clear market leader is likely to establish some of the ground-rules for competition in that industry. A dominant firm is likely to promote price leadership and leadership in other dimensions of strategy too, which will allow all firms to make more profits.

- Industry growth rates: Industry growth rates are important since in an expanding market all firms can expand without beating any of their rivals, but in a shrinking one expansion is only possible at the expense of rivals. There is clearly a link between the industry growth rate and its environment, because of the influence of such things as income, population and fashion.

- Likelihood of price competition: As we have seen, price competition damages profitability in a way that non-price competition usually does not. Price competition is more likely when there are many firms and no price leadership emerges, perhaps because there is no dominant firm. It is also more likely when fixed costs in the industry are high since in this case firms will want to keep production levels up, even if this means cutting prices. If the product is perishable we may also get price competition; since it cannot be stored, selling it at any price is better than letting it rot. If cars rotted quickly, for example, the current over-supply would ensure dramatic price reductions rather than fields full of unsold models. Price competition may also be greater in industries where production is lumpy rather than incremental, or subject to long time lags between the start and finish of the production run, since periods of over-supply and thus price falls are likely. Often in the chemical, steel and shipbuilding industries, the opening of a new plant (which of necessity are big) can lead to a sudden jump in supply and a fall in prices. Another factor involved in determining the likelihood of price competition is exit barriers, for if these are high firms may accept lower profits and price competition because there is nothing else they can switch to.

Case study

IS MARKS AND SPENCER LOSING ITS LEGENDARY GRIP ON ITS SUPPLIERS AND CUSTOMERS?

M&S has for some time been Britain's most profitable general retailer but things seem to be slipping of late. The main problems are firstly that there has been an increase in competition, over the years, with many supermarkets moving into M&S territory. They have done this by improving the quality of the best of their products and by emulating some of the practices that traditionally set M&S apart. Secondly, the economy is slowing, in particular consumer demand is weakening. A few years ago M&S achieved increases on the sale of clothes in excess of 5% per annum, whereas today there is apparently no growth at all; even falls are in evidence on some lines. This creates a problem for the firms that supply M&S since traditionally M&S expects to buy all their output, which is fine until they want less, rather than more, as now. The third problem stems from the M&S board's decision to buy clothes on the open market rather than rely so heavily on its traditional British manufacturers. The board made this decision in response to the fact that their rivals were gaining a considerable advantage over them by making their clothes in the Far East, where wages are significantly below those prevailing in the UK. This decision has affected their 'made in Britain' image, and has led, in the opinion of many, to a reduction in quality. The problem is that with the open market purchases M&S can no longer employ their legendary quality control techniques. It has also meant that once an order is placed it is up to M&S to sell all that they have bought. In the past, if a line was not selling they could instruct the supplier to switch to something else instead. Now they have to put unsold stocks on the sale rail, so that the sight of relatively low-quality clothes 'piled high' for a quick sale has blighted many stores. This further undermines the belief that M&S is a cut above the rest and, perhaps worst of all, puts a big dent in the reputation of the management. On the other hand, with 70% of its goods still coming from within the UK, M&S has a higher input cost structure than its rivals, who buy more on the open market than M&S do. So, until it learns how to buy from the open market and maintain quality as its rivals do, M&S will find itself in something of a cleft stick. It also means that those who buy most on the open market will have benefited greatly from the strength of the pound relative to other currencies over the past few years, as this makes foreign produce even cheaper. This also means that in its foreign operations, selling British goods has become more and more difficult for M&S since the high pound makes our goods more expensive for foreigners (for the same reason that it makes their goods cheaper for us; see Chapter 11).

5.3.6 Summary of five forces

1. Bargaining power of suppliers: Our firm's profit margins are inversely related to the power of our suppliers since a powerful supplier can charge higher prices and push our costs up.

2. Bargaining power of buyers: Our firm's profit margins are inversely related to customer power, since a powerful buyer can push our prices and profits down.

3. Threat of substitutes: Our firm's profit margins are inversely related to the number of substitutes.

4. Barriers: Exit barriers, and in particular entry barriers, such as patents, economies of scale and so on, keep rivals out and profits up.

5. Intensity of rivalry: More competition lowers profits.

If we add all the forces together, we get a picture of how attractive a niche is (industry or segment), since taken as a whole the five forces indicate the profit potential of that niche, and the strategic options available in the niche. The specifics of what a firm can do are given by considering each force and seeing what opportunities and threats are likely in respect of each, and which if any can be manipulated to the benefit of the firm.

Five-forces analysis case study

A BRIEF FIVE-FORCES ANALYSIS FOR TESCO PLC

Suppliers

- A few big brands such as Cadbury's, Bass, Lever.

- However, many supplies are purchased on the open market to ensure the lowest possible prices are paid. For example, currently less than 3% of the price of a banana bought in UK supermarkets is paid to the growers, as the suppliers are numerous, poor, and relatively powerless.

- Own brands have been developed using locked-in suppliers, or by take-over.

- Its ability to buy in bulk means that Tesco is often a very important customer for suppliers.

- The production of many foods is heavily subsidised by the EU and EU policies have driven world food prices down; both factors reduce the cost of food to supermarkets.

- Tend to use mainly low skilled workforce, which helps to keep costs down.

- Have several routes to raising finance, including their own profits.

- Result: Costs are low.

Buyers

- Many buyers but well informed on price and quality issues.

- Customers' expectations are rising regarding degree of in-store complements and facilitators, insofar as consumers expect not only a large product range of foods but easy parking, restaurants and crèche facilities. Some trends may be identified, such as the increased interest in healthy eating, and the rise in popularity of Far Eastern and Indian foods.

- There is also a rise in consumers' interest in 'ethical shopping', which entails the supermarkets reducing the extent to which they exploit producers, particularly in the Third World. Some supermarkets (not Tesco) have been targeted for continuing to buy from producers that use child slave labour. In effect, some consumers are collaborating to use their power as buyers to increase the power of suppliers to the supermarkets. The effect on supermarkets' profit margins will be avoided if consumers are willing to pay more for such 'ethical' goods. Otherwise, it means reduced profits for those adopting a cheap-at-any-cost approach.

Substitutes

- Large-scale shopping arcades, both in and out of town, have been developed.

- Rejuvenation of town centres now being given priority by some local councils.

- Internet shopping, and TV shopping, are also increasing in popularity although currently still very small in the UK.

Barriers to entry

- Relatively high margins make the UK market a potential target.

- But large network of stores makes it very expensive for an outsider to come in on a big scale.

- Massive advertising spend is also a barrier to entry into this market.

- High degree of awareness by the public of who the main firms are and their key characteristics. There is also some brand loyalty.

- Possibility of increasing penetration from foreign rivals seeking to develop a pan-European pretence.

Rivalry

- A few big firms dominate main food market, generally separated geographically.

- There is considerable non-price competition and price wars are rare.

- Location is an important differentiator between firms since many local councils do not permit rival stores to open near each other.

Conclusions

This analysis suggests that profits will be high for the main oligopolists because of large volumes of sales. Being cheap and being different are both viable strategic options for incumbent firms since for own-brands produced by tied, or taken-over, suppliers, costs will be low and PeDs high, which suggests a low-cost strategy. On the other hand, the environment for complementary services suggests that the firm can differentiate by marketing non-food products and by providing more customer services.

Implications of anticipated changes in the five forces

- Increased competition may put pressure on margins as the main threat is from firms offering products at lower prices. The fact that European and US rivals operate on lower margins may increase the pressure on the government to intervene in this sector; already the Office of Fair Trading is investigating practices in this industry.

- Internet shopping may one day eliminate the need for supermarkets, but not for some time.

- Increasing concern about the demise of town centres may see increased use of smaller in-town stores. Tesco is responding to this, with its 'Metro' stores.

- 'Ethical shopping' could lead to a squeeze on margins, unless consumers are willing to pay more. However, the fact that only some are willing to pay more may lead to a further differentiation between products (as has happened with free-range eggs). If this occurs, ethical shoppers will have their own range of products without narrowing margins for the supermarkets.

Five-forces analysis case study

A BRIEF FIVE-FORCES ANALYSIS FOR THE PHARMACEUTICAL INDUSTRY

Suppliers

- Cost of ingredients in drugs generally low.

- Most plant is capital intensive and different products can be created with similar production and thus suppliers techniques – therefore switching of production is possible, including geographical switching.

Buyers

- Many chemists are small and in a poor bargaining position relative to the big pharmaceutical firms.

- Customers' brand loyalty is often strong.

- Doctors who – up to a point – tend to recommend the best products regardless of cost prescribe many drugs in the UK, with the patient generally paying only a fraction of the cost. There is also an arrangement with the government that ensures that prices paid give firms a return of around 20% in order to encourage them to come up with and supply new products to the NHS.

● Combined this means inelastic demand and high prices. However, doctors are becoming increasingly cost-conscious owing to government reforms and growth in distribution by agents who buy in bulk rather than by the individual chemists.

Substitutes

● Drugs patents ensure that immediate copying is limited.

● However, there is a general rise of cheap alternative 'generic' drugs such as Aspirin replacing brands like Anadin.

● Improved biochemistry technology means that close substitutes can be produced increasingly rapidly.

Entry

● Large barriers to entry include legal patent system, high set-up costs, high costs of research and development (R&D) and requirement for prolonged safety testing. Only a fraction of drugs tested ever make it to market and those that do are generally over a decade old before they become established. So this kind of investment is risky and creates an exit barrier since such investment costs are often sunk costs.

● Increasing threat from global competition spurred in part by advances in biotechnology and computing that make it easier to create new drugs.

Competitive rivalry

● Dominated by a few big players.

● Significant merger activity to cover increasingly homogeneous global market leading to increased concentration.

● Brand reputation and product differentiation are more prevalent than price competition. The 'market skimming' pricing strategy is invariably adopted for new products, since market penetration is assured (if the drug works).

● Growth in market likely to continue due to ageing population and rising expectations amongst customers regarding treatment levels.

● Access to customers is important, especially large chemist chains such as Boots plc, and NHS hospital trusts.

Conclusion

Currently very profitable for those with big selling drugs.

Likely implications of anticipated changes in the five forces

● Increased price competition and pressure on margins owing to rise in use of cheap 'generic drugs' and improved use of similar drugs by rivals brought to market increasingly quickly after new products are launched.

● Increased merger activity likely to ensure economies of scale are made to enable cost advantages, which will become increasingly important in the face of copycat drugs.

● Main source of competitive advantage will continue to be the efficacy of products and the R&D required to create them. However, pressure on margins may mean firms become more inclined to look for efficiency gains in this respect. This could lead to developments in the way R&D is organised through, for example, the use of new technology, research networks and links to universities.

● Access to customers is likely to remain crucial and so developing links with major purchasers is likely to remain important.

5.4   STRATEGIC GROUPS

We can of course apply the five forces to any firm or industry but, we can also apply it at the level of the individual product or Strategic Business Unit (SBU). The SBU is some grouping of products that managers feel are similar enough to treat as one for strategic purposes. Products or SBUs occupying the same niche within an industry are called 'strategic groups' as the successful strategies, or at least the paths of least resistance, are likely to be similar for each of them. Looking at strategic groups will also help a firm's decision-makers identify the most attractive positions to occupy within an industry. In Figure 5.19 we identify some strategic groups for SBUs in the newspaper industry, using two dimensions: regional focus and the social class of the readership.

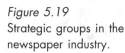
Figure 5.19
Strategic groups in the newspaper industry.

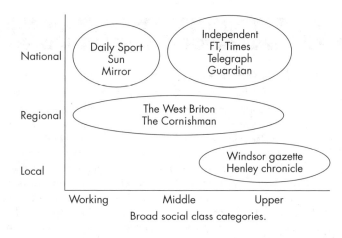

Broad social class categories.

5.5 THE COMPETITIVE ENVIRONMENT AND STRATEGY

We are a long way short of identifying the strategic paths of least resistance that apply to different environmental niches, but Porter (1985) believes that there are, in most cases, two overriding strategic choices to be made – between cost leadership and differentiation.

Because profits are the difference between what the firm gets for producing something and the cost of making it, a firm's competitive advantage must ultimately come from offering customers something different at the same or higher price than their rivals, or offering customers something similar at a lower price. This dichotomy suggests that firms face a basic choice between 'differentiation' and 'low cost' strategies. These two are what Porter terms 'generic strategies' as they always apply and always work. **Cost leadership** always works but to do it requires that the firm has more economies of scale, and is further along the experience curve than its rivals. **Differentiation** always works since it means the degree of substitutability is reduced. A firm can make its products different from those of its rivals in terms of quality, branding, aesthetics, durability, taste and so on. Simply doing something that it has never done before without providing customers with anything different does not count however, as the Laura Ashley company has recently found out: in the mid-1990s the Laura Ashley company introduced a range of new lines that represented a radical departure from its traditional country look. This did not, however, make it different from the customers' point of view, since in this case the lines were similar to those offered by almost every other clothes shop. In fact, insofar as the traditional Laura Ashley look is different to what Next and Principles offer, the differentiation of Laura Ashley products actually went down. In fact, Laura Ashley found itself 'stuck in the middle' between the two generic strategies as it had failed to differentiate but could not compete on price with its rivals.

Cost leadership vs. differentiation case study

THE MOTOR CAR INDUSTRY

To facilitate mass production, Henry Ford froze the design of the Model T in the early 1900s and limited the range of options on it (leading to the famous saying that you 'could have any colour as long as it's black'). The hope was that this would give Ford a significant cost advantage, as Adam Smith and all subsequent economists had predicted. Prices were cut in anticipation of this and, fortunately for Ford, demand was price elastic and costs did indeed fall as economies of scale came into play. This allowed the Model T's price to be cut further from $950 to around the $290 mark in the early 1920s with Ford's share of the US market increasing from 9% to over 55% by 1921. A great success story. However, by 1926 Ford's share was below 35%. What had happened? The answer is that other firms had differentiated their products from Ford's in terms of quality – with innovations in engines, transmissions and bodywork, as well as in terms of styling, and the provision of add-ons. All this combined to reduce the relative elasticity of demand for Ford's rivals who could therefore find buyers who were willing to pay more for their cars and who, by the same token, expected to pay relatively less for Fords. This battle between cost leadership and product differentiation continues in the car industry today.

5.5.1 Getting stuck in the middle

Differentiation and cost leadership allow the firm to succeed generally across a market's niches. If, however, a firm finds that it is unable to compete on price or add value to the product and charge a higher price, it may still nonetheless succeed by targeting a part of a market. This 'focus' strategy means it can win with a certain type of customer, or within a certain region, for example. It is, however, important to realise that this is not a middle path between the generic strategies since that leads to firms getting stuck in the middle. This means that the firm has no advantage in terms of price, or in terms of its ability to offer something better. Because: 'unless a firm strictly separates the units pursuing different generic strategies, it may compromise the ability of any of them to achieve competitive advantage' (Porter 1985, p. 18), since the two cultures may clash and since the two are 'usually inconsistent, because differentiation is usually costly'. This is not to say that a firm can never succeed in both, many Japanese firms have increased their share of manufacturing markets throughout the world by raising the quality of their goods and lowering their prices, this is, however, only possible in certain circumstances:

- If every other firm is stuck in the middle, a winner can emerge that does both. If all firms are cost-inefficient, a cost-conscious firm can differentiate its products and still end up producing something cheaper. In Porter's estimation such circumstances seldom last since one firm will eventually choose and implement a successful generic strategy. Much of UK industry in the 1970s may have been in this position, having been both protected from foreign competition by fixed exchange rates and featherbedded by government policies that ensured a high level of demand and support for industry.

- If economies of scale are very large, gaining market share can reduce costs sufficiently to enable the firm to achieve both better quality and lower prices.

- If the firm introduces a significant innovation – this might be a better production technique, or a better method of distribution, or of organisation, or of improvements in the products themselves – then again both can be achieved.

Competition and strategy

BUILDING SOCIETIES

In the 1890s, there were thousands of building societies, today there are less than a hundred. Building societies were first established as clubs where people would pool their funds to build a house for the eldest in the club, and when the last brick was put in the last house of the youngest of the club it was wound up. Some, however, initiated a rolling system of taking deposits and offering mortgages and thus never came to an end. However, some commentators today say environmental changes will put an end to them for a number of reasons. The first of these concerns competition. Before the 1980s, monetary controls effectively precluded banks from offering mortgages, while building societies, who for some time had operated an open cartel, were not permitted to offer proper cheque accounts and loans to business. So, in other words, there were legal barriers stopping each entering the others' established lines of business as well as clear collusion eliminating competition within each market too. But in the 1980s all that changed as a policy of deregulation was introduced by Margaret Thatcher to increase competition and bring down prices (interest rate margins) in the provision of financial services. This was part of a general programme of deregulation but was also seen as a means of encouraging home ownership through boosting the availability of mortgages. This played a part in the

late 1980s housing boom and the recession of the early 1990s that was required to eliminate it, as discussed in Chapter 4. However, for the building societies it was a time both of great opportunity and of great threat. On the plus side nearly all of them took the opportunity to issue cheque accounts and many dipped their toes into the massive business lending market, with varying degrees of success. On the negative side, their grip on UK mortgage business was loosened, with banks and new types of lenders entering the market at will. The second change was a legal one. The deregulation policy was enshrined in law as all such things must be, but in addition the 1986 Building Society Act enabled the societies to convert from mutual to 'public limited company' (plc) status, in effect, to become a bank. In their traditional mutual set-up, each saver and borrower (who constituted the members of the society) had one share in the firm. Converting to plc status would mean that shares in the firms would be sold on the open market to whoever could afford them. Such conversion would, in addition, give them more strategic options because, despite deregulation, there were still things that banks were allowed to do that building societies could not. In addition, conversion would mean small windfalls for the existing members, big windfalls for some of the senior staff, and a big inflow of money for the firm to invest in all the new markets that were to come within its grasp. The first to convert was Abbey National, but since then, many have followed, although a few remain tied to the idea of mutuality. However, those who remain mutual, such as the Nationwide, are subject to pressure from many of their members to convert, to allow them to take the windfalls that are their due. On the other side, the Nationwide's board and many other members emphasise how by not having to make profits for shareholders it can enhance the returns to its borrowers and savers. In conjunction with these changes to the specific environment of building societies, there have also been broader environmental changes at work on them. In particular, there is the continued opening up of the European market to UK firms, and the entry of foreign firms into our market. In addition, there have been considerable improvements in information and communication technology that make it ever easier for firms, whether from a building society, bank or insurance company background, to provide for all of an individual's financial needs.

It was, of course, hoped that pitting the building societies and banks against each other would mean more competition. However, although initially it had that effect, because competition reduces profits it was not long before erstwhile competitors were merging. Indeed, in the opinion of many, there are three clear niches in which long-term profits are likely, of which the primary one is to be big. Moreover in a European, and increasingly global market, big means very big. The Halifax, for example, was the biggest of the building societies before it converted. In 1998, it made nearly £1.8bn profits (before tax) and it has assets of over £144bn. But still its management feels that it is too small, which is why it is currently seeking to merge with Barclays Bank. However, even this strikes many in the City as too parochial, so that what may happen is an even bigger tie-up with a European partner. The second niche is that of the regional lender. As long as trust is important in this industry, some competitive advantage will remain in being known to be associated with a particular area. So, for example, the Monmouthshire Building Society does particularly well in Monmouth and south Wales in general, because it has a tradition of service to that community. Finally, there is the 'specialist' niche. In this case, there is an advantage to firms who target a small subset of the market. The Ecological Building Society, for example, will attract customers who associate themselves strongly with the 'green' movement. The Teacher's Building Society will survive by targeting teachers and tailoring their product to the specific needs of teachers. As you may have realised, these are nothing more than the expression of Porter's generic strategies of being big, different or focused.

5.6 SUMMARY

- The importance of the number of competitors in a market helps determine the behaviour of firms in that market, with different levels of competition in an environment leading to different routes to survival.

- The number of firms in a market must be somewhere between none and infinity.

- At one end where there are an infinite number of rivals, we have the perfectly competitive environment, in which all firms make only normal profits and survival depends only on price competition.

- In an environment characterised by monopolistic competition, in which there are many firms with each selling a slightly different product, some super normal profits can be made and there are more strategic choices than simply price competition.

- In an environment characterised by oligopoly, in which there are a few principal players, huge super normal profits can be made if firms do not destroy each other in price wars. Competitive advantage in this case therefore comes from collusion to avoid price wars, non-price competition, and the ability to predict strategic move and countermove.

- When there is no competition, we have monopoly and in this case, the most profit that could possibly be made from any given market can be extracted by the monopolist. The key to success in this case is to keep competitors out and stop regulators legislating the firm's super normal profits away.

- We can conclude that less competition produces more market power for the remaining firms, which results in increased profits and a greater scope for strategic choice.

5.7 QUESTIONS

1. Can you name some markets that are close to perfect competition?

2. Name one good or service that you buy from a market where there is only one supplier available to you. If this market was turned into a perfectly competitive market, do you think the price would go up or down?

3. What goods and services do you buy from oligopolistic suppliers?

4. (a) What is collusion?
   (b) Why is collusion particularly prevalent amongst oligopolists?
   (c) What forms of collusion are there?
   (d) Explain why an oligopolistic firm, that does not aim to collude, but which does aim to maximise profit, will not change its prices unless its costs change considerably. Illustrate your answer with a diagram.
   (e) Why does the Competition Commission allow some forms of collusion, and mergers, despite the fact that this increases the power of the firms to exploit customers?

5. The majority of domestic detergents (washing powder, washing up liquid, etc.) are supplied by just two firms – Procter & Gamble and Lever Brothers. They each produce a huge number of branded products. Why?

6. What kinds of XeDs might the following have?
   (a) Porsche 911   and   Fiat panda
   (b) Margarine   and   Butter
   (c) Coke   and   Pepsi
   (d) Shoes   and   Shoe polish

7. Glaxo Wellcome is the world's largest pharmaceutical (drug) company. In this industry, firms are allowed patents on drugs for a period of time. This is to allow firms to reap monopoly profits as a reward for the research and development needed to create major new drugs. One of Glaxo Wellcome's most important products worldwide is Zovirax, an anti-viral drug which fights cold sores and other types of herpes. It is estimated that 1 in 5 people in Europe (and presumably in the world) suffer from cold sores which are painful and distressing. Zovirax is widely believed to be the only effective formulation and hence this is the world leader in the anti-cold-sore market. However, Glaxo Wellcome's world patent on this product ran out in 1998 (1999 in Japan).
   (a) What is the likely effect of the ending of the Zovirax world patent on:
       (i) the market for anti-cold sore drugs;
       (ii) on Glaxo Wellcome;
       (iii) on Glaxo Wellcome's competitors.
   (b) Devise a strategy for Glaxo Wellcome to minimise the effect of this change on them.

8. The matrix below shows the extra Christmas total revenue associated with the pricing options facing two oligopolists. The figures relate to delivery to a supermarket chain before the start of the Christmas rush. Once entered into, the contract with the supermarket chain cannot be broken, even if it means making no additional Christmas sales because you have priced too high.
(a) What does this matrix show?
(b) Which is the best pricing strategy for the firms?

Strategic options for Murphy's stout beer

		Low price	High price
Strategic options for Guinness stout beer	Low price	Murphy's 30 *Guinness 30*	Murphy's 0 *Guinness 80*
	High price	Murphy's 80 *Guinness 0*	Murphy's 60 *Guinness 60*

All pay-offs are in £ million
Pay-offs for Guinness are in italics

CHAPTER 6

Different theories of the behaviour of firms

After studying this chapter, you should be able to:

● understand how the impact of environmental changes is dependent on the assumptions made about the aims of firms;

● appreciate how the separation of ownership from control and the prevalence of market power give rise to the possibility of non-profit-maximising behaviour by firms;

● appreciate the differences between managerial and behavioural theories of the behaviour of firms;

● understand and appreciate the differences between various managerial theories of the firm;

● understand how in behavioural interpretation of firms the interplay of power within the firm determines what firms do;

● appreciate how the interplay of power within firms can lead to indeterminate results.

6.1   A COMPARISON OF DIFFERENT THEORIES OF THE BEHAVIOUR OF FIRMS

The aims of firms affect the way they behave, including the way they respond to changes in their environment. So far, we have only considered one model of the behaviour of the firm, in which we stipulate an overriding aim to maximise profits. In this chapter we will consider some alternatives and investigate their implications for our analysis.

Formal models (simplifications) of the behaviour of firms can be divided into two types. '**Managerial**' theories show what types of behaviour result from maximising managers' objectives. '**Behavioural**' theories attempt to show how firms arrive at their decisions; in these theories no assumption of maximisation is made. We will begin by looking at the model we have thus far been using and against which we will compare the rest.

6.1.1 Short-run profit maximisation

Figure 6.1 shows the relationship between revenues, costs and output as calculated in Chapter 3. To this is added a curve representing the size of total profit, in other words the size of the gap between TR and TC.

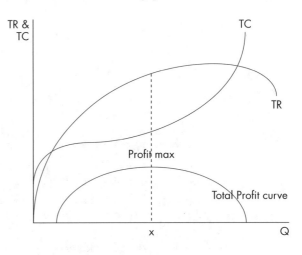

Figure 6.1 Typical TR, TC and total profit curves.

Response to a change in demand

We can use this diagram to illustrate what a profit-maximising supplier will do when demand shifts. If, for example, there is a recession and the firm is selling normal goods, then TR will be less and the firm's profit-maximising output will fall; it will therefore supply 'z' rather than 'x' in Figure 6.2. (In this case, the best the firm can do is to minimise its losses, as is common in a recession.)

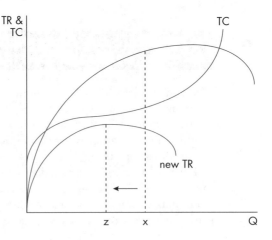

Figure 6.2 Profit maximisers reduce supply when demand falls.

This result – that supply is less when demand is less (and up to full capacity more, when demand is more) – is shared by all the approaches below and amounts to no more that stipulating that supply curves are upward sloping. The different theories do, however, have different implications for firms' price elasticity of supply.

Change in fixed costs

In this model a fall or rise in fixed costs does not change the level of output; as can be seen in Figure 6.3, profits shrink when such costs rise, but the place where the biggest gap between TR and TC lies is unaffected.

Figure 6.3 Changes in fixed costs do not affect the profit maximiser's supply decision, only the level of profit.

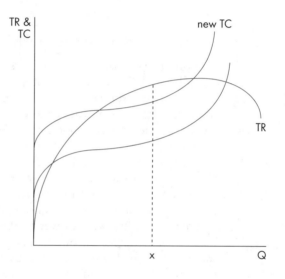

So environmental changes such as a fall in business rates or a cut in the tax on profits, or a fall in the wages of those who are paid for the job rather than how much they produce, do not affect the firm's supply decision; they simply earn it more profit. The extra profit may act as a magnet to other firms so at the level of the market supply will go up, but no more is supplied by each incumbent firm.

Change in variable costs

A rise in variable costs, including those caused by environmental changes such as a rise in indirect taxes like excise duty, will affect supply. A rise in variable costs will shift supply to the left, in Figure 6.4 from 'x' to 'y'.

This confirms what we have seen already: if wage costs or other variable costs go up, supply shifts left. If they fall, supply shifts right.

Figure 6.4 A rise in variable costs reduces the profit maximiser's supply.

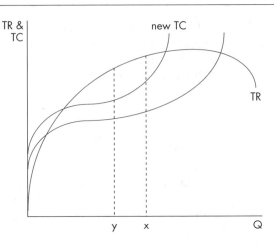

6.1.2 Do firms aim to maximise profits?

The profit-maximising assumption is criticised on two main grounds. Firstly, that it is difficult to equate MC and MR in practice; however, as we have seen, there are simple rules of thumb that firms employ that push them towards this. Secondly, that owners cannot force firms to act solely in their interest since owners are not the only powerful stakeholders in a firm. In many large joint stock companies, the shareholders are dispersed and the power over the firm of any one of them is low relative to the managers who run it. There is therefore a separation of ownership from control, so although managers may attempt to reach a level of profit that avoids shareholder revolt, this is not their only, or even their main, goal. The question then becomes: how high is the level of acceptable profits? The answer to this is that it varies, but many small and medium-sized firms are owner managed and even a number of large firms' shares are owned predominantly by one individual, family, or institutional investor, rather than millions of powerless shareholders. Indeed, Nyman and Silberston (1978) estimate that 56% of the largest 224 UK firms are effectively controlled by their owners. We should not therefore discount the importance of maximising profits as an objective. Although difficult to measure, it is also probably true to say that since Thatcherism reasserted the importance of the wealth creation process and the need to maintain global competitiveness, there has been a renewed focus on profits by firms. Even prior to the full effect of this change in attitude, Jobber and Hooley (1987), in a sample of nearly 1800 firms, found that 40% put profit maximisation as the overriding objective of the firm, while Shipley (1981), in a study of 728 UK firms, found that 73% described profit as their principal goal in setting prices. In addition, as we saw in Chapter 5, it is argued that competition results in a need to maximise profits in order to survive, regardless of whether managers actually prioritise it or not. So, clearly these criticisms do not prove that the assumption of profit max-imisation is redundant; they do, however, prove that there is scope for the pur-suit of other objectives too, in particular to maximise what managers rather than owners want, particularly in oligopolistic and monopoly environments, where environmental selection pressures are less.

6.2   MANAGERIAL THEORIES OF THE BEHAVIOUR OF FIRMS

6.2.1   Short-run sales revenue maximisation

W.J. Baumol (1959) developed a model of the firm that takes two things into account: the separation of ownership from control; and the fact that environmental selection pressures do not ensure that only strict profit maximisers survive since most firms do not operate in perfectly competitive environment. These two together mean that there is continuing scope for managers to pursue their own goals, which Baumol argued was predominantly to maximise sales revenue (TR) rather than total profit. The main consequence of this is that firms will sell their products cheaper than profit maximising firms (and may have to do more advertising and so forth too in order to achieve more sales). In Figure 6.5, the two cases are compared and the difference between the profit-maximising amount 'x' and the sales-revenue-maximising amount 'a' is apparent. Indeed, the only time when a revenue maximiser will not supply more than a profit maximiser is when the top of the TR curve is by coincidence also the profit-maximising point, in which case they will supply the same amount.

Figure 6.5 Sales revenue maximisation.

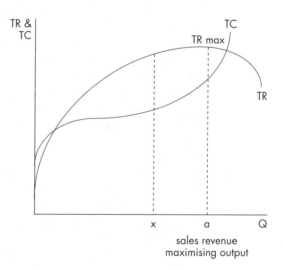

Managers are likely to want to maximise TR since their pay is likely to be higher if they do. There is more output to be managed, more costs to be managed, and more workers and other inputs to be managed; in short, the management task is bigger and therefore so is the pay. It is the case, for example, that the manager of a multinational will be paid more than the manager of a corner shop, even if the corner shop makes a profit and the multinational does not.

Although managers are depicted here as aiming to maximise revenue and not profit, Baumol argued that in practice they will be constrained by shareholders pushing them to make more profit. Firms with quoted shares have to pay an acceptable 'dividend' and keep the share price high enough to ensure a good press, and avoid a shareholders' revolt. This will also maintain the firm's ability to raise funds, through issuing more shares or by borrowing, in future. We can picture such a constraint on our diagram as the minimum profit that shareholders will settle for. The amount the firm supplies will then be between the point of profit maximisation and sales maximisation, that is, 'b' rather than 'x' or 'a', in Figure 6.6.

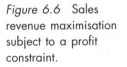

Figure 6.6 Sales revenue maximisation subject to a profit constraint.

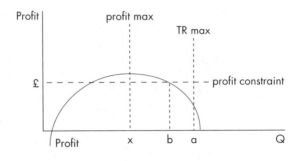

The actual value of the profit constraint depends on the bargaining power of the managers and shareholders respectively. Although the shareholders own the firm, the managers control it and a lot of the information regarding its performance, which means that shareholders can find it difficult to work out if managers are aiming to maximising profits or not. If there is a very similar firm with which to compare their performance and the other firm is more of a profit maximiser, then shareholders may be able to identify under-performance, otherwise they have to rely on their own intuition and the guesstimates of stock-brokers' analysts. These analysts evaluate firms' performances for stockbrokers who buy and sell shares on behalf of their clients in light of such analyses, and as anyone can own shares, these reports are often freely available in libraries and on the Internet.

In comparison to profit maximisation, Baumol's model suggests that in addition to selling their products cheaper than a profit maximiser, the sales-revenue-maximising firm will alter supply in the face of a change in fixed costs. For example, a rise in fixed costs will reduce supply, from 'b' to 'd' in Figure 6.7, whereas the profit-maximising supply 'x' will be unaffected (unless the rise in costs is so much that the firm shuts down).

Figure 6.7 The sales-revenue-maximising amount of supply is affected by a change in fixed costs.

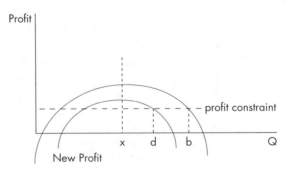

The empirical evidence suggests that a rise in fixed cost often reduces supply, as Baumol's model suggests. It is also possible that not only is there an element of sales revenue maximisation going on, but that the amount of it varies. Indeed, it may be contingent upon the environment, so, for example, supply might reflect the aim of sales revenue maximisation for a shift left in demand, and profit maximisation for a shift right. For example, in a recession firms may be more willing to accept smaller profits, or even losses, than strict profit maximisation dictates, in order to keep sales up in preparation for the recovery and revert to profit maximisation when the recovery comes.

6.2.2   Williamson's model of managerial discretion

As with Baumol's model, the assumptions in Williamson's (1963) model are that there is a separation of ownership from control and that the environmental pressures to maximise profit are weak. In Williamson's model, managers are assumed to be maximisers but what they maximise is their own utility, which involves more than the simple maximisation of sales revenue. Williamson argues that managers' utility is a function of the number (and grade) of staff reporting to them, the size of their emoluments (perks, size of office, expense account, etc.), and the amount of discretionary investment spending they have at their disposal. Williamson shows what maximising managers' utility implies for supply, but in doing this he accepts the need for firms to make an acceptable level of profits and so this maximisation is subject to a profit constraint. Solving this in a manner akin to the solution of the maximisation problem discussed in Section 2.6 suggests that a firm run in this way is likely to engage in greater spending on staff and investments that do not directly contribute to profits, than a profit-maximising firm would. Also, as with the Baumol model, a rise in fixed cost, in this case, will reduce supply.

In testing his theory, Williamson found that this model applies to varying degrees and that the degree depends on how the firm is organised, which has led him to look at how organisational form affects what firms do, which takes his later work largely beyond the scope of this book.

6.2.3   Marris's growth maximisation model

Instead of looking at contested territory between shareholders and managers, Marris (1964) looks at the aims that they can agree on. In particular, he argues that both managers and owners share an overriding desire to see the firm grow. In the Baumol model, managers are in effect aiming to maximise the size of the firm, but the difference is that for Marris the aim is to achieve growth rather than bigness *per se*. Managers, he argues, derive more satisfaction in seeing a firm expand than in simply working for a big firm, and owners want their wealth accumulation to be maximised (capital growth) rather than their current income (distributed profits). According to Marris, the constraints on growth are twofold. Firstly, managers want job security and too fast a growth rate could undermine this by leading to too fast an absorption of new personnel into new roles. Secondly, growth is constrained by a limit to the availability of funds to finance expansion, which gives us a 'financial security constraint'. The growth aim can then be restated as the desire to maximise the rate of growth of the demand for the firm's products and the firm's capital. This constitutes what Marris calls 'balanced growth'. The growth of the capital supply function for each combination of the rate of growth and profitability (profit rate) is shown by the line gC in Figure 6.8; its slope depends on the security constraint, or in other words in the attitude to risk of the managers. If the managers are willing to take more risks, the line will become flatter. The growth of demand is for Marris largely the result of diversification rather than increasing revenue from existing products. Marris argues that the growth in demand function (gD in Figure 6.8) that results from diversification is dome shaped because as the firm diversifies, and thereby grows, the things that it initially diversifies into are likely to be the most profitable new products. Diversification also stimulates managers to perform well, so again, the profit rate is likely to go up. Gradually, however, the rate declines as management becomes over-stretched and experienced new personnel cannot be absorbed fast enough. Together, the demand growth curve and capital supply growth curve determine one balanced rate of growth 'a', which exceeds the profit-maximising growth rate 'b' in Figure 6.8.

Figure 6.8 Marris' growth maximisation model.

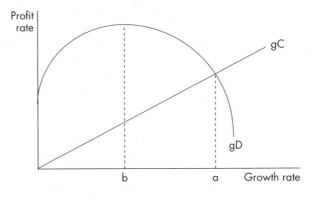

Studies show that some firms seem growth orientated and earn fewer profits as a result, which suggests that for some firms at least the two are separate objectives and that some are choosing to go down the path described by Marris.

6.3 | BEHAVIOURAL THEORIES

Assuming one of even a small number of primary objectives is simple and has considerable empirical support; it is, however, not the whole story, as it hides a lot of detail and tends to ignore how decisions are made. An alternative, or complementary, approach depending on your point of view, is to see the firm as too complex to be depicted as attempting to maximise anything. These approaches look instead at what managers do and how they, in effect, 'muddle through'.

6.3.1 Bounded rationality

In looking at what managers do, a good starting point is to recognise, as Simon (1959) did, that managers base their decisions on imperfect understandings, as they do not have access to all information and could not process it all even if they did. So, although they may rationally maximise the use of the information they have, such rationality is inevitably 'bounded' by the limits of that information. One aspect of this bounded rationality is that managers do not know how to maximise, so instead they aim to produce satisfactory profit levels, and satisfactory levels of any number of performance indicators that they have to juggle. They are therefore inevitably 'satisficers' rather than 'maximisers', with the outcome depending more on the process involved than on what constitutes the optimal decision.

6.3.2 Firms as political coalitions

Cyert and March (1963) argue that decision makers, when confronted with their bounded rationality, or in other words the uncertainties of the world, form political coalitions and alliances within organisations in pursuit of career progression rather than in pursuit of anything as grand as an optimising decision for the firm. This is not to deny that individuals can act rationally, just that the firm's strategy can seldom be traced back to any unified act of rationality. This means that understanding the behaviour and aspirations of the main groups involved is crucial to finding out how major decisions are made, and why. In considering this, Cyert and March conclude that large organisations are made up of separate interest groups, linked together by contracts. These contracts are often between one group who hire another group to act as their agents in achieving some objective or other; the nature of this relationship has particular consequences which authors following Cyert and March have developed, and to which we now turn.

6.3.3 Principals and agents

The relationship between shareholders and managers can be defined as a **principal–agent relationship**. In this case, shareholders are the principals who employ managers to maximise profits on their behalf. However, shareholders cannot monitor everything that their agents do and so there is scope for the agent to do their own thing. This is called the **agency problem**; generally, agents can:

1. pursue their own goals;

2. avoid applying the maximum effort (shirking);

3. act 'opportunistically'; that is, they can act deliberately to take advantage of the principal.

Although Baumol's sales revenue maximisation model is based on recognising the problem that arises from one principal–agent relationship, there are a number of others within firms to which these issues of control may apply, such as:

	Principal	*Agent*
1.	*Shareholders*	*Directors/senior managers*
2.	*Directors/senior managers*	*Other managers*
3.	*Managers*	*Employees*
4.	*Managers*	*External consultants (auditors etc).*
5.	*Banks and other creditors*	*Managers*

In designing the contracts that define the relationship, principals need to consider what incentives the agent has to do what the principal wants, and in recent years a number of new-style arrangements have come into play to ensure that principals get their way. Profit-related pay, for example, ensures that managers have an incentive to maximise profits, while annual assessment for employees is an arrangement to align staff motivations with firms' objectives. An alternative form of control to incentives is monitoring; agents' ability to avoid work (shirking) or to feather their own nest, for example, can be reduced simply by monitoring their progress, in short by keeping an eye on them. In the case of shareholders, there is the annual audit and a constant stream of stockbrokers' reports on the prospects and performance of the firm that can be used to monitor the performance of managers. These are backed up by the possibility that bad performance will lead to dismissal since, as Manne (1965) argues, poorly performing management leaves a firm open to take-over. This means that, in effect, there is a market for management teams to control corporation, in short a market in 'corporate control'. However, a large survey by Hughes (1993) suggests that the take-over threat does not force firms to act in the interest of shareholders. Hughes found that firms that were taken over did not generally show improved profitability thereafter and that the main difference between the predator firm and the victim was simply size, so that, in short, big firms take over smaller ones regardless of relative profitability. This is generally believed to be the case in the West, although in some countries that have less dispersed share ownership, monitoring may be more effective. Prowse (1992), for example, argues that this is one of the reasons for the success of Japanese firms. Fama (1980) discusses a related form of control. He argues that the market for managerial staff, both within and between firms, means that managers, in effect, rent their skills and the value of these depends in part on the success of the firm. This means they have some incentive to help ensure the success of the firm as well as to maximise their own progress within it. The firm can encourage managers in this by ensuring that there is a clear link between the success of the firm and the success of the individual through a profit-sharing scheme or something similar, although at present, as Jensen and Murphy (1990) found, managerial pay systems do not provide a significant incentive for managers to side with shareholders. On the other hand, an increasing number of senior managers have share options and thus have a significant direct stake as a shareholder too. The banks, and other lenders, may also exert some control over managers insofar as very poor performance could lead to liquidation. This, however, amounts to control over riskier expansions rather than day-to-day control, and may apply mainly to small firms. The product market may also act as a discipline on managers, with a more competitive market for firms' products leading to greater efforts amongst both managers and workers. However, as mentioned in Chapter 5, Leibenstein (1966) argues that if this stimulus to efficiency is absent, as it commonly is, then a firm can use its resources in a less efficient, (X-inefficient), way and yet still survive.

In general, as long as the environment does not dictate that firms must maximise profit then there is scope for different stakeholders to push for what they want and some form of compromise decision is therefore likely. Indeed Arrow (1950) has shown that even with very few objectives, optimising any one of them can prove impossible when groups interact.

6.3.4 Arrow's impossibility theory

Even if we ignore all the political complexities of firms' decision-making processes, Arrow (1950) has shown that it can still be impossible for anyone to get what they want when groups with different objectives interact. Arrow's 'impossibility theorem', as it is called, can be illustrated by considering three different groups and three objectives. The groups are the shareholders, the firm's marketing department, and the firm's corporate planning department. The strategies are: profit maximisation, a merger strategy, and a sales revenue maximisation strategy. We may then find that the shareholders like profit maximisation most and sales revenue maximisation least, while the marketing department favour sales revenue maximisation (which involves more marketing than profit maximisation) and do not like the merger strategy (since it could mean they lose their jobs). The corporate planners, on the other hand, like the merger strategy most (because it would be fun for them and a useful addition to their CVs) and like profit maximisation least (since this means more technical analysis of margins and the like, and very little fun). In a straight vote, none of the strategies would win as each group has a separate favourite. We can illustrate this using a matrix showing the preferences in terms of numbers, with 100 showing the most preferred options, and zeros indicating the least preferred option for each group.

	profit maximisation strategy	merger strategy	sales revenue maximisation
shareholders	100	50	0
marketing dept.	50	0	100
corp. planning dept.	0	100	50

To end the deadlock, the Chief Executive Officer (CEO) suggests they consider ignoring the merger option. Looking at the matrix again, we can see that this creates a winner, with corporate planning and marketing choosing sales revenue maximisation in preference to profit maximisation.

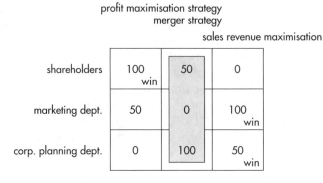

However, if the CEO simplified matters by rejecting profit maximisation, then shareholders and corporate planners would choose the merger policy over sales revenue maximisation, as shown below:

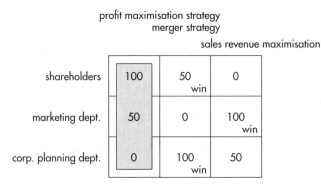

However, if the CEO had simplified matters by rejecting sales revenue maximisation, then profit maximisation would be chosen, as shown below:

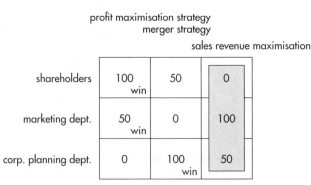

In other words, sales revenue maximisation is preferred to profit maximisation and merger is preferred to sales revenue maximisation and profit maximisation is preferred to merger and yet sales revenue maximisation is preferred to profit maximisation! In short, it is impossible. Of course, this does not always happen; the point is that it can, and in quite a simple example, without any consideration of the social and political complications that characterise even small firms.

6.4 NOT FOR PROFIT ORGANISATIONS

Some organisations do not have to make a profit; they have different aims and different stakeholders from a privately owned firm. These include many co-operative organisations, the best known being the retail co-op. These operate as other firms except that the workers have more say at board level and the customers are the shareholders. Mutual insurance companies and building societies are also owned by their customers, each customer having one annual vote on the policies of the firm. There are also charities whose profits accrue not to the owners but to a good cause as defined by the Charities Commission. These differences do not, however, mean that these organisations need behave differently from a privately owned firm; they too can aim to maximise efficiency and profit even charities, since in their case it simply means maximising the returns not to private shareholders but to the good cause. Indeed, the relative efficiency of charities can be gauged by their customers in terms of what proportion of each pound donated actually goes to the good cause. In this way charities compete for our donations. (The spanner in the works of the market for charitable donations is the National Lottery since this acts as a substitute to charitable giving, despite the fact that only 6% of the money collected via the lottery goes to traditional 'good causes').

Another type of organisation that does not aim to maximise profit is the public sector organisation.

6.5 THE PUBLIC SECTOR

Over the past 20 years, market forces have been introduced into the public sector in the belief that competition will encourage efficiency. However, it is still generally the case that public sector organisations such as hospitals and schools are allocated a budget rather than being expected to raise money from their customers, with the money coming from the government who raise it largely through taxation.

This does not of itself preclude profit maximising behaviour, as in such a case this simply amounts to being cost efficient within the budget, (and trying to secure a budget in the future). Suppose, for example, that the NHS currently produces an output of 'x' in Figure 6.9 then profit maximisation simply means that the organisation aims to reduce TC.

Figure 6.9 The public sector.

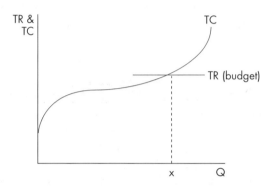

In practice, however, there are certain barriers to this: firstly, suppliers only have administrative controls on costs rather than the discipline of the market. Secondly, in the absence of profitrelated performance indicators others must be invented; in other words, the authorities must decide what 'x' actually is, as we cannot easily define the output when there are so many different treatments and combinations of treatments. Finally as the funding level is determined through a political process that involves public consultation and in which the media take an active interest, the level of TR depends on a very complex bargaining process. On the one side, we have governments trying to ensure that, in the face of increased demands, spending rises little. On the other side we have a coalition of employees, the public and the media trying to ensure that spending does not decline.

6.6 SUMMARY

- Because in many modern firms, particularly big ones, the owners no longer run the firm, the decisions of firms now reflect the wishes of a broader spectrum of stakeholders, especially those of managers.

- Given that profits are the income of the owners of the firm, the fact that they no longer have full control over managers means that the maximisation of managerial goals may take precedence in many firms, particularly those outside of perfect competition in which there is less environmental pressure to maximise profits.

- A number of theories have been developed to encapsulate the aims of managers to maximise a number of different things, with different consequences for the behaviour of the firm arising from each, including how they respond to environmental changes.

- An alternative range of theories takes this one step further by dispensing with the idea that managers maximise anything, but are instead involved in a dynamic interplay of power within the firm.

- In these 'behavioural theories', it is this interaction that is the key to understanding what firms do.
- Within the behavioural approach, we acknowledge the possibility of indeterminate outcomes, which means that collective behaviour can be meaningless and that therefore no aim can be attached to an organisation in the way than it can to an individual.

6.7 QUESTIONS

1. 'Building societies do not have to make any money for shareholders, whereas banks do. Building societies can therefore always offer their customers a better deal, and will therefore ultimately emerge as the winners in the banking game.' Discuss.

2. Devise an objective that you would like a public sector organisation such as a school or a hospital to achieve, and then create a performance indicator that creates incentives that are consistent with that objective.

PART 2

Components of the business environment

In this part, we look at the business environment in terms of components that correspond to different areas of traditional enquiry. In doing this we need to bear in mind two things: firstly, that we are fragmenting these components in order to understand each more fully, but in doing so we should not forget that in truth they interact; and secondly, that each chapter provides only an overview of the topics therein.

CHAPTER 7

The resource environment

After studying this chapter, you should be able to:

- define factor markets and appreciate the differences between them and goods markets;
- appreciate the properties of labour markets, including the role of human capital accumulation and of barriers to occupational and geographical mobility;
- show how the level of competition for resources affects the price of them;
- show how the level of competition amongst resources affects the price of them;
- show how an indeterminate market result is obtained when both workers and firms are powerful, and appreciate the role this gives to trade unions in the bargaining process;
- understand the principle of economic rent;
- appreciate the main features of the UK labour market and the effect of regional policy on this;
- understand the impact on firms of changes in this element of the business environment.

7.1   FACTOR MARKETS

Factor markets are different to other markets. The labour market is particularly unique since the factor being supplied is us, and there are a number of social constraints on who can be employed and in what cicumstances. Nonetheless, most of the things we have discussed in terms of the supply and demand for goods and services can also be applied to factor markets. Even individual workers exhibit upward-sloping supply curves in terms of the labour they are willing to supply at different wages (the fixed factor in the production of this is, of course, time). There are, however, some aspects of factor markets that are worth considering as a separate topic.

159

The prices of the factors of production are given different names depending on what factor is involved. For the use of capital, either the leasing of equipment, or more usually the lending of money to buy the equipment, the payment is called **interest**. The return to the risk taker, the owner of the firm's capital, is of course profit. For using land, the price is usually called **rent**, while for workers the payment is called **wages**. In the UK, the ownership of capital and land is unevenly distributed amongst the population. Profits, interest and rent are therefore a source of income for some people more so than for others (Figure 7.1).

Figure 7.1 The distribution of wealth in the UK.

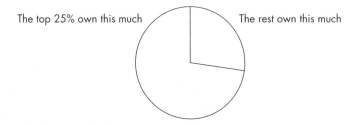

Source: Office for National Statistics (ONS).

The distribution of work is more equal, but even within the labour market there is a relatively slow flow between different jobs and different income levels. Therefore, someone from a poor background tends to remain poor, with restricted access to capital, land, and the better paid jobs. Some of the barriers to mobility within the labour market are:

- Geography: Many people do not like to move even if there are better employment prospects in other regions. Regional differences in house prices and costs of living also mean that moving can prove impossible.

- Formal barriers to entry: Qualifications and the rules of professional bodies act as a barrier stopping unqualified workers from entering a market, and this helps to keep wages in the professions (in particular) up.

- Discrimination: All forms of segmentation of the labour market are practised, depending on the particular preferences of the firm. Research has found discrimination to varying degrees against ethnic minorities, certain religions, people with disabilities, the working class, women, people who are overweight, short people, and people with spots (in a study in the hospitality industry). No doubt there are many other forms of discrimination too, and of course all employers, even those who claim neutrality, will tend to recruit in their own image. Legislation seeks to combat discrimination on a number of fronts, with some successes against discrimination by gender and race.

7.2 COMPETITION AND THE PRICE OF INPUTS

The discussion in the previous chapter can be extended to look at the effect of the level of competition on the price of an input. In what follows we shall focus on labour, which for many firms constitutes the main input cost.

7.2.1 Wage determination when both workers and firms are numerous and powerless

If there are many workers with similar skills then they will be unable to force their wages above the 'going rate' determined by the market. If the firms are also powerless, because they are in perfect competition with each other, they will also have to accept the going rate too. In effect, both parties in this market will take the market 'price', as in Figure 7.2. In the diagram, the supply curve bends up to indicate that even if wages go up, the population level and the desire for leisure put a limit on how much is supplied.

Figure 7.2 Wage determination when both sides are powerless.

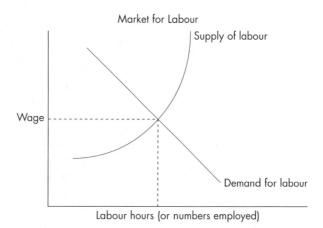

The question then is what will the going rate for the job be? If we assume that firms aim to maximise profit then they will employ workers until the marginal cost of the worker equals the marginal revenue that they create, which is called their **marginal revenue product** and is simply their marginal product multiplied by the marginal revenue associated with that product (MRP = MP × MR). The rule for employment is then to employ more workers until MC = MRP. Under perfect competition, the firms are wage takers; for each firm the supply of labour curve is perfectly elastic and the MC of labour is simply the going rate for the job. Therefore, if, for example, the last worker employed adds one kayak a week to production and it sells for £300, then it is worth employing this worker unless the going rate is more than £300 per week. The MRP curve follows the shape of the MP and MR curves and, since the firm picks points where MC = MRP, this line shows how much labour they demand at different wage rates. It is, therefore, the demand for labour curve (Figure 7.3).

The demand for labour depends therefore on three things: the wage rate (MC of labour), productivity (MP), and the demand for the goods they are employed to create (MR). Indeed, the demand for labour and other factors are described as **derived demands** since the demand is not for them in themselves, but for their ability to create something that is in demand. If the good or service they create is not in demand then the factors will not be needed to create it. If there is an increase in demand for the product, or an increase in productivity, or a rise in the price of substitute factors, then the demand for labour

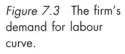

Figure 7.3 The firm's demand for labour curve.

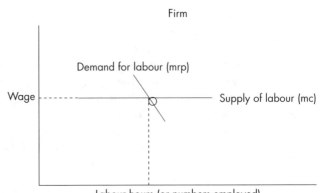

Firm

Demand for labour (mrp)

Wage - - - - - - - - - - - - - ⭘ - - - - Supply of labour (mc)

Labour hours (or numbers employed)

curve will shift right and wages will rise, as shown in Figure 7.4, using straight lines for convenience.

Figure 7.4 An increased demand for labour.

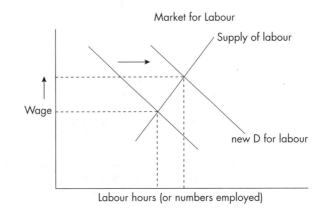

Market for Labour

Supply of labour

Wage

new D for labour

Labour hours (or numbers employed)

How much wages will rise depends on the elasticity of supply, which depends on factor mobility. Generally, in this market high wages are paid to people who are in short supply relative to the demand for their services. In Figure 7.5 vets earn more than vets' nurses do because it takes longer to train to become a vet and hence fewer are supplied.

Figure 7.5 Relative wages in the veterinary care market.

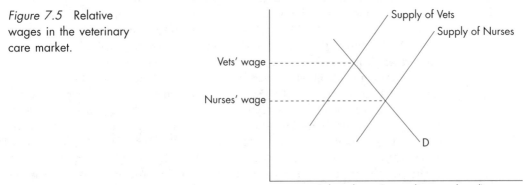

Supply of Vets

Supply of Nurses

Vets' wage

Nurses' wage

D

Labour hours (or numbers employed)

The fact that vets are scarcer than their nurses because it takes longer to train vets indicates that workers have a choice between employment today or investment in their **human capital**, that is, their stock of saleable skills and knowledge resources. In this case, vets are paid more because they have invested more, having sacrificed seven years' wages while training to become a vet, and their higher wage is partly a reward for that investment.

7.2.2 Wage determination when firms are powerful

Wage determination when firms are powerful is slightly different since the firm can affect the wage. This is rather obviously so for big employers, but it can also apply to small firms under imperfect competition. A local garage, for example, may not be a big employer nationally but by virtue of being the only one in a village can have some bargaining power over the workers it employs and may be able to pay them less than they would get working for a city garage. When firms have some power because they are large in relation to the labour market that they pick their employees from, they will have to pay more to attract more labour. In other words, they will face an upward-sloping supply of labour curve. To see why, consider a firm that is a monopsony; it must by definition face the market labour supply curve and in less extreme cases the firm faces a part of the market but not such an infinitesimally small part that the supply curve becomes perfectly elastic. If firms have to pay more to attract more workers they will tend to find that the marginal cost of hiring extra workers is greater than the wage they pay. This is because other workers already employed by the firm to do the same job will expect the same (or better) pay than a newcomer. Therefore, the MC of labour will exceed the **average cost** of labour (which is the wage), as shown in Figure 7.6.

Figure 7.6 The market for labour when firms are powerful.

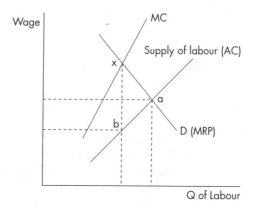

In this case, equating MRP and MC (point 'x') means that fewer workers are demanded than in the competitive case, which would be at 'a'. However, although MC indicates the profit-maximising amount of employment, the wage associated with this is still read off the supply curve, so the wage is given by 'b' rather than 'x'. Both wages and employment are therefore lower when firms are powerful.

7.2.3   Wage determination when workers are powerful

Counteracting the tendency for powerful firms to push wages down, we have organised labour attempting to push wages up. This is not simply a case of reducing supply, however, since firms themselves may allow wages to rise if it helps motivate or keep staff, while workers can try to increase wages by increasing labour demand; by enhancing their skills, by ensuring industrial relations work well, and so on. If, however, the trades unions or professional associations manage to increase wages simply by restricting the entry of labour, then this must be at the expense of jobs, as shown in Figure 7.7.

Figure 7.7 One possible effect of powerful workers.

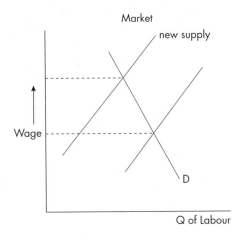

7.2.4   Wage determination when both firms and workers are powerful

It is seldom the case that one side is powerful and the other side powerless, so now we will see what happens if we have some power on both sides. Unsurprisingly, the result depends on the relative bargaining power of each side. If we start with the monopsony case, where the firm has all the power, we will find ourselves at wage 'b' in Figure 7.8. If then we introduce a monopoly supplier of labour, it could raise wages to 'x' without reducing employment in this industry (and in so doing simply transfer money from profits to wages). On the other hand, if workers wanted to, they could raise wages only as far as 'a', which would actually increase employment. Therefore, what will happen to both wages and the numbers employed in this market depends on the power of the bargainers and what their objectives are. It will be somewhere in the triangle 'bxa', but where exactly is an empirical issue.

Figure 7.8 Wage determination when both workers and firms are powerful.

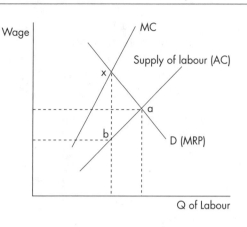

7.3 COMPETITIVE ADVANTAGE

One route to competitive advantage is to have inputs that are better or cheaper that those of rivals. As the discussion above shows, the route to cheaper costs is to have buyer power. However, the degree of buyer power a firm has will vary. For some of its workers, for example, it may face relative abundance and lots of substitutes; for these the firm can adopt a more mercenary approach than with workers who are harder to replace. This gives rise to two different sources of competitive advantage. For core workers it means flexibility in terms of training, career progression and transfer between departments. This should stimulate these workers so that the firm can get the best from them and should also encourage them to stay with the firm. This is known as **functional flexibility**. However, for those in relative abundance on the periphery, flexibility means something else entirely: for these workers **numerical flexibility** is more advantageous for firms as it means they can adjust their use of labour to suit market conditions and thereby minimise costs. This means employing people on a part-time, or casual, or subcontracted basis.

7.4 THE PAYMENTS TO FACTORS: THE GENERAL PRINCIPLE OF ECONOMIC RENT

The payment to factors, wages, rent and profit, is made up of two components: firstly, the payment necessary to ensure that the factor is supplied known as 'transfer earnings', and secondly, anything above that sum that the factor is able to extract from the buyer, which is called **economic rent**. When firms earn super normal profits, they are earning more than is necessary to stay in business; that is a form of economic rent. The reason it is called 'rent' is due to the fact that David Ricardo (1772–1823), who did the pioneering work on this subject, focused on land. He treated the supply of land as perfectly inelastic as it has no alternative uses (which was not entirely true even then), and in so doing found that rent or the price of land was determined solely by the demand for it. This means that the payment to this factor is an unearned surplus, and if the rent goes up it is simply an increased transfer of income to landowners, as shown in Figure 7.9.

Figure 7.9 All the earnings are 'economic rent' when the supply is perfectly inelastic.

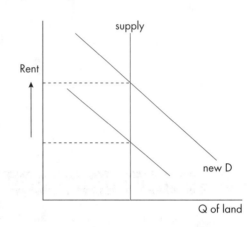

Today, the term economic rent is used to depict the additional payment that reflects the power of the supplier relative to the buyers regardless of which factor of production is under discussion. In the case above, all the earnings are economic rent. In the case of labour and goods, some is rent and some is necessary to maintain the supply of the factor or goods. Consider the market for vets again. Suppose £10,000 per annum is the minimum necessary to get anyone to work as a vet, as shown in Figure 7.10; then all earnings above this is rent. In the case of workers who will do the job for £10,000, they are getting £20,000 more than they need to stop them transferring to another line of work. In contrast, the person (Mr X) who will only do it if the wage exceeds £29,999 is only getting £1 in rent.

Figure 7.10 Economic rent in the market for vets.

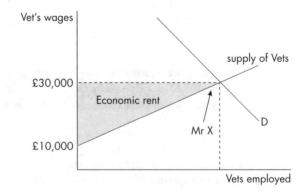

In the case of rock stars, or land in central London, we would expect an inelastic supply and a correspondingly high proportion of their earnings to be a form of economic rent.

7.5   LABOUR MARKET TRENDS IN THE UK

There are four main trends evident in the recent history of the UK. Firstly, there is a long-term downward trend in employment in the agricultural and manufacturing sectors and a rise in employment in the service sector. Secondly, since the 1970s there has been a rise in unemployment, as well as an increase in part-time working. Thirdly, there has been a rise in the proportion of women in paid employment, with women now constituting half the paid labour force in the UK. This reflects both an increase in the options facing women but also economic necessity for many, since this coincides with a rise in family breakdown, the reluctance of employers to pay men a 'family wage' and a decline in the status of child-rearing and home-making activities. Finally, there has been a rise in the numbers of people employed on a casual or temporary basis as firms attempt to maintain a competitive advantage by using labour as a flexible resource. This means that the key to lifelong employment for many workers has shifted from the acquisition of a particular skill to the ability to be flexible and re-trainable.

7.5.1   Regional policy

The shift in employment from manufacturing to service industries mentioned above has been regionally segmented. Jobs have been lost in traditional industries in the north of England and south Wales and service jobs have been created predominantly in the south east of England. Many of these jobs were lost in the early 1980s because of an overvalued pound, rather than any natural evolution from manufacturing to services and since the environmental changes were set in motion by the government, it was to the government that many turned for help. Only limited help was given, however, since the new Thatcher government of the day had set its face against supporting industry through subsidies, regional or otherwise. The predominant belief at the time was that, left to their own devices, markets would eliminate regional imbalances. A precondition of this is that labour and capital are flexible and geographically mobile, so that either workers move to where the jobs are, or wages fall in depressed regions to attract firms to take advantage of the cheap labour. The problems with this approach are firstly that while workers have an incentive to go where the jobs are, there are barriers to job mobility. There are occupational barriers such as the number of qualifications and the amount of experience required. In addition, there are geographical barriers to labour mobility such as high house prices in the more affluent areas where the jobs are. These make it impossible for some workers to move from one line of work, or region, to another. Secondly, the evidence on capital mobility suggests that it does move, but slowly, and thirdly as a solution it ignores the fact that depressed regions have depressed demand too. This means that firms have to weigh the advantages of access to cheap workers against the costs of transporting goods to faraway markets if local markets have insufficient demand to absorb the firm's output. The failure of market forces to work sufficiently quickly means that, despite many years of government by those who believe in free markets, we have had a continual subsidisation programme for depressed regions, albeit on a decreasing scale (with regional assistance taking 0.34% of GDP in 1981, but only 0.05% in 1996). On the other hand, some areas have become recognised for assistance for the first time during this period, including a number of urban 'enterprise zones' where allowances are available and simplified planning makes setting up and expanding relatively painless. The two main type of grants currently available are Regional Enterprise Grants and Regional Selective Assistance. The former are discretionary and mainly set aside to help small and medium-sized enterprises (SMEs) to facilitate growth and to enable new ones to start up. The latter are for any size firm and are designed to top up private investment as long as the firm can demonstrate that the project contributes to the local and national economy. There are also various schemes available at a regional level; the Business Links scheme, for example, offers a range of services, including consultancy of all sorts. There is also special assistance for firms involved in certain urban areas, in recognition of the fact that some urban areas may be in the middle of affluent cities and yet still require assistance. There is also assistance provided by the European Union for relatively poor member countries such as the Irish Republic, Spain, Portugal and Greece, and for regions, like south Wales, within the more wealthy ones (although this may decline as the Union expands to encompass the poorer countries of eastern Europe).

Case study

NURSES WAGES

For many years, the real wages (after adjusting for inflation of all wages and prices) of nurses serving in the NHS have fallen relative to those of comparable occupations. We can see this in the huge gap between the wage of a private agency nurse and an NHS nurse. For example, Thornbury Nursing Services of Bristol supplies nurses to Bristol hospitals for £60 an hour, of which £38 goes to the nurse. This works out at £70,000 per annum, whereas the average NHS nurse gets a mere £15,000 per annum. In effect, successive governments have put a price ceiling on NHS nurses' wages, as indicated by the dotted line in Figure 7.11.

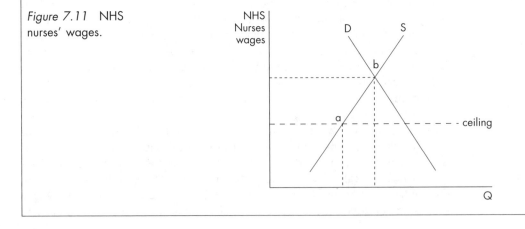

Figure 7.11 NHS nurses' wages.

Of course, this diagram is a static portrayal of a dynamic historic process. Nonetheless we can use it to show the essence of the problem, which is that the supply of NHS nurses (at 'a' in the diagram) is less than it would be if wages had gone up as others have (to 'b'). The government has initiated a pay review, in response to what has become for some hospital trusts a recruitment crisis. In the meantime, however, some trusts are boosting the supply at the current wage by importing nurses from poorer parts of the world who are willing to work at the going rate. In 1998 there were over 1200 non-European-resident nurses working in the NHS, just under half of whom have work permits allowing them to work in the UK for a year at most.

7.6 SUMMARY

- Factor markets are different from goods markets in a number of ways. For one thing, firms are generally the buyers in these markets. In addition, they have some unique features.
- The labour market is unlike other markets because we are the factor and a host of social constraints operate on what can and cannot be done with us.
- There are also significant barriers to the free movement of labour both occupationally and geographically.
- By applying supply and demand analysis to the case of labour, we can see that if firms are powerful relative to workers, wages will be pushed down. Alternatively, if workers are powerful relative to firms, wages can be pushed up.
- If both firms and workers are powerful we do not get a definite result from applying supply and demand analysis; in this case it depends on relative bargaining powers and the strategies of both sides.
- When both sides are powerful in a labour market, workers can increase both wages and employment.
- A distinction can be made between the payment to a factor that is required to keep them in their current use and payments above and beyond that, which are labelled 'economic rent'. This principle can be applied to firms' profits; since normal profits are all that is required to keep the firm engaged in its current activities, anything above that is economic rent. Super normal profits are, in other words, a type of economic rent.

7.7 QUESTIONS

1. 'Firms would be better off without trade unions to deal with.' Discuss.
2. Why are trade unions better at raising wages in some industries than in others?
3. With reference to a firm that you are interested in, devise a way of reducing its labour costs.
4. Why is the demand for labour often described as a 'derived' demand?
5. What barriers are there to labour mobility in the UK?

6. Assuming the validity of marginal productivity theory, show how the wage level and the level of employment are determined in labour markets in which:
   (a) neither firms nor workers have market power;
   (b) firms have market power but workers do not;
   (c) both firms and workers have market power.

7. Using partial equilibrium supply and demand diagrams, explain what is likely to happen in the market for bricklayers in the UK when:
   (a) there is a significant fall in the price of bricks;
   (b) there is a decrease in the demand for new houses;
   (c) there is a significant increase in demand for bricklayers in Germany.

CHAPTER 8

The public sector environment

After studying this chapter, you should be able to:

- appreciate the nature of the welfare state and the history of recent reforms of it;

- appreciate the nature of the public sector as a replacement for, and a tax burden upon, the private sector;

- appreciate that the public sector is also a significant source of support for the private sector and may provide things that would not be provided by the private sector, because of 'market failure';

- understand the different forms of 'market failure,' and appreciate which are relevant in the UK today;

- appreciate why each type of 'market failure' gives cause for government intervention and appreciate what form such intervention might take (and does take in practice);

- appreciate the nature and difficulties of cost benefit analysis;

- understand the impact on firms of changes in this element of the business environment.

8.1   THE WELFARE STATE

Public provision has been a feature of the UK economy since feudal times but the growth of the public sector to around 40%[1] of total spending in the UK is largely due to the introduction of the welfare state, mostly in the immediate aftermath of the Second World War. The term **welfare state** encompasses the introduction of free health care, free education, financial 'social security' support for people with low incomes or who are unemployed, and the nationalisation of key industries. However, rising concern that the public sector was becoming too much of a burden on the taxpayer and was leading to an emasculated private

---

1 This figure includes 'transfer payments' – see Chapter 10.

sector has, in recent years, resulted in policies that have stopped any further growth in the public sector as a proportion of total UK spending. There have been reforms aimed at reducing the size of the public sector and improving its efficiency, as well as a number of reforms to increase the competitiveness of the private sector, some of which are discussed below.

8.2 CONSERVATIVE REFORMS

Since the 1970s, successive Conservative governments have encouraged competition in four main ways. Firstly, they reduced regulations and restrictions on who can compete in a market. This deregulation covered a number of markets but is perhaps most noticeable in financial markets; it was, for example, not until the 1980s that banks were allowed to sell mortgages and building societies were allowed to issue cheque-books. Although encouraging competition has been the touchstone of the reforms, the exercising of market power has not simply been ruled out, as each case is considered in turn on its merits. For example, any proposed merger or acquisition that creates a firm that has 25% of an industry is considered by the Competition Commission. The Commission takes into account a broad range of possible costs and benefits associated with each proposal. They might consider, for example, the need to have firms big enough to compete in Europe or in world markets, as in an increasingly international marketplace a big UK company might well be a small player. Secondly, they reduced the power of trades unions in order to limit wage growth and keep firms' costs low, and to reduce the number of strikes and other forms of industrial disputes that adversely affect the performance of firms. They even introduced some minor reforms to curb the power of the most established workers associations – the professions. Thirdly, they reduced direct taxation, that is, taxation from earnings, particularly for those on high incomes. The UK tax burden, (the proportion of income that is paid in tax), has not fallen, however, because indirect taxes have gone up. Nonetheless, by allowing people to take home more of what they earn, Conservative governments believed they were encouraging work effort. Fourthly, they introduced various reforms in the public sector, in particular the following:

- They sold many nationalised industries to the private sector (to anyone willing to buy shares in them). Companies sold include the electric and water companies, British Gas and British Telecom, which were all originally taken into public ownership because they were thought to be natural monopolies. There are many reason why Conservative governments were keen on privatisation: it raises money that does not therefore need to be raised in taxation; it reduces government interference in the running of the firms concerned; it can be used to open a market to competition, which should result in greater productive efficiency (although many privatisations have turned public monopolies into private ones with few of the benefits of competition being achieved yet). Indeed, the benefits for the state of privatisation are large enough to have convinced the new Labour government to continue with it, despite their earlier antagonism to the idea.

- They introduced **competitive tendering** so that any firm can tender for contracts to provide some elements of public services, such as street cleaning, operating leisure centres, and doing hospital catering.

- They introduced internal (or quasi) markets into areas of public provision. **Internal markets** mimic the working of a market while retaining some of the features of public provision. For example, while a doctor may decide on which hospital to send a patient to for an operation on the basis of different prices charged by different hospitals, the patient is not aware of this and is not personally charged. Market forces are at work; efficient hospitals will win more customers and more funds. However, allocation is still largely according to need and payment through taxation still dominates, so market forces are at work while major features of public provision are retained. An element of competition between schools has also been introduced by allowing parents more choice over which school to send their children to and by publishing performance tables to help them make that choice. Schools are then allocated funds depending on how many pupils they attract, which, with parents choosing those with the best records, acts as a spur to efficiency. Similar information may in the future be made available regarding the performance of hospitals too.

These reforms have produced some gains, but they have also caused problems. Reforms in the NHS, for example, have led to a large increase in administrative costs, of the order of several hundred percent since their introduction. This is disappointing since the pre-reform NHS had very low costs relative to its output and lower administration costs than in market-led systems such as that used in the USA. Part of the reason for this is that any system, planning or otherwise, can work well if all those involved are committed to it, that is, if the firm has **social capital**, which in the case of the NHS may have been dented by the reforms rather than enhanced. In light of this, the new Labour government plans to continue with some of these reforms but has already undone some that they consider to be failing, including the use of internal markets in the NHS, as they see this as leading to more bureaucracy rather than more efficiency.

8.3 MARKET FAILURES

Despite all these reforms and despite the avowed intention of successive Conservative governments to leave things to market forces (the laissez faire approach), the public sector still accounts for around 40% of UK spending (as it does with most of our European partners). Clearly then, there must be important reasons why governments continue to intervene. These can be divided into two types: firstly, those interventions that reflect a simple desire by politicians to control things (which are impossible to classify), and secondly, those interventions based on the belief that a market will fail to achieve some of the goals that governments set themselves. The existence of these failings does not imply any shortcomings in our supply and demand analysis, simply that the results we get with markets are not always considered best for society. These 'market failures' can be categorised as follows:

- Natural monopolies: In some cases, it would be unprofitable to have more than one firm in an industry. In this case, it can be argued that it is better to nationalise the industry and have a publicly accountable monopoly, rather than an unaccountable private one. Although the current trend is to return nationalised industries to the private sector, because many of them are natural monopolies, competition is difficult to introduce and the privatised firms continue to have considerable market power. The result is that governments have introduced official watchdogs such as OFWAT to try to ensure that public exploitation is minimised (albeit with varying degrees of success).

- Winners and losers: Market power tends to become concentrated as some firms win and some firms lose the battle for market share; this results in oligopoly, and monopoly, and all the efficiencies associated with competition can be lost. In response to this, governments have deregulated many markets and increased the competition in others by strengthening various rules and codes on acceptable business practices. In addition, the Competition Commission and European regulators act to limit the spread of individual firms when this is not considered to be in the 'public interest'.

- Externalities: These are the costs or benefits that may be overlooked by buyers and sellers in a market because they apply to a third party not represented in the market. For example, a firm could pass some of the costs of production on to the community in the form of pollution that everyone pays to have cleaned up. Graphically the real costs of production in this market are greater than the costs borne by the firm, so supply is greater than it would be if the firms paid the real costs (Figure 8.1).

Figure 8.1 External costs.

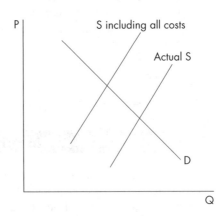

The government might deal with this pollution by persuasion, as many firms are aware of the need to be seen to be green. Alternatively, they could make it illegal but this may stop the goods being produced at all and it will cost public money to enforce. On the other hand, they might use a carrot and stick approach using taxes and subsidies. For example, heavy traffic in large cities creates the external costs of noise, pollution, and extended travel times.

While, public transport might be seen as creating the external benefit of less traffic. Therefore, the government could tackle the problems associated with car congestion either by increasing taxes on cars to discourage their use, or by subsidising public transport to make it cheaper and thereby encourage its use instead. We should not, however, conclude from this that indirect taxes can be explained in this way. Products that do have a large indirect tax applied to them are often products that have significant external costs, but usually those that also have inelastic PeDs. This means that a tax rise that shifts supply left will do more to raise tax revenue than to eliminate the externality. So, for example, each year the government increases the tax on tobacco to raise revenue rather than to stop people smoking and thereby eliminate the externalities associated with smoking.

- Public goods: These are goods that might not be provided at all if left to the private sector, because the benefits of the good are shared. This has two dimensions, firstly 'non-excludability' and secondly 'non-rivalness'. This means, firstly, that no one can be stopped from enjoying the benefits of the product, and secondly, that by the same token one person's consumption of it does not preclude others from enjoying it at the same time. The problem is that who would buy something just to see it shared by all in this way? Ship owners in the past faced just this dilemma with respect to paying for the building of lighthouses, since every ship owner would benefit equally from the light they throw out. Indeed, any firm that did pay for a lighthouse would lose out insofar as all would benefit but only it would bear the cost. As a result, prior to public provision there were too few lighthouses around the British Isles, and those that were provided were often paid for by philanthropists concerned with the loss of life from shipwrecks, rather than by ship owners themselves. This kind of problem is occasionally solved by firms collaborating, but more often than not, by the intervention of the government.

- Markets allocate goods and services according to price, not need. This means that a rich person can have things that a poor person cannot, regardless of who needs it the most. In some cases people find this unacceptable and prefer instead a system that focuses on need directly and disregards income. The NHS is based on this idea because people want health care to be allocated according to need, with the sickest rather than the richest being treated first.

- Unstable markets: Particularly where suppliers have to anticipate future demand, then what suppliers expect to happen (their 'expectations') can have significant consequences. If, for example, a farmer anticipates a high price for potatoes in the next season, he will increase his plantings of seed potatoes now. If, however, lots of farmers do the same then there will be an unexpectedly large rise in supply of potatoes and the price next season will fall, not rise. The following season, if farmers form their expectations on the basis of last season's disappointing price, they will plant fewer seedlings and consequently next season's prices will rise. This cyclical up and down of prices can be eliminated if the government steps in. It might simply provide information to help farmers coordinate their plans, or it might fix the price entirely, by, for example, setting a price floor.

- Price floors: Some industries experience large rightward shifts in the supply curve, which in combination with an inelastic demand can result in large falls in revenues and possibly the destruction of some firms. In such a case, the government may intervene by guaranteeing a minimum price and buying any resulting surpluses (Figure 8.2). This is done in the Common Agricultural Policy of the European Union, to protect the income of farmers, particularly those with relatively high costs, and to eliminate any possibility of a cycle like the one discussed above. These objectives are often achieved but at the cost of high prices and growing surpluses, 'food mountains' and 'wine lakes' in the case of the CAP.

Figure 8.2 A price floor.

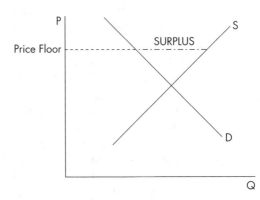

One much-discussed price floor is the minimum wage. This is a floor for the price of labour. If we look at individual labour markets such as the market for 'bar staff', then a rise in wages implies an increased surplus of workers, which in labour markets means more unemployment. However, when we look at the market for all labour, combined supply and demand are inter-related since most consumers are workers too, and therefore whether more unemployment results from a minimum wage or not is an empirical issue.

- Price ceilings: Occasionally governments intervene directly in markets in the other direction to stop prices rising to the equilibrium. This is done to protect consumers. For example, during the latter part of World War I and for the whole of World War II, many goods were not allowed to rise above a certain price. This, however, creates a shortage of the good (Figure 8.3).

Figure 8.3 A price ceiling.

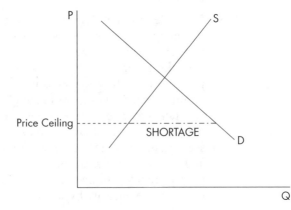

The shortage creates an incentive for firms to illicitly supply at a higher price; a 'black market' is therefore likely to develop. Supply can only be raised to cure the shortage by governments becoming directly involved in supplying the good, which during the war is exactly what happened. After the war such intervention was felt unnecessary in the West but continued in the former Soviet bloc, until recently, when the removal of price ceilings led to significant price rises.

- The distribution of income: Conservative governments tend to intervene in the labour market to encourage workers to be geographically mobile, and to reduce the power of the unions. On the other hand, those on the political left suggest measures to reduce income inequalities since they see these as largely determined by what class people were born into, their gender, and the colour of their skin rather than their economic contribution to society.

- Customer ignorance: When consumers buy a jar of coffee they probably know what they want, but when they go to the doctor they often do not know what product or procedure they need. In this circumstance doctors could, if they wish, make money by offering patients more treatment than is necessary. So, if health care is left to the market, the fact that doctors know more about the product than patients means there is a potential for artificially inflated demand, and indeed there is evidence that this is a feature of the American health system.

- Uncertainty: Because the rewards from investment occur in the future and are therefore subject to uncertainty, firms may do less of it than is necessary to achieve national economic prosperity. In response to this, governments throughout the world subsidise investment and undertake much of it themselves, particularly where the project is a big one with very distant returns. This also applies to investment in human capital, particularly as any firm that invests heavily in its staff can literally see that investment walk out the door. This is particularly true of 'general training' that could be of use to other firms rather than 'job-specific' training that only relates to the particular tasks of an employee's currently job. Consequently, we find governments subsidising general education and training even in the most market-orientated economies.

- Speculation: Since traders can benefit from changes in the price of some goods and services while they hold them, some traders will be driven by the desire simply to make money from the dealing activity itself, by speculating on which way the price will go. For example, property speculators will buy houses in a street where they expect prices to rise, in order to sell them at a profit at a later date. Similarly, currency speculators will buy US dollars if they expect the dollar to rise, in order to sell them later at a profit. This activity may be destabilising; for example, if currency speculators all anticipate a rise in the dollar, that in itself will tend to push it up as they demand more dollars. They can, therefore, create a 'self-fulfilling prophecy' which means that non-speculators will have to pay more than they otherwise would; indeed, in the case of a currency any importer or exporter using that currency will be affected by such a rise. Speculation can, however, also be stabilising. A speculator buying a share that nobody else wants, for example, keeps the price from falling, and a currency speculator that anti-cipates that a currency is near its peak will sell and therefore help to stop the rise. Nonetheless, insofar as it can be destabilising, governments act to thwart speculators as and when the need arises (if they can).

- Macroeconomics: Even governments that believe in laissez faire have been unable to let go of trying to run the national economy. Indeed, the management of this is entrenched in the institutions of government and increasingly in institutions which are beyond direct democratic control, such as the Bank of England, the European Commission and the European Central Bank in Frankfurt.

- Merit goods: Free markets would under-provide these goods or services because the consumer is ignorant of the full range of benefits of the prod-uct when they buy it. The benefits are, of course, a matter of judgement, but one of the reasons the government subsidises education and sport is that the benefits of both may not be apparent at the start, and consequently they feel that we should be encouraged to consume them.

These are all reasons why we may need a public sector; they do not prove that governments are better than markets, and indeed many argue that the failings associated with government provision may exceed the failings of the market that they are meant to address. In addition, in the discussions above it was assumed both that the extent of the problem – and therefore the size of the solution – could easily be calculated, and that the government would act in society's best interest. In fact, the nature of the problem is often elusive and the government can be the culprit rather than the saviour. For example, while discouraging pollution by others, successive governments have allowed their own polluting activities, such as pollution generated by the nuclear power programme, to continue. Moreover, in assessing the value of intervention the benefits have to be weighed against the costs in terms of the additional tax burden placed upon both the general public and firms. On the other hand, to the extent that it supports a level of educa-tion and health amongst workers that exceeds what would otherwise occur, the existence of the public sector will benefit both people and firms as well as burden them.

8.4 COST BENEFIT ANALYSIS

One problem that the government faces, when intervening in the economy, is to decide what the costs and benefits for society as a whole actually are. This is the subject of **cost benefit analysis**. An early use of this technique was in evaluating the costs and benefits of the first motorway, the M1. Some of the factors that were taken into account were obvious, such as the cost of building it, but evaluations were also made of the cost to the environment, including the costs of noise, and so on. Indeed, the issue of noise pollution is one of the key issues in the current public enquiry into the building of a new runway at Heathrow airport. There is, however, no market for such things, yet they must be given a value if costs and benefits are to be calculated. The alternative is to ignore them, which effectively gives them a value of zero, which cannot be right. Even in the health service dealing with life and death decisions, such calculations can be made, since each pound spent should be spent where it has the greatest benefit, which means comparing the costs and benefits associated with treating different complaints. However, although some ways of measuring the number of extra years of good health that accrues for each pound spent are considered, the difficulties of measuring them means that no NHS funds are allocated in this way as yet.

8.5 SUMMARY

- The UK is not unusual in having a large public sector. Most economies are mixed, including those of our European partners.

- Most of the public sector involves the provision of services that collectively we call the welfare state.

- There have been various reforms of the welfare state in the recent past because of concerns regarding its size. However, the existence of 'market failures' gives a role for continued government intervention in the economy.

- Market failure is where markets operating in the private sector fail to provide some of the things that societies decide that they want, such as public goods like national defence, or merit goods such as general education.

- Market failure also occurs when free markets over-provide some things that societies do not want, such as pollution.

- Market failure also occurs when the nature of the provision of something that societies want is unacceptable in some way, if, for example, it becomes monopolised or subject to large fluctuations in supply, as with some agricultural products.

- Before intervening in specific cases, governments may undertake a cost benefit analysis in which an attempt is made to weigh all the pros and cons of any proposal.

8.6 QUESTIONS

1. The NHS provides a lot of health-care goods and services for free. Does this mean that there is an infinite demand for it?

2. Analyse the effect of a reduction in the public provision of health care.

3. Analyse the effect of a reduction in public transport.

4. There are four pubs in a coastal village in Cornwall, and the owner of one of them, the Ship Inn, believes that a few signposts from the main road would help attract passing trade, as the village is easily missed. The council will not pay for any, but neither will the owner of the Ship Inn, because she believes the signs will be a 'public good'.
   (a) What does she mean?
   (b) What can be done to sort this problem out?

CHAPTER 9

The investment and financial environment

After studying this chapter, you should be able to:

- understand the nature of investment in building both tangible and intangible assets;
- understand the determinants of the supply and demand for investment;
- appreciate the main characteristics of the UK investment environment and its effect on the productivity of UK firms;
- understand the different types of financial intermediary currently in operation in the UK;
- explain the types of services provided by firms that act as financial intermediaries;
- explain the role of financial intermediaries in supporting other businesses through the provision of funds and through support for mergers and acquisitions;
- appreciate the role of bonds and shares in channelling funds to firms;
- understand how bond markets and share markets work;
- understand the importance of uncertainty in the determination of bond and share prices and the importance of this for individual firms and national economic performance;
- understand the impact on firms of changes in this element of the business environment;
- be aware of the key financial ratios that are used to gauge the health of a firm and as a guide to investment.

9.1 THE INVESTMENT ENVIRONMENT

The term investment is often applied to people's purchases of stocks and shares, and their holdings of bank and building society deposits. However, strictly speaking these do not become investments until someone somewhere uses these funds to divert production away from the creation of consumer goods and into the creation of more or better factors of production. So, we will confine our analysis of investment to looking at the use of resources to create machines, offices, and other forms of physical capital as well as the enhancing of human capital through investments in education and training. In other words, we will be looking at both 'tangible' investments in physical assets and 'intangible' investments in knowledge, competence and organisation. This encompasses all of the factors of production that we have thus far labelled land, labour, capital and knowledge. We will also include 'working capital', which consists of stocks of raw materials, semi-finished goods, and stocks of unsold goods that a firm holds, since this is a form of investment, albeit unintended.

The first question we have to answer is why anyone would want to divert resources to create more resources. You may, however, have an insight into this since you may be doing this yourself. As a student you may be sacrificing the opportunity to work and earn money today as an investment in getting a better-paying, or more interesting, job when you graduate. The motives involved are undoubtedly complex and unique to each individual, and so it may be for firms too. However, as usual, we can both simplify matters and encompass an awful lot of the motivation of firms by looking at the revenue and profits angle.

The profit-maximising firm will want to invest if it expects that the revenue resulting from it will exceed its costs. The complicating factor is that with investment the pay-offs, and often some of the costs too, occur in the future and spending £100 today in order to make £100 in 10 years' time, say, does not look like a good deal. For a start, during those 10 years inflation is likely to erode the value of the future £100, and we also know that we could turn it into a larger sum simply by putting it in the bank and watching the interest accrue. Firms need to take this into account when weighing the costs and benefits of an investment, and this can be done by the application of a mathematical formula that discounts the future so that it is as if we were getting the returns today. This 'present value' of the revenues returned by the investment, R, to be received t years from now is defined as:

$$PV = \frac{Rt}{(1 + i)^t}$$

The same formula can be applied to future costs too, by simply replacing revenues with costs. The term 'i' is the rate at which we are discounting the future values. Ideally, for firms, this should reflect the opportunity cost of capital, which is to say it should be the rate of return on the next best alternative investment. In our case, the option was simply to put it in the bank, hence it will simply be the rate of interest that the bank is offering savers.

For the example above, using t = 10 years, R_t = £100 and i = 10% (or 0.1 in decimal) gives us:

$$PV = \frac{100}{(1 + 0.1)^{10}}$$

$$PV = \frac{100}{2.594} = 38.55$$

This means that the present value of £100 in 10 years' time, with interest rates of 10%, is only £38.55p, which confirms our earlier suspicion that it would not be a good return for investing £100 today. An investment pays off in cash terms only if the present value of the revenues exceeds the present value of the costs involved, or in other words if the **net present value** (NPV) is positive. A firm can then compare different returns for different investments. One complicating factor is that with most investment projects the receipts accrue over a number of years, as might some of the costs associated with the project (such as operating costs). This means that we have to look at the sum of the expected cash flows (Revenues less Costs) discounted into present value terms for each year of the lifetime of a project to get our profit value figure. For example, for a project with a life of three years

$$PV = \frac{(R - C)_1}{(1 + i)} + \frac{(R - C)_2}{(1 + i)^2} + \frac{(R - C)_3}{(1 + i)^3}$$

Generally, using summation notation for t = 1 to n we have to calculate:

$$PV = \sum_{t=1}^{n} \frac{(R - C)_t}{(1 + i)^t}$$

We can then compare this value with the initial investment cost to get our NPV, which as before if positive indicates that the investment pays off. Another complicating factor is that if we want to look at the NPV for a different interest rate scenario we will have to do all the calculations again, which for the case above may not be too onerous. But, for projects involving different costs and revenues each year, it can be even when using a computer spreadsheet. An alternative that gives us a measure of the returns per pound which can be compared for any interest rate we choose involves calculating the **internal rate of return** (IRR) of a project. The IRR is the discount rate that would make the NPV = O, in other words it will make the returns equal to the investment. If the IRR exceeds the interest rate that has to be paid to fund the investment then the project will be a winner, and the investment with the highest return is the best investment. This is, of course, one of the considerations that a firm will take into account in making investment decisions. However, the outcome depends on a number of environmental factors, such as the changing state of the economy, (since revenue projections will be affected by the level of demand, and inflation could put future costs up), or the nature of planning rules and regulations which, may also change. In fact, there is almost a limitless range of factors that will have an effect on the outcome of the investment and its costs that do not appear in the calculations made above and although an assessment of the risks involved can be attempted, there are a host of costs, benefits and influences that even if included cannot easily be quantified.

9.2 THE MARKET FOR INVESTMENT

The price of borrowing money for investment is the rate of interest that has to be paid on it; we need therefore to look at this market in terms of the supply and demand for investments plotted against interest rates.

We can see how interest rates can affect the investment plans of firms by looking at what happens to the PV of £100 in 10 years' time using several different interest rates (Table 9.1).

Table 9.1 Present value over time.

Interest rate	PV of £100 in 10 years' time
20%	£16.15
15%	£24.72
10%	£38.55
5%	£61.39

Clearly a rise in interest rates reduces the attractiveness of investment; it is likely therefore that the firm's demand for investment reflects this, and that there is therefore a downward-sloping demand curve for investment plotted against interest rates.

9.3 THE DEMAND FOR INVESTMENT

If we were to rank all investment projects according to their IRRs, we would expect to find that a few have very high IRRs but more have lower ones. This means that, since the go-ahead for a project depends on its IRR being equal to or greater than interest rates, more and more projects become viable as interest rates are lowered. This coupled with the consumers' increased desire to borrow and invest at lower interest rates produces a downward-sloping investment demand schedule as shown in Figure 9.1.

Figure 9.1 The investment demand curve.

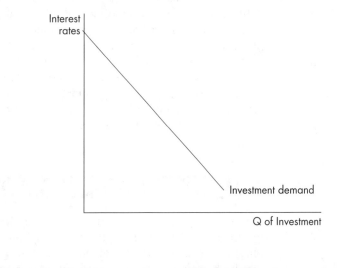

9.4 THE SUPPLY OF INVESTMENT

The supply of funds for investment is likely to be upward sloping since more funds are likely to be available when rates are high as people are likely to save more. The amount of investment that will occur is then given by the intersection of supply and demand in this market (Figure 9.2). Note, however, that where we end up is largely determined by the rate set by the Bank of England and that, even if it were not, interest rates would be determined by the supply and demand for money for all purposes, not just investment.

Figure 9.2 The supply and demand for funds for investment.

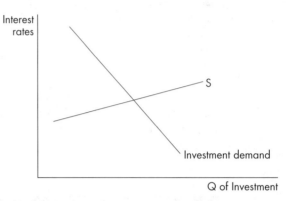

The main shifters in this market are the 'base' interest rates set by the Central Bank of England on the supply side and expectations of future costs and revenues on the demand side. This can be problematic for, as J.M. Keynes (1883–1946) argued, since the future is uncertain, optimism, and pessimism, can play a big part in this market, and since investment spending is a major part of total national spending this can affect the whole economy too. Indeed, investment spending can be switched on and off in a way that consumer spending cannot, which means it can and does lead to a general fall in national demand and output. This is why controlling inflation by keeping interest rates up, as is the current practice, is often considered akin to using a sledgehammer to crack a nut. In addition, it can exacerbate any change in demand since a simple slowdown in demand can act as a signal to firms to stop investing altogether. On the other hand, a small increase in demand can see investment spending switched back on again. This speeding of any changes in demand helps to explain the fact that national economies go from boom to slump and back again every decade or so (as we shall see in the next chapter), and is known as the **accelerator effect**.

9.5 THE INVESTMENT ENVIRONMENT IN THE UK

Figures on tangible investment are provided by the Office for National Statistics (ONS), but given the ephemeral nature of intangible investment we only have rough estimates of this. This is a problem insofar as it is obvious that both are necessary to ensure investment success. Even a simple machine like a bike is useless until you acquire the skill to ride it; this means that in practice it is difficult to judge the extent to which UK firms' relatively poor output and productivity performance can be attributed to under-investment in either tangible assets or intangible ones.

Nonetheless, some patterns in this element of the UK business environment are worth discussing. For example, there does seem to be an increasing recognition of the importance of human capital by firms and by the government, which has initiated a number of programmes to support training in industry both in terms of providing financial subsidy and by improving the communication between universities and industry. This awakening is partly due to the realisation of the importance of intangible assets within a business. But it is also in recognition of the shift in the focus of economic activity and wealth creation from heavy engineering to high-technology industries, and information and knowledge-intensive services, such as financial services, in many of the advanced industrial nations, including the UK.

One feature of the UK investment environment is the business cycle, for although a rise in demand might be expected to raise investment in the same way that a fall in investment reduces it, there is no symmetry in this. Investment in an economy that exhibits steady growth exceeds that of an economy that goes up and down, even if the average rate of growth in the two economies is the same, because the instability itself is a deterrent. Volatility in inflation may also put investors off, as it will make predicting the costs of a project impossible. Instability in both output and inflation have been features of the UK business environment in recent decades and cannot be dismissed as possible constraints on any current investment plans that a firm may have, despite the Labour government's avowed commitment to low inflation and stable growth. However, an obsession with keeping inflation down will not help British industry either if it means that our interest rates remain double those of the rest of Europe as they have been of late. One solution to this that would put our rates in line with the rest of Europe is to join the European single currency, which is discussed in Chapter 11.

Firms may also find it difficult to determine the real cost of capital, since investment can be financed by retained profits or by borrowing, the price of which not only varies with general interest rates but depends on which lender you talk to and how well you present your proposals. It may also depend on how the banks view the economic prospects, since in the last downturn there was something of a 'credit crunch' with banks defending their own balance sheets by reducing their financial support to industry. Investment may also be financed by issuing equity, but again how and when, and through whom, this is done is crucial. It also depends on the tax system, not only in terms of corporate taxes and investment allowances as applied to the firm, but also taxes on individuals which will affect the level and balance of savings and equity purchases by them.

At the national level, it seems fair to say that the UK's investment performance is below that of some of the leading industrial nations. This in turn may help to explain why it is that, although our best firms are as productive as any in the world, our productivity taken as a whole is below that of the best. The government is addressing this by trying to create a stable macro environment, keep inflation down, and thereby ultimately keep interest rates down too. It is also showing an increased willingness to provide support for investment projects both directly and by improving the links between universities and firms. In addition, the Labour government has expressed strong commitment to supporting training in general, and is actively supporting the development of arrangements for information sharing through which firms can see what best practice is in their industry. The idea being that they can 'benchmark' their performance against the best and thereby learn from them.

In considering investment in training, a distinction can be made between training that is relevant to a wide variety of tasks that will enhance an employees' productivity across a number of firms, and training that is relevant only to one firm. This distinction is made because, as Becker (1975) argues, while a firm might be happy to provide job-specific training it may be less willing to provide general training which makes the employee more employable elsewhere, since if they leave the firm their extra productivity will accrue to rival firms. It is generally believed, therefore, that there is a market failure here, since left to their own devices firms will provide less of this than is required to maximise national productivity. This market failure is seen as a reason why governments need to support this kind of training, which includes all general education, such as learning to read and write, and a lot of non-job-specific higher education too. Consequently, most countries provide support for education and training of this sort, which means that developments in the education and training provided by governments are an important part of the business environment of firms, since changes in the amount and content of it have profound effects on them.

9.6 THE FINANCIAL ENVIRONMENT

Before a firm undertakes any investment, it must usually borrow some money. This is where financial intermediaries come in, so called because the firms specialising in providing finance act as intermediaries between people who have surplus funds (savers) and those who want to use those surplus funds (borrowers), including firms looking for funds for investment.

The main financial intermediaries in the UK are:

1. The Bank of England: This is what is termed a **central bank**. It regulates the day-to-day workings of the financial system in the UK and is responsible for interest rate policy; simply by announcing a rate at which it will deal it can move all UK interest rates up or down. The interest rate set by the bank, because it forms a base for other rates to cluster around, is often called the 'base' rate. The rate is set to achieve the government's inflation targets, so if inflation looks like it is exceeding the target, the Bank of England will put interest rates up. Within the European single currency bloc, which the UK may one day join, interest rates are set by the European Central Bank based in Frankfurt.

2. Commercial banks: This includes the **retail banks** that are found in the high street, like Barclays plc, National Westminster plc, and so on. Their main business is taking funds from the general public and lending it to business. They also enable people to use their money without carrying too much cash by providing cheque-books and debit cards, as well as provid-

ing other banking services. This category also includes foreign banks that do business in the UK.

3. Merchant banks: These banks do not have extensive retail networks, but tend to operate in major financial centres where they arrange major deals. An example is Rothschilds.

4. National Savings Bank: This bank operates largely through post offices to collect savings that it then lends exclusively to the government.

5. Building societies: These are mutual societies that were established in the late eighteenth century to collect savings to fund house purchase. This is still their main area of business, but since the deregulation of the financial sector in the 1980s the societies have introduced a range of banking services. Many building societies have converted from mutual status to plc status, with shares bought and sold in stock markets.

6. Finance houses: These specialise in providing car loans and loans for consumer durables. If you buy a car, for example, the retailer will normally offer you some form of easy payment terms, which is where the finance house comes in.

7. Discount houses: These do not deal with the public; they are solely involved in buying and selling bills (discussed below), including government ones.

8. Insurance companies: The fact that unforeseen events like accidents or thefts can be very costly to the victims means that there is a demand for insurance to pay financial compensation if they occur. Because we do not know who will be hit, we are all willing to pay a regular amount (the premium) just in case. The insurance company pools the money so that the cost of compensating claimants is borne by many people, not just the victims. The insurance company makes its profit from the fact that the premiums add up to more than the payouts. The firms are able to predict payouts in total with a fair degree of accuracy, as the 'law of large numbers' means that the number of accidents or thefts when taken as a whole can be predicted more accurately than individual cases. A similar thing happens when we look at savings. While we cannot predict who will withdraw their funds on any one day, we can predict quite accurately how many funds in total will be withdrawn on that day, and the more savers the easier it is.

The fact that insurance companies are experts in dealing with risk makes them suitable for organising pensions too, as the premiums and amounts to be paid out depend on the number of people living beyond pensionable age.

9.7 WHAT DO FINANCIAL FIRMS DO?

The financial services sector is a major employer in the UK and accounts for nearly a quarter of UK output. It is not obvious, however, what we get from financial intermediaries and hence some explanation is required:

Customers benefit from financial intermediation in four principal respects:

1. Expert advice: In a complex financial system one service that intermediaries provide is finding the right method of saving or borrowing to suit individual requirements.

2. Channelling of funds: Intermediaries have devised methods to reduce the carrying of cash by providing cards and cheque-books to enable people to access their funds.

3. Maturity transformation: People can be both borrowers and savers. For many people their wage is paid straight into the bank, and until they spend it, they are saving it. At the same time, they may have a mortgage or other loans, or an overdraft facility, and are thus also borrowers. However, only a tiny fraction of their deposits are sitting there waiting for people to spend them; the rest are being lent to someone. Some of it is being lent to people taking out mortgages for 25 and 30 years to buy a house, and some is being lent to firms taking out business loans for investment, which again could be very long term. The banks and building societies are able to do this and still give savers their money back whenever they want it. They are able to do this not because they have the money waiting idly by for savers to withdraw, but because they know that on any one day few customers will take all their money out. There are also arrangements amongst banks and with the Bank of England to ensure the stability of the financial system if they did, since the destruction of major firms in this sector can destabilise the whole economy. The result is that the banks and building societies have a stock of money from which they can make long-term loans; effectively they bundle up lots of small, short-term loans from savers, transforming them into fewer but bigger long-term loans. This process is known as **maturity transformation**, as the term maturity is banking jargon for the length of a loan. Without this maturity trans-formation, most long-term loans would be impossible and investment and economic growth would be undermined. Savers enter this arrangement because it is convenient not to carry too much cash around and because they are paid interest on their savings. The banks can afford to do this because they in turn charge borrowers interest. They make a profit with-out necessarily charging people for their services, unless they become overdrawn, because the interest they give savers is less than the rate they charge borrowers.

4. Risk pooling: A modern financial intermediary can reduce both the risks and the consequences of people not repaying a loan. They can reduce the risks by looking at what borrowing firms plan to do with the money, or if the money is for mortgages, evaluate the financial status of the pro-spective borrower. They can reduce the consequences of non-payment because they can pool the risk. That is, they can share it amongst all the savers so that the burden carried by each saver is relatively small, and default simply means a fractionally lower rate of interest is received than would have been possible with no defaulters.

9.8 THE ROLE OF FINANCIAL MARKETS AND INTERMEDIARIES IN SUPPORTING BUSINESS TO GROW

Firms can grow in a number of ways. One way is to plough back all the super normal profits they make into expanding the firm. This route to growth need not involve any financial intermediation but the remainder usually do:

- Mergers and acquisitions. Both mergers and acquisitions allow firms to grow by integrating one business with another. A firm can move either 'upstream' into the business of the firms that supply it, or downstream towards the end user of their products. For example, a fashion house that buys cloth to make clothes that it sells to shops could move either upstream or downstream. It could move upstream into cloth production, or even further upstream into cotton growing, and downstream into the retail clothing market by opening its own retail outlets. Moving up or downstream is often called vertical integration to contrast it with a sideways, or horizontal joining of firms in the same stage of the production process. For example, when BMW took over Jaguar, that was a horizontal move since both companies are car manufacturers. Horizontal integration can involve two types of benefits, as it can eliminate substitutes and add complementary assets to the acquirer. For example, Abbey National's acquisition of National & Provincial meant that one of its rivals had been eliminated. However, it also meant that it had added all the N&P branches, which were mainly in the north, to its own set of branches mainly in the south, giving it an improved geographical coverage in the UK. There is also what is termed a **conglomerate** merger or acquisition, which involves firms in unrelated industries integrating to form a conglomerate. Hanson Trust is an example of a conglomerate with a diverse range of businesses in the one company. Mergers and acquisitions are usually arranged and supported by financial intermediaries, in particular merchant banks.

- By accessing the markets for long-term loans (from months to any number of years). Firms can get loans from this source by issuing bonds or issuing shares:
  - Issuing 'bonds': These can be either debentures or stocks. **Debentures** are loans that are secured on the assets of the firm, which means that if the firm goes bust, they have priority; **stocks** on the other hand are unsecured. Bonds are simply IOUs (I owe you); in other words, pieces of paper saying that a firm owes the amount of money printed on them. The investor gets more than a piece of paper and the promise of their money back at some future date (the 'maturity date' of the bond), they also earn interest in the meantime. Investors can also make money if they sell a bond for more than it cost to buy, as bonds can be sold before they mature, and in fact, most bonds for sale have been sold many times, through 'stock markets', such as those in the City of London.
  - Firms that are public limited companies, which includes most of the biggest ones, can issue shares (equity) in the company to the public; these have no payback date, but they do confer ownership of the firm

on the holder. This entitles them to a vote on the major strategic issues affecting the firm, in addition to a regular payment called a **dividend**. The size of the dividend depends on the success of the firm in making profits, although the firm may still manage to pay a dividend if it makes no profit, by using reserves. If, however, it looks as if a firm will continue to make losses, shareholders will sell the shares, forcing the price down, as shown in Figure 9.3, because reserves will soon run out. This is a problem for the firm as well as the shareholders since shares are the ownership certificates of firms; if the firm's shares are worth less then the firm is worth less, the firm's value being calculated as the price of shares multiplied by their number.

Figure 9.3 A fall in the price of a company's shares.

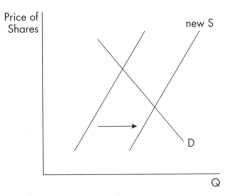

Shareholders can make money from the dividend but also from selling a share at a higher price than they paid for it, although, of course, they can also lose money by selling at a lower price than they paid for it, which they will do rather than hang on to it if they expect the price to fall even further. The number of times shares can be sold is limitless, so although shares are perpetual as far as the firm is concerned, for each individual investor the commitment can be as short term as they choose; there is in effect, therefore, a maturity transformation involved. The resale price of shares depends on two factors. Firstly, the prospects for the firm's environment of all firms will have an influence, this being assessed on a regular basis by stockbroker's analysts. If the prospects for the national economy look good, share prices tend to rise; as this is such an important element in all firms' environments, when all prices rise in this way we have what is known as a **bull** market. On the other hand, a poor outlook will lead to a fall in share prices, which is known as a **bear** market. If, therefore, stockbrokers and their analysts begin to predict recession then share prices will drift down, with possible waves of pessimism about the future pushing them down more dramatically on some days rather than others. These **crashes** can cause problems; a big crash in 1929 precipitated the Great Depression of the 1930s. Nowadays, while governments cannot stop share prices falling, they can limit the extent of any fall by putting money into the market, or by changing policies to suit the City and thereby generate more optimism and investor confidence because insofar as the future is unpredictable, sentiments matter. Although crashes tend to get a lot of publicity, for most of the time economies are growing, which means that the output of firms is getting bigger, so that in the long term the normal course of share prices taken as a whole is upwards. Indeed, on average, more can be made by investors buying into firms direct than by putting their money in the bank, and as a result banks make some deposits work for them by investing in shares, as do all financial intermediaries. In doing this they will, however, ensure that they have a portfolio of shares to reduce the impact of any one share doing badly, since not all shares rise and fall together. This brings us to our second influence on the price of shares – the prospects for individual firms. The prospects for different industries will vary and so will the performance of different firms within an industry, even within a strategic group, and share prices will reflect these differences.

Recently we have seen significant share price falls, and the onset of recession in the Far East, which will hit the prospects and share prices of some firms in the UK. However, the big questions, at the moment, for British firms are whether we will go into a recession in the next few years and whether we will enter the European single currency, since both will have a major impact on all share prices.

As with bonds, resales of shares rather than new issues tend to dominate the market. Most shares are owned by institutions such as insurance companies and pension funds that have large pools of cash from their clients – the public. Privatisation issues have generated considerable interest from smaller investors, but mostly to **stag** the issue, which means that they bought in order to sell quickly for an immediate gain. This was made easy in this case by the fact that the issue price of privatisation shares is kept low in order to ensure a successful launch.

- By accessing the markets for short-term loans (from days to several months). These cover a variety of short-term loans, including 'bills' that generally have a three-month life, but can be resold up to the date of maturity. Unlike bonds, they do not specify a rate of interest on the piece of paper (the IOU) that the investor gets, but instead are simply sold for less than their value at maturity, with the investor pocketing the difference between the two values.

  Governments also borrow money to bridge the gap between their spending commitments and what they are able to raise in tax. They issue both bonds and bills; the bills are known as Treasury bills because Her Majesty's Treasury, which is the main economic management branch of the UK government, sanctions them. Bonds are called gilt-edged bonds (commonly abbreviated to gilts), as the certificates are edged with gold. Some bonds issued by the government are perpetual bonds, with no maturity date. They are nonetheless tradable, because a rate of interest is paid and a gain can be made by selling them for more than they cost to buy.

- Finally, in our list we should include the fact that firms can finance growth by simply taking out a loan from their local bank. In fact, most business start-ups are financed by bank loans on receipt of a sensible business plan from an applicant.

Case study in the financial and investment environment

THE RUSSIAN FINANCIAL AND INVESTMENT ENVIRONMENT

During the early 1990s, the Russian central bank started pumping money into the economy in an effort to shore up Russia's inefficient industrial sector, and thereby lit the inflationary fuse. In response, the Prime Minister, Victor Chernomyrdin, dramatically reversed the policy but, with cash support suspended, Russian firms resorted to issuing their own IOUs, which are now being used instead of money. The inflationary pressures therefore remain, but in addition, since firms are issuing IOUs in excess of the value of their enterprises, it has become impossible to estimate the true worth of firms. Therefore, investment in Russian firms has ground to a halt since there is nothing for investors to base their calculations on.

The Russians acknowledge that they have to rebuild their political and legal framework to establish the legitimacy of capitalists and managers' right to decide what to produce, how to produce it, and who to sell it to. But in addition, it looks as if they will have to rebuild their whole financial environment too. Indeed, many British and American banks have become financially involved in Russia in the expectation of huge returns, only to come unstuck. Reality is turning out rather different than the investors had expected, with huge losses being recorded in some cases. Indeed, one American intermediary has been forced into liquidation because of its dealings in Russia.

9.9 SUMMARY

- Investment means using resources to create more resources.

- Firms will invest if the discounted sum of future revenues exceeds the costs involved, bearing in mind the risks.

- National prospects for output and inflation as well as the costs of funds have an impact on investment.

- Investment can even be affected by sentiments, which can be a problem as pessimism can stop investment dead, and since investment is a major part of national spending this can have a damaging effect on the economy.

- The UK investment environment is unfavourable in certain key ways, when compared to other major industrial nations, and this may contribute to our relatively low average productivity.

- Financial intermediaries are firms that specialise in linking savers with borrowers.

- In the UK there are a number of different types of financial intermediary, including commercial banks, building societies, and insurance companies which all specialised in different things, at least in the past.

- Financial intermediaries provide four main services: expert advice, the channelling of funds, maturity transformation and risk pooling.

- Financial intermediaries support business expansion by providing money, negotiating access to money markets and capital markets, and by supporting firms engaged in mergers or take-overs.

- Issuing bonds and issuing shares allow firms to access funds, and both are traded openly in such places as the City of London.

- Bond prices and share prices are subject to all manner of pressures over time since they can be resold time and again. One consideration in determining their price may be the prospects of the firm, but it may also be speculation or even simply the result of herd behaviour by traders.

9.10 QUESTIONS

1. Analyse the effect of a cut in interest rates on the savings market and firms involved in that market.
2. Analyse the effect of a cut in interest rates on the market for loans and firms involved in that market.
3. Discuss how an investor can make money by investing in company shares.
4. Pick a firm that has a quoted share price in the paper that you read and monitor what happens to its share price over the next few months. See if you can relate the performance of the share to
   (a) events that are specific to the firm;
   (b) the general prospects for the economy.
5. When the price of bread falls we treat this as good news, but when the price of shares falls this is treated as bad news. Why?

APPENDIX A — PREDICTING BOND PRICES AND SHARE PRICES

Bond prices

One major influence on the price of bills, and in particular bonds, is interest rates. This is because bonds pay a fixed return. For example, a perpetual bond with a face value of £100,000 may stipulate that it will pay a fixed interest of 5%, or in other words, that it will pay £5,000 per annum. If subsequently general interest rates rise to 10%, no one would be willing to pay £100,000 for a bond that pays only 5%. To match 10%, the bond needs to sell at £50,000 because then the £5,000 will provide a 10% return. In general therefore, we find that interest rates and bond prices are inversely related, with bond prices rising if interest rates fall, and falling if interest rates rise. The most successful investors in bonds tend, therefore, to be those best able to predict interest rates.

Share prices

Although share prices grow as the economy grows, it is at any one point in time difficult to explain why they are where they are. The problem is that there are so many significant influences on share prices. Firstly, they reflect what people think about the future of the whole economy. Secondly, they reflect what people think about the prospects for individual companies. Thirdly, as no one knows exactly what will happen to the economic 'fundamentals' that underpin a share, investors are sensitive to what other shareholders think is important, because if it affects their buying or selling behaviour then it is important. This means that if people think share prices are going to fall, they will sell shares and that will drive prices down. This is another example of a self-fulfilling prophecy and it means that share prices can be subject to waves of pessimism or optimism. For the influential economist John Maynard Keynes, writing in the 1930s, the scope for share prices to fall prey to waves of sentiment was a problem, since if they fall far enough, investment in industry will stop and recession will ensue. Indeed, he argued that the 'Great Depression' of the 1930s, in which the whole world went into a deep and prolonged recession, really began when share prices fell dramatically in the 1929 'Wall Street Crash' (so named because the New York stock exchange is on Wall Street).

APPENDIX B | **EVALUATING THE PERFORMANCE OF FIRMS**

There are a number of financial ratios that are commonly used as a guide to the health of firms and as pointers to which one to invest in.

Profitability

Profits

Profits can be reported simply as a figure, or in comparison to something, such as last year's profits, or the profits of the firm's closest rivals, or in relation to the average profits for the industry.

Profit margin

This is another measure of profit, but in this case, we express profit as a percentage of '**turnover**' (which is total revenue after excluding the payments for VAT, but before other tax and interest payments).

Profit margin = Profit/Turnover   (/ means divide by)

As an example, consider the world's largest retail food company – Nestlé. In 1996, its gross profit was 2,535 million. Turnover was 45,091 million. Both of these are recorded in dollars, but one of the advantages of ratios is that this does not matter:

Nestlé profit margin 1996 = 2535/45091 = 0.056

The percentage equivalent of the decimal number is found by simple multiplication by 100. This gives us a figure of 5.6% in this case. This is small compared to many industries but Nestlé is a big firm, with a high turnover, so despite a small margin it makes big profits. My local shop would close down if it could not get a 30% margin, but its rival Tesco had only a 6% margin in 1996. However, Tesco has an enormous turnover, and so unlike my local shop it made a total gross profit for that year of £724 million. Some firms are both big and have high margins; gross profit margins for big drugs firms, for example, are frequently over 30%. This is partly because patents can protect the market share of new drugs, to enable firms to make big profits on their discoveries, at least for a while, to encourage them to keep investing in the search for new medicines.

Return on capital employed (ROCE)

This represents the return on funds invested in the firm, as measured by 'capital' employed, against the output from that investment, which is net profit before tax and interest (net profit is profit after taking out overheads such as rent, and so on). In this case, the term capital refers to existing funds rather than existing physical capital.

ROCE = Net profit/Capital employed (share capital + reserves +
long-term loans)

Shareholders invest money to make money and so, to attract funds, a firm needs to offer a better return than investors can get from substitute uses for their funds. For example, since putting the money in a firm is more risky than putting it in a bank, at a minimum investors would expect to make more than bank deposit accounts are currently paying. In 1994, the ROCE for Cadbury's was 22%, for Tesco it was 16%, and for Glaxo Wellcome it was 36%.

Efficiency

We can measure efficiency using published accounts in a number of ways:
Total asset turnover ratio: this measures how well a firm is using its assets (the things it owns) to generate sales (total revenue):

Total asset turnover ratio = sales/total assets

In looking at this figure, firms would like to see an upward trend to indicate efficiency gains, and a higher figure than rivals would indicate relative efficiency. The same can also be said if we look at efficiency in terms of turnover per employee:

Turnover per employee = sales/total number of employees

Our final efficiency ratio relates to the holding of stocks. It is expensive for firms to carry unfinished, or finished but as yet unsold, goods and therefore an indicator of the amount of such stocks needed to support sales is required:

Stock turnover ratio = average stocks/turnover

The most efficient firms will carry least stocks but again it depends on the industry; with fast-moving consumer goods (FMCGs) the figure is likely to be lower than is possible in other industries.

We can also view the company's performance in terms of its credit control by looking at how long on average it takes for the firm's debtors to settle their debts to the company. An accepted norm is 30 days after the issuing of an invoice. On the other side, we can look at how long a firm takes to pay its creditors as an indicator of the goodwill extended to it by its suppliers, or of course as an indicator of problems in being able to pay the bills. This indicator may also show the relative power of firms; many big firms can get away with late payment that they would not tolerate from those that supply them. Many firms, however, even some of the biggest, pride themselves on their prompt payment of bills.

Finally, a firm's efficiency can be gauged in terms of its ability to self-finance future operations by comparing working capital (current assets minus current liabilities) with turnover. Working capital is an indicator of the funds available internally after meeting liabilities that have to be paid within a year.

$$\text{Working capital/turnover ratio} = \frac{(\text{current assets} - \text{current liabilities})}{\text{turnover}}$$

A figure of below 50% is often sought, but again it depends on the industry; retailers, for example, will have very low (possibly negative) numbers.

Liquidity

Measures of liquidity give an indication of the firm's short-term financial position, in particular whether it has enough cash, or saleable assets, to meet its current liabilities (those requiring payment within a year). It is essential that a firm can pay its debts within a reasonable time of them falling due as, although big firms can stretch what is reasonable, they cannot do this to the extent of indefinitely delaying payments. If there is a question mark over the ability of a firm to pay its debts, confidence amongst those who lend to it and amongst suppliers that extend it credit can evaporate.

Current ratio

This measures the extent to which currently available assets cover current liabilities.

$$\text{Current ratio} = \frac{\text{Current assets (stocks + debtors + cash)}}{\text{Current liabilities (creditors + tax + dividents + overdrafts)}}$$

Generally, a figure around 2 is considered prudent. A higher figure than this implies large holdings of stocks or debtors or cash, which is not efficient. However, again circumstances matter, and in some industries a higher figure may be acceptable because of the nature of the goods produced. A figure much lower than 2 can indicate a problem, but again it depends on the industry; in fast-moving consumer goods markets, where stocks are often tiny compared to turnover, lower figures are acceptable. In 1996, for example, Tesco's current ratio was a mere 0.36. A similar ratio is the 'acid test' ratio; this is the same as the current ratio except that stocks are taken out to focus exclusively on those assets that are easily converted into cash. The acceptable figure is correspondingly lower.

Leverage ratio

Indicators of this attempt to measure the extent to which the firm has to rely on external borrowing, that is, loans from outsiders, as well as its ability to service and repay such loans.

Gearing ratio

This measures the extent of external borrowing relative to the total capital employed (all the financial inputs to the firm).

$$\text{Gearing ratio} = \frac{\text{External borrowing}\ (\text{bank overdrafts} + \text{loan capital})}{\text{Capital employed}\ (\text{external borrowing} + \text{ordinary shares and reserves})}$$

The figure calculated gives an indication of the extent of external borrowing and of the burden of interest payments to which the company is liable, regardless of profitability. A figure around one-third is considered prudent and unlikely to see the company struggling to repay interest on its loans even if profitability falls. Again, however, it depends on the context; a big firm in a growing economy may be confident of generating sufficient revenue and profits to be able to operate with higher gearing ratios than this. Another indicator of gearing is the debt/equity ratio.

$$\text{Debt/equity ratio} = \frac{\text{External borrowings}}{\text{Shareholders' funds (ordinary shares and reserves)}}$$

This is the same as the gearing ratio except that external borrowings are removed from the denominator; the acceptable figure is correspondingly a bit higher at around a half. For example, in 1994, Glaxo Wellcome had a debt/equity ratio of 0.53, indicating that for every pound contributed by shareholders to finance the firm, lenders and creditors contributed 53 pence.

Investment ratios

These ratios are used by potential investors to indicate the level of risks and returns in buying shares in a company. We cannot simply look at profit to do this, since the returns to shareholders depend on the price of shares and the number of shares issued. To adjust for the number of shares issued we can calculate the profits per share. This is referred to as 'earnings per share' as it represents the earnings of shareholders.

Earnings per share (eps) = Net profit/Number of shares

In 1995, each share in BskyB earned 8.7p, while Tesco shares earned 18.9p each. This indicates how well the firm is doing per share; the bigger the figure, the more profits available for each shareholder. However, it does not show how much a shareholder will actually get. What shareholders actually get for holding shares is called the dividend. Normally, if profits rise, the dividend will go up but not necessarily by the same amount, as the firm may keep some profit to plough back into the firm. On the other hand, even if no profits are made, a dividend may be paid. The firm's managers decide the size of the dividend but the shareholders have to approve the decision. In 1995, BSkyB paid a dividend of 2.5p and Tesco 8.6p. In 1992, British Aerospace had earnings per share of minus 45.9p, since it was making a loss, but nonetheless managed to pay a dividend of 7p.

To indicate the dividend as a fraction of the share price we can simply divide one by the other; this gives us the 'yield':

Yield = Dividend per share/Share price

How investors view a firm depends on the dividend but also on the price of the shares, which fluctuate daily as they are resold repeatedly. The Stock Exchange collates the prices and they are quoted in national newspapers, the most detailed reporting being found in the *Financial Times*. The simplest way of seeing the popularity of a share is to divide its current price by past earnings per share, which produces the price/earnings ratio:

P/E ratio = Share price/Earnings per share (eps)

This tells us the number of years it would take the previous year's earnings (profits) to add up to the current price. This figure is taken as the key indicator of what value investors are currently putting on the future performance of the shares and thus the firm (future because buying now means getting a return later). Some yield and P/E ratios for 2 May 1997 are shown in Table 9.2.

Table 9.2 Some yield and P/E ratios.

	Yield	P/E
Laura Ashley	1.2	24.0
Burton	2.3	19.6
M&S	3.0	20.4

Of these three, M&S had the best yield, and Laura Ashley the worst, but Laura Ashley was the most popular stock of the three. As we shall see later, a full company analysis of that stock might have suggested that it was in fact over-valued.

Investors can also calculate the ease with which the previous year's dividend was met out of profits, by dividing the amount of dividends by the amount of profit. The result is termed the 'dividend cover' as it shows the number of times the profits cover the dividends. A small figure indicates that the firm is having difficulty providing the dividend. This could be taken as a warning that the firm might lower the dividend next time, or pay no dividend unless profits improve this year.

Composite indicators

We can combine key indicators of a firm's performance into a composite score, often called a 'Z score', using regression analysis (discussed in Chapter 15). If this combining is done with care, the 'Z score' will indicate which firms are performing well and which face problems. Although 'Z scores' are useful in identifying firms that are likely to fail, for many firms the results are not very useful because firms vary in the details of how they report their figures. The same problem, of course, applies to all comparisons using accountancy data. Other factors therefore need to be taken into account; an innovative, fast-growing firm with great prospects might have a low yield or P/E, for example, so further analysis, beyond looking at ratios, is nearly always required. Such an analysis should encompass consideration of the environment in which the firm operates; an example of such an analysis for British Aerospace can be found after Chapter 16.

Public sector indicators

In the public sector a number of performance indicators have been devised. For example, schools are now ranked according to the attainment grades of their pupils, Police forces produce 'clear up' figures, while hospitals may in future publish their success rates for different operations. In some cases, some if not all funds are allocated according to measured performance. In the private sector, shareholders' funds tend to flow towards those who perform best in terms of profits and growth, so in both the private sector and increasingly in the public sector there is an incentive to present data in the best light. This means that we have to take care in interpreting the data we receive and should always look for corroborating evidence. The potential to use indicators to allocate funds also means that when designing an indicator for the first time, considerable thought has to go into considering exactly what incentives the indicator creates. If, for example, the government wishes to increase the number of operations done in a hospital, then using numbers of operations would do. Hospitals that do well on this score should be allocated more funds because they are clearly efficient. However, such a narrow definition of efficiency could mean that more trivial operations are done, or that they are done quicker and with greater loss of life, because the incentive is to do more operations, not to be more successful in the operations that are done.

CHAPTER 10

The macroeconomic environment

After studying this chapter, you should be able to:

- appreciate the significance of the difference between a microeconomic and a macro-economic approach to employment and output;
- appreciate how aggregate demand and aggregate supply interact to determine the level of output, employment and inflation in an economy;
- understand the purpose of depicting the economy as a circular flow of income, and appreciate the role of injections and leakages within it in determining the level of aggregate demand and national income;
- understand the multiplier principle and its significance for the management of the macroeconomy through the manipulation of the level of aggregate demand;
- appreciate the difficulties of managing the macroeconomy by manipulating aggregate demand;
- appreciate the benefits and difficulties of boosting aggregate supply;
- understand the approach to macroeconomic management of the current government;
- appreciate how macroeconomic changes impact upon individual firms;
- explain how different macroeconomic variables are measured;

10.1   MACROECONOMICS

In looking at macroeconomics, we are looking at the workings of the economy taken as a whole. As a separate subject it is a relatively new branch of economics, as until the 1930s economists thought that neo-classical microeconomics explained the workings of whole economies too. In this view, employment, for example, was seen as the product of the interaction of the supply and demand for labour. This leads to the conclusion that unemployment can be eliminated by lowering wages; since wages are the price in the labour market, unemployment must by definition be due to high wages, as shown in Figure 10.1. In this, the numbers who want to work at the current wage is shown by 'b', while the number that employers want at this wage is only 'a'. Therefore, at wage 'w' we have a surplus, which in this market we call unemployment.

Figure 10.1
Unemployment.

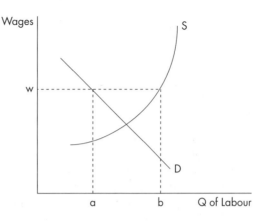

10.2 THE GENERAL THEORY OF JOHN MAYNARD KEYNES

Problems with the microeconomic approach came to a head during the depression of the early 1930s when wages fell but unemployment went up. For Marxists, it was evidence of a fundamental flaw in capitalism, for which there was no cure. But many non-Marxist economists felt that it could be fixed if only policy makers would stop seeing unemployment as a labour market phenomenon to be tackled by cutting wages, and instead see it as the by-product of the economic system taken as a whole. This view was developed by several economists, but the outstanding contribution was by John Maynard Keynes (1883–1946) in his book *The General Theory of Employment, Interest and Money* (1936). A lesser-known economist called Michael Kalecki (1899–1970) developed a similar approach in the early 1930s, but it was Keynes' approach that came to dominate the debate, so much so, that people working along similar lines after Keynes' death became known as Keynesians. In the Keynesian framework, rather than looking at individual markets we look at the relationships between the key participants of society and how the money flows between them.

For simplicity, we start our investigation of the Keynesian approach by looking at two types of institutions, firms and households (individuals, or families). Firms coordinate production and supply households with goods and services in return for money; that is, they provide the total, or **aggregate supply**, of all goods and services that equates to the total, or **aggregate demand**, for them. We can represent this in terms of a supply and demand diagram as shown in Figure 10.2. (Note that although we are often involved in adding a lot of supply and demand curves together when we look at markets, we only use the terms aggregate supply and aggregate demand when we are looking at all markets combined.)

Figure 10.2
Aggregate supply and
aggregate demand.

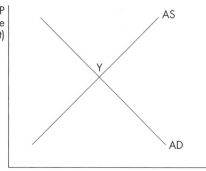

The money that firms make from selling the goods to households is, however, given back to households in payment for use of the factors of production, as these are all owned by somebody in the household sector: capitalists earn profits, workers earn wages, and landowners receive rent. Suppliers of raw materials are also paid, and they in turn pay their own workers, owners, and so on. Therefore, ultimately all the money received for selling the goods – the total revenue (and by definition therefore, total expenditure too) for the whole economy (P × Q) – ends up back in one household or another as income, denoted 'Y'. This in turn gets spent by households on firms' output, and on it goes round and round in a circle, as shown in Figure 10.3.

Figure 10.3 The
circular flow of income.

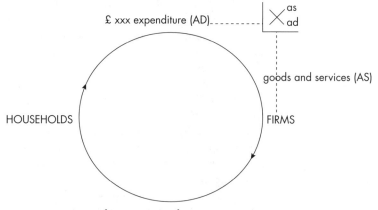

One consequence of this circularity is that the value of the output produced in the economy, national output, must be the same as national income (Y) and national expenditure. However, in practice, because of the difficulties of measuring these huge aggregates, the official figures for output, such as 'gross national product' (GNP), are similar to figures for 'gross national income' and 'gross national expenditure', but they are not identical (as shown in the appendix below). In 1996 GNP at 'factor cost' (after removing the effect of indirect taxes and subsidies, which hide how much we spend on the actual output of firms) was £653 billion (billion – bn for short – being a thousand million).

The question for Keynes was: what determined the level of national income? What, in other words, made xxx in Figure 10.3 £400bn in a year rather than, say, £700bn, and what level will produce 'full employment', for regardless of the level of technology there will always be a level of economic activity great enough to provide everyone with a job. (Although, of course, full employment in this sense means a level of employment where everyone who wants to work at going wage rates can find a job, rather than zero unemployment, since there will always be some people between jobs, or who do not want to enter paid employment). For Keynes it was the level of spending (AD) that determined Y. He had observed that spending fell when investment confidence evaporated after share prices collapsed in the Wall Street crash of 1929. This led to less investment spending and a rise in unemployment in the capital goods and other investment-intensive industries. But more than that, Keynes noticed that this also led to less spending on other goods (especially in the absence of unemployment benefit), which in turn led to more layoffs and lower incomes all round. In the USA, it also led to the collapse of several banks, which further exacerbated the original investment crisis. This process continued until ultimately we had economic stagnation on such a scale and for so long (the whole of the 1930s) that it became known as the 'Great Depression'. In Keynes' interpretation of events, while there may have been logical reasons why share prices should have fallen (after the bullish 1920s), it was nonetheless clear that the suddenness and severity of the switch from optimism to pessimism in investment markets was a direct cause of mass unemployment in labour markets. In contrast, the neo-classical economists of the time viewed the world in an essentially microeconomic manner, seeing labour market problems as addressable in isolation, rather than in a macroeconomic context, and they therefore concluded that the unemployment could be cured by cutting wages. But as mentioned earlier wages were cut and instead of curing the problem this actually made things worse, suggesting that Keynes was right in believing that the problem was not that wages were too high but that spending was too low. Although the neo-classical economists of the time did not tend to think in terms of aggregate supply and demand, we can summarise their view in terms of it by showing total demand affecting only prices and wages, not output or employment, by drawing a vertical AS curve, as in Figure 10.4.

Figure 10.4 The neo-classical view on AS and AD.

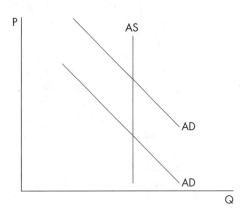

For Keynes, the question was not whether aggregate demand affects the level of output; in his opinion, the depression had proved that it did. The big question, as he saw it, was whether the free market contained a mechanism to ensure that spending bounces back, for if it does not, or if it is unacceptably slow, then government intervention to raise spending is called for. Keynes' conclusion was that nothing could be relied on to increase spending except governments, who can spend quickly regardless of how pessimistic everyone else is. He recommended spending on 'public works' such as large constructions projects (like road-building) to do this, since these do not suck in many imports, often require lots of labour and once built, support the activities of firms and thereby improve supply too. This suggestion was taken up successfully in the later part of the 1930s throughout the Western world. To see why Keynes came to his conclusion that AD was the villain of the piece, we need to look at the various routes by which spending can be withdrawn from the economy and the mechanisms by which it may be injected back.

10.3   WITHDRAWALS AND INJECTIONS

If we look at the whole economy, we find that not all income is spent; some is saved. Savings are a withdrawal, or a leakage of spending, from the circular flow. There are two elements in savings: firms' retained profits, and households' unspent earnings. Most of these funds end up in the hands of a bank which can then lend the money on to firms for investment spending, in other words to buy capital goods. If money saved is available for investment, is there any reason for supposing that it will not be passed on? For Keynes, investment spending was likely to be volatile, as a firm that is pessimistic about the future can stop investment spending altogether and still stay in business, and at a later stage switch it back on again when its decision makers become more optimistic. So investment need not reflect how much is saved, and this is one reason why aggregate demand could fall below the level of income. The pre-Keynesian view was that savings would be brought into equilibrium with investment, by interest rates, since savings are the supply of funds for lending, investment is the demand for funds for lending and interest rates are the price of funds for lending. Keynes realised that interest rates equate the supply and demand for all money and that there are various reasons for demanding money in the financial system unrelated to investment needs, so that in fact interest rates do not work simply to equate savings and investments.

Spending on imports is another leakage from the circular flow of income since the money is paid to people abroad and becomes a part of their income, not ours. The counterpart to this is the amount foreigners spend on our goods, which is export spending. The question then is: will exports balance imports? For Keynes, this was not guaranteed; if the rate at which one currency exchanges for another is determined by the amount of import and export spending then the two will tend to balance. However, there are reasons (discussed in the next chapter) why this does not happen, not least of which is that governments like to intervene in the determination of 'exchange rates'. The result is that export spending and import spending rarely balance and we have a net export figure that can be a positive number, or more usually in the case of the UK, a negative number. Again therefore, this is another weak link; another route through which aggregate demand could fall below the level of income, with spending effect-ively leaking abroad.

Our final leakage is taxation. Most tax in the UK is 'direct tax' taken directly from income; from the 'disposable income' that remains, further 'indirect taxes' are taken at the point of consumption, such as VAT and excise duty. In what follows, for simplicity, we will depict all taxation as if it were taken out of house-holds' expenditure rather than out of their income. The counterpart to this leakage is the injection of government spending on the output of firms. This does not include the money that is simply transferred between households, from taxpayers' pockets into the pockets of those in receipt of such things as student grants, social security payments and pensions, as this affects the level of net taxes being taken, not the level of spending. In contrast to such 'transfer payments', what governments spend on roads, schools, public sector salaries, hospitals, and so on does add to the aggregate demand for firms' output. For Keynes, the fact that this did not have to balance with the level of taxation was the answer to getting out of the depression, since more could be spent than was raised in tax. For neo-classical economists, the fact that governments could add to, or subtract from, total spending made it imperative that they do not. Instead, they should balance their budget by spending no more than they raise in tax, since in their view governments are the primary source of instability in the economy.

Figure 10.5 shows the circular flow diagram with the injections and with-drawals discussed above added in.

Figure 10.5 The circular flow diagram with injections and withdrawals included.

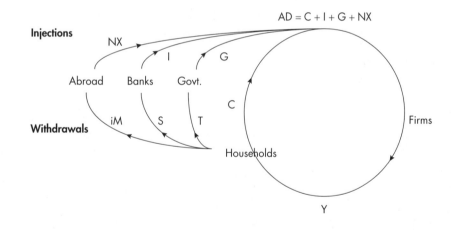

In this diagram C = Consumer spending (on domestically produced goods), iM = Import spending (spending on foreign-produced goods), NX = Net exports (export spending by foreigners on our goods minus import spending, or X – iM), I = Investment spending (on domestically produced goods), S = Savings, G = Government spending (on domestically produced goods), T = Taxes.

Since injections were, in Keynes' view, determined largely by factors other than the level of income, it followed that it was changes in AD that led to changes in national income. Indeed for no better reason than a lack of optimism AD could fall, resulting in fewer sales for firms and ultimately therefore lower incomes for all. The result could be a level of national income below that necessary to maintain full employment, which is an equilibrium insofar as there is nothing to say it will not last except the political will of government not to tolerate high levels of unemployment. However, to do anything about it the government must be able to calculate how much extra spending is required. To answer this they need to find the equilibrium level of national income and compare it with the full employment level of national income to measure the size of the gap to be closed.

10.4 **FINDING THE EQUILIBRIUM LEVEL OF NATIONAL INCOME**

The first step in this is to find out how income and consumption are related. How much is spent on consumption depends on many things, but mainly people's current income. Keynes argued that the relationship between incomes and consumption contained two dominant features. Firstly, when incomes are very low people will spend all their income on consumption, even if this means selling their assets or borrowing; after all, people have to eat. Secondly, as incomes rise people spend more but also start to save, and the higher the income the more they save. So, as incomes rise consumption rises too, but slightly less so. Although Keynes did not draw a line to represent these ideas, we can, since his first point gives us an intercept, which shows that some level of spending occurs even when incomes are zero (at £90bn in Figure 10.6, for the line labelled C). His second point suggests a linear relationship between income and consumption that is less than one, which is to say a line with a slope less than one. In Figure 10.6, the slope of the C line is 0.6, which is to say that 60p of every extra £ of income is spent (40p is saved).

Figure 10.6 The consumption function.

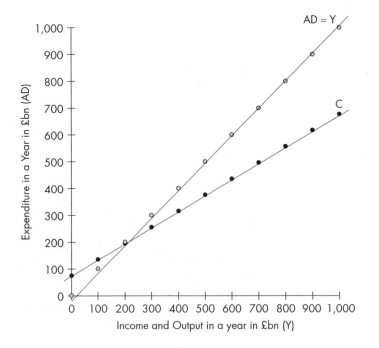

The algebraic equivalent of the line is using 'a' for the intercept and 'b' for the slope:

$C = a + bY$ (which in this case is $C = 90 + 0.6Y$)

Keynes called 'b' the **marginal propensity to consume** (MPC). Since Keynes, there have been numerous refinements and developments in the theory of consumption, but the basic insight here that the MPC is less than one remains central to modern Keynesian thinking. All we have done here is to turn Keynes' thoughts about people's consumption into a graph, or **consumption function** as it is often called. We can now use this graph to explain how in Keynes' opinion it was possible for the equilibrium level of national income to be less than is necessary to create full employment. Since, for Keynes, injections are determined largely by factors other than the current level of income, we can for simplicity draw injections as entirely independent of Y, so that as Y gets bigger injections stay the same, in the first case at £80bn per annum in Figure 10.7. If, subsequently, injections go up, perhaps because investor confidence goes up or because the government spends more, then we get an upward shift in the line, as for example indicated by 'Inj 2' at £200bn per annum.

Figure 10.7 The level of injections, assuming no relationship between injections and income.

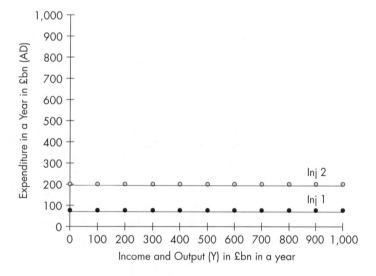

We can now depict graphically how aggregate demand determines the level of income. In this simplified model AD = C + Injections, which, starting with 'Inj 1' (£80bn), gives AD 1 in Figure 10.8. This is simply our C line with £80bn added all the way along it. For 'Inj 2' we simply add £200bn, which gives AD 2. These AD lines show us what total spending will be for every level of Y. For equilibrium, AD and Y must be the same, therefore all the potential equilibrium points are indicated by the line of equality between AD and Y. For AD 1, equilibrium is therefore where GDP = £400bn. To see why this is the equilibrium, consider what happens when we are to the left of this. To the left of £400bn AD will exceed Y. In other words, demand will exceed output. Firms will respond to this by increasing output, if they can. (We will look at what happens when they are unable to do this later.) As a result, output and incomes will rise, pushing us up to £400bn. If, on the other hand, we are to the right of the equilibrium, then output will exceed demand, firms will not therefore be able to sell all their output, and stocks of unsold goods will accumulate. Consequently, firms will cut output until we get to £400bn.

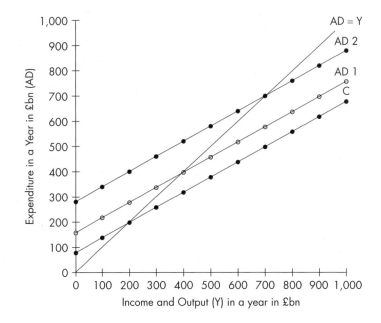

Figure 10.8
Equilibrium national income for two different levels of injections.

Suppose the government estimates that £700bn is the full employment level of national income, but finds the economy is currently at £400bn; it can then calculate the increase in demand needed to get the economy back to full employment. In this case, it needs to put injections up from £80bn (Inj 1) to £200bn (Inj 2), which we know will get AD up from AD 1 to AD 2. However, the difference between the two levels of spending is only £120bn (200 − 80), whereas the difference between the national income levels for AD2 and AD1 is £300bn (700 − 400). This means the government needs to spend less than half of what is required to get the economy back to full employment, as somehow the impact of the rise in spending is being multiplied. It is not magic, or a 'free lunch'; it simply reflects the extra spending and productive effort that newly employed people and previously idle machines bring in response to the initial rise in spending. So, when the government spends the £120bn, the money is spent on goods that generate incomes for the people who make them. They in turn spend 0.6 of this income (i.e. £72bn) on the output of others, who then spend 0.6 of the income (i.e. £43bn) that generates on the output of others and so on, until we find that output has risen by 300, as shown below:

120 + 72 + 43 + 26 + 16 + 9 + 6 + 3 . . . and so on = 300

The same would happen regardless of the source of the initial boost to spending; a rise in confidence that raises investment spending by £120bn will have the same sort of effect. The fact that in each case 0.6 of the rise in income gets spent means that we can use the MPC to work out the size of the multiplier effect:

$$\text{Multiplier (k)} = \frac{1}{1 - \text{MPC}}$$

In this case the multiplier is 2.5, since $\frac{1}{1 - 0.6} = 2.5$

10.5 THE MULTIPLIER

Given that what is not spent is withdrawn, $1 - \text{MPC}$ must equal the marginal propensity to withdraw, so we can also write the multiplier formula as:

$$\text{Multiplier (k)} = \frac{1}{\text{MPW}}$$

Our list of withdrawals is savings, imports and taxation, and we can therefore disaggregate our MPW into the **marginal propensity to save** (MPS), the **marginal propensity to import** (MPiM) and the **marginal propensity to tax** (MPT). Of course, the government does the taxing, so this propensity is simply the marginal rate of tax (that is, how much is taken per additional pound of income). This is, however, a bit more complicated than our formula suggests, since most is not taken at the point of spending but directly from incomes. In addition, it is not a flat rate (say 35% for everyone) but rises (up to a point) with income in the UK (and indeed most other countries). To keep things simple we shall ignore these details and simply add MPT to our list of withdrawals, while acknowledging that the government, in deciding how much to increase (or reduce) spending, will use a more complicated version of the multiplier than the one below:

$$k = \frac{1}{\text{MPS} + \text{MPiM} + \text{MPT}}$$

The following figures are based on broad brush estimates of the size of the UK government spending multiplier in the early 1990s.

$$\text{MPT} = 0.35, \text{MPiM} = 0.25, \text{MPS} = 0.1$$

$$k = \frac{1}{0.35 + 0.25 + 0.1} = 1/0.7 = 1.43$$

This low multiplier reflects the fact that in the UK only a small part of spending accrues directly to domestic firms; most goes in taxes, savings, and spending on imports. Using these figures we can see what may happen if the government decides to increase output from our starting point of £400bn up to £700bn by increasing government spending.

10.6 INCREASING G

When Y = £400bn we can work out the size of withdrawals by multiplying Y by the respective marginal propensities. For example, since the MPS = 0.1 the total savings figure is 400 × 0.1 = £40bn. Also, since injections = withdrawals, once we have calculated S, T and iM we can work out I, G and X too (Table 10.1).

Table 10.1

Withdrawals	Injections
S = £40bn	I = £40bn
T = £140bn	G = £140bn
iM = £100bn	X = £100bn

The multiplier for the figures here is 1.43, which means that if the government is to raise Y by £300bn it will need to increase G by £210bn, as 1.43 × 210 = 300. After a while the new equilibrium will be established and the withdrawals will rise, so, for example, S will go up to £70bn since this is 700 × 0.1 (Table 10.2). G will also go up, by £210bn of course, giving a total spend of £350bn (210 + 140). However, there is no reason why investment should necesarily be higher; as argued earlier, it is independent of Y (in practice it is at least partly independent of Y). Neither is there necessarily any reason why foreigners should buy any more of our goods (although with flexible exchange rates, our expansion could lead to more exports insofar as it leads to a fall in the value of the pound relative to other currencies).

Table 10.2

Withdrawals	Injections
S = £70bn	I = £40bn
T = £245bn	G = £350bn
iM = £175bn	X = £100bn

So now, although injections still equal withdrawals, the components of each no longer correspond (although for the reasons mentioned above, these figures overstate the case). Taking each inconsistency in turn:

1. Budget deficit: The government now has a budget deficit; G is bigger than T, since it has spent £350bn, but its tax haul has only gone up to £245bn (0.35 × 700). The government has therefore a deficit of £105bn that it can only plug by borrowing money. Governments' budget deficits are measured in a number of ways, but the best known measure is the Public Sector Borrowing Requirement (PSBR). If tax revenues exceed government spending, which they may do when the economy is in a boom, the government would have a budget surplus and be able to pay back some previously accumulated 'national debt'. A budget deficit is a problem insofar as the government has to offer a rate of interest on National Savings

certificates that will attract savers in order to fund it. This means that banks and building societies will lose some custom and there will be less money available for private investment, so that in effect some private investment may be 'crowded out' by the public investment. The alternative is to borrow the money from the banks, but as we shall see, this leads to an expansion of the money supply and may therefore be more inflationary than intended. Either way, a budget deficit tends to act as a constraint on governments' ability to 'reflate' the economy.

2. Balance of Payments problem: There is now a problem with the balance of payments between exports and imports as we are now spending £175bn on imports and only £100bn is being spent on exports. This produces a deficit of £75bn, which again will act as a brake on reflation, since such deficits cannot be sustained for long (as we shall see in the next chapter).

The analysis above suggests that in reflating the economy to get to full employment, two types of deficit may appear, and the problems associated with this may mean that AD cannot be expanded as much as required. We should also note that the multiplier represents a complex process that takes time to work and has uneven impacts not apparent in our simplified story. There is, in addition, one final constraint on reflation, which we shall look at later, namely that it can cause P to rise rather than Q.

10.7   CUTTING TAXES

An alternative to increasing spending is to cut taxes; this, however, has a smaller multiplier effect because the reduction in tax applies largely to income (since most tax is actually taken at this point). Therefore, the amount that actually goes around the circular flow is reduced; if, for example, the MPC is 0.6, only 60% of it goes around, as Figure 10.9 shows.

Figure 10.9 A part of the circular flow showing why the multiplier for cutting T is smaller than for raising G.

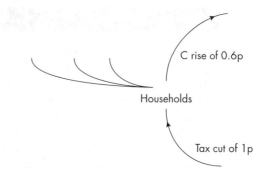

This means that the tax multiplier = spending multiplier × MPC, so for a multiplier of 1.43 it is 1.43 × 0.3 = 0.43. In fact, the tax multiplier is always one less than the spending multiplier. For controlling aggregate demand therefore, tax changes are a less powerful instrument of policy than changes in government spending. Another drawback with the tax-cut option is that the increase in spending cannot be focused on UK goods and UK jobs in the way that spending on 'public works' can. Tax cuts in the 1980s, for example, seemed to feed quite quickly into increased spending, on imports in particular. On the other hand, tax cuts may have certain advantages; they have an immediate effect, can encourage work effort and make it easier for people to take low-paid jobs, none of which is taken into account in our simple Keynesian model.

10.8 THE BALANCED BUDGET MULTIPLIER

Because the tax multiplier is smaller than the spending multiplier, governments can also reflate the economy by increasing spending and increasing taxes by the same amount. This will avoid a budget deficit, but insofar as the reflationary effect of the spending exceeds the deflationary effect of the tax rise, output should go up. If, for example, the government increases spending by £10bn with a multiplier of 1.43, that will increase Y by £14.3bn. If, at the same time, to avoid increasing its deficit it increases taxes by £10bn with a tax multiplier of 0.43, this will reduce Y by £4.3bn. Therefore, in total, spending and taxing more increases Y by £10bn. This will be the case as long as the government spends every penny that it raises in extra taxes on domestic goods, since that way none is withdrawn in the first spending round. This adds weight to the argument for reflation in a recession even if a government is keen to maintain a balanced budget. It is not, however, an argument for big government, since it relies on an increase in production for it to happen and big government can, by crowding out the private sector and by necessitating high taxes, undermine the productive capacity of the economy on which the multiplier effect depends.

10.9 MONETARY POLICY

Thus far we have been focusing on **fiscal policy**, that is, changing aggregate demand by changing government spending or taxation. However, aggregate demand can also be changed using **monetary policy**: this means changing the amount of money in circulation since money facilitates spending. For example, by putting interest rates up the Bank of England can make people demand less money and spend less, as it will reduce borrowing, reduce the spending power of those with variable rate mortgages, and cut investment spending by businesses (as these are often funded with loans). It will also push the value of the pound up against other currencies, which will also be deflationary. On the other hand, lower interest rates encourage borrowing and stimulate spending. Governments can, in this way, affect the demand for money, but they may also try to control the money supply directly; to understand how, we need to consider what money actually is.

10.10 MONEY

In order to understand monetary policy, we need to be clear about what we mean by money. Anything that can be spent is money. Cash is very easy to spend, and is very powerful insofar as it can be spent anywhere. It is often therefore described as **liquid** and in addition as **high-powered money** or **the monetary base**. However, despite all the grand titles, most spending is done without this stuff, since as long as someone makes some deposits with a bank or building society they can draw on that money (or someone else can when taking out a loan), using cheques, cards, or even electronic transfer. Because of this variety of forms of money there are different definitions of the amount of money (the money supply) in the economy, from 'M0' (which is just cash) to 'M3H' (which includes all sorts of deposits with banks and building societies). So, that explains what it is, but where does it come from? People tend to assume that it all comes from the government since they are in charge of printing notes and pressing coins; however, banks can create money too, because they only have to keep a small fraction of deposits in their tills to cover any cash withdrawals. How much they keep on hand is called the **cash reserve ratio**. If, for example, a deposit of £1,000 is made, the bank may keep 10% in cash (in practice it is much less), which means keeping £100 sitting idle in the tills and lending the remaining £900 to someone. In doing this, the bank earns interest on the loan that exceeds the savings rate they pay to depositors. However, the person taking out the loan will spend it, perhaps they buy a car from Frank Butcher. If they do then Mr Butcher will be able to deposit the £900 with the rest of his day's takings in his bank, which in turn keeps 10% as cash and lends £810 to someone else, and so on in a sequence summarised in Table 10.3.

Table 10.3
Money supply.

	Money supply (deposits) in existence
Original deposit	£1,000
Frank Butcher's deposit	£1,900
The next deposit	£2,710
The next . . .	£3,440

At each stage the amount of money available for spending goes up; after three rounds it is £3,440, but eventually it will be £10,000. One deposit of £1,000 will ultimately increase the money supply by ten thousand pounds; there is clearly a multiplier process involved.

10.11 MONEY MULTIPLIER

In fact, we can see that the money supply rises by 10 times the original amount of cash (the monetary base). In other words, there is a money multiplier the size of which is determined by the reserve ratio:

Money multiplier = 1/b   (where b = banks' cash reserve ratio)

In the case above, the money multiplier is 1/0.1 = 10. In practice, it is more complicated since not every pound borrowed is returned to the banking system as some is kept in consumers' pockets. We can include this in our formula as follows: If 'c' is the fraction of cash held by the public outside the banking system we get:

$$\text{Money multiplier} = \frac{1}{(b + c)}$$

For example, if c = 0.1 then the money multiplier = 1/(0.1 + 0.1) = 1/0.2 = 5.

As with the macroeconomic multiplier, adding more leakages lowers the size of the multiplier, and again, as before, we can refine this further if we wish by adding more leakages. However, for our purposes this is sufficient detail to appreciate how a government might go about controlling the money supply and what difficulties it might encounter in so doing.

10.12   CONTROLLING THE MONEY SUPPLY

If the government wishes to reduce the money supply and thereby reduce spending and deflate the economy, one option is to cut the monetary base, since if there is less cash to begin with the money supply will fall. The money supply is equal to the monetary multiplier multiplied by the monetary base, and so printing less money would certainly have an effect; however, the main effect of denying people access to the cash that they have legitimately earned is likely to be the destruction of the banking system. Consequently, governments tend to print as much money as people want and focus on other ways of managing the economy. Another option is to try to control 'b' and this has been tried; before 1971, for example, banks were required to keep 8% cash reserves. However, the Bank of England is committed to keeping the system liquid, which makes it very difficult to stop banks calling on them for cash and thereby effectively keeping less in reserve. This policy also creates an incentive for banks to find ways around the controls and, because financial intermediaries can produce services in a number of different ways, in this business: 'To target is to distort' as Charles Goodhart put it. Another alternative for the government is to try to persuade banks to cut their lending (or increase it if reflation is required). But although all governments bring pressure to bear on banks their success in this is limited, as what banks do is ultimately driven by the need to make profit. Another alternative that has been tried is for the government to reduce the PSBR, for if budget deficits are financed through the banking system this will increase the money supply. Generally, however, a lot of it is raised directly from the public in the form of receipts from National Savings, which means that reducing the PSBR is usually not a particularly powerful tool for controlling the money supply. Finally, the government can raise interest rates to reduce the demand for money and cut spending or lower interest rates to increase it. Since the 80s, this has been the primary tool of monetary policy, but recently, control over interest rates has been passed to the Bank of England on the understanding that they are used solely to ensure that inflation is kept within its target range. To this end, they have recently put interest rates up, since, as we shall see, too much spending is inflationary.

10.13 ANOTHER PROBLEM WITH REFLATION

Regardless of whether the reflation is initiated by fiscal or monetary expansion, there is one final but very significant constraint that the government needs to take into account, namely the possibility of 'demand–pull inflation' occurring before we get to full employment; that, in other words, P rises rather than Q. This means that although nominal national income will go up, real income, output and thus employment will be unaltered. For Keynes writing about the Depression inflation was not seen as a major constraint on expansion. Although he recognised that even in a recession there would be some 'bottleneck' industries where workers were in short supply, he believed that the vast majority of firms would deal with an expansion of demand during such times by hiring more workers and expanding production, not by raising prices. We can picture this in terms of aggregate supply and demand as moving from 'a' to 'b' (Figure 10.10). If, however, we start from 'c' we can see that the same rise in demand, in this case to 'd', does nothing but pull prices up since firms are already working flat out, and if prices on average rise we have inflation. But even before we get to full employment, we can see that a rise in demand from 'b' to 'c' has some inflationary impact. This may not look like a major problem in terms of this diagram. However, it can lead to a wage–price spiral with workers seeking higher wages to pay for the higher prices and firms seeking higher prices to compensate for the rising wages. In such cases, inflation can rapidly get out of hand. In response, therefore, governments tend to stop reflating, before we get to full employment even when inflation is only of the order of a few percent per annum.

Figure 10.10
Increasing AD can be inflationary.

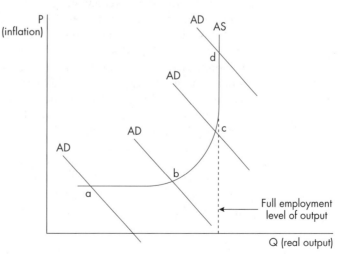

The different methods employed by economists

The contrast between the way Keynes approached the analysis of the Great Depression and those of the neo-classical economists of his day is clear. They looked at markets and took as their starting point individual behaviour. They believed that ultimately they could show how the economy works by reference only to the natural order (of scarcity), and to people's innate psychological givens, such as self-interest. He looked at how everything worked together in the implicit belief that this was somehow greater than, or at least different from, the sum of the parts. The neo-classical method that has since been labelled 'methodological individualism' by Schumpeter (1883–1950) can be compared with Keynes' approach by looking at the 'paradox of thrift'. This paradox occurs when an increase in savings, which as an individual act is expected to increase our wealth, produces the opposite effect if we all do it when it pushes the economy into recession. In such a case, what is rational for an individual becomes irrational for all individuals taken as a whole. We encounter a similar problem in looking at supply curves.

As we have already noted, the elasticity of supply will be affected by how many suppliers wish to increase supply. If many do, then the costs of inputs may rise since they will be fighting for the same resources, so that individual plans become affected by how many firms share the same plan. Keynes was not the only one to adopt a more methodologically holistic approach; other less famous economists of his generation did and Karl Marx (1818–83) and David Ricardo (1772–1823) had both done so some time before. These thinkers can usually be spotted by the fact that they tend to announce their work as grand theories that encompass the way everything works (albeit at the expense of some detail). In addition to these, there is an approach that falls somewhere between holism and individualism, called institutionalism, which we shall look at in Chapter 16. Institutionalists emphasise the importance of looking at how institutions such as established arrangements of power, behaving, and thinking are crucial to understanding the economy, and more broadly for understanding the business environment and firms' relationship to it.

10.14 UK ECONOMIC POLICY SINCE THE WAR

To discuss the path of economic policy since the war we will use the aggregate supply and demand diagram (Figure 10.11), but before we proceed, we need to mention some of the specific terms that apply to it. Firstly, while the level of P is not very interesting, increases in it are, since that is inflation and, as discussed in the appendix, there are a number of problems associated with this. Q shows us how many things are produced in the economy in a given period, but again that is not very interesting in itself. The real output of the economy is, however, interesting insofar as if it goes up, which it will if the equilibrium moves rightward on the graph, then the economy is growing, and our material wealth is increasing. If, on the other hand, it falls for half a year or more then we have a recession, and *ceteris paribus* a recession will create 'demand deficient' unemployment; indeed, this is the major cause of unemployment in the UK today.

After World War II, Keynesians (Keynes died in 1946) argued that if aggregate demand could be used effectively to cure depressions then it could be used to iron out the smaller, but still undesirable swings in economic activity, known as the **business cycle**. This cycle has pushed economies from boom to recession every decade or so, since records began, and it is something that

Figure 10.11 The various possible outcomes for growth and inflation.

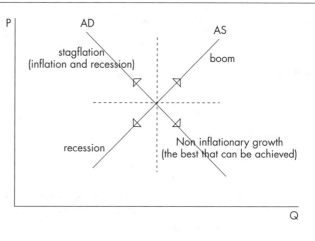

since the 1970s we have had to get used to again. The principle of Keynesian demand management is simply to raise AD when recession looms and lower it when the economy starts to show signs of overheating. This sounds simple enough; however, because the lag between action and impact is generally a few years, the government must act some time ahead if it is to manage demand sufficiently well to stabilise the economy. The Keynesian view held sway until the 1970s and, as can be seen from Figure 10.12, major ups and downs in growth were eliminated insofar as no major recessions occurred and full employment was maintained without raising inflation. Since this time, although it is still true on average that the figures remain above zero so that collectively people become materially better off over the years, we have nonetheless had three major recessions, with output being negative in the mid-1970s, early 1980s and early 1990s. In each case, the result was unemployment, as shown in Figure 10.13, and for those who become unemployed, knowing that growth on average is positive is little consolation.

Figure 10.12 UK real growth rates 1950–98.

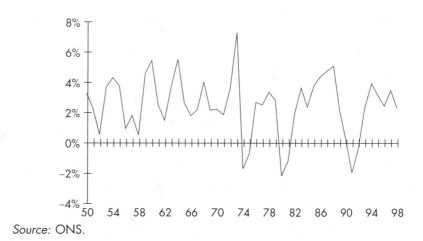

Source: ONS.

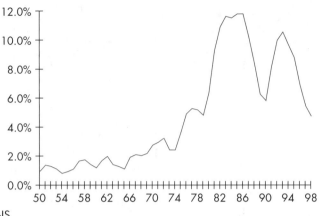

Figure 10.13
Unemployment as a
percentage of the
workforce in the UK,
1950–98.

Source: ONS.

When oil prices went up dramatically in the 1970s, demand management hit a crisis. Because oil is used to make petrol, plastics, and a lot more besides, if it goes up in price all firms' costs go up too, therefore aggregate supply shifts left. The result, as can be seen in Figure 10.14, is more inflation and recession: At the time we had got used to the idea that if demand goes up too much or down too much we get either inflation or recession, but in this case we got both. This became known as **stagflation** as it involves economic stagnation and inflation.

Figure 10.14 When
AS shifts left we get the
worst of everything.

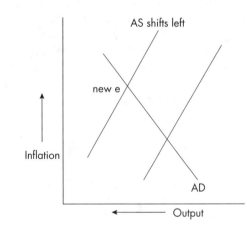

In such circumstances, aggregate demand cannot be managed to reduce inflation and increase output, since raising it will add to inflation while reducing it will cure the inflation but make the decline in output worse. The possibility of such a 'policy dilemma' was first considered in detail by Tinbergen (1952), who realised that one tool cannot be relied on to do two jobs. The problem is that a leftward shift in aggregate supply means that as a nation we are poorer, because we are giving more to the oil exporting countries (which, prior to the discovery of North Sea oil, did not include us). The question then is simply one of how to share out the misery. The Keynesian response was have an 'incomes policy' that, by forcing wages to rise slower than prices, would make everyone a little poorer. This, they felt, was better than letting any one group of firms or workers bear all the burden, particularly as it tends to be new firms and unskilled workers who would otherwise bear the brunt of any such changes. However, the incomes that the government has most control over are those in the public sector, so in effect this policy put the onus of adjustment on them. Given that for the most part they are poorly paid, their reluctance to be used in this way was understandable. On the other hand, from a Keynesian government's perspective it is difficult to see what else could have been done, and so, with right on both sides, the government and the public sector workers collided in a series of bitter disputes that culminated in the 'winter of discontent'. An alternative was suggested by a group called the **monetarists** led by Milton Friedman (1912–) who argued that reducing the money supply would reduce demand in such a way that the effect on employment would be minimal. But when in 1979 the new Conservative government, led by Margaret Thatcher, adopted their policies, they resulted in the first recession since the war, which decimated manufacturing and increased unemployment dramatically. This no doubt led to the clearing out of some dead wood but the scale of the decimation of the manufacturing sector suggests that it destroyed a lot of efficient firms too and ruined the career prospects of a generation of school leavers. So deep was this recession that the following upturn was slow to materialise and eventually developed a momentum that surprised those in office in the late 1980s, which may have contributed to the depth of the subsequent recession in the early 1990s. On the other hand, there was a strand in the policies of successive Thatcher governments that outlived any adherence to money supply targets and the like, which can be summarised by the term 'supply-side policies'.

10.14.1   Supply-side policies

The Keynesian era led to low inflation and low unemployment but in the view of some led ultimately to 'Britain's Economic Problem; too few producers' as Bacon and Eltis (1976) described it in the title of their influential text. There were two main dimensions to the problem: firstly, the growth in the size of the public sector had crowded out private production, and secondly, that what private production remained had become 'featherbedded' and strike prone since Keynesian policies effectively bailed firms out of any difficulties. In short, the accusation was that Keynesianism led to a disregard for the supply side. Renewed interest in the supply side became a feature of 1980s Thatcherism and remains central to Labour government policy today. The aim of supply-side policies is to shift AS to the right. Although this tends to be harder to achieve, and takes longer to work, than changing aggregate demand, the advantage is that it produces non-inflationary growth. As we can see graphically in Figure 10.15, shifting AS right increases output (and thus employment) and reduces inflation.

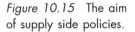

Figure 10.15 The aim of supply side policies.

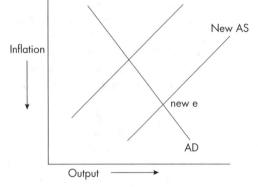

Anything that reduces the costs, or increases the productivity, of inputs will shift aggregate supply to the right. One route to this, much favoured by Conservative governments in the 1980s, is to improve the 'flexibility' of the labour market. This was to be achieved by reducing days lost through strikes, and reducing workers' power to raise wages. The means to this end was to reduce trades unions' power, by ending secondary picketing, closed shop and demarcation rights, and by supporting firms in disputes, most noticeably to assist the employers during the miner's strike of 1984. In support of this belief, Layard and Nickell (1985) estimated that around 25% of the rise in unemployment between 1956 and 1983 was due to the actions of trade unions in pushing wages up.

As well as reducing the power of unions to push wages up, another supply side way of reducing employment was to encourage people into low-paid jobs by reducing the **replacement ratio**; that is, the ratio of income received out of work compared to income received in work. If, for example, social security pays £200 per week and working pays £200, the ratio is one and the individual is less likely to take the job than if the ratio is lower. If, for example, social security only pays £100, then the ratio is $1/2$ and the incentive to take the job at £200 per week is increased. Indeed, if the replacement ratio is greater than 1, we have an 'unemployment trap' in which people are trapped into staying unemployed because they are better off than if they work. However, according to official figures in 1982 when concern on this first came to the fore, only about 3% of people had a replacement ratio in excess of 1, while for 40% it was less than 0.5. These figures may understate the problem, however, since many people on social security may do undeclared work. Nonetheless, the lack of noticeable employment effects from reducing social security payments in real terms confirms that the generosity of the benefit system is one of the lesser causes of unemployment.

Another route to improved labour productivity is to make people work harder or longer, and one way to achieve this is to let people keep more of the money that they earn from work by reducing income tax. To this end, successive Conservative governments cut direct taxation, particularly at the top end, so although overall during their reign from 1979 to 1997 the total tax burden did not fall there was a significant shift from direct to indirect tax. In 1987, the Treasury commissioned C.V. Brown to look at the effects of this on work effort. He concluded, however, that there was no clear link. The final way to shift

AS to the right that we shall look at is to encourage a more entrepreneurial, risk-taking attitude, and certainly in the 1980s the pursuit of money as an end in itself became more legitimate. Lower wages and reduced taxes played their part in this but so did the privatisation programme and deregulation, especially of the financial sector that supplies funds for risk takers.

All of these policies have their advantages and disadvantages but overall productivity in the UK has risen little over the past two decades. It might be that the current period of non-inflationary growth is the result of a supply side miracle and that it will last for some time. However, this was how the Conservatives felt at the end of the 1980s when they allowed demand to expand dramatically and ultimately disasterously. Perhaps we should conclude therefore that creating a healthy macroeconomic environment depends on getting both AS and AD right.

10.14.2 Labour government policies

Although many of the supply side measures taken by previous Conservative governments were not popular with the Labour party at the time, now that we have a Labour government they seem willing to continue with them although the emphasis and presentation are likely to be different. So, for example, rather than reduce replacement ratios by cutting social security, they may look to reduce replacement ratios by making low-paid jobs more attractive to workers. They are also putting renewed emphasis on training as this can increase aggregate supply by making workers more employable. This should encourage employment amongst indigenous firms and encourage new firms to set up in the UK; in addition, it should reduce the tendency for expansion in aggregate demand to lead to skill shortages and a wage–price spiral. Critics of the New Labour approach is that it continues the Conservative emphasis on improving the supply of labour, and fails to acknowledge problems on the demand side, that in short there are too few jobs. There is little of the reflationary job-orientated macroeconomics that characterised the American version of the 'New Deal' of the mid to late 1930s in Labour's 'New Deal'. However, some of the ideas contained in the government's 'Welfare to Work' programme do recognise the need for some sort of push to the demand for labour side too. There are, for example, 'new deal' arrangements that provide a number of links and financial incentives to encourage firms to take people off the unemployment register as well as providing incentives and encouragement for the potential employees. Training may, nonetheless, be in danger of becoming the panacea of the 1990s and may, like previous panaceas, prove to be based on something of a myth, since how much training is required to actually create a job is by no means clear. On the demand side, the main policy instrument is interest rates, but control of these have been passed to the Monetary Policy Committee of the Bank of England, with only one stipulated objective – to keep annual inflation down to around 2.5%. This is a problem insofar as high interest rates tend to reduce demand, and thus inflation, by destroying firms and jobs. This means that unless the Bank's committee takes a broader view of their role, interest rates may not be cut far enough to avoid recession as we enter the millennium (particularly against the backdrop of a slowdown in world growth sparked by problems in several Far Eastern economies). On the other hand, the Monetary Policy Committee is made up of Bank officials and independent experts, some of whom have pushed for interest rates low enough to avoid recession even if it means breaching the 2.5% inflation target.

10.15 THE EFFECT OF CHANGES IN THE MACROECONOMIC ENVIRONMENT ON FIRMS

The obvious effect of changes in the level of income is that the amount spent on individual firms' products will be altered, as Figure 10.16 shows, and as argued previously, spending and income are correlated.

Figure 10.16 Annual percentage changes in real disposable income (Yd) and real consumer expenditure (Cd), 1971–97.

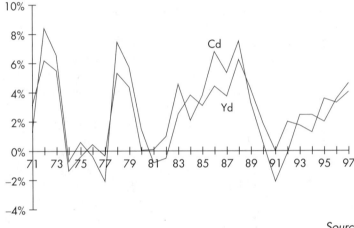

Source: ONS.

So if, for example, incomes fall (as might happen during a recession), the demand for normal goods will shift to the left, and firms' revenues will fall. If, on the other hand, the firm sells inferior goods, demand will shift right and revenues will rise. The link between shifts in demand for a firm's output and its total revenues is shown again in Figure 10.17.

Figure 10.17 The relationship between TR and shifts in demand.

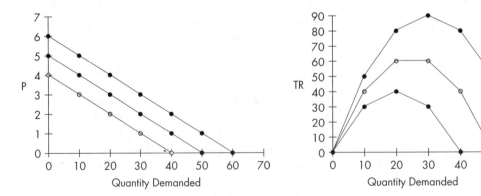

This is important since, as we have seen, national income fluctuates between boom and recession during the business cycle. Firms can calculate the likely percentage increase or decrease in the demands for their products at different stages in this cycle using the elasticity formula. In this case, firms are interested in **income elasticity of demand** or YeD for short:

$$YeD = \frac{\% \, \Delta Qd}{\% \, \Delta Income}$$

If a firm finds that a rise in income makes consumers buy more then the good in question is a normal one, whereas if it makes them buy less then it is an inferior good. Calculating YeD can help firms in three main respects: firstly, to predict what will happen to their business as the economy grows or shrinks; secondly, to find out which of its products are inferior in order to be ready to promote them in a recession, in order to keep the business going when the demands for normal goods fall. Finally, firms can use YeD to establish whether changes in performance are due to internal factors or simply to a change in the macroeconomic environment. If a firm's decision makers mis-attribute their relative success in a recession to their own brilliance, rather than the fact that they have more inferior products than their rivals, they will be caught out when the economy starts to grow again.

The effect of changes in the supply side are obviously important for firms too, since their main purpose is to make firms more innovative, entrepreneurial, and of course cost-efficient. However, this is not to say that all supply-side policies are aimed unequivocally at benefiting firms; Labour's minimum wage may be a case in point since it may both help and hinder firms. The minimum wage can benefit firms in two respects: firstly, by reducing replacement ratios it will encourage the supply of labour; secondly, by raising incomes it will lead to more demand. However, it will also put labour costs up, which, unless matched by rises in productivity, will reduce profitability.

10.16 SUMMARY

- A macroeconomic approach that takes into account the interrelationship between markets can be contrasted with a microeconomic one by reference to unemployment. In the micro interpretation, it is due to wages being too high; in a macro interpretation, it can be due to too little demand for goods.

- The whole economy can be depicted in terms of a circular flow of income that allows us to investigate the role of injections and leakages in determining the level of aggregate demand and national income.

- This approach also allows us to investigate the multiplier process and the implications of governments' attempts to manipulate the economy through managing the level of aggregate demand.

- We can add aggregate supply to this story to picture the aggregate demand and aggregate supply which, together, determine the level of output, employment and inflation in an economy.

● Using aggregate supply and demand analysis allows us to further investigate the benefits and constraints on the management of the economy by means of fiscal and monetary policy.

● In addition, using aggregate supply and demand analysis allows us to see the advantages and difficulties of improving aggregate supply rather than aggregate demand.

10.17 QUESTIONS

1. With reference to the circular flow of income, explain what a leakage (withdrawal) is and give an example.

2. Why do leakages/withdrawals matter?

3. What is fiscal policy?

4. What is monetary policy?

5. What is a government spending multiplier?

6. What is Tinbergen's rule and why is it relevant today?

7. Use a diagram to explain the difference between supply-side policies and demand-side policies.

8. Analyse the consequence of a recession occurring in the next five years on a firm of your choice. What can the firm do today to prepare for this outcome?

9. Analyse the consequence of continued economic growth over the next five years on a firm of your choice. What can the firm do today to prepare for this outcome?

10. The Kingfisher group is a holding company. Its holdings include Woolworth's, Superdrug, Comet and B&Q. B&Q is a large store retailer of gardening equipment and DIY products. During the early 1990s it went through a bad patch. The state of the economy led to low profitability in the DIY sector. In addition, B&Q experienced a decline in its market share. At the time its products were more expensive than those of its main rivals but as Dr Alan Knight says, 'if you believe in what we're doing, shop at B&Q, if you just want a cheap hammer, go somewhere else.'

    (a) What particular facets of the state of the economy in the early 1990s are likely to have been responsible for the poor performance of firms in the DIY industry?

    (b) What factors are likely to have been responsible for the poor performance of B&Q in particular?

11. (a) Prepare a forecast of next year's:
       (i)   UK inflation;
       (ii) UK output growth;
       (iii) UK unemployment.
    (b) Discuss the basis of your predictions.
    (c) Discuss the implications of your predictions for UK firms.

12. The following approximate marginal propensities to save, tax and import have been calculated for the UK:

    $MPS = 0.1$
    $MPT = 0.4$
    $MPiM = 0.3$

(a) Calculate the size of the government spending multiplier implied by these figures.
(b) Given these figures, if the government wishes to increase national income by £10bn, how much should it increase government spending by?
(c) If the government can increase national income by spending more, as these figures suggest, then why is it so reluctant to do so?

APPENDIX A

MEASURING NATIONAL INCOME, EXPENDITURE AND OUTPUT

Figures on these are collected by the Office for National Statistics (ONS) and published in official booklets such as the National Income 'Blue Book', and on the Internet. In looking at these figures we are considering the flow of newly created goods and services and the incomes that are thereby generated. We are not measuring the accumulated wealth of the economy, so we must exclude transactions in second-hand goods, like used cars, non-new houses, financial assets and so on. We exclude these from all our calculations since these do not create any additional flows of goods and services. (The estate agents' fees and such like involved in these types of transactions are counted since what they provide each time is new.) What we are trying to measure is the value of output produced in an economy in a given time, such as a year. We can look at this in three ways: at the value of all output, or the value of all incomes, or the value of all spending. Therefore, we are measuring the same thing when we measure national income, national output, or national expenditure.

National income

This is the sum of all factor incomes, generated in a given period. We include in this people's pre-tax incomes, since that is what firms pay them, and we include any subsidies that they receive from the government since it will be available to the firm to pay as wages or whatever. On the other hand, we exclude the amount that is paid in indirect taxes since that is not available to the firm to be paid in wages or whatever, and we exclude transfer payments since this is just money taken out of one pocket and put into another. These adjustments allow us to calculate the value of income at 'factor cost'. Figure 10.18 shows the composition of income in the UK in 1996.

Figure 10.18 The composition of national income.

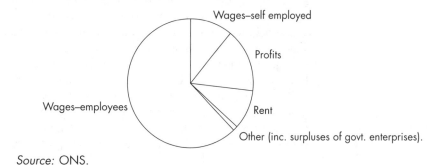

Source: ONS.

National output

National output is also known as national product; it is the value of all output sold in the period in question. Some goods are not sold; for example, the services of the NHS are not bought and sold, but instead paid for through taxation. In such cases, the value is measured by the cost of the inputs, although that may tend to understate their value. In measuring the value of output, it is important to avoid double counting since many products involve the output of other firms as inputs. For example, a car that sells for £10k might include wheels that are the output of another firm, selling at £500 a set, which includes tyres made by another firm selling at £200 a set. If we include all these, and all the prices that firms receive for supplying the car firm with other components and raw materials, we would be counting the same thing repeatedly. We could get around this problem by measuring only final goods, but in practice, it is easier to measure the value added by each firm in the process and then add them all up. Figure 10.19 shows the composition of UK output in 1996.

Figure 10.19 The composition of UK output.

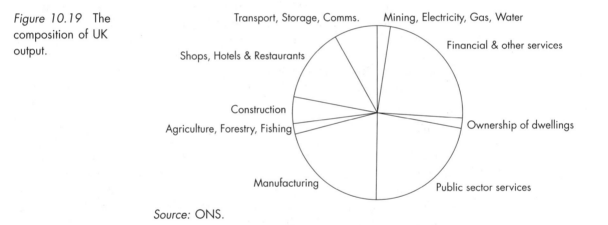

Source: ONS.

National expenditure

Our final way of calculating the value generated in the economy in any given time is to add up all the spending. This becomes firms' total revenue, which is then paid to factors in the form of income. The total amount spent on goods is called **national expenditure**. As before, we need to subtract indirect tax and add subsidies to get the true 'factor cost' figure; and for government expenditure we need to exclude transfer payments. Figure 10.20 shows the composition of spending by category for the UK in 1996. Note that when we subtract imports from exports to get net exports we get a negative number, since imports exceeded exports in 1996; this means that when we count GDP those figures would drop out, as shown on the right in Figure 10.20.

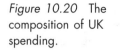

Figure 10.20 The composition of UK spending.

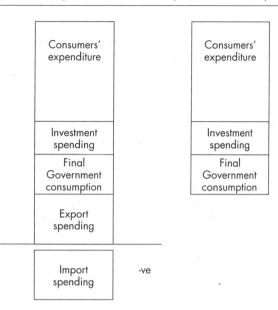

The figures produced by the different approaches differ slightly in practice, as they are collected in different ways from different sources. The income and output figures are probably the more reliable, because income figures are collected by the Inland Revenue and to declare a false income is illegal; while a lot of work goes into the output figures, whereas the consumer expenditure figures are based on a relatively small voluntary survey.

In addition to being measured in three different ways, the figures can be quoted net or gross of depreciation, in real or nominal terms, and as national or domestic. This last distinction sounds rather important but in fact is rather trivial since the only difference is that national figures include net property income from abroad and domestic figures do not.

Problems with measuring national income, expenditure and output

Since these kinds of figures are important to macroeconomic management, many countries throughout the world collect them. We might therefore be tempted to think that they indicate the standard of living in different countries, particularly if we divide the total figure by the population to get 'per capita' figures. However, they are not recommended for comparing living standards between countries for a number of reasons. Firstly, it is difficult to get accurate figures for such big aggregates in countries that put a lot of effort and expertise into collecting them, as in the UK. In poorer countries, few resources can be spared for their collection so they are likely to be even less reliable. In addition, some things are intrinsically hard to measure, such as depreciation. Secondly, many goods are not marketed, and therefore not counted, housework for example. Moreover, what is and is not marketed varies between countries and in the same country over time, so, for example, many of the services provided by the extended family now have to be paid for, but this does not prove that our welfare is improved by such a change. Thirdly, some things are bought and sold but not declared; this is the so-called 'underground (or black) economy'. Again, this may differ in size between countries or in the same country over time. Fourthly, the figures ignore a variety of factors that may increase output but reduce the quality of life, such as the destruction of the environment, the exploitation of workers and other externalities; destroying the rainforests, for example, adds to Brazilian GNP. Fifthly, additions to GNP are assumed to be good, when in fact we may have preferred not to buy the good, so, for example, buying home security adds to GNP although it may actually reflect a decline in the quality of life. Finally, the figures do not show who benefits, in other words, how the value is shared out. Because of these difficulties, W. Nordhaus and J. Tobin (1972) have suggested an alternative 'Measure of Economic Welfare'. This, however, has not been adopted by government statistical agencies since many of the things that are left out of GNP figures, are left out because they are difficult to measure and putting them in would therefore require more expense, and entail more guesswork, than at present.

APPENDIX B | **MEASURING INFLATION**

In general, inflation can be **demand pull**, where a rise in AD is the source of the problem, or **cost push**, where costs rise and supply shifts left. The most commonly quoted indicator of general inflation in the UK is the Retail Price Index (RPI), which is based on a monthly survey of the prices of 130,000 products in a variety of shops up and down the country. Inflation has several effects. Firstly, failing to keep it down is perceived to be indicative of government incompetence and can therefore reduce business confidence. Secondly, volatile inflation introduces additional uncertainty about the costs of inputs and the likely selling price of outputs for firms. Thirdly, if wages rise by more than the amount firms can pass on to customers then firms' costs go up. Fourthly, inflation has a redistributive effect as it makes debts shrink in real terms, which would be bad for savers but good for borrowers. If, for example, prices and wages were to rise so fast that by next year a pint of lager costs £5,000, then anyone with a £5,000 loan, taken out today at a fixed rate of interest, could pay it off next year for the price of a pint. Fifthly, anyone unable to secure wage rises to match any price rises will lose out, and these are likely to be the poorest groups in society. Finally, if we have higher inflation than other countries our exchange rate will fall (as discussed in the next chapter).

Inflation means that the value of money, how many goods it will buy, is falling. Occasionally inflation can be so bad (hyperinflation) that money rapidly becomes worthless. In this situation people have to resort to barter, which is very inefficient, as it means finding people who have what you want and want what you have got. This is what happened in Germany between the wars when annual inflation reached 7,000,000,000,000% (big but not a record). In response, people reverted to barter, and extreme poverty ensued. Although inflation is a concern for modern governments, hyperinflation is unlikely since to fuel it the government must keep expanding the money supply, as no other mechanism can increase AD that quickly. Generally, governments will only do this if they have a political reason for accepting the hyperinflation as a way out of some greater problem. (In the German case, the greater problem was the huge debt that the allies put upon Germany to pay for the First World War.)

Figure 10.21 show the annual inflation figures for the UK since 1950. The high inflation period 1973–83 was of the cost–push variety, stemming mainly from the oil price hikes, but also from the wage–price spiral that this led to. On the other hand, the last surge in the late 1980s came from a consumer boom and is therefore mainly of the demand–pull type, and corresponds therefore to a period of strong growth.

Figure 10.21 Annual inflation in the UK 1950–98.

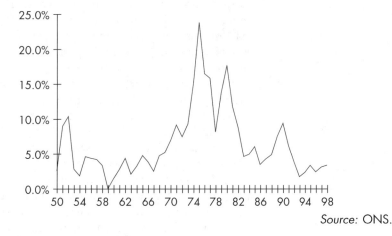

Source: ONS.

Falling prices

Rising prices are undesirable, but what may be less obvious, given how familiar we have become with worrying about inflation, is that falling prices are also undesirable. Indeed, when Keynes was writing the General Theory, the big worry was how bad things were despite falling prices. Although the emphasis therein is on the dangers of insufficient demand, falling prices can be a problem in themselves since they mean that real debts get bigger. A 25-year mortgage loan for £50,000 today might not be much of a burden for the average house buyer. However, if all prices and wages fall for each of the next 25 years then by the time this debt has to be paid off £50,000 could be a fortune. The same would, of course, apply to firms, who in such a world would be very wary of borrowing to fund anything but the shortest of investment projects. In addition, if prices are falling consumers will tend to wait for further falls before spending and any such delay will reduce aggregate demand. However, since the end of the Great Depression, inflation has been the rule in the West and it is hard to imagine that we would accept falling wages these days even if prices fell first. Nonetheless, we cannot entirely rule out the possibility of a period of **disinflation**, (sometimes referred to as 'deflation', but as this also means to slow the economy down the term disinflation is used here). After all, world commodity prices are currently falling, there is excess supply in the car market that should push prices down and the Far Eastern economies are moving into recession, which may force them to become even more cost competitive than they currently are. If in the unlikely event that disinflation does take hold, it will be the lot of the economist to point out that generally falling prices can be as bad as generally rising prices.

Measuring unemployment

The new Labour government prefers figures on the number of people actively seeking work compiled from the 'Labour Force Survey', but in the past, the figures related to people claiming unemployment benefit. However, regular redefinitions have made the unemployment total smaller, which should be borne in mind when looking at past figures. Previous governments also reduced the unemployment count by creating a financial incentive for people to move from the unemployment register to the sick register. Despite the adjustments, a clear rise in unemployment can nonetheless be seen in the official figures as shown previously in Figure 10.13, with particular bulges in the early 1980s and early 1990s.

Unemployment can be caused by a number of things. Firstly, it could simply reflect time spent on benefit looking for the right job. If benefits are generous or last a long time, this 'frictional unemployment' will go up. Secondly, it might be that someone is unemployed for a part of each year. This kind of 'seasonal unemployment' is common amongst those living in holiday areas such as Cornwall. Thirdly, 'structural unemployment' can result when the structure of industry changes; the increasing exposure of the UK to competition from the Far East for example has had a significant effect on many traditional industries in the UK. In addition, there may be changes that simply reflect declining demand; for an industry's output for example, a fall in the demand for coal is partly the result of a straightforward decline in its use, as well as subsidised competition from abroad. Again, there may be a regional dimension to this; in the case of coal, for example, a lot of the jobs were lost in South Wales. Fourthly, we might find an element of 'technological unemployment', where improvements in technology reduce the demand for labour. This does not mean that technological progress must reduce employment, since by reducing costs it can shift supply to the right and thereby encourage demand for the product, and thus possibly result in more jobs, not fewer. Today, for example, cars are produced using technology undreamed of 100 years ago, but the demand for cars, and the number of car workers employed, is much greater now than it was then. Fifthly, unemployment can result from an increase in labour supply if this does not lead to a fall in wages. An increase in supply may be due to demographic changes or the entry of new participants in the labour market. In the 1980s, for example, there was both a rise in female labour market participation rates and a bulge in the population of working age. Sixthly, unemployment can result from wages being driven above the labour market equilibrium. This, of course, was the explanation for unemployment that dominated before Keynes. However, although his work showed that it was not the main cause of the mass unemployment of the Depression, it cannot be dismissed entirely, as mentioned previously, Layard and Nickell's (1985) calculations suggest that it may have accounted for a quarter of the rise in unemployment from 1956–83. Finally, and according to the statistical evidence the main cause of unemployment in the UK, we have the Keynesian 'demand deficient' unemployment, which results from a reduction in AD, and in particular from periods of recession.

Unemployment is considered to be bad for the economy insofar as it means less is demanded and less is produced; it is also expensive to fund and administer. It might be considered good for the economy to the extent that if it is rising it tends to reduce wage demands from those in work. However, the relationship between inflation and unemployment is by no means as clear as it appeared when A.W.H. Phillips (1958) first identified the 'Phillips curve' that purported to show a trade-off between the two.

CHAPTER 11

The international environment

After studying this chapter, you should be able to:

- explain the importance of international trade;
- explain the workings of the Forex market;
- understand the principles of the balance of payments account;
- explain the three ways in which changes in the exchange rate can affect firms, and discuss the macroeconomic implications of such changes;
- outline the economic arguments for and against flexible and fixed exchange rates;
- comprehend both the economic and political arguments for and against the UK joining the European Monetary Union and adopting the European single currency;
- appreciate the implications of European Monetary Union for firms.

11.1   THE ADVANTAGES OF INTERNATIONAL TRADE

All economies are open economies, which means they trade with the rest of the world. Some, however, are more open than others, with the UK being relatively open. Although we often get the impression in the media that we are in an economic war with other countries, unlike a war international trade benefits all, as David Ricardo (1772–1823) argued in his 'Theory of Comparative Advantage'. In this, Ricardo shows that even countries with no absolute advantage in anything benefit by trading since it allows them to focus on what they do best, in other words on what they have a comparative advantage in, as discussed in a different context in Chapter 1. This is not to say that international trade benefits everyone equally, or all the time, since individual firms can both win foreign orders and lose out to foreign competition. Confirmation, however, that Ricardo was right came during the Depression when things got dramatically worse as countries responded to collapsing demand by erecting barriers to protect their own markets from foreign competition. Nowadays, in order to avoid this kind of 'protectionism', world leaders meet regularly to sign a commitment to free trade, although most countries continue to protect their industries to some extent, either by making life difficult for foreign firms or by subsidising indigenous industries. Indeed, UK and European support for certain banana-exporting nations, with whom we have historical ties, is currently under attack from the American authorities because it is thought to be harming the interests of the American-based firms that dominate world banana markets. The body that adjudicates on such matters is the World Trade Organisation.

11.2   EXCHANGE RATES

Different countries have different currencies, so if they are to trade, then they must use each other's currencies in order to buy each other's goods, services and assets. This means that they need to exchange currencies, pounds (£) for dollars ($), yen (¥), German marks (DM), or whatever. This means that there is a market for pounds for foreign exchange (Forex market) as shown in Figure 11.1 for the pound and US dollar, in this case showing a rate of exchange of 1.5 dollars for each pound.

Figure 11.1 The pound–dollar market.

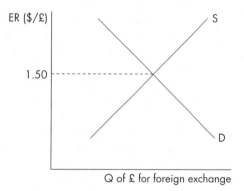

Some terms have come to be used in looking at exchange rates and these need to be mentioned. Firstly, the price at which two currencies exchange is their **bi-lateral exchange rate** rather than their price, while the general term **exchange rate** usually refers to the level of one currency relative to a basket of other currencies. Secondly, if the value of a currency rises, it is often referred to as an **appreciation** and if it falls a **depreciation**, rather than simply saying that it goes up or down. Thirdly, because a number of other countries have pounds too, we often refer to the UK pound as **pound sterling**. It should also be noted that the supply and demand drawn in Figure 11.1 relates to the money required to do transactions, which means that they are not supply and demand curves in the usual sense. Fortunately, this does not matter for the limited uses to which we will put this diagram in what follows.

The supply of pounds in the markets for foreign exchange comes from people who want foreign currencies to buy foreign goods (such as a BMW car, or a holiday in Greece) or to invest abroad. These are **imports**. A holiday in Greece is an import since the money is spent on foreign goods, just as surely as if the money had been spent on taramasalata in Tesco. In order for us to buy these goods, the Greeks will need to be paid in drachma. In the case of the supermarket, it is they who do the actual importing and paying in drachma of course. However, in the case of the holiday it is up to the individual traveller to go to a travel agent, or bank, and supply pounds in order to get drachma to take on holiday. The demand in these markets is from foreigners, who want to buy our goods or transfer funds here; in other words, it is for **exports**. In addition some of the supplying and demanding will be done by people speculating on likely changes in the rates in order to make money on the transactions themselves rather than with an eye to buying or selling goods, or investing in foreign countries *per se*.

Exchange rates can be fixed by the government; for example, the government may decide that the best rate in the market above is $1\pounds = 2\$$, and fix it there. Alternatively, they can be allowed to float freely, with supply and demand determining the rate on a daily basis. There are advantages and disadvantages to both fixed and floating (flexible) exchange rates. Consequently, different approaches have dominated the scene at different times; before 1914 and between 1925 and 1931 the UK, and indeed most of the world, was in a rigid system in which currencies were fixed in respect of gold, called the 'Gold Standard'. Between 1945 and 1971 the 'adjustable peg' system was used, which allowed some adjustments, but less and less as time went on, and, having become too rigid, was abandoned in favour of a 'dirty float' (1972–90) in which currencies floated with occasional government interference. In Europe, a new fixed system, the Exchange Rate Mechanism (ERM), which allowed currencies to float within a limited band, was introduced in 1979. The UK entered this in 1990 and left two years later (leaving it in tatters). The ultimate form of fixed exchange rate is to have a single currency, as England, Wales, Scotland and Northern Ireland currently do, and as all members of the European Union except Britain and Denmark, under the programme for European Economic and Monetary Union (EMU). With a single currency, the rate of exchange is fixed irrevocably so that the need for separate currencies disappears.

Whether the UK should join the EMU is the biggest economic decision of our age which will have a profound effect on British industry, whether we enter it or not. Before, however, we discuss this we need to look at how we record the UK's transactions with the rest of the world.

11.2.1 The balance of payments

The balance of payments between us and the world is recorded in an accounting table, which, like all such tables, must balance, although individual elements within it can be in surplus or deficit. The accounts are divided into three parts. Firstly, there is the **current account**, in which we record net transactions in the import and export of visible goods. At the moment, this 'trade balance' is in deficit, but not on the scale that it was in the boom years of the late 1980s, when we sucked in a lot of foreign-made goods. The current account also includes net transactions in 'invisibles' like tourism and financial services (invisible because you cannot see them as such). Finally in this category we have the income generated by international investments (but not the investments themselves which appear in the financial account discussed below). Taken together, these produced a UK current account surplus in 1997 of £6.3bn. Secondly, there is the capital account which is a small category covering such things as payments of EU grants. In 1997 this was a surplus of £0.8bn. Thirdly there is the **financial account** (which contains most of what used to be in the old definition of the capital account). This shows the net transactions in the vast amounts of short-term monies that flow in and out of a country in search of the best rate of interest for deposits that are handled by banks and other financial intermediaries. In addition, this category includes long-term flows for things like building factories abroad, or for foreigners building factories in the UK. Finally in this category we have international 'portfolio investments' in equities, bonds and so on. If expenditure (on imports) by UK residents is not matched by receipts (from exports), then we will have to borrow or run down reserves of foreign currency in exchange for the surplus pounds. This is where the government comes in, and in 1997 the government used £2.4bn of reserve assets in this way. Adding this to the financial account gives us a figure for 1997 of minus £8.6bn, which balances the surplus on the current and capital account, give or take £1.5bn. The third element of the balance of payments is the **balancing item**. This is simply a number added to or subtracted from the total balance to make it actually equal to zero, since the figures never add up, as they are cobbled together from a number of different sources.

11.2.2 The effect on firms of changes in the exchange rate

Even if the UK joins the single currency, before it does, firms will remain subject to changes in the exchange rate and even after entry, exchange rates will still apply for trades with countries outside the Union, since the Eurocurrency floats against all the other currencies of the world. It is important, therefore, for us to consider how changes in this part of the business environment affect firms. Firms can be linked to this part of the business environment in three main ways: firstly, they can use imported raw materials; secondly, they can export their goods and services abroad; and thirdly, they can produce outputs for the home market that are in competition with foreign imports. We can analyse the effect of changes in the exchange rate for each of these using supply and demand analysis; for example, for a fall in sterling against the dollar from 2$ for every pound down to only 1$ for every pound we get:

1. Firms using imports: A fall in the value of the pound makes imports dearer, which adds to the costs of UK firms that use foreign imports as inputs. A firm that uses American peanuts to make peanut butter, for example, will find that the price of the peanuts goes up. The American suppliers will continue to sell it at, say, $100 a batch, but the UK firm will need £100 to buy a batch instead of £50, since as far as the Americans are concerned the pounds are worth half what they were previously. In terms of the sup-

international environment

ply and demand for the output of firms affected in this way, such as our peanut butter producer, supply will shift left as costs have risen, and profitability is likely to fall.

2. Firms producing exports: A fall in the pound makes exports cheaper. A sports car manufacturer that exports to the USA might, for example, calculate that it should price its supercar model at £100,000, which before the exchange rate fall means pricing at $200,000 in America. However, after the fall it means pricing at $100,000. Our firm will still make £100,000 on each car but the price for Americans has halved, which means more will be demanded and sold in the USA. Revenues for the car firm will go up regardless of elasticity (unless PeD = 0 and no more are sold), because the price it receives in pounds has not gone down. It is in fact therefore more demand at unchanged UK prices, which is, in other words, a rightward shift in the demand curve for the firm's products.

3. Firms producing goods that are in competition with imports: A fall in the pound makes imported goods dearer. So, unless the Americans are willing to sacrifice revenue to keep market shares up, they will have to raise their prices, and the demand for UK products will therefore shift to the right. Almost all firms produce goods that are in competition with goods produced abroad and will benefit if foreign rivals lose their competitiveness in this way.

A rise in the pound, as we are now experiencing, will have the opposite effect; it will make exported goods more expensive abroad. It will put the costs of imported raw materials down and will lead to more competition from imports. Overall export spending is likely to fall, and import spending rise, but for any one firm the net effect will depend on the balance of the three effects. Consider, for example, how a hotel in Cornwall might be affected by the current rise in the pound. Taking each effect in turn:

1. Input costs: The rise in the pound may reduce the cost of some of its inputs, such as food, and foreign waiters (there is scope for paying them less as each pound is worth more when they go home).

2. Exports: The hotel is an exporter if it gets some foreign visitors. The rise in sterling will make UK holidays more expensive for foreigners since more of the visitors' own currencies are needed to buy each pound. Consequently, fewer foreigners are likely to be coming this year.

3. Competition from imports: The firm is in competition with imports because foreign holidays are a substitute for domestic customers. The rise in the pound, by making foreign holidays cheaper, is likely therefore to reduce the hotel's summer trade from UK residents.

Table 11.1 summarises the effects on firms of changes in the exchange rate.

Table 11.1 The effects on firms of changes in the exchange rate.

	Firms using imports	Exporting firms	Firms competing with imports
ER down	S shifts left	D shifts right	D shifts right
ER up	S shifts right	D shifts left	D shifts left

11.2.3 Macroeconomic effect of changes in the exchange rate

In terms of its overall macroeconomic effect, a lower pound means export sales are boosted, and in a relatively open economy like the UK, any increase in exports is good for growth. On the other hand, a lower pound means import prices go up, which means we import some inflation but should also demand fewer imports; indeed, if the PeD for imports exceeds 1 import spending will fall. A rise in the exchange rate has the opposite effect; it reduces the price of imports, which is good for inflation, but increases the price of exports, which is bad for growth. Whether a fall in the exchange rate puts total UK revenues up overall depends on the elasticities involved. If the PeD for exports and imports combined exceeds 1 then the rise in export spending and fall in import spending are together large enough to cause a net rise in spending on UK goods. This rise in revenue means an inflow of money, and a surplus on the current account (or a fall in the deficit). The requirement that the combined elasticities add up to more than 1 for a fall in the exchange rate to cause a rise in revenue (and a rise in it to cause a fall in revenue), is termed the Marshall–Lerner condition after the economists who first drew attention to it. However, even if this condition is met there may nonetheless be a temporary deterioration in the trade balance when the pound falls. This will happen if firms have to pay more for their imported raw materials before they can sell the exports they are going to make with them. This gives rise to what is termed the **j curve**, which, starting on the day of the fall in the exchange rate, shows the current account falling before it rises (Figure 11.2).

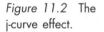 *Figure 11.2* The j-curve effect.

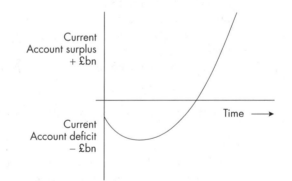

11.2.4 Fixed versus flexible exchange rates

There are a number of interrelated issues in the debate over what kind of exchange rate regime is best, the main points of which are summarised below.

Fixed exchange rates encourage trade

With flexible exchange rates, the rate can be influenced by footloose funds. These are funds that do not relate to imports and exports, but arise from money dealers looking for the best rates of interest or simply speculating on which way the rates are going to go next. Therefore, flexible exchange rates can be more volatile than the underlying trade patterns, and as we have seen, changes in exchange rates hit firms. Firms can insulate themselves from some of the changes in exchange rates by **hedging**, which involves a financial manoeuvre to cover the risk. If, for example, the sports car manufacturer mentioned earlier agrees to sell a supercar to the USA at $200,000 for delivery next month and finds that in the meantime the pound rises, then when it gets the $200,000 it will be worth less than expected. The firm can cover this risk by taking out an option to buy $200,000 worth of sterling in one month's time at today's rate. Then if the pound rises the firm will lose on the car deal as before but will make money on the option deal. However, hedging is an imperfect and costly process, and in many cases impossible, since some options simply do not exist (especially for contracts more than a few months ahead). So, most firms cannot do much of it, and it remains therefore an empirical fact that changes in the exchange rate hit firms. Indeed, the current strength of sterling is hitting UK exporters. The result is that if exchange rates are allowed to float freely it can mean less international trade than if rates are fixed, because firms involved in international trade do not know in advance what their costs or revenues are going to be. This means that in effect, with flexible exchange rates, any firm entering into import or export trade will come under the influence of a part of the business environment that is very 'external', being almost entirely beyond their control with effects on firms that are difficult to mitigate. Becoming involved in foreign trade is therefore a riskier business with flexible exchange rates than with fixed ones, and we would expect to get more trade of this sort with fixed rate regimes. In terms of EMU, estimates vary but it seems very likely that if trading in Marseille, Munich or Madrid becomes as easy as trading in Morecambe, Manchester or Macclesfield, then there will be more of it.

Flexible exchange rates insulate a country from the economic problems of its neighbours

With fixed exchange rates countries become interdependent, so that our economic performance has to follow that of the countries to which we are fixed. Consider, for example, what happens if there is a recession in Europe, which reduces the demand for our exports, as shown in Figure 11.3.

With a fixed exchange rate regime, we get a surplus of pounds equal to the gap between 'a' and 'b', since the fixed rate is now above the equilibrium. In response to this the Bank of England will sell foreign currency for pounds. In effect, it will demand the pounds that nobody else wants by drawing on the UK's foreign exchange reserves (or even gold if need be). But these reserves will not last long. Indeed, in 1931, when the UK returned to the Gold

Figure 11.3 Fixed exchange rates mean that our neighbour's problems become our problems.

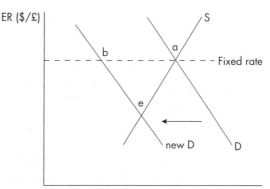

Number of pounds for foreign exchange.

Standard at too high a rate, we literally ran out of gold, and in 1992, the government, facing a similar unsustainable drain, decided to pull out of the ERM rather than fight a losing battle. Ultimately therefore, if the government is locked into an exchange rate that is too high, its only long-term solution is to raise interest rates to attract foreign funds and deflate the economy, since the rise in interest rates will reduce consumers' spending on imports. This will shift supply left, making 'b' the equilibrium, but the side effect is that the UK catches the recession that is affecting the rest of Europe. In 1992 the option of further interest rate rises was ruled out since we were already in a recession. In general, we can conclude that with fixed exchange rates the whole economy has to adjust to suit the exchange rate, which makes the economy open to recessionary, or indeed reflationary, pressure from outside. In contrast, with flexible exchange rates, the domestic economy is more insulated from outside shocks. In the case of Figure 11.3 the European recession would lead to less demand for UK exports, and thus less demand for sterling and a 'depreciation' in the ER to 'e'. This depreciation will make exports cheaper, and therefore, some more are sold (compared to 'b'), and we thereby escape the full effect of the recession.

With flexible exchange rates a country can pursue its own path to prosperity

With flexible exchange rates insulating it from the performance of its neighbours, there is more scope for a country to pursue policies that are different from those of its neighbours. It can, for example, expand faster than them, whereas with fixed exchange rates, if a country reflates faster than its neighbours it will suck in imports, develop a trade deficit, and ultimately have to deflate the economy to eliminate it. With flexible exchange rates the adjustment falls on the exchange rate, as this falls as the supply of pounds rises when the desire for imports grows. Indeed, even if the expansion leads to more inflation in one country than another, with flexible exchange rates the adjustment will tend, in the long run, to maintain the 'purchasing power parity' of different currencies so that competitiveness is unaffected. Consider, for example, what happens to the sports car manufacturer mentioned earlier when prices in the UK double. If the firm normally sells its cars for £100,000 then if the exchange rate is 1£ = 2$ it will need to sell them at $200,000 in the USA. If the exchange rate is fixed and UK prices double they will be selling the cars at £200,000 in the UK; however, that means they need to sell at $400,000 in the USA. The price as far as the Americans are concerned has doubled, and the UK has therefore lost competitiveness. On the other hand, with flexible exchange rates the inflation of pounds means that each is worth less. In fact, each is worth half what it was in terms of how many goods can be purchased with it, or put another way, more are needed to buy the same value of imports. The extra supply pushes the exchange rate down to 1£ = 1$, so that the £200,000 car will therefore continue to sell at $200,000 in the USA. In this way our international competitiveness is maintained and we can have a higher inflation rate than our trading partners if we want to, since real (after inflation) exchange rates and their purchasing powers are maintained by the movement in the exchange rate, although never as neatly as this story suggests.

11.2.5 Government policy in an open economy

One implication of the effect of inflation on the real costs of imports and exports is that we need to look at real (inflation removed) exchange rates to see what is happening to our competitiveness, which we need to do in this section. If we do not make this adjustment then a fall in the exchange rate might simply reflect a higher level of inflation in the UK than elsewhere, and will imply nothing for our competitiveness, while a rise might simply reflect lower inflation and imply no deterioration in our competitiveness. Figure 11.4 shows the depreciation in sterling in the early 1990s which leaving the ERM allowed. This cut import spending and boosted export spending, and was a major factor in getting us out of the recession of the early 1990s. The graph also shows the more recent rise in the exchange rate that has resulted from rises in interest rates in the late 1990s authorised by the Bank of England in its fight against inflation. This appreciation is currently causing a deterioration in our export performance, which is a worry given that exports account for such a large part of our output. With this in mind, and in light of its success on inflation, the Bank of England is now cutting interest rates, although whether it is doing it fast enough to avoid recession in the next few years remains to be seen.

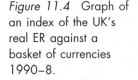

Figure 11.4 Graph of an index of the UK's real ER against a basket of currencies 1990–8.

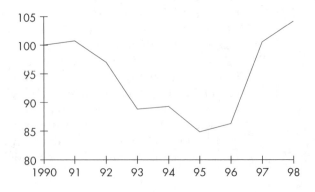

If a government reflates faster than its trading partners, having a fixed exchange rate results in a trade deficit and the economy has to be slowed down again. This was a feature of economic policy in the 1950s and 1960s; it involved a lot of short-term policy reversals between reflation and deflation, or 'stop-go' as it became known. With flexible exchange rates the government has more scope to go its own way, but in managing the economy it may still want to take the exchange rate effects into account. As we have seen, the level of the exchange rate has several effects on firms, but generally a high exchange rate keeps inflation down but destroys exporting firms and tends therefore to slow the economy down. A low rate tends to be bad for inflation but good for export-led growth. So what exchange rate is right depends on the overall state of the economy and whether the government is more worried about inflation or recession.

11.3   EUROPEAN ECONOMIC AND MONETARY UNION

The main benefit of economic and monetary union is the likely expansion of trade discussed earlier. However, the fact that with fixed exchange rates countries must deflate or reflate together means that entering the single currency can be viewed as imposing either an intolerable constraint or a useful disciplinary force upon us. We will look at each point of view in turn.

11.3.1   Intolerable constraint

It can be viewed as entailing an intolerable constraint insofar as it means that the UK cannot go it alone; if we need more expansion (or contraction) than other states we will not get it. It was, for example, lower interest rates and a lower exchange rate that got us out of the last recession. But with a single currency neither option would be available, as although differences in fiscal policy and tax rates will continue for some time, there will be one monetary policy from day one for those entering EMU, with the European Central Bank in Frankfurt in charge of it. This is necessary because differences in monetary policy would undermine the single currency, since separate countries simply cannot have separate money supplies or interest rates, that is, cannot have separate amounts of money or prices for money, because everyone will be using the same money. This is clearly a diminution of our economic sovereignty, although it should be borne in mind that some of this sovereignty has already been lost as the new Labour government has handed control of interest rate policy over to the Bank of England. However, although, the decision over the most significant tool of monetary policy has already been passed to a small cadre of unelected bureaucrats and academic advisors in London joining the EMU would mean passing their power, (and more besides in future), to the

European level in Frankfurt where the British voice would be just one amongst many.

11.3.2 Necessary discipline

On the other hand, it can be viewed as necessary discipline since the central bank that will dictate the degree of expansion is likely to be dominated by the Germans, who have a better track record in recent times on inflation than the UK has. It also means that because of their credibility in tackling inflation, interest rates inside EMU are likely to be lower than we would otherwise have in the UK. A single currency will also eliminate the possibility of countries pushing their currencies down to steal markets from their neighbours, which, if they respond in kind, can create a competitive depreciation cycle, as has occurred recently in the Far East.

11.3.3 Other advantages and disadvantages of economic and monetary union

If it turns out that within the single currency different countries would benefit from different amounts of reflation (or deflation), in the same way that particular regions within a country currently do, then some mechanism for some kind of regional policy for poorly performing countries needs to be established. Currently there is aid for depressed regions and there are plans to correct imbalances by fiscal transfers to accommodate any greater need that the single currency generates in respect of this, but few details have been worked out as yet. Which regions will need long term help is not entirely clear either, since with one currency firms will be able to work out which regions have the most productive firms and labour, (which is not easy with flexible exchange rates) there is likely to be some movement of investment funds that could significantly affect which regions need assistance. One thing that is clear is that there will be pressure on us to raise our corporate taxes, as the relatively low rates in the UK will be seen as an unfair incentive for firms to come here, which means that this particular lessening of our economic sovereignty might come sooner rather than later. In addition to questions about how it will work, there are also some questions about how the late entry of such a big economy as the UK can be achieved. How to achieve it is by no means clear; there are 'convergence criteria' to ensure that our economy is in step with Europe before we enter, but there is likely to be considerable fudging on this with destabilising effects that may not be apparent for quite some time. There will also be adjustment costs for businesses; all wages, prices and thus tills and menus in the UK will have to change. If, for example, we join when the Euro is worth 75p, or in other words when you get 1.33 Euros for every pound, then workers on £10,000 per annum will find that they are on 13,333 Euros, and that a pint of beer will cost E2.40 not £1.80. Since all prices and wages will need to be adjusted in this way, this will take some getting used to for customers as well as being costly for firms to do. However, this is not to say that EMU will not work, since people, and firms, have a great capacity for muddling through. Although we are not planning to enter the currency union for some time (if at all), firms can get used to using the Eurocurrency simply by accepting payments in Euros now. If, for example, you wish to buy a CD from the Virgin Megastore in Oxford St, you can now do so as easily with Euros as you can with pounds and pence.

The government has promised that although we should prepare for entry into the EMU, whether we will enter or not will be decided by a referendum. However, this 'prepare and decide' approach is criticised for assuming the outcome of the decision. There are also problems with this wait and see approach insofar as the Euro is beginning to act as a strong substitute for sterling, which means that if EMU is working well the Euro will rise and the pound will fall. On the other hand, if EMU is not working well then the pound will rise. Either way, staying outside the EMU could cause us to have currency problems, and will open the door to speculative flows of money between the Euro and sterling. This means that although staying out may seem to give us the option of seeing how it works, that decision will affect how it works. The Euro itself will be less affected by speculation, for although being new it is a prime target for it, being big offers it some protection. Because there are currently 11 countries using the Euro as their main currency, it has financial backing and moral support in excess of that of any of the old European currencies, including sterling. This may be of growing importance as the globalisation of instantaneous computer-assisted foreign exchange flows and the sheer size of this market make it ever harder for any one nation to exert any influence. So, unless and until a new order of international regulation is introduced, ganging together by governments may be the only way to reverse any major speculative movement against a currency.

Case study in forming a monetary and economic federation

THE UNITED STATES OF EUROPE

Predicting what further European unification will do to the economies of Europe is impossible since it has never happened before. However, something similar happened with the forming of the USA. So if we combine their experience with some economic theory we might make some broad-brush comments as follows. Firstly, it seems likely that trading in the bigger market of Europe rather than trading predominantly in the smaller UK market will give even more advantage to bigness. If tomorrow's winners are going to be even bigger than today's winners then we can expect further bouts of merger mania, as this is a quick route to increased scale. Secondly, specialisation in production will be further enhanced and noticeable national specialisations may become apparent. For example, the Germans may do more car production, the UK may do more financial services, and the southern European states may do more food production and tourism. External economies of scale are likely to result from such clustering of firms in the same industry in the same place. In addition, we would expect all the economies of scale that would come from this increase in specialisation and size. Thirdly, although national specialisation will bring benefits of economies of scale there may be a significant risk that our sensitivity to business environmental changes as a nation may increase. The problem is that if regions, maybe even whole nations, become more dependent on one or a small number of related industries, then any major disruptions to that industry will have a more extensive impact. In effect, countries will be 'carrying all their eggs in one basket' as the saying goes. Having more variety of firms acts as a barrier to the destructive effect of any

adverse environmental change, since the impact on different industries is likely to vary and thus become more diluted than it does within a single homogenous industry. On the other hand, we might expect that the firms in such an industry would have more power over, and knowledge of that industry's environment. However, they will also then be dealing directly with global environmental forces. Whichever turns out to be the more telling factor, what is certain is that individual national political institutions will be relatively powerless and that the business environment will change radically.

11.4 SUMMARY

- International trade is desirable in the same way that any other form of trade is, and when protectionism becomes widespread, the world goes into recession.
- Because different countries use different currencies, they must be exchanged if trade is to take place between countries. The exchange of foreign currencies constitutes the market for foreign exchange, or 'Forex' market.
- The balance of payments account shows the different inflows and outflows of money into and out of an economy. Although as an accounting table it must balance, elements within it do not, and the UK has experienced significant deficits on the current account during booms because of our high propensity to suck in imports.
- Changes in the exchange rate can affect firms in three ways: firstly, by changing the price of inputs; secondly, by changing the price of any exports made by the firm; and thirdly, by changing the price of imported competitor goods.
- The UK currently has the option of joining the biggest experiment ever in establishing a fixed rate currency zone by becoming a member of the European Economic and Monetary Union and adopting the single currency.
- In addition to the economic arguments for and against fixed exchange rate regimes, entering the European Economic and Monetary Union raises many political issues since it means that much of the running of the UK economy will be ceded to the European Central Bank in Frankfurt.

11.5 QUESTIONS

1. Analyse the effect of changes in the exchange rate on a firm of your choice.
2. Analyse the consequences of European Economic and Monetary Union for a firm of your choice.
3. All strategies contain risks. In international trade there are additional risks to be taken into account by firms, such as:

- Extra political risk – foreign governments have to be considered as well as our own.
- Extra legal risk – the rules that we apply may not apply elsewhere.
- Extra crime risks – new entrants to foreign markets are a relatively easy target.
- Extra credit risk – the likelihood of non-repayment of any loans given and credit extended is greater when the firm has little local knowledge.
- Exchange rate risk.

Given the following information, outline what you think are the main threats and opportunities involved in the following proposal:

> Brewed in the North West of England, McCarthy's produce what are generally considered expensive but very fine ales. A few years ago, they conducted a trial in the north east of the USA. Their ales sold well in this high-profile test in 20 bars from Boston to Augusta. They now plan to ship ale brewed in the North West of England to America on a regular basis.

4. (a) Explain the effects that high interest rates are likely to have on the hotel described below, particularly if the high interest rates lead to a rise in the pound relative to other currencies.
   (b) Explain the likely effect of the UK entering the single currency on this hotel.

> The hotel is a large one near a beach on the Isle of Wight. A lot of its customers are young people from London having short breaks. Many of them will go abroad instead if it is cheap. On the other hand, the hotel also attracts some foreign customers. It also employs a number of foreign waiters and uses imports from abroad. Indeed, its wine is entirely bought, by the owners, on regular trips to northern France. The firm has considerable borrowings on a variable rate basis from its local bank.

5. Recently the chief economist of General Motors (owners of Vauxhall) stated on the radio that if Britain does not join the European single currency bloc British jobs will be in jeopardy. Asked if Vauxhall would be inclined to shift production (and thus jobs) from a UK that remains outside monetary union to a country inside it, he replied 'yes'.
   (a) Explain why he might hold such a view.
   (b) Outline the arguments that could be used to justify the UK staying out of the Economic and Monetary Union.

6. The fact that everyone now interacts within a global environment means that the effect of recession in the Pacific Rim area may be far-reaching, with global recession as we enter the next millennium a possibility. Indeed, we may feel the impact earlier than this, as financial markets react these days to the news as it happens, regardless of where in the world it happens.
   (a) Discuss the ways in which modern communications technology affects the pace of economic change.
   (b) Discuss the mechanisms through which global instability could undermine a local market with which you are familiar.
   (c) Which markets are most likely to disappear if we have a major recession as we enter the millennium?
   (d) What market niches are likely to appear or develop if we have a major recession as we enter the millennium?
   (e) What strategies might organisations consider in order to avoid the threats and take advantages of the opportunities that recession brings?

CHAPTER 12

The social and demographic environments

After studying this chapter, you should be able to:

- understand the importance of shared culture, sub-culture, reference groups, social class, religion and ethnicity on firms, both in terms of demand and in terms of inputs and how firms operate;

- appreciate the importance of the differences between the cultural and religious traditions of different nations;

- understand the nature of the debate on the power of national cultures to resist the logic of increasingly dominant pan-global enterprises;

- appreciate the cultural context of business ethics;

- appreciate the effect of demographics on firms, both in terms of demand and in terms of resource availability;

- understand the importance of particular cultural institutions, such as the family, in shaping the destiny of firms.

12.1 SHARED CULTURE

Although people have different demands depending on their social class, sex, ethnicity and so on, certain codes of conduct represent what is considered normal behaviour within a society. These behavioural norms, coupled with the values that underpin them, constitute the dominant culture of the society. This determines what is ethical behaviour, and what demands are considered legitimate. It also determines what work practices and patterns of ownership are tolerated and thus it influences how the supply side works too.

For markets to exist at all there must be established property rights; you must own your own labour if you are to sell it, the firm must own capital if it is to use it, and so on. There is also a set of shared understandings about how different factors of production will relate to each other, and the rules by which firms will interact as suppliers and buyers of each other's products and as rivals. Some of these codes are enshrined in law but many are not and rest instead on shared norms, implicit understandings, and trust. Even what constitutes a tradable activity is not simply a matter of legal definition but of social and cultural considerations too. For example, in the UK it is illegal for children to work; however, most local councils turn a blind eye to children working late nights in family-run take-away restaurants, or working as carers for sick relatives, because both activities occur within the family setting.

There are three central shared understandings in the organisation of economic relationships in capitalist economies. Firstly, that the distribution of property rights is acceptable. In 1789 in France and in 1917 in Russia, it clearly was not. Secondly, that consumers want more material possessions, since if consumers were to wake up one morning not wanting goods and services anymore then the production system would be redundant. Thirdly, that in some contexts cooperation is seen as the most effective institutional arrangement, such as within the family for example, but between firms we expect (but do not always get) competition. However, the details of the allocation of property rights, the governance structures (that is, the organisational arrangements of power within and between firms), and the rules by which exchange takes place within different capitalist countries result from a continuing interplay of social and political processes. These processes involve all sorts of interested parties, from the general public to organised groups such as pressure groups, the media, government and, of course, firms themselves. That this is an ongoing process means that not only do firms operate within the constraints and enjoy the freedoms provided by the social context, but that many of the opportunities and threats facing firms come about from social change of one sort or another. So, for example, the firms that first identified the rise of the yuppie in the 1980s had, for a while at least, several new markets to themselves; indeed, Filofax had a near-monopoly for a number of years simply from being the first mover into the upmarket personal-organiser market.

12.1.1 Influence on firms' supply decisions

Cultural change can alter supply by changing attitudes to the use of factors of production. Changing attitudes to the use of labour, for example, led to the widespread abolition of slavery in the nineteenth century and a rise in the power of organised labour to, in some cases, the extent of near-equality with capitalists and managers in the decision making of firms. More recently, while Thatcherism curtailed the rise of the power of workers in general, it did not stop changing attitudes to the role of women that have enabled them to enter areas of employment that for centuries had been largely out of bounds. Even more recently, a level of concern for the natural world has developed to such an extent that certain polluting production processes have been eliminated, such as the use of CFC as a component in aerosols, fridges and freezers, and as an input in the production of polystyrene.

12.1.2 Influence on the demand for firms' products

Cultural change can precipitate change in demand by influencing the overall level of spending and the kinds of demands that are considered socially acceptable. As an example, consider gender differences. In this there is an element of biology since men and women exhibit different spending patterns because they are physically different; however, there are also differences that relate to different norms that apply to the sexes. For example, differences in what is considered normal (gender norms) in the UK means that women wear make-up and men generally do not, whereas in the distant past men generally did and in many tribal societies throughout the world men generally still do. In addition, although there has been some convergence in the roles of men and women in recent decades, differences remain. The differences between the kinds of roles that men and women have within a marriage, for example, are still significant enough for marketers to target most of their domestic chore-related products at women.

Case study in the effect of social changes on demand

THE YOUNG CONSUMER

Women have always worked outside the home, particularly working-class women. In addition, evidence suggests that, taking all forms of work into account, women do more of it. Nonetheless, it is true to say that more women spend more time working outside the home today than in the 1950s, 1960s and 1970s. In addition, although the evidence is patchy, it seems that the length of time spent on work by men has also gone up. Both of these have squeezed the amount of time available for childcare and it may in part be compensation for this that the spending on children, particularly on toys and clothes, has risen dramatically over this period too. Combined with the decline in the birth rate, it means that spending per child has rocketed dramatically. Firms are aware of this and much of their marketing efforts focus on this group. At Christmas, for example, the emphasis on toys is unmistakable, but at other times of the year it is still in evidence in the advertising of fast food restaurants, soft drinks, and even holidays. That youngsters respond to this is perhaps not surprising given that they watch more TV than anyone else. Indeed, regular surveys of the extent of TV viewing show that they spend more time in front of a TV than in front of a teacher. The other side of the coin is that where parents cannot afford to give their children all the things that advertisers have convinced them they need, tensions within the family are likely. Indeed, that pressure may induce some to underinvest in their human capital, by seeking the first job that comes along, and may make them more willing to seek illegal means to material rewards.

12.2 SUB-CULTURE

People do not, however, simply accept the norms and roles societies impose on them, so that although we might be able to identify a dominant culture, there will be variation. For example, people have different aspirations and attitudes that reflect their idiosyncrasies and experiences but also the reference groups that they relate to, which encompasses friends, family, social class, religious group, ethnic grouping, or simply lifestyle choices. We can, for example, see a clear difference between the 'traveller' life style and the 'yuppie' lifestyle both in terms of overall levels of spending and its pattern. It would, therefore, be a mistake to view firms as operating within a one-dimensional cultural environment, so, to think of a firm as working within the British culture for example, is to risk ignoring the multiplicity of cultural dimensions within which British firms are embedded. Nonetheless, we can identify such a thing as 'national culture' that cuts across other cultural dimensions, as Hofstede (1983) argues. Hofstede categorised 50 countries according to:

1. the extent to which the dominant culture stresses the importance of the individual or the collective;
2. the extent to which the dominant culture is tolerant of uncertainty (that is, whether it encourages a relaxed attitude to life's ups and downs or not);
3. the extent of power differences between people;
4. the extent to which the dominant culture expresses what might be termed masculine or feminine traits.

In terms of these four we can contrast different cultures, so, for example, a UK firm thinking of expanding into France, Germany and Holland may find that these value collective action more than is common in the UK today and that the individualism that characterised 1980s Thatcherism is less evident. This may affect how the UK firm targets its markets in these countries as well as the work practices and organisation that it will encounter in each country. The French and Germans, for example, are intolerant of firms that hire and fire too quickly, since they view firms more as part of the collective, with responsibility to that collective. German workers are also likely to expect a level of training support, even in easily transferable skills, as a part of the responsibility of firms to the collective training effort. In terms of the second of Hofstede's dimensions, while there are large power differences between people in British society, in terms of firms, while this exceeds that commonly encountered in Germany and Holland, it is less marked than in France. So despite the deep-rooted call to 'liberté, egalité, and fraternité', there is often precious little of it in many of their firms. French managers will expect, therefore, to be treated in a manner that differentiates them from the rest of the workforce more than their Dutch or German counterparts will. In terms of the third dimension, the French and Germans are more control orientated than most UK firms and are likely to expect a higher degree of formal planning and attempts to control their environments as a result. Lastly, while in Holland the distinctions between the roles and responsibilities of men and women are less than in the UK, in France the roles of men and women are in many ways more strongly defined than here. Also, and partly because of this, behaviour that would be frowned upon (or indeed give rise to litigation) in the UK can be a part of the daily organisational dynamic in the French context.

Even how people approach problems may have a national cultural dimension. Adler (1991), for example, argues that problem solving activities are approached in one of two main ways in different cultures. In some, the emphasis is on problem solving, while in others it is on problem accepting. In the West we tend to focus on how to deal with a problem, whereas in Asia and Latin America a greater willingness to accept situations as they are is found, which may be reflected in how firms from these countries deal with their environments too.

Case study

CHRISTMAS

Social changes are often hard to spot since they can involve subtle changes and can take generations to unfold. Spotting them is made doubly difficult by the fact that we live in and are a part of the social milieu ourselves. However, some social changes are very clear. The festival of Christmas, for example, is easy to spot since it occurs every year and is widely accepted as a temporary period of increased indulgence and reverie. This, however, tends to make us forget its importance commercially as well as socially. The effect it has on some products is enormous. For example, in 1997 an unsurprising 95% of annual Christmas pudding sales occurred in the Christmas period. In addition, 85% of packets and tins of assorted biscuits were sold at this time, as well as 60% of cranberry sauce, 45% of port and liqueurs, 40% of loose nuts and Scotch whisky, 30% of champagne, and 20% of all chocolate and wine sales. Because of all year round marketing and the development of turkey burgers, only a relatively small 25% of turkey sales occurred in the Christmas period.

12.3 NATIONAL CULTURE VS. THE LOGIC OF INDUSTRY

The thrust of the discussion above is that there is a multiplicity of cultural environmental niches, so that while a bank in Dover finds it can sell variable rate mortgages, one 20 miles away in Calais finds that it cannot. Not because it is forbidden, but because French culture dictates that the payments due on a loan are established at the outset. Even within the same street different firms can appeal to different subcultures. In south Croydon, for example, there are two shops separated by a breezeblock wall that are culturally miles apart. On one side of the wall, there is a shop that is organised along cooperative lines selling vegetarian food and Buddhist literature. On the other side of the wall, there is a fast food store that sells all manner of dead animals. In addition, it is organised as a franchise, and is promoted as a way to a fast buck for anyone willing to suffer the long hours that the parent company demands of its franchisees. Nonetheless, there are those who argue that industrial production, being concerned in essence with the same process regardless of where it occurs in the world, has its own overriding logic.

There has always been a feeling in some of the leading American and British universities and business schools that best practice was best practice wherever you were in the world, and some influential thinkers of the past believed this, including Alfred Marshall and Max Weber (1864–1920). This view was undermined as people began to adopt a less ethnocentric view of the world and began to appreciate the efficiencies of firms from other cultures, particularly when they began to steal American and UK markets. However, the work of Kerr *et al.* (1973) put this idea back into discussion, for although it could not be disputed that national cultural differences matter currently, it could be argued that they would matter less in future, which is what Kerr *et al.* felt. This is possible since global competition between firms, globalisation as it is known, may ensure that those who employ best practice win, regardless of their geographical location, and that by this process best practice will spread until all production is organised along similar lines everywhere and anywhere. This, as Levitt (1983) argues, would make national cultural differences a non-issue for firms. The fact is, however, that it has not happened yet and there is little evidence that it is happening yet except insofar as the biggest firms are running more of industry internationally as well as nationally, so that what they do, regardless of whether it is best or not, wins.

Case study in why national differences matter

NATIONALITY AND COMPETITIVE ADVANTAGE

In looking at monopolistic competition, location is often cited as a major source of competitive advantage. In any town with a waterfront, for example, any pubs, clubs and restaurants on the waterfront have an advantage over those in the hinterland. What is not so obvious is that this can apply at the national level too, as we find it easier to trade with people who speak the same language and share the same culture. Even if two nations share a common boarder, use the same language, and have a similar culture as Canada and the USA do, most trade is still done within, rather than between, nations. National differences, however, can also be a source of competitive advantage for firms, their different characteristics acting as a springboard for differentiating products. The Englishness of a Rolls-Royce car, for example, and the Americanness of Levi's are part of their appeal. This facet of nationality is apparent across whole industries too. Consider food, for example; there is no country in which all types of food and styles of cooking developed simultaneously. So, although the range of cuisines in any supermarket now encompasses the world, we are all aware that different styles originated in different regions, and that even adjacent countries have (or at least did have) recognisably different cuisines. This means that it is still easier to convince someone of the authenticity of a dish if it has the right name: Patak's Indian pickles, Dolmio Italian sauces (albeit actually made in Holland), for example.

Another effect of nationality is that some things are better done in some regions, or under some cultural conditions. There is, in addition, a less obvious effect of nationality that Porter (1990) refers to in discussing the creation of national diamonds. These are products or processes that, because of the difficulties of producing them in one country rather than another, have, instead of being replaced by things that come easier, been perfected under pressure. This often means they become among the best in the world, in the same way that lumps of coal subjected to great pressure become diamonds.

| 12.4 | **BUSINESS ETHICS** |

One important dimension of the cultural environment is the degree of legitimacy afforded to different courses of action, which means that some activities, even if legal, are considered unethical in some way or by some groups. What is generally considered ethical depends on the norms and values of the society, but society does not provide strict rules for firms to follow. So, for example, every stakeholder in a firm might accept that exploiting customers is unethical. However, that does not tell us whether raising the price of a good in the face of an inelastic demand to save the jobs of everyone in a firm is justified, since this entails weighing one ethical consideration against another. This requires not just that the stakeholders in the firm know what is right or wrong but that they know how wrong and how right, and this kind of calculation cannot be made by reference to the norms of society. So, in effect, while societies exhibit some shared ethical codes defining what business decisions are ethical or not, firms will find that many decisions relate to these codes in ways that are not entirely clear, so that in practice there are significant 'grey areas'. Indeed, the very basis of what firms do rests on an ethical conundrum, since as Adam Smith argued, it is the pursuit of self-interest that produces what consumers want. 'It is not from the benevolence of the butcher, the brewer, or the baker, that we expect our dinner, but from their regard to their own interest' (1776, p. 26). In the modern world, the butcher and the baker are firms and maximising their self-interest means maximising profits. This is not to dismiss the issue of how firms pursue profit, or to ignore the social constraints on this pursuit, as Smith (1759) himself recognised in his 'Theory of Moral Sentiments', it is simply to recognise that there is a social benefit to the pursuit of profit itself. Indeed, with this in mind Milton Friedman cautions firms about accepting ethical considerations that get in the way of the pursuit of profit, since in his view: 'Few trends could so thoroughly undermine the very foundations of our free society as the acceptance by corporate officials of social responsibility other than to make as much money for their stockholders as possible' (1962, p. 133).

The view typified by Smith and Friedman can be summarised as recognising that as long as we value the creation of material wealth, and for as long as it is organised along capitalist lines, then we must accept that the maximisation of profit is an ethical pursuit in itself. This means that the pursuit of profit has a value to be weighed against other ethical considerations. There are, however, some broad ethical constraints, such as honesty and openness, that are broadly consistent with the pursuit of profit, and might therefore be thought of as constituting a set of minimum ethical requirements for business. If, for example, a firm is dishonest then in the long run its performance will be less than that of honest rivals, as those with whom it deals will learn of its dishonesty and switch to rivals that are more honest since the dishonesty imposes costs on them. Similarly, a degree of openness can be beneficial to both the firm and society.

Although the pursuit of profit can be interpreted as promoting the public good, when we take the power of firms into account (in other words, when we move away from perfect competition), this argument breaks down in three main respects. Firstly, a firm with market power can exploit its customers by pushing prices up and a monopsony can push workers' wages down. In both cases, we might describe that as unequivocally unethical as the costs are clear and the benefits accrue not to society but solely to the firm. Secondly, firms can exercise their power by passing some of the costs on to society in the form of externalities such as pollution. So, for example, although people's desire for cars makes some level of pollution acceptable as the inevitable by-product of current engine technology, a powerful firm can exceed that level of pollution without loss of custom. Thirdly, some sources of competitive advantage may impose costs on society. For example, because one of the main ways for a firm to gain a competitive advantage is to differentiate its product, one of the features of the modern industrial world is the rapid pace of product innovation and change. This can cause a problem insofar as the effects of some product innovations on human health or the ecology may not be apparent for decades, and may be harmful. If, for example, a chemical firm discovers a new chemical that improves agricultural output, the firm will benefit if it can get the product on to the market as quickly as possible. There are some checks to be made to ensure that its effect is not immediately detrimental to human health. However, there is no way to check what its long-term effects are when it is in the environment combining with all the other things that have been put there. So, in effect, the benefits to the firm and the society (in terms of improved agricultural output in this case) appear before all the costs have become apparent, possibly decades before.

The pursuit of profit may also be unethical when the national political context is oppressive, since then it amounts to helping something which is intrinsically unethical to work. With an increasing number of firms operating throughout the world it is worth remembering this, for although on witnessing the demise of undemocratic regimes in South Africa and the Soviet bloc, one commentator, Francis Fukuyama, declared that history was at an end (meaning that the big debates had been settled), nonetheless, it is still the case that many countries in the world are authoritarian. Firms in these countries work in very different environments to those prevailing in the UK. It is not only that they are subject to state oppression, or that they promote it simply by making the system work, but also that they often become wittingly or unwittingly agents of state oppression themselves. In such circumstances, what is good for the firm is impossible to justify ethically, even in Friedmanite terms.

12.5 BUSINESS ETHICS AND THE ETHICS BUSINESS

Firms have been hit by consumer groups lobbying them to reduce pollution, and, as in the case of supermarkets, to use ethical considerations in choosing their suppliers. In addition, we have seen the rise of 'ethical investment' funds in which brokers agree only to use investors' money to fund firms that meet certain criteria. Being seen to be ethical is therefore not only good for business, but becoming essential, and as a result, there is a growing business relating to the presentation of firms' ethical credentials. So, while many firms have found it necessary to change what they do, an increasing number have also begun to realise the value of communicating these changes in the media and through their advertising. Some are even attempting to display their ethical credentials in total by conducting 'social audits' of all their activities.

12.6 THE EFFECT OF FIRMS ON CULTURE

The sources of cultural change are many and varied. Historical events play a part; the shooting of a president, for example, can lead to a wave of social reform and cultural reassessment at the revulsion of the event. Technological change can have an impact; the technology of TV, for example, exposes us to other cultures in an immediate visual way in the news and on travel and lifestyle TV, and this may influence our willingness to be open to different perspectives. On the other hand, the TV can also act to reinforce the mores and values of the establishment, from the moral codes written into children's entertainment to the patronising stereotypes of working class and ethnic subcultures that appear in many soaps. Another source of cultural change is the migration of people into a country, since this brings in new ideas and new ways of thinking and behaving; indeed, many of the new work practices that you will learn about in business school are imports of this sort. Finally, we should not forget that because firms are embedded in culture it is inevitable that they affect it as well as being affected by it. This reciprocity occurs all the time, of course, since firms contribute to the replication or adaptation of culture in everything they do; every sale reflects on what we value as a society, and every order obeyed at work confirms the legitimacy of the boss to issue orders. It can, however, be more deliberate than this, as occasionally firms have to work at it. In the 1970s, for example, the profitability of firms was low and declining, bankruptcy levels were returning to those of the Depression, and trade unions were managing to squeeze profits at the same time that the macroeconomy was doing its best to undermine even the biggest firms. In response, some firms, in conjunction with a number of academics in the Mont Pelerin Society, began to reassert the legitimacy of the needs of industry, in particular of the legitimacy of the pursuit of profit, which had become marginalised in the dominant culture of the time. The dominant culture of the time emphasised the importance of the rights of the individual to benefit from the collective, such as the right to equality of opportunity, the right to work, the right to a living wage, and the rights of workers to have a say in the organisation of production. This, of course, reflects the forces at work in other areas of the environment, so that, for example, the belief in the right to work reflects in part the success of the Keynesian era in providing work. However, for Western firms looking to the docile, obedient and cheap workforces then available to their Far Eastern competitors, these rights were increasingly seen as an environmental constraint that could in the face of increasing global competition no longer be tolerated. Therefore, the cultural change that many firms worked towards and which became the cornerstone of Thatcherism was the expunging of the belief in these rights from the dominant culture. This worked in large part, so that today few would think it legitimate to argue that a firm should stay in business just to keep them in work.

12.7   THE DEMOGRAPHIC ENVIRONMENT

12.7.1   Influence on the demand for firms' products

The demographic environment affects the demand for firms' products in three main ways.

Firstly, the size of the population helps to determine the total number of things demanded. At the moment, the UK population is currently growing more slowly than in the past, although because of immigration the population itself is not declining. The reason for the slow growth is that although people are living longer, fewer children are being born; this largely reflects a lifestyle choice, that people are deciding to have fewer children, although the decline seems now to have levelled out. Because the total evolves slowly and at 59 million seems like an awfully big number, it is easy to dismiss the total population as a non-issue for firms, whereas in fact for some it is crucial. For some firms, having a mere 59 million people in the UK is a problem insofar as it means that they are unable to reach their minimum efficient scale. For them, increased global competition from low-cost rivals makes expansion into Europe, with its total of nearly 400 million EU inhabitants, a strategic imperative.

Secondly, the age structure of the population will affect the types of products demanded. Young people, for example, will have some demands in common with old people but some demands that are almost exclusive to them, indeed there are agencies that undertake market research for firms to pinpoint what different age groups want. The main trend in the age distribution of the population in the UK, and indeed the whole of Europe, is that it is ageing, owing to fewer children being born at one end but more people living longer at the other. This will shift the pattern of demand away from youth-centred products towards mature-centred products. We have already seen a massive expansion in the elderly care/residential home markets, and in future, as the government finds it harder and harder to fund the pension debt, we are likely to see similar expansion in the private pensions industry. No doubt, all manner of other industries will expand while others decline as a direct result of this demographic trend. Firms can respond to this by refocusing their activities, with the more proactive of them being able to anticipate these in some way. Retailers, for example, are having to expand their product ranges to suit the ageing population. This, of course, is sometimes difficult to do within one store; in clothes retailing, for example, once a shop becomes associated with elderly people's products it is hard to redeem it in the minds of the young. So, in this sector the importance of demographic differences means that large firms have portfolios made up of different types of stores. The Burton Group, for example, owns a number of stores aimed at different age groups, including Top Shop, which is aimed at the youth market, Principles which is aimed at the thirty-somethings, and Debenhams which is largely aimed at those of forty or more.

Thirdly, the regional distribution of the population will determine the locations of most demand. In the UK, the population is unevenly spread out in two ways; firstly, the vast majority of people live in towns or cities, and secondly, most people in the UK live in the Southeast and Midlands regions of England. Not only does location affect the pattern of demand but other influences on this, such as class, income and ethnicity, can be cross-referenced by location too, since people of similar class, income and ethnicity tend to live in similar areas. This means that location is a good predictor of spending patterns at a very disaggregated level, which is why firms such as CACI have developed databanks relating people's spending patterns to their postcodes. The main trends in the geographical spread of the UK population is deurbanisation, that is, the movement of population out of towns into suburbs and to an increasing extent into the surrounding countryside. This creates new patterns of demand, for example, for rural housing and for better road links from rural areas to towns and cities, while at the same time it contributes to the running down of many urban areas.

12.7.2 The changing nature of the family

Apart from these population changes, there are a number of patterns to do with the composition of the family and suchlike that have social roots but geographic impacts. In particular, two trends are worth noting. Firstly, high rates of divorce have led to a demand for housing that outstrips the growth in the population, since divorced couples add to demand by demanding their own homes rather than returning to their parents' homes. Indeed, despite little projected growth in population, the government is anticipating the building of four million new dwellings in the UK in the next decade. Obviously this is good news for house builders but has implications way beyond that, since where these will be built will affect all kinds of local services and will help determine the location of firms that gravitate to where the demand and labour are to be found. The second major trend is the entry of women across class divides into paid labour markets outside the home; this has contributed to the rise in demand for convenience food, convenience shopping, and convenient child-care services.

12.7.3 Influence on firms' supply decisions

Labour is one of the factors of production and a change in population can affect the supply of labour, which will affect the price of labour, that is, wages. Fewer young people resulting from the slowdown in the birth rate could therefore raise the price of young labour in the future. Indeed, fewer young people combined with more old people means that the children of today will have to be more productive than we are. This may or may not be a problem; it can be achieved by more use of capital, and with tens of millions of people unemployed in Europe it would be premature to talk of labour shortages, but it does suggest that they will warrant higher real wages than we pay ourselves. However, it is not the only factor involved in determining the demand for labour that we would need to take into account before making any forecasts.

12.8 SUMMARY

- Within any country there is what might be called a dominant shared culture that determines the legitimacy of behaviour, including what firms can and cannot do.

- Springing from this are particular institutional arrangements, such as the family, which have widespread legitimacy and a profound importance for the activities of firms.

- Within this overarching shared culture, there are subcultural differences, since people have different reference groups, belong to different social classes, have different religions, and have different ethnic backgrounds. All of these shape people's patterns of demand, and their attitudes to work. It can even shape the way firms react to environmental changes and the aims of firms, since firms are made up of people.

- National cultural differences exist and therefore firms in different countries are inevitably operating in qualitatively different environments.

- On the other hand, as pan-global firms increasingly dominate the business world, there is a debate about whether the logic of industry is dissipating the importance of cultural differences and creating an increasingly homogeneous global business environment.

- The demographic environment affects the demand for firms' products since demographic changes will affect the number of consumers in total and their age distribution.

- The demographic environment affects firms on the supply side too, since labour is a major input for most firms.

12.9 QUESTIONS

1. Analyse the effect of a growing emphasis on lowering the fat content in our diets on the market for potato crisps and firms involved in that market.

2. Analyse the effect of a rise in the rate of divorce and remarriage on the market for catering at wedding receptions and firms involved in this market.

3. Analyse the effect of an increased rate of participation by women in paid labour markets on both supply and demand.

4. Analyse the effect of paying people to stay at home, do housework and raise children.

5. 'Every day there's some new college report claiming that yet another product causes cancer. They can't all be right.' Discuss.

6. Analyse the effect of an increasing number of old people on the market for health care.

7. Analyse the implications of a low birth rate on markets for goods, services and factors of production.

8. Discuss the differences and similarities in the patterns of demand of the following age-related groups: young singles; DINKYs (Double Income No Kids Yet); young married/cohabitees; nesters (couples with children); empty nesters; retired.

CHAPTER 13

The political
and regulatory
environments

After studying this chapter, you should be able to:

- understand the principal political institutions affecting firms in the UK today, from local authorities to international organisations, and appreciate the increasing role of Europe in this;

- appreciate the ways in which political institutions and ideas can affect firms;

- appreciate the major UK political partners' different perspectives and their implications for firms, including the main tenets of New Labour, and be aware of their pledges to business;

- understand the regulatory arrangements governing the conduct of firms in the UK;

- identify the ways in which laws affect firms, and be aware of the basics of the main laws affecting firms today and of the nature of current competition policy;

- appreciate the way in which the legislative focus in the UK is moving towards Europe;

- appreciate that the relationship between this element of the business environment and firms is a reciprocal one.

13.1   THE INTERNATIONAL CONTEXT

The spread of global competition means that UK firms are open to the influence of political changes not only within the UK, but outside it too. Probably the biggest international political development of our age is the demise of major world empires based on national identity and military power, such as the British, French and Soviet ones, and the rise of corporate empires based on pan-national identities and market power. The British and French empires were run down over many decades with relatively few transitional problems for the countries involved, but the Soviet system collapsed. Historically, collapse of empires creates adjustment problems that are enormous; the faith in markets that has replaced Soviet-style central planning is therefore likely to be severely tested over the coming decades in Russia and its ex-dominions. This means that while their embracing of capitalism is good news for UK-based firms, who know how it works and how to meet consumer demand better than their indigenous firms do, the opportunities have to be weighed against the threat of political turmoil. Another major change that in part stems from the collapse of the Soviet empire is that countries in Eastern Europe who were within its sphere of influence now wish to join the EU. This would enhance their attractiveness to UK firms since it reduces the prospect of turmoil, although it also means further low-cost-based competition to deal with in the short term. It may also mean a reduction in the regional aid available for UK-resident firms since these newcomers are relatively poor and will merit assistance before depressed regions in the UK. Another consequence of the end of the Soviet empire is that there is a reduction in spending on armaments by the major powers as they are no longer in direct ideological opposition. For many UK firms this 'peace dividend' is bad news as selling armaments is something that UK firms do well.

Of course, some would argue that increased global competition is itself the greatest political development of our age; however, looking at this as a new development is somewhat misleading, since the spread of global competition is nothing new. What changes is who is involved and how they are dealt with. Today it is the newly industrialising nations of the Pacific Rim, 20 years ago it was Japan who could do no wrong and had the answer to every business problem, before that the Americans, before that it was our turn, and in future it may be China's. It is important therefore to see this as a long term trend, rather than a change that will perhaps peter out, because the production of manufactured goods using cheap labour is one of few ways for non-industrialised countries to industrialise, while the names may change low-cost competition is likely to remain a feature of the world economy for the foreseeable future.

13.2   POLITICS IN THE UK

While global political trends are important, national differences remain; therefore for UK firms it is the UK political context that we shall focus on. We can picture the political process as a production process in order to give us a framework to work within, as shown in Figure 13.1.

Figure 13.1 The political process of the UK government.

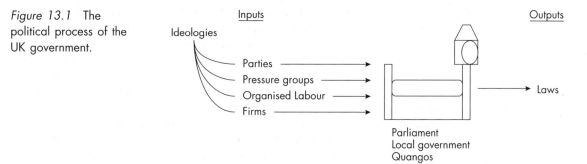

The prerequisite for having an input into the political process is to have some aim, or desire, which we can divide into two types. Firstly, there are those involving the activation of people on the basis of a single idea which is normally pursued through the setting up of a 'pressure group', such as CND who campaigned for nuclear disarmament, and the CBI who campaign to promote the interests of business. Secondly, there are those involving a set of principles for governing, which we refer to as ideologies, and which give rise to political parties whose goal in the UK is to implement their ideas by winning elections and becoming the government. The main ideologies in the UK are summarised below, but before reviewing these it is worth mentioning that these approaches are not necessarily mutually exclusive or clearly defined in the minds of all adherents, since people hold all manner of apparently inconsistent views. So, for example, we find Marxists who deplore the exploitative nature of capitalism but are quite happy to exploit their wives (indeed, some would include Karl Marx himself in this category).

13.2.1 The right wing

In the UK, the Conservative Party is the dominant right of centre party. It was traditionally associated with a belief in self-reliance, industry, the importance of law and order, strong defence and small government, although in the 1950s and 60s it also grew to accept the importance of the welfare state, and the need for Keynesian intervention to keep unemployment down. However, in the 1980s it became dominated by those with more 'New Right' ideas, embodied in Margaret Thatcher. The New Right place less emphasis on the need to provide a welfare state and to intervene in the economy than other Conservatives do, since they believe strongly that markets work. In particular, they reject Keynesian demand management to maintain low unemployment, since they believe that the level of unemployment is determined by the workings of the labour market and cannot permanently be reduced by raising aggregate demand. This means also that as trade unions represent only one side of the labour market, they must be biased against the needs of industry and should, therefore, play no part in politics. In addition, they see the rise of the state sector as a threat to capitalism, because they see the failings of state provision as far outweighing any market failures that they are meant to correct. This leads them to the view that markets are better left alone, even to the extent of abandoning intervention in the macroeconomy completely. Indeed, they argue that rather than dampen the swings of the business cycle, governments set them in motion as they often reflate prior to an election to encourage a 'feel-good factor' in the election run-up. This 'let it be' (laissez faire) approach rests also on the belief that the state sector crowds out private business, leaving too few producers as Bacon and Eltis (1976) put it. This also creates a dependency culture amongst what private sector firms remain, since they will be artificially supported and generally 'featherbedded', as discussed in Chapter 10. This is how the New Right explained the poor performance of domestic firms when exposure to foreign competition increased in the 1970s. We should not assume that because the New Right favour markets that business necessarily favour them, however, for as we have seen more competition is not necessarily what firms want. Indeed, many firms, particularly in the manufacturing sector, are currently calling for a level of traditional Keynesian intervention beyond that currently on offer from the Labour government.

13.2.2 The centre

In the centre of the political spectrum the belief is that markets are able to provide most consumer needs adequately but fail in some respects to promote social welfare, which means that there is a role for the state to intervene. Generally, people in the centre believe that business needs regulating to protect the weak and to encourage fair play and are, therefore, best described as believing in the benefits of a mixed economy. In the UK, the party that traditionally occupies the middle ground is the Liberal Democratic Party, although the current Labour government adheres to many centrist ideas too.

13.2.3 The left wing

The left tend to argue that democracy is rather limited in the UK, since the right to vote every few years does not convey the right to own capital, or to run industry, or the City. The reason is that there is an establishment involving power and privilege that continues to run a lot of the nation's affairs regardless of who gets elected. The members of this establishment are greatly rewarded for doing this and are largely there by virtue of their privileged background. Left-wing ideas are based on the primacy of the need to treat people equally, which generally means that production cannot be left in the hands of capitalists, since most inequality stems from unequal access to resources. Left-wing ideas predate Marxism, but inevitably are influenced by many of the concepts and terms used by Karl Marx (1818–83), because he was so influential and prolific. However, the tarnishing of this intellectual history by Stalin in the establishment of the totalitarian Soviet system has led many to seek a new form of collectivist and reforming ideology that minimises the links to the Marxist tradition, and words such as 'socialism' and 'communism'. This seems to be amalgamating into what is termed the 'Third Way', but which more parochially we might term New Labourism or even 'Blairism' in recognition of the contribution to this ideology made by our current prime minister.

13.3.4 New Labour

There are certain features of the approach of the current Labour government that make it different from the traditional Labour approach, which is why it has become known as New Labour. These generally give it a more centrist appeal than previous Labour governments, which were largely Keynesian and expansionist, which (thus far at least) the current government is not. In addition, while Labour traditionally expressed redistributive aims, support for the trade unions (from which the Labour party evolved), and a belief in the viability of full employment in the UK, none of these are specified in the New Labour approach. As the opening statement of their election manifesto explains, 'New Labour is neither old left nor new right . . . Instead we offer a new way ahead, that leads from the centre, but is profoundly radical in the changes it promises.' Amongst the promises are a set of 'pledges to business'. The following are taken from its 'New Opportunities for Business' document:

1. To set tough rules for government spending and borrowing; ensure low inflation and strengthen the economy so that interest rates are as low as possible.

2. To establish a central role for Britain in a Europe that is outward looking and anti-protectionist.

3. To raise standards in all our schools and promote new opportunities for people at work to learn new skills.

4. To promote the interests of small business, by improving their access to financial backing, more eaective information and support services, and by taking tough action on late payment.

5. To establish a new partnership between government and business to improve Britain's competitiveness, including a revitalised Private Finance Initiative to renew Britain's infrastructure.

One additional aim of the New Labour approach to business and society that is worth mentioning is to involve everyone who is affected, and is therefore a stakeholder, in the decision-making process. Although as yet there have been few new practical applications of this 'stakeholder approach', it can be seen as a common thread running through many of the objectives listed below, which are taken from a number of Labour pamphlets and press releases:

- The economy:
  1. To keep inflation down by passing control of interest rates to the Bank of England and by keeping a tight control of government spending.
  2. To determine whether the UK should join the single currency on the basis of the practicalities, not ideologies.
  3. To tackle long-term unemployment by offering firms a tax rebate for every worker they hire who has been unemployed for two or more years.
  4. To tackle youth unemployment by ensuring that every young person who is unemployed for more than six months is offered training.
  5. To introduce a minimum wage.
  6. To introduce low starting rates of tax and thereby reduce 'replacement ratios'.
  7. To encourage local investment projects by councils through allowing them to spend the receipts they have accrued from the sale of council houses.

- Investment:
  1. To investigate ways to simplify and quicken the planning process so that major infrastructure projects are not delayed.
  2. To reform the Private Finance Initiative, by simplifying it and making clear which projects are to be given priority.
  3. To train and recruit more civil servants able to support the Private Finance Initiative (where public and private money is used for investment projects), and provide greater 'creativity and energy' to it.

- Corporate governance:
  1. To establish an expert panel on corporate governance with a 'broad membership' to draw up codes of conduct on the running of firms.
  2. To investigate ways of encouraging people who are not currently directors of one firm to sit as non-executive directors on other firms, in order to reduce the degree of interlocking directorships at the top of British industry.
  3. To introduce voluntary supervisory boards drawing members from all the firm's stakeholders to act in an advisory capacity for firms, to ensure that a greater number of views become represented in the decision-making processes of firms.
  4. To introduce a legal right for shareholders to vote on the remuneration packages for the firm's management and directors.
  5. To encourage long-term investment in British firms by the institutional investors such as insurance companies and pension funds by forcing them to publish codes of conduct and reports on their voting decisions.

- Competition policy:
  1. To ensure that UK competition policy becomes harmonised with European policy.
  2. To investigate the possibility of amalgamating the competition authorities.
  3. To investigate the possibility of transferring the burden of proof on to the firm that is proposing a merger or take-over to prove that it is in the public interest, rather than on to the Competition Commission to prove that it is not in the public interest.

- Regulation:
  1. To broaden and strengthen the constitution of the regulatory authorities.
  2. To investigate the possibility of combining OFFER and OFGAS because of the increasing overlap between these two industries (electricity and gas).
  3. To expose the firms to 'greater transparency' in their activities; this may include the regulators having access to internal memos and the like.
  4. To expose the regulators' activities to 'greater transparency' by getting them to publish reports on their activities and the rationale for their decisions.
  5. To investigate the replacing of the RPI-x formula (discussed later in this chapter) with something a little more complex, in particular to link it to profits so that if profits exceed a pre-agreed norm customers get rebates on their bills.
  6. To strengthen the regulation of financial services, by simplification and amalgamation of regulatory bodies in this sector.

7. To introduce a new regulatory body for television and telephony infrastructure, OFCOM.

- Education and training:
  1. To cut class sizes to 30 or under for all 5–7 year olds.
  2. To replace YTS with 'Target 2000' in which employers have an obligation to ensure that their young staff are studying towards recognised qualifications, such as NVQs.
  3. To make the 'University for Industry' a major source of adult learning for those unemployed as well as those in work.
  4. To introduce a system of incentives for firms to become 'Investors in People'.

- Transport:
  1. To increase the amount of joint public and privately funded projects for improving transport infrastructure.
  2. To integrate land use and transport planning.
  3. To introduce a regulatory framework for bus services.
  4. To increase tax on company cars.
  5. To encourage more use of railways, and to shift the subsidy for railways towards infrastructure and away from operators.

- Employment:
  1. To introduce a national minimum wage.
  2. To accept the EU 'Social Chapter'.
  3. To work within the trade union reforms of previous Conservative governments, including the abolition of 'secondary picketing' and 'closed shops'.
  4. To introduce compulsory acceptance of trade union membership within firms where the majority of workers vote for it.
  5. To review the workings of industrial tribunals.

- Pensions:
  1. To make it easier for people to make their own pension arrangements.
  2. To simplify and strengthen the regulation of the pensions industry.
  3. To introduce rules enabling people to transfer between pension schemes more easily and to make the costs and benefits of each scheme more transparent.

- Constitutional reform:
  1. To decentralise power from Westminster by introducing elected assemblies in Scotland and Wales, and regional chambers in England.
  2. To introduce elected mayors for major cities.
  3. To adopt the European convention on Human Rights.
  4. To reform the House of Lords; changes proposed include the removal of hereditary peerage.
  5. To review the work of QUANGOs and ensure that appointments to them are made on the basis of 'merit and community representation rather than political patronage'.
  6. To introduce a Freedom of Information Act to allow access to information held by government, public bodies and QUANGOs.
  7. To ensure that political parties disclose the source of large donations.

13.3 — THE CURRENT ARRANGEMENTS IN THE UK

In the UK the main political institution through which these political ideologies are crystallised is parliament, which is made up of an hereditary monarch as head of state, the House of Lords which is largely hereditary, and a House of Commons that is elected. The political party with the most members in the House of Commons becomes the government, and the leader of that party becomes the Prime Minister. It is in the Commons that most of the 'bills' that eventually become law are initiated, and the vast majority are initiated by the government, although a limited time is set aside for 'private member's bills' when an individual Member of Parliament (MP) can propose legislation. This means that most legislative power in the UK results from the winning of the General Election, which is normally held every 4–5 years. In the UK we have a form of democracy in which, for each local constituency, the winner is whoever polls the most votes in that constituency; this is referred to as the 'first past the post' system. The winner then becomes the MP for that constituency, and what they do as an MP is open to comment by those that elect them, although they cannot normally be removed until the next election. Some countries are more democratic insofar as they allow people to vote more frequently on more things; on the other hand, there are many countries that are run by dictatorships, and where comments on issues, let alone votes on issues, are forbidden. There are also differences within democracies on how the voting works. In some countries 'proportional representation' of one sort or another is used as this better reflects the distribution of total votes cast than the first past the post system. In the UK this system is supported by the Liberal Democrats as it would give them a bigger representation in parliament, which their share of the total vote suggests they are entitled, but which is denied them by the current system.

Each of the main functions of the state are divided into government departments, so there is a department for education, a department for economic management (called the Treasury) and so on. An MP appointed by the Prime Minister, referred to as a 'minister of state', heads each of these. The departments are staffed by civil servants who, unlike MPs, are not voted in or out of office every 4–5 years. The Prime Minister and the ministers of state form the 'Cabinet', which meets regularly to formulate and coordinate government policy. Although much of the power rests with the Prime Minister, the fact that the Cabinet as well as all manner of pressure groups, lobbyists, advisors and civil servants have an input into this process means that we often talk of 'policy communities' determining government policy in the UK.

There is also another tier of government at local and county level, which is also elected and to which we now turn.

13.3.1 Local authorities

Local authorities are run by elected councillors, local political parties (since many councillors are elected on a party ticket), unelected bureaucrats and local pressure groups such as residents' associations and local business representatives.

Traditionally, local government in the UK has involved a number of tiers, from counties down to districts down to parishes; however, following a Commission report in 1992 there have been reforms to simplify this structure. The main change has been the introduction of 'unitary authorities' in which the functions of county and borough councils are merged. For many firms this is a welcome change as it means fewer levels of regulators to deal with. In addition, many former responsibilities of elected local councils have been passed to unelected QUANGOs, although, as we have seen, Labour plans some reforms in this area.

Under the Conservatives, power has been taken away from local government by central government. New Labour may reverse this trend with the introduction of regional assemblies and the like (as discussed below), but in the meantime central government sets limits on councils' total expenditure as well as how much they can raise in council tax. In addition, over half of councils' income now comes from the Department of the Environment, and councils can no longer set local business rates. Local authorities also have little discretion regarding the range of services they provide. They remain responsible for the provision of some services that firms use, such as roads. However, the day-to-day management of much of what they used to provide has been turned over to the private sector through the introduction of compulsory competitive tendering, in services such as leisure centre services, rubbish collection, and so on. Councils are, however, responsible for the regulation of local business in terms of ensuring compliance with public health regulations and the like, and by dealing with planning applications to build or develop houses and factories. Other reforms to local authorities include the introduction of competition within the services they provide, with schools for example, and a greater scrutiny of their activities, through the activities of the Audit Commission and suchlike.

Much of the power lost by councils has been transferred to unelected agencies and QUANGOs, to which we now turn.

13.3.2 Agencies and QUANGOs

Two-thirds of civil servants do not work directly for the government but instead for largely autonomous government agencies that are run as private business but with aims and budgetary parameters set by the government. There are around a hundred of these, including the Student Loans Company, the Prison Service and the Benefits Agency, which is the largest. In addition, there remain some public corporations such as the BBC for which similar rules apply.

The acronym QUANGO stands for 'quasi autonomous non-governmental organisation', which describes what they are. There are over five and a half thousand of these in the UK controlling in excess of £50bn of taxpayers' money. They are controlled by committees, the chair of which is appointed by a minister. Many business people are appointed to these committees and it is clearly in a firm's interest to get its views represented in this way. Examples of QUANGOs include the NHS Trusts, TECs, the Competition Comission, and advisory bodies such as the Hearing Aid Council. The main advantage of QUANGOs is that decisions can be taken quickly.

13.3.3 Labour's constitutional reforms

The new Labour government has initiated a number of constitutional reforms; plans include the ending of the traditional role of hereditary peers in the House of Lords, and the introduction of voting by proportional representation in some cases, and most importantly of devolution: A Parliament in Scotland, and assemblies for Wales and Northern Ireland are being established. Even regional assemblies in England are being considered, with the establishment of regional development agencies to coordinate economic development, and the election of a mayor to oversee a new strategic authority for London, being the first steps in this direction. The new Scottish Parliament has been granted extensive legislative powers over transport, industrial assistance, policing, education, training, and even taxation. The National Assembly for Wales has much less power; it has not been granted tax-raising powers and cannot enact primary legislation, and will simply have the executive functions of the former Secretary of State for Wales. This may not seem like much of a change but it will open these executive functions to democratic debate, and the possibility of future extension of the assembly's powers cannot be ruled out, particularly if the people of Wales believe it to be doing a good job. The proposed Northern Ireland Assembly will have extensive devolved powers, including some that Scotland does not have such as social security, but not such things as control over policing and the administration of criminal justice because of its recent history, although that can, of course, change.

13.3.4 Government influence on the demand for firms' products

Governments legislate on what can and cannot be bought and in what circumstances. So, for example, the demand for pleasure and relaxation cannot legally be met by smoking cannabis but can be met by smoking tobacco, but not everywhere, and not if you are under 16. Governments also have a significant role in determining the distribution of wealth and income in the country through the taxation and welfare systems, and changes in either of these will affect the pattern of demand. In addition, governments can influence national cultural values and thereby affect demand. Recent Conservative governments, for example, encouraged the view that people should be more independent of the state and should make more provision for themselves. This led them to reduce and reform the role of the welfare state and has led to an increase in the demand for private pension provision, private healthcare provision, and so on. Governments can also influence the level of total demand in an economy as well as the demand for specific products through its management of the macroeconomy, which can often be politically motivated to ensure that the economy looks healthiest in the run-up to an election for example. In addition, governments can affect the pattern of demand directly through their influence on the public sector, which, as we have seen, accounts for 40% of total spending in the UK. Public sector organisations are especially open to the political element of the business environment as all are subject to debate about how they should be organised, whether they provide value for money and so on, and the way they are organised and even their very existence is a political issue. Finally, governments have also intervened to promote the interests of consumers, through the setting up of the National Consumer Council (NCC), which represents consumer opinion to the government, and through various consumer 'charters' that lay down standards of service, particularly in respect of public or ex-public utilities.

13.3.5 Government influence on firms' supply decisions

Governments affect supply in three main ways: firstly, by passing laws that govern what firms can make, how they can make it, and what inputs can be used in its production; secondly, by legislating on how certain goods should work, so that, for example, electrical appliances must all meet certain standards; thirdly, governments can affect firms' costs through indirect taxes (which reduce supply) and subsidies (which increase supply). Which industries are targeted for this kind of help or hindrance is often a political decision; Conservative governments in the 1980s, for example, were keen to subsidise farming but not coal production because of the long-standing enmity between them and the coalminers.

Although we have looked here at the effect of the political actions of governments on firms, we should not overlook the fact that an increasing source of political threats and opportunities comes from Europe. It is estimated that half the new legislation that affects firms comes from Europe and so, in looking at the political institutions in the UK, we need to cover the institutions of the European Union too.

Managing the environment case study

GENETICALLY MODIFIED (GM) CROPS

The controversy in the UK over GM crops centres around Lord Sainsbury, who has connections with the GM industry and whose supermarket interests are likely to benefit greatly from selling genetically engineered foods. However, the links between the genetic engineering firms and politics are more extensive than that, since they have several lobbyists, advisers and financial backers in operation in the UK and abroad. For example, the widespread initial acceptance by politicians in Britain that GM foods did not have to be labelled reflected the practice in the USA. We tend to follow the USA in this respect since their regulatory arrangements regarding the labelling of food additives is considered the best in the world. The question then is: how did GM foods apparently slip through the net? The answer is that Monsanto, the leading GM firm, convinced Ronald Reagan in the 1980s that adding a different gene to a food is not an additive and does not therefore need to be labelled as such, or investigated by the US Food and Drug Administration. This means that issues raised about it were not likely to go before Congress where searching questions might have been put and media interest sparked. Virtually the only regulation imposed was to ensure safe practice in the process of the research. Whether the final results of the research are safe is what the current controversy is all about, and this is only now being addressed, when already an estimated 50 million acres of US soil are planted with genetically modified crops.

The potential rewards of genetic engineering for GM firms are astronomic. If this kind of engineering works, and has no side effects, all food production will become dependent on Monsanto and other genetic engineers, as will much of the clothing industry (cotton) and the wood and paper industries (trees). It should also be remembered that what we have here is an example of political management of a firm's business environment by the firm. But before you make any moral judgements on the action of the GM firms, it is important to remember two things. Firstly, this type of activity is not unusual or illegal, and secondly, GM crops have the potential of increasing agricultural production in areas with poor soils, which encompasses some of the poorest countries in the world.

13.4 THE EUROPEAN UNION

The European Union began in the 1950s when France, West Germany, Italy, Belgium, Luxembourg and the Netherlands established a zone in which reduced barriers to trade and some harmonised policies on energy and agriculture applied. This 'European Economic Community' (EEC) has expanded since then in two ways. Firstly, as its current name suggests, it has become more unified, with more coordinated policies and few barriers to trade. Secondly, it has expanded geographically as more countries have joined. Currently the members are the six listed above plus the UK, Ireland, Denmark, Spain, Portugal, Greece, Finland, Austria and Sweden. In 1992, all formal barriers to trade between member states were removed, creating the Single European Market. For UK-based firms this has opened up a market of nearly 400m people to head-on competition from us, although of course it also gives European firms greater access to our market too. In 1992, the Treaty of European Union, commonly known as the Maastricht Treaty, laid down the rules for common security, foreign and justice policies, as well as establishing the mechanism by which all member states would join an Economic and Monetary Union (as discussed in Chapter 11).

The key bodies of the EU are:

1. The European Commission
2. The Council of the European Union
3. The European Parliament
4. The European Court of Justice.

These four form the main legislative, executive and judicial bodies of the EU. There are, however, also a number of bodies with specific roles in areas such as health and safety, training, and regional aid, and there is the European Central Bank, which is responsible for the operation of the single currency and monetary policy within the EMU currency bloc.

1. The Commission consists of 20 commissioners appointed by national governments, to specific portfolios, such as transport. The main purpose of the Commission is to make policy proposals which after consultation

with the Council of the European Union become laws. The UK sends two commissioners to the EU, usually ex-politicians. Their role is to take responsibility for one of the EU departments and initiate legislative proposals relating to that responsibility. For example, Neil Kinnock, ex-leader of the Labour Party, is one of the UK's commissioners, his responsibility being transport. After its proposals have been accepted by the council of the EU, the Commission issues then as 'directives' to member nations, each of which must become national law, by being enacted within each member state. The Commission is also responsible for the day-to-day running of the bureaucracy of the Union and it allocates funds to comply with EU regional and social policies.

2. The Council of the European Union (formerly known as the Council of Ministers) is the main legislative body of the Union. However, it makes the laws by accepting proposals from the Commission (which the Commission then issues as directives), so that in practice over 90% of the laws passed by the EU originate in the unelected Commission. The Council is made up of ministers from each government of all member states.

3. The European Parliament is directly elected by member states, with members being referred to as MEPs rather than MPs. There are 626 of these in total, of which the UK returns 87. The term parliament suggests that this is where the legislative power lies, and maybe in future it will, but at the moment it does not initiate much EU legislation. It does, however, have control over the EU budget and must approve proposals made by the Commission and the Council before they are turned into law. It can also amend any such proposals and can ultimately dismiss the Commission if it does not get its way.

4. The European Court of Justice is charged with ensuring that all states comply with the laws of the EU as interpreted by it. Governments, firms or individuals can bring cases to it, and all member states are bound by its rulings. A subsidiary court called the 'Court of First Instance' is used for a lot of cases involving firms, as these tend to be rather technical and often very time consuming.

13.4.1 European regional aid

There is regional aid available from the EU, from one of three sources. The European Social Fund is aimed at reducing barriers to labour market participation by supporting training and suchlike. The European Regional Development Fund is aimed at infrastructure and development projects. The European Agricultural Guidance and Guarantee fund aims to assist farming and other rural industries. There are also specific funds relating to specific technology initiatives and the like. The eligibility of an area for assistance is decided upon with reference to five objectives, as outlined by the European Commission (1993):

Objective 1: Development and structural adjustment for regions lagging behind.

Objective 2: To support regions affected by industrial decline.

Objective 3: To combat long-term unemployment and help young people and other excluded persons into the labour market.

Objective 4: To help in training of personnel and adjustment to industrial change.

Objective 5: The promotion of rural development, either to speed up adjustment of agriculture to changes in the Common Agricultural Policy (CAP), or to support the development of new industry in rural areas.

Currently the UK is the fifth-largest recipient of regional aid in the EU, mainly under objective 2. However, proposed future expansion of the EU to encompass the poorer eastern European countries is likely to see the UK fall down this particular pecking order.

Case study in the power of Europe to influence firms

THE WORKING TIME DIRECTIVE

The recent European Union Working Time Directive requires that (apart from a few exemptions) firms of all member nations do not allow their employees to work more than 48 hours in a week (taken as an average over a 17-week period). The Directive, which has the force of law in the UK, also stipulates that after three months' continuous employment each employee is entitled to four weeks' holiday. In addition, there must be a 24-hour continuous break each week, and a 20-minute break after six hours' work. In addition, anyone normally working three hours or more between 12 a.m. and 5 a.m. must be given a regular health check. The owners of the Royal Hotel, although employing less than 100 people even at the height of the season, calculate that this will add £10,000 to their costs, because in this industry long hours are common. The Directive does, however, provide for flexibility when it comes to seasonal employment, so that the additional staff taken on at the height of the season can be treated in the usual manner. There is also scope for getting the written consent of staff to opt out of the 48-hour maximum. What is permissible is not yet clear, however, as the relevant wording of the Directive is open to interpretation. In addition, it depends on how rigorously the government chooses to implement the spirit rather than the letter of the law. Despite the possibility of dodging some of the implications, the owners of the Royal have decided instead that they will embrace the changes in letter and in spirit in the belief that the more they support the staff the more they can count on their loyalty The hope is that, in an industry with average staff turnover rates in excess of 40%, this will have an indefinable but no doubt positive effect on the firm's social capital. Also, the thought of how much money they will make on the millennium party keeps the owners smiling, if they can get the staff that is. Nonetheless, there are lots of changes afoot in this firm's business environment. In addition to the Working Time Directive, there is the minimum wage coming, which at £3.60 exceeds the current wage of some of the Royal's employees. Luckily, for the Royal those under 21 can be paid only £3 an hour, so in future, older cleaners, and bottle washers and the like, will have to make way for students. There is also a strong possibility that the UK will join the single currency in the next few years, which will mean changing all the tills and much more besides. Added together, all these changes mean that the owners of the Royal, like many small businesses, feel that their futures are very much in the hands of the politicians.

Although it was suggested in Figure 13.1 that pressure groups and firms act to influence the UK parliament, I have left the discussion of their influence until after looking at the European dimension, as the focus of lobbying is shifting to encompass this increasingly powerful super-national tier of government too.

13.5 PRESSURE GROUPS AND LOBBYING

Pressure groups can be classified in a number of ways. One distinction is between insider and outsider groups depending on whether governments typically seek their views as a part of the political process, or whether the pressure group only gets heard when it is shouting loudly in the right direction. We can also divide them into interest groups that promote the interests of members, or single-cause groups that promote an idea. But whatever their make up or purpose, there are a number of ways they can exert an influence; they may have contacts within parliament or within a political party, they may try to mobilise public opinion or have some powerful support within the media, or they may hire professional lobbyists. Clearly, with many levels and forms of governance to deal with, including now the regional assemblies, firms engaged in lobbying will have to target their activities at the right level for the decisions that they seek to influence. However, the increasing centralisation of power within UK government in the hands of a small group around the prime minister means that lobbyists who manage to get on the inside of this small cabal can exert influence on all rather than just a few, major decisions. Above this there is the increasing need for firms to focus their lobbying at the European level, since an increasing number of decisions are being made there and as the continued geographical expansion of the EU means that the power of the UK government to influence its decisions are correspondingly diminished.

As UK firms begin to focus their attention to the European level another political issue arises with which they may have to deal and that is that on periphery of Europe the very stability of the political system which is a prerequisite for firms to invest in a country, may be in doubt. For example, some ex-eastern bloc countries, such as Russia, as discussed in the case study on Russia's economic problems later in this chapter, and most obviously in the former Yugoslavia.

13.6 THE REGULATORY ENVIRONMENT

The main regulatory aspect of the environment for most firms is laws, so although you will be covering the legal environment separately as a part of your studies, we need to look at certain aspects of this part of the business environment here too.

Laws can be divided into two main types, civil and criminal. Criminal law defines the actions that will be punished by the state, such as murder. Those found guilty of breaking these laws will normally be fined or imprisoned, but to be found guilty requires proof 'beyond reasonable doubt'. Civil law, on the other hand, establishes the rules for conduct between people and organisations, and redress is normally sought by the injured parties themselves. Those found guilty of breaking these laws will normally be fined and ordered to adjust their behaviour, but the burden of guilt is weaker than for criminal cases as it is based simply on the 'balance of probabilities'. In the UK, smaller civil cases are taken to the County Court, bigger ones to the High Court. For criminal matters, most are dealt with by local Magistrates Courts, or if they are deemed serious enough in the Crown Court where the defendant's innocence or guilt is established by a jury.

We can also categorise laws according to their source. There are three principal sources of law: EU law as discussed above, statute law as legislated by parliament, and case law. Case law is formed by previous judicial decisions, since by the doctrine of judicial precedent, judges are bound to follow the interpretation of previous courts, and as no legislation can cover every angle there will always be a need for judicial interpretation.

13.6.1 The effects of laws on firms' supply decisions and on demand

On the supply side, laws help determine what inputs can be used, and in what ways. There are laws in the UK to restrict anti-competitive practices, and to limit the exploitation of the natural environment and employees and to ensure their safety at work. There are also laws to protect firms' inventions (they are patented so that copying is limited), and to protect firms' trademarks and logos. On the other side, laws help determine what demands can be met and in what ways. For example, the demand for relaxation and pleasure can be met by alcohol but not by cannabis. There are also laws regarding the operation of markets, what information has to be given to customers, the level of danger involved in using a product, and what can be said about substitutes and complements. All these are aimed at ensuring that buyers are not misled about the nature of the good.

Some of the most important laws governing the behaviour of firms in the UK are as follows.

The Patents Act 1977

New inventions have been protected for many years to ensure that firms continue to invest in new ideas, and the 1977 Act is just the latest version. In effect, patents allow firms a monopoly position in a market if they can prove that they created the product being demanded, and that there is something unique about it. Eventually competitors come up with something similar but not identical and the monopoly power is lost. A firm's trademarks are also protected under the Trademarks Act 1938.

The Fair Trading Act 1973

This act established a role for a Director General of Fair Trading to encourage firms to adopt codes of practice agreed with relevant trade associations. Much of the behaviour of firms is governed by these codes.

The Sale of Goods Act 1979

There are a variety of acts to ensure that consumers know what to expect of products and get what they expect. The Trade Descriptions Act 1968 prohibits false statements about products and the Sale of Goods Act 1979, and amendments to it in 1995, attempt to ensure that all goods do what the customer expects them to do.

The Trade Descriptions Act 1968 and Consumer Protection Act 1987

Both of these cover misleading advertising, and there are a number of voluntary codes too. In addition, it is an offence to give a false description of a good, by, for example, claiming it to be new when it is not.

The Industrial Training Act 1964

This established industrial tribunals where employees who believe they have been unfairly dismissed can seek redress.

Consumer Credit Act 1974

This contains a set of requirements for firms issuing credit such as the need for the firm to quote APRs and for a five-day cooling-off period in which customers can change their minds, and so on.

The Consumer Protection Act 1987

This stipulates that firms have a general duty of care to sell only goods that are safe and comply with British standards where necessary.

The Equal Pay Act 1970

This made it a duty of businesses to treat men and women equally in terms of pay and conditions for work of a 'broadly similar nature'. However, since part-time workers continue to have fewer employment rights than full-time workers do and since most part-time workers are women, we find empirically that they still generally get paid less for comparable work than men.

Race Relations Act 1976 and Sex Discrimination Act 1975

These were aimed at ensuring that firms do not discriminate on the basis of sex or race, with varying degrees of success.

The Trade Union Act 1984

Along with a number of employment acts in the 1980s this Act established new responsibilities and reduced the power of the unions to engage in industrial disputes.

Health and Safety at Work Act 1974

This lays down certain minimum requirements and a mechanism to ensure their compliance. The main mechanism is a Health and Safety Executive whose inspectors have legal rights to enter and inspect premises, question people, take photographs and measurements and remove substances for analysis. Generally, those in breach of the regulations are fined. Health and Safety issues are now largely developed and legislated upon by the EU, and increasingly cover all aspects of the working environment, such as temperature and ventilation.

Fire Precautions Act 1971

This established that all premises in which 20 or more people work must have a fire certificate to prove that they have adequate fire escapes and extinguishers.

There are also laws that attempt to deal with externalities, with action being taken against firms for releasing dangerous chemicals, nasty smells, and excessive noise. Most new consumer and firm-specific legislation now originates in the EU. For example, the Directive on Unfair Terms in Consumer Contracts, which became UK law in 1994, is aimed to counter any contract that leads to a 'significant imbalance in the parties' rights and obligations', which in other words seeks to protect the weaker party in any contract.

13.6.2 The criminal environment

People acting deliberately in breach of the law influence many firms too. In the UK, many small firms encounter bullying tactics and other anti-competitive practices to push them out of a market, while theft is a particular problem for retailers. In some countries the bribing of officials is considered to be a routine business expense, while in the UK, on the whole, it is not, although whether that means there is less of it or that it is just less open is a matter of debate.

13.6.3 Regulation of privatised firms

Privatised firms make up a significant part of the UK economy, currently accounting for nearly a quarter of UK output. They are major suppliers to other firms of electricity, water, gas and communications. In addition, they have many millions of customers; BT, for example, has 25 million customers, including individuals and firms. Since in most cases they were privatised with their monopolies intact, their scope for exploiting their customers, and their workforce and the firms that supply them, is huge. Therefore, a system of regulation was established to oversee them, based on bodies that are nominally independent of government. These were established with the intention of steering the privatised firms away from the temptation to exploit, until competition had developed sufficiently to make this unnecessary. The main regulatory bodies are OFTEL, which monitors the activities of British Telecom, OFGAS, which monitors British Gas, OFWAT, which monitors the water companies, and OFFER, which monitors the 12 regional electricity distribution firms, and the generators National Power and PowerGen.

The regulators' main control levers over their industries are firstly publicity, since what they do is of interest to the media, and because what they do is supported by a number of user groups and government-appointed consumer bodies. Secondly, they have a price-cap formula that means they can limit the price rises of the firms they regulate. The formula is simply RPI – x, where RPI is the retail price index and 'x' is the limiting factor. This limiting factor is set by the regulator on the basis of the scope that the firm has for reducing costs. So, if, for example, the regulator feels that the firm can cut its costs by 2% and inflation is 3% then the firm can only increase its prices by 1%. This creates an incentive for the firms to cut costs and be as efficient as possible. However, because the regulators have to guess at how much scope there is for cutting costs, they started with rather cautious values for 'x', which meant that the firms could in practice cut costs more than anticipated and thereby increase their profits. In response to this, the regulators have pushed the value of 'x' up, but that of course diminishes the firms' incentives to cut costs since whatever they do in that respect does not benefit them. The problem is that the regulators do not know the right value for 'x'. There may also be the possibility that some of the regulators have succumbed to 'regulatory capture', that is, have started to align themselves with the firm, who will obviously try to sway their sympathies, and with whom the regulator can expect a lucrative future career. In addition, since they are unelected and largely unaccountable, being captured in this way does not meet with the same kind of disapproval that it would do if they were elected. For the water companies, rather than an 'x' factor there is a 'k' factor, as in their case they are allowed to raise charges above inflation each year to finance the investment costs that stem from having to meet the water quality standards laid down by the EU. However, again the firms have generally been able to work this to their advantage and put profits up. Indeed, their ability to outwit the regulators and push profits up means that the main beneficiaries of privatisation have been the firms' managers and shareholders, while for other stakeholders the results have been less positive.

For many workers, for example, it has meant redundancy, while for consumers the position is rather mixed. In the case of BT, prices to customers have fallen in real terms, while significant rises in real prices have occurred in the water industry, with few of the promised benefits in improved services or water quality. There have also been significant moves by these firms into new markets, both new areas of business in the UK and the same areas of business in different countries. However, since few of these have been successful they can be interpreted as experiments subsidised by the public, which was not an obligation written into any of the regulations and may be something that the regulators do something about in future.

13.6.4 Competition policy

There are a number of business practices that governments have tried to eliminate in law or to regulate in practice. These include the setting up of cartels, (where suppliers act together to avoid competition and exploit customers); 'retail price maintenance' (where manufacturers refuse to supply retailers who charge less than recommended prices), 'predatory pricing', (where a firm prices well below costs just to force a rival out of business); and 'price discrimination', (where a firm charges different prices for the same good simply to make more profit, not because the costs of supplying customers differ). In addition, there are a number of arrangements that dominant firms can enter into that will shore up their dominant position, and these can be appealed against. All appeals against unfair practices are referred to the Director General of Fair Trading, at the Office of Fair Trading (OFT), who can ultimately send offenders to trial at the Restrictive Practices Court, or the Competition Commission. The Commission reviews the activities of privatised firms and assesses whether proposed mergers, where the combined assets exceed £70m or 25% of the market, are against the public interest, in which case they will not be allowed to proceed. In addition, any abuses of power by dominant firms, defined as those with 25% of a market or more, can be investigated. Generally, there are no absolute blanket bans, with each case being considered on its merits. The tendency within the EU is rather different; the EU tends to prohibit rather than adopt a more pragmatic approach, so over time we can expect UK policy to change as it comes in line with EU policy.

There are a number of laws relevant to competition policy:

- Monopolies and Restrictive Practices Act 1948, Monopolies and Mergers Act 1965, and Competition Act 1980. The first of these established the Monopolies and Mergers Commission (MMC), which has now developed into the Competition Commission. The second allowed for mergers to be referred to the MMC, and the last made it possible to take public bodies before the MMC.

- Restrictive Trade Practices Act 1956. This allowed for a register of unfair practices relating to the sale of goods to be established.

In addition, the EU has a number of regulations relating to competition policy. Article 85 of the Treaty of Rome prohibits anti-competitive agreements except where significant efficiency gains can be made and where those gains are shared with customers. Article 86 of the same treaty concerns the abuse of market power, although in this case it is deemed to come into play only if a firm has 50% or more of a market. These Articles are applicable to UK firms when trade between member states is affected. Two other Articles act as important regulatory devices too: Article 90 which prohibits governments granting special rights to protect public enterprises, and Article 92 which aims to stop governments giving financial aid to firms that distorts trade between member states. However, British mining firms have made this complaint against their European rivals for some time, to little effect.

The EU Commission also has arrangements to limit mergers and joint ventures that are big enough to have Europe-wide ramifications. However, the ability of the EU to impose controls on firms in member states is resisted by those states. This is because in most member states the purpose of current competition policy is not to stop big firms emerging, as antagonism to the abuse of market power is tempered by the desire to have firms big enough, and efficient enough, to compete on the world stage. Indeed, firms in some industries rely on the protection of the states, so, for example, we find that in some countries the state protects firms from competition by ensuring that only registered firms do certain activities. Even in the UK, where for some time we have espoused the virtues of competition, the monopoly position of many privatised firms remains largely intact because of, rather than despite, government rules and regulations. Many privatised firms, for example, still benefit from protections from competition that were established by the government, so that while on the one hand they are being opened to some forms of competition, on the other they are protected from the full force of it. Similarly, while the control of some facets of competition, such as predatory pricing, may limit monopoly power, it tends also to help existing firms protect their niches, and can therefore also be viewed as a form of regulatory protection for uncompetitive practices.

13.6.5 Difficulties of regulation

Defining the boundaries of individual firms is becoming ever more difficult, firstly because an increasing number of firms straddle the boundaries between markets, and secondly, because alliances and tactical tie-ups are becoming ever more popular as they reduce the 'problem' of competition reducing profits. The result of both of these trends is that in an increasing number of cases it is becoming impossible to say where one firm ends and another begins. This also makes it harder for regulators to exert any influence, as generally they act when the size of a firm's market share becomes a concern, but if the boundaries of the firm are unknown such assessments cannot be made. Increasingly therefore, regulators will have to adopt an ever more ad hoc approach, with less emphasis on generally applicable rules and more emphasis on the costs and benefits to society of particular arrangements and agreements between firms.

NATIONAL REGULATION AND POLITICS VS. GLOBAL FOOTBALL. NO CONTEST

How do you get your TV programmes into every country in the world? The answer for Rupert Murdoch seems to be sport. Murdoch has developed a satellite TV entertainment and communications network based around News Corp. Ltd, which can truly be said to be global. The success of this firm, or perhaps more accurately network, is based upon the overcoming of national barriers through the acquisition of the rights to show popular sporting events. This seems to work, as every country, regardless of politics, religion or ethnicity, seems to like sport of one sort or another.

In the UK the fact that Murdoch's firm 'Sky TV' came to dominate the UK satellite services in such short time was a surprise to some, since the UK had an official BSB satellite. In addition, Murdoch was widely regarded as unlikely to get a licence as he would have fallen foul of rules on cross-media ownership since he owned so many UK newspapers. In addition, even if permission had been granted, Sky would have been restricted to a 20% share of the market. But Murdoch out-foxed everyone, by broadcasting before BSB by using the Luxembourg satellite Astra. This allowed Sky to build a market presence before BSB got off the ground and to by-pass all the restrictions and quality programme obligations that were placed upon BSB. By 1990, Sky had consolidated its lead to such an extent that BSB was forced to merge with it to create BSkyB (now 40% owned by News Corp.).

However, having access is not enough to get people to buy a TV service (and the satellite dish that is required to receive it); you need to offer a unique service and this is where sport comes in. In the UK BSkyB's pre-eminence was underlined when in 1992 it secured the almost exclusive rights to broadcast premier league football; within a year BSkyB sales doubled. BSkyB does, of course, offer a lot more than football but it seems that sport is a major access vehicle into all nations. Of course, countries vary in what they like, so that what is required in each case may be different. In the USA, American football is very popular and Murdoch's 'Fox TV' has acquired the exclusive rights to broadcast the National Football League. Murdoch changed his nationality to become an American citizen to forward his ambitions in this market, but does not confine his ambition to this market alone. In Asia, for example, he bought 'Star TV', which broadcasts throughout the region. However, since the day that Murdoch publicly declared that satellite broadcasting had the power to undermine totalitarian regimes by by-passing state controlled TV, the Chinese have placed restrictions on what Star can broadcast to them. In response, Murdoch has done a lot of personal negotiating, a 'charm offensive' in effect, with politicians and has tailored the outputs of Star TV to suit local sensitivities. In our part of the world he already has a huge influence on politicians and the regulators who work for them through his ownership of the majority of the best selling newspapers in the UK, including the *Sun*, while in the country of his birth Murdoch's papers are held largely responsible for the election of Gough Whitlam, who in 1972 became Australia's first Labour Prime Minister for 23 years. They are also held largely responsible for his subsequent downfall a few years later through their vociferous insistence that his policies would spell ruin for the economy, when they realised that he was more radical than they had thought.

RUSSIA'S ECONOMIC PROBLEMS

In this case study, we look at the social, political and legal problems that lie behind the economic difficulties of modern Russia.

Some of the economies that used to be in the Soviet bloc have acclimatised relatively quickly to capitalism. Some, however, are having great difficulty in making the transition to a market economy. How they fare in this depends on the historical background and the culture of the populace as much as on the precise method by which the economies are opened up to competition and the way the central planning systems are dismantled. One of those finding it hard to adjust is Russia. One reason is simply that its size makes the scale of change and therefore the coordination of change harder. It has many natural resources but the price of these is volatile and the experience of Third World countries that trying to grow by focusing on producing one or two primary commodities is not easy. Inward investment is occurring, and this represents one way in which Russia can rapidly introduce the technologies, organisation and management practices that are successful in the West. However, barriers to inward investment remain and political turmoil simply makes investment in Russia all the more risky.

One problem stems from the removal of price controls that result from the abandoning of central planning as this has had inflationary repercussions (unsurprisingly as it amounts to the removal of a plethora of 'price ceilings' as discussed in Chapter 8). The resulting price rises must mean that in the short run at least, consumers' real wages will fall. This prospect has, however, encouraged workers to seek higher wages in compensation and so a wage–price spiral has been set in motion. This may prove particularly damaging in the Russian context since the public sector in Russia remains large and inefficient, with a large fiscal deficit financed by expanding the money supply. This means that there is a risk that a wage–price

spiral could lead to hyperinflation if the authorities begin to believe that monetary expansion is the only way out and despite having recently flirted with it and rejected it; that they might choose this option remains is a possibility since the alternatives are equally unpalatable. The alternatives are to abandon the public sector and allow unemployment to rise or to fund the deficit by increasing taxation (although that could be inflationary too). This may be the best option in this case since currently taxation revenues are very low in Russia as taxation is easy to evade and the whole system is riddled with corruption. The economics of it are clear cut – no country can have a public sector that is not funded in this way, but the political and social barriers to it in Russia; of vested interests and petty criminality are entrenched.

Another barrier to inward investment in Russia is that they currently levy corporation tax on turnover rather than profit, so an automatic distortion is built into business planning. There is also a lack of agreed legally enforceable accounting standards that makes it hard for outside firms to know if they are being robbed by their Russian managers, which means the possibility for exploitation is high. On the social side, there is little social capital in any firm in Russia so any possibility for exploitation or corruption, let alone shirking or satisficing behaviour, is likely to be taken. Another barrier is that the laws of contract in Russia are not clear and there is little legal redress for breaches, which means that firms are reluctant to enter into relationships with Russian firms that would be considered routine in the West.

13.7 SUMMARY

- There are a number of political institutions affecting firms in the UK today, from local authorities to international organisations. Some of these are directed by elected officials, but many, such as QUANGOs, are not.

- European institutions are increasingly important in determining both the legislative and regulatory framework within which UK firms operate, and are also a source of political ideas and controversies.

- Political institutions and ideas can affect firms by determining what demands are legitimate and by determining how and in what circumstances such demands can be met.

- The major political perspectives in the UK can be divided into left and right, with the right more sensitive to the needs of firms and the left more sensitive to the needs of workers.

- Currently the ideas that make up the New Labour approach are in the ascendancy and these seek to strike a balance between left and right.
- Competition policy in the UK is complex and increasingly based at the European level, since the level of business links and trade between the UK and the rest of Europe has increased substantially in recent years.
- Laws relating to business are something of a growth area. This reflects both the growing legislative power of European institutions and the difficulty of controlling increasingly international networked firms.

13.8 QUESTIONS

1. Analyse the effect of the banning of tobacco advertising on the market for tobacco and firms involved in that market.
2. Analyse the effect of the legalisation of Sunday trading on the market for retail food and firms involved in that market.
3. Analyse the effect of a rise in average sentences for burglars on the market for burgled goods.
4. Analyse the effect of a rise in the fear of crime on the market for home security products and firms involved in that market.
5. Analyse the effects of the legalisation of any previously banned product.
6. Read the newspapers and analyse the effect of any current trend or expected change in the political or legal environment that you come across in your reading.

CHAPTER 14

The technological environment

After studying this chapter, you should be able to:

- appreciate that technological change does not take place in a vacuum but is the result of social and economic pressures;

- identify the ways in which technology influences the demand for firms' products and the role it has in converting general demands into specific ones;

- identify the ways in which technology helps determine what inputs can be used and in what ways to meet demand;

- appreciate the role of technological innovation on product life cycles;

- understand the relationship between technological progress and economic growth;

- appreciate the reciprocity between firms and the technological environment;

- have an appreciation of the possibility of long waves and be aware of the role that technology may have in creating them;

- be aware of the major technological innovations affecting firms in the UK today.

14.1 TECHNOLOGY

The term technology encompasses anything that, to paraphrase Galbraith (1967), involves applying organised knowledge to practical tasks. We should not therefore equate it simply with what is new. We should also be careful not to treat it as the result of inexorable scientific advance, since technology is an output too, and like all outputs it occurs within a social and economic context. What gets invented depends partly on what has gone before, so in that sense we see a progression. However, it also depends on what the inventor perceives to be the needs of society, and its take-up will depend on how well it meets those needs, not on how much progress it represents or how clever it is. In other words, technological progress is determined by both the supply of and demand for new technologies.

The supply of new technologies consists initially of an invention or a discovery. The rate of new inventions depends on investment and the culture of the society, as some societies embrace technological change more than others. It also depends on whether it is profitable or in other ways rewarding to develop technological advances; a patent system, for example, allows an inventor to benefit financially from a certain monopoly over the invention's use. Of itself, the invention is insufficient to ensure its take-up; a demand must either exist or be created for it. Moveable type printing, for example, while invented in the fourteenth century, was not taken up in a big way until the nineteenth, when it became the dominant form of mass communication in the UK. The education required to learn to read is costly to provide, particularly if parents cannot read either, and it was not something that feudal lords felt the need to subsidise. Therefore for centuries there was little demand for it. It was not until the nineteenth century that this changed. Some of the pressure came from people wanting to read, but most came from capitalists wanting better-trained workers, and from a state that needed literate clerical workers to run the empire. Demand may also stem from broader social changes; the increased interest in low-emission technology, for example, is a direct result of people's increased concern for the ecological environment. Similarly, the demand for labour and time-saving products, which has encouraged firms into numerous innovations in convenience foods and the like, stems in part from changes within the structure of the family over recent decades.

One factor in determining the level of demand for a new technology is how entrenched the existing technology that it seeks to usurp is. David (1985) points out that this does not just depend on relative efficiencies, but on many things besides, including inertia. Indeed, David argues that many arrangements, devices and ways of working, which all combine to form a firm's environment, remain in existence simply through usage. As an example, he looked at the persistence of the 'QWERTY' keyboard. This keyboard arrangement is ubiquitous, and yet it is widely acknowledged to be hard to use; in fact it was partly designed to be hard to use to stop early typewriters jamming, and if efficiency prevailed, this keyboard would have been replaced years ago. However, its use has become locked-in since nearly everyone learns how to use it, and once learnt few are willing to change. The implications are expanded on by Arthur (1996), who describes how difficult it is for new ideas to usurp technologies that have become locked-in; he finds that it is often only by pricing significantly below costs that new inventions are able to get a foothold in a market. Because of this, even ideas that with hindsight seem sure-fire winners (because they themselves have now become locked-in) were nonetheless risky investments at the start.

14.2 THE INFLUENCE OF TECHNOLOGY ON FIRMS

On the supply side, technology influences not only what can be produced but also how it is produced. The biggest trend in this is the strides made in production-related technology; indeed, improvements in the efficiency of machinery are one of the main reasons why the real cost of producing things tends to go down over time. This may involve the substituting of technology for labour, and could therefore add to unemployment. However, since it also moves us down a demand curve it can increase the demand for all factors including labour too, so the net result is an empirical issue. The effects on competitive advantage are also not clear cut; we might expect an innovation to increase or reduce the need for whole industries. However, the innovation can be more or less competence-enhancing or competence-destroying, depending on the firm, and hence technological innovations can significantly alter the distribution of competitive advantages within an industry as well as between industries.

The absorption of technology may also be problematic because although in the long run it does not appear to cause unemployment, in the short run it does. Indeed, it is probably true to say that changes in this part of the business environment have most impact on this group of stakeholders in the firm above all others, with, on occasion, the immediate consequences for workers being so dire that bitter industrial disputes result. The actions of the Luddites in resisting the introduction of mechanisation in the cotton mills in the early nineteenth century and the picketing of new newspaper production facilities at Wapping by the print unions in the 1980s are two well-known examples involving violent action on both sides.

Because technology determines what specific types of product are supplied and how they are made, it acts to translate our general demands into demands for specific products. For example, the general demand for news and stories in the UK has been met in different ways over the centuries, depending on what technology was available. In the distant past, the development of the technology to make fire allowed tribal elders to tell tales and relate news well into the night. By the nineteenth century, the widespread use of printing meant that the dominant specific demand was for printed stories and newspapers. Earlier in this century, this dominance was reduced with the inventions of radio and cinema. Today, our general demand for stories and news comes out as specific demands for books, papers, radio, cinema, and of course television. Similarly, the general demand for transportation can be traced through many specific products reflecting the technology available at the time, from horse-drawn vehicles, through boats and trains, to planes and cars. Technology also helps determine how trade takes place and the geographical spread of trade; without the technologies of railways, lorries or boats, trade was largely confined to local areas and face-to-face dealings. With modern transportation and communications, we can trade with anyone anywhere in the world.

Technology also facilitates organizational change; for example, communications and computer technology combine to make it possible for office-based staff to move from the office and work from home. The more managers and office staff that take advantage of this, the more the firm can economise on overheads; however, the question of its effect on organisational arrangements, authority structures and the nature of working relationships is anybody's guess.

Case study

THE OTHER HIGH-TECHNOLOGY CHIP

Technological advance can be a source of competitive advantage even in the production of the humble chip (French fry). In an attempt to further undermine the market dominance of the world's largest fast food chain, the McDonald's franchise network which encompasses 25,000 outlets in 112 countries, Burger King has introduced the heat-retaining chip. Market research has shown that one of the few disappointing things about a burger meal for most customers is that the chips go cold too quickly. One answer would be fatter chips, but this is not so easy to do with processed potato, and using whole potatoes would introduce too much irregularity into the product and is more costly. In addition, people seem to prefer the taste of the thinner chip.

In response, Burger King, a subsidiary of Diageo, invested heavily in the science of integrating heat-retaining materials into the chip mix. This investment now seems to have paid off, with the unveiling of a heat-retaining chip made from a combination of modified potato, corn starch, corn syrup, sodium bicarbonate, sodium acid pyrophosphate and xanthan gum. The new chip not only retains heat better than its rivals, but market research suggests that nearly 60% of customers preferred it to the McDonald chip too. So, it looks as if technological advance has once again tipped the balance in an industry, although how this affects overall sales will, of course, only become apparent over time.

14.3 PRODUCT LIFE CYCLES

The fact that general demands tend to endure but are, over time, met in different ways means that products and industries tend to exhibit a life cycle in terms of sales and profits. If new improved products are quick to come along then the life cycle of products will be short. Indeed, many people argue that this is exactly what is happening today, with a faster rate of technological 'progress' leading to a shortening of product life cycles in many industries. If, on the other hand, new products are few and far between, the life cycle will be longer, and there are cases where products seem to remain as popular today as they have always been, like bread, alcohol and bikes. Indeed, if no new substitutes come along, the product will endure for as long as the general demand. With newspapers, for example, the demand shifted right as more people learnt to read and supply shifted right as mass production techniques became widely used, resulting in massive sales, but then came radio and TV, which led to a decline in the sales of newspapers. However, although newspaper sales continue to decline, the product is far from dead as it still has features that are unmatched by other products; there are, in other words, no perfect substitutes as yet and so rather than die out sales have simply levelled out as shown in Figure 14.1.

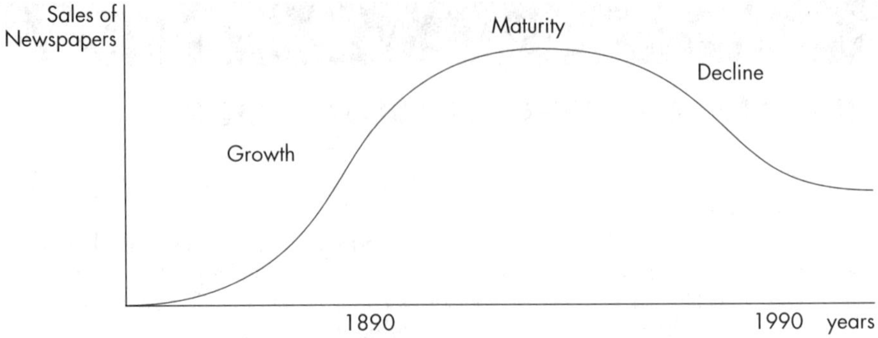

Figure 14.1 Stylised life cycle for newspaper sales in the UK.

DO RECENT TECHNOLOGICAL ADVANCES SPELL THE END FOR THE CD?

Although still very profitable, the recording company EMI (whose labels include Virgin and Chrysalis, and whose bands include best selling artistes Robbie Williams, the Spice Girls and The Verve) suffered a decline in sales and profits in 1998. For many commentators this has been taken as heralding the beginning of a time of upheaval in this industry that can largely be attributed to technology. On the one hand, it seems that sales of groups like the Beatles and Queen, who can produce nothing new, have declined significantly. This is believed to reflect the fact that all those consumers who throughout the 1980s began converting their record collections from vinyl to CD have virtually all done so. In addition, no such revamp is happening for new formats, since in sound quality terms new developments, such as the mini-disc, make little difference. This means that while new formats may pick up new sales to the extent that they are more convenient or whatever, they are unlikely to be purchased simply to replace existing CDs.

Another technological advance that may cause a problem for CDs is the increasing speed, availability and power of information technology, in particular of the Internet, since anyone can put digital-quality music directly on to the Internet for everyone to share. The only thing currently stopping this is the time it takes to download the material at the user end, but advances in computing are making this easier day by day. Indeed, many commentators argue that ultimately the only source of competitive advantage in information technology is in the information, not the

technology. This means that before long, those who benefit from the information, such as advertisers and firms making direct information contact with end users, will ensure that computers are given away rather than sold. It is currently estimated that there are 80,000 songs currently available on the Net, and nothing can be done to remove them as they can be replicated anywhere in any home in any country anywhere in the world. It is likely that this, as with everything else on the Net, will grow exponentially in the future. The source of profits for record companies will shrink as a result to a limited number of sales of first-issue new releases before the record 'pirates' have a chance to upload the information. So, unless the record companies like EMI can think of some way of protecting this information, their niche will shrink spectacularly. Music will, of course, endure but the means of profiting from it will change, and that inevitably means that there will be winners and losers. Whether EMI is a winner or loser only time will tell, but what is clear is that there is no future in what it currently does. This does not, however, mean that EMI should pack it in, since every threat contains an opportunity. In this case, if no one needs to go into a shop to buy records, that cuts out the retailer, and this could have benefits for EMI, for although it owns HMV most of its output is sold through other retailers. Eliminating the retailers' slice of the profits would boost EMI's profit potential if only it can devise a way of protecting its information assets so that customers pay it, and it alone, for hearing the sounds of their favourite artistes.

14.4 | **TECHNOLOGY AND GROWTH**

At any given stage in the business cycle, some firms will be expanding, some contracting; in a boom the expanders significantly outweigh the contractors while in a recession they do not. However, throughout this, some growth will result from new techniques and technologies reducing costs and shifting supply curves to the right. Technological change is therefore a source of long-term economic growth, but even in this there may be a pattern.

14.4.1 Long waves

In 1922 Nikolai Kondratieff (1892–1931), having looked at the performance of Britain, France and the USA from 1800, concluded that there was a long-wave cycle of peaks and troughs in economic prosperity (as measured by a number of indicators of output, wages and stock prices), every 50 years or so. His ideas were developed by Joseph Schumpeter (1883–1950), who argued that the main cause of this cycle was that technological innovations come in waves, each upswing being associated with a cluster of changes 'in the method of supplying commodities' to use Schumpeter's words. The innovations that lead to the upswing actually occur in the trough of the downwave when new ideas are needed and old technologies are becoming redundant, so that a period of 'creative destruction' occurs. However, it is not until the new technologies become diffused throughout the economy that we see a general economic upswing, and this may take decades. Once the innovations are widely integrated into the production process it becomes harder and harder to gain any competitive advantages from their use, as further technological improvements on the same piece of technology tend to become incremental. This means that cost competitiveness becomes the dominant strategic option, which in turn, by giving the advantage to the biggest firms, further reduces the chance of any additional radical innovation. This lack of innovation then sets off the next downwave and the process starts again, producing a wave pattern as depicted in Figure 14.2.

Figure 14.2 Stylised long waves.

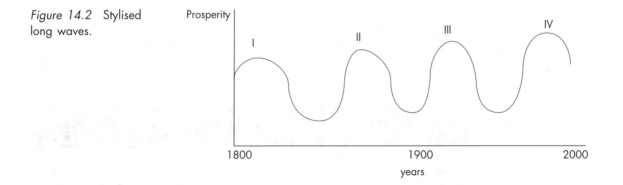

The first wave was associated with the start of the Industrial Revolution and in particular the huge productive gains associated with mechanised production in the textile industry, which was made possible by the technology of steam power. The gains from this petered out by the end of the Napoleonic wars. The second wave is associated with the railways, which relied on the invention of portable steam power and the rise of the new steel industries, which was only possible given a number of inventions since steel is not simply dug up and melted down. The third wave is associated with the invention of the car and the harnessing of electricity, which relied on a number of inventions. Since Kondratieff and Schumpeter, we have seen what may be another, fourth wave, associated with the invention of the transistor and related developments that led to modern electronic products, such as the TV, and of course the development of computers. Some would argue that this last wave peaked in the 1970s. However, there is nothing in the theory to say that innovation clusters must be evenly spread, so a long slide is not inevitable. In addition, any theory based on long-term historical data is always open to debate, given the paucity of reliable data. You may also reject this idea on the basis that computer technology has so clearly advanced since the 1970s; computers in those days did relatively little. However, this is to jump from the fact that technological change promotes long-term economic growth to assuming that there is a simple and direct link between computer processing power and economic growth, or indeed between spending on IT and productivity, when in fact there is not. The USA, for example, is the most technologically advanced country in the world, with the highest levels of investment in IT too; indeed, in the 1990s spending on IT is growing at up to 50% per annum in the USA. However, productivity and output growth have remained below par throughout this period. This is not to deny the link between technology and growth, simply to suggest that it is not a straightforward one, and is not simply a matter of processing power. It is possible, therefore, that despite the obvious acceleration of processing power, the peak of the fourth wave has indeed passed. On the other hand, Schumpeter argued that there were three stages to technological change: invention, innovation and diffusion. Innovation is when the invention is turned into a usable device or product, but it is not until the diffusion stage, when the full benefits of the change become spread and absorbed into the production process, that the productivity gains accrue. So while, for example, the second wave in the 1830s was based on steam power, the invention that really made it possible occurred over a hundred years earlier in 1709. As argued previously, this may be due to a lack of demand for the innovation, but whatever the reason, such delays seem typical. It may therefore be the case that we are in the diffusion stage of computer and communication technology and that the main benefits are therefore yet to come.

14.5 HOW FIRMS AFFECT THE TECHNOLOGICAL ENVIRONMENT

Although for each firm nearly all the technology it uses is external to it, there are ways of internalising technological change. The obvious one is for the firm to try to make the inventions that will affect it most. In some cases this 'research and development' is given a low priority as the chances of success are low. The owners of a chip shop, for example, are unlikely to put any effort (or money) into devising new types of fryers, preferring instead to take, or leave, whatever innovations come along. On the other hand, some firms will put considerable effort into this. Pharmaceutical firms, for example, realising that the invention of new drugs is a major source of competitive advantage in their industry, spend billions on R&D. The level of spending on R&D also varies with the state of the economy, since, like all investments, it is a discretionary form of expenditure; so when profits are high, as they tend to be in a boom, more is spent on R&D than when profits are low. Indeed, in a recession, when profits are likely to be particularly low, one of the recessionary forces at work is the fact that investment spending gets switched off. There are also national differences in the level of R&D that reflect national attitudes and institutional arrangements in the different countries. So, for example, while in the UK over the past decade just over 2% of GDP was spent on R&D, in Japan, Germany and the USA it was nearer 3%. This seems to be a consistent feature of the UK investment scene and, insofar as it leads to a lower level of long-term growth, this may represent a problem for the UK economy and of course for UK firms too. The blame for this is laid at a number of doors. Firstly, firms are accused of underinvesting; this is supported by the fact that UK firms often take more profits than equivalent firms in other countries before making the same level of investments. Secondly, financial intermediaries are blamed for their 'short-termism' insofar as they seem to look unfavourably at projects with long-term pay-offs. In addition, many firms complain that banks effectively cut them off in a recession, which makes firms unlikely to invest during downturns and unlikely to invest in a boom in anything long-term enough to still require financial support when the boom ends. Thirdly, successive governments are blamed for failing to invest enough in research themselves, or to provide the tax breaks or institutional arrangements that encourage long-term investment by firms. They are also blamed for their poor management of the macroeconomy, which over the past decade has meant that our interest rates have tended to be above those of our major international competitors. This deters investment since interest rates are the major cost involved in borrowing money, and therefore high interest rates mean that firms will borrow less to invest than they otherwise would and will look for quicker payback periods too. For UK firms the long-run effects of relatively low investment levels will be relatively low levels of growth and productivity, which makes it even harder to compete with rival firms based in low-wage 'newly industrialising countries' (NICs). A lack of investment and low rates of innovation and absorption of innovations, which comes from failure to invest, may therefore represent the erosion of a major source of competitive advantage for UK firms, since relatively high wages must be accompanied by relatively high productivity if they are to survive.

The individual firm can also internalise a technological innovation not by investing itself but by taking over another firm that does. The importance of new drugs in driving profits for pharmaceutical firms means that not only do the biggest spend a lot on R&D, but they also take over other firms that look likely to make, or have just made, a breakthrough. For example, in 1995 Glaxo

Wellcome spent nearly £900m on R&D, but also spent $533m buying a firm that specialised in a type of chemistry that looked likely to deliver results.

14.6 THE CURRENT SITUATION

Some of the most important technological changes affecting firms now are computer related, in particular the combination of computer and communications technology to transfer information via the Internet. In addition, we have seen more use of computers in product design (computer aided design, CAD), in manufacturing (computer aided manufacturing, CAM), and in coordination and control. In retailing, for example, a computer reads the barcodes on products and the information is fed into the stock reordering system when customers buy a product. This ensures that shortages do not usually occur, so that no customers are turned away, and it also minimises surpluses as carrying too much stock is a waste of space and can be costly. With these types of facilities, many firms can operate a just-in-time (JIT) production and distribution system so that they effectively hold no stocks either along the production line or at the point of sale.

Today, many people argue that we are entering a new 'post-Ford' era, meaning simply that we are entering an era that no longer relies on mass production (as exemplified by Henry Ford's use of assembly lines for car production). They argue that computer technology and the amount of control that computer monitoring brings are allowing a greater degree of flexibility in the organisation of production. This may require a more flexible workforce in terms of the variety of tasks performed and the amount of training required. It is also affecting where the work can be done, with increasing numbers of people finding it possible to work from home.

14.7 SUMMARY

- Technology influences the demand for firms' products by creating new products and thus new demands, and by altering the nature of existing products or their mode of delivery.
- Technology helps determine the precise form that general demands will take, which means that it turns general demands into specific ones.
- Technology helps determine what inputs can be used to produce a desired output and in what precise ways.
- Technological innovation creates products with new characteristics that act as substitutes (at least in part) for existing products. It therefore leads to a decline in demand for existing products, and shortens their 'product life cycle'.
- Although individual technological innovations may destroy jobs, taken as a whole technological progress has a positive impact on economic growth and (thus far at least) jobs too.

- Firms are in a reciprocal relationship with the technological environment, since they are affected by it but also initiate technological change and block or encourage the adoption of anything new that emerges.
- There is the possibility that there are long waves of economic activity based on the clustering of technological innovation.
- There are significant major technological innovations currently having a significant impact on firms, including computer technology and the Internet.

14.8 QUESTIONS

1. Analyse the effect of the growing use of catalytic converters (which use platinum) on the market for platinum and firms involved in that market

2. For £5, you can compile your own music CD using any of several thousand tracks (and in future probably any recorded track), using the Internet. Discuss the likely implications of this for the market structure and profitability of 'record' companies.

3. Read the newspapers and analyse the effect of any current trend or expected change in the technological environment that you come across in your reading.

APPENDIX — SOURCES OF DATA ON THE BUSINESS ENVIRONMENT

The EU and the Organisation for Economic Cooperation and Development (OECD) are increasingly important sources of data on European and world trends. For the UK specifically, the main source of economic, financial and business information is the government's Office for National Statistics, which publishes a number of booklets including *UK Economic Accounts*, *Social Trends*, *Regional Trends* and *Financial Statistics*. These, and many more besides, can be found in the libraries of colleges and universities, and an increasing amount of the data they contain can also be accessed directly from the ONS via the Internet (much of it for free). In addition, the Department for Trade and Industry publishes the results of the annual census of production that looks at the output of each industry (and many parts thereof) for the whole of the UK. Regulatory bodies such as the Competition Commission, OFGAS and OFWAT also publish reports in their area of jurisdiction. Non-governmental sources include professional and trade associations which collect data in their areas of business, with, for example, the Council for Mortgage Lenders publishing booklets that contains information and reports on the UK mortgage and loans markets, and related topics such as house prices. In addition, there are a plethora of private companies that supply detailed reports and information for a fee, including Economist Publications, Mintel Market Intelligence, Euromonitor, Key Note Publications, Market Research Great Britain, and ICC Information Group. Finally, we should not forget that many reports and forecasts from all sources are discussed in the media. The *Financial Times* newspaper and the *Economist* and *Investor's Chronicle* magazines, in particular, contain all kinds of information about the business environment and its likely impact on firms. In addition, political issues are discussed at length with representatives of the government, including members of the Cabinet, on TV and on Radio 4's 'Today' programme.

ASSIGNMENT

Part A: Describing a firm's relationship with its environment

Choose a company to analyse and find out what you can about the company. Then answer the following questions:
(Notes on what is expected are given in italics.)

(i) Who are the firm's stakeholders?
Customers, suppliers, workers, owners. Need to discuss who they are; for example, customers are seldom 'everyone', often they are people from a particular location, or of a particular age, or class, or sex, or aspirational group.

(ii) Why do customers buy this firm's products?
What need do the products satisfy and why are they preferred to the alternatives? Links into subsequent questions on substitutes, complements, and amount of competition in the markets they supply.

(iii) What complements and facilitators are there for the firm's products and who supplies them?
Types of goods and types (possibly names) of suppliers.

(iv) What substitutes are there for the firm's products and who supplies them?
Types of goods and types (possibly names) of suppliers.

(v) What things are likely to cause shifts in the demand curves facing the firm?
Should include some of the factors listed in iii) and iv) above but should include some other factors as well, such as changes in PEST factors. Focus here should be on factors that may change rather than everything you can think of.

(vi) What inputs does the firm use?
Need to encompass different types of inputs – land, labour, capital and knowledge. Some figures to help quantify these, and any trends in the use of different factors need to be mentioned.

(vii) What market structure is the firm in?
Classification and implications for firm.

(viii) What things are likely to cause shifts in its supply curve and those of its rivals?
Draws on vi) and vii) above but should include some other factors as well and, as before, focus here should be on what might change.

(ix) Why did the firm make a profit (or loss) last year?
Discussion of costs and revenues, where possible drawing on links with the external environment as discussed above.

Part B: Analysing changes in the firm's environment and how the firm deals with them

(x)   What developments in the business environment (trends or changes) could affect the firm over the next five years?
Can be anything but need evidence that the topic was not just plucked out of the air. This might involve a discussion on the part of the environment chosen and can include the use of some form of impact assessment grid, or similar device. Need to make some attempt at quantifying the changes envisaged.

(xi)   Analyse the impact of these developments on the firm.
Should use the analysis outlined in the book to do this, at a minimum a simple supply and demand diagram and some consideration of the opportunity and threats implied. Possibly some mention of strategic options for the firm to deal with these developments. This should draw on your understanding of how the firm works as described in Part A of the assignment.

(xii)   What changes in the external environment in the past have been of particular importance to the firm? Evaluate the reactions of the firm to these changes.
In deciding what developments in the business environment have been important for your firm, you have to distinguish the effect of particular changes. To evaluate their reactions you will need to consider what was done and why. You should assess the outcomes in terms of the relative success, or otherwise, of the firm insofar as it can be related to what was done and consider what it tells us about how the firm's decision-makers analyse and deal with the firm's environment.

ASSIGNMENT ANSWER

Example based on a small local firm: AW's Fish and Chip Shop, Mytown, South Wales.

Introduction

The data in this report is based on discussions with the owner, a Mr Alan Williams, coupled with evidence from a sample survey of AW's customers. This entailed asking opinions of customers as they entered the shop. It was carried out one Tuesday (the quietest day of the week) and one Friday (the busiest day) in May. The survey would have been improved if I had conducted it on more days. However, I thought that by picking a quiet day and a busy day I would cover the range of the firm's upper and lower demand levels for the week, and could extrapolate from this. This survey might also have been improved by covering more weeks; however, the demand for fish and chips is not very seasonal and Mr Williams's experience suggests that 'there's not a lot of difference between weeks'.

(i) Who are the firm's stakeholders?

The main stakeholders in this firm are A.W. and his family, their food suppliers (mainly local farmers and a local fish wholesaler) the local community, and of course their customers. They have no employees outside the family. My survey revealed that all AW's customers were locals from within a five-mile radius. Most (over 80%) were regulars coming at least once a week. The vast majority (over 90%) of the customers at lunchtime were young people, buying mostly chips as a substitute for school lunch. In the early evening, the majority of customers were women, mostly buying for their families. Between 5 p.m. and 7 p.m. there were 16 customers on the Tuesday and 84 on the Friday night. This suggests that most families treat Friday as fish and chip night, since there is a long tradition of eating fish on Friday. In addition, being the end of the working week makes Friday the natural day to treat the kids. On the Friday, Mr Williams informed me that there was virtually no trade between 8.30 and 11.00. He suggested that I continue my research in the New Inn, The Plough and the Red Lion public houses, as this is where most of the late-night custom would come from. As anticipated by Mr Williams, several people went from the pubs at closing time to AW's. Between 11 and 12 (when AW's closes), over 80 orders were taken, mostly men in the age range 18–35; however, the orders were of relatively low value on the whole, many being just chips and curry sauce. The orders were noticeably different from those of customers earlier in the day, involving a greater diversity in the use of complements such as pickled eggs, gherkins and onions, and in particular curry sauce. In contrast, during the day there were very few orders for curry sauce and none for pickled eggs at all. This pattern may reflect the tendency for alcohol to increase the desire for spicy food, which moves us on to issues of why they buy the products, which is the next question.

(ii) Why do customers buy this firm's products?

Generally, people buy food to live, but in modern societies, there is a lot of choice for most people about what they eat. Therefore, the characteristics of the food, its price, its taste and so on, are important determinants of demand. With AW's fish and chip shop, the main selling point is that it offers filling and tasty meals at relatively low prices. Convenience is also a major characteristic of this type of food, since people do not have to cook it; they just unwrap it and tuck in. The popularity of this type of food with women, particularly on the Friday night, can be explained in terms of these characteristics, in particular convenience, since many mums in Mytown work in paid employment. Another reason why people buy from AW's is the degree of complementarity amongst the foods that make up the firm's portfolio of products. Fish and chips are clearly complements, but these are, in addition, complemented by the peas, beans, curry sauce, pickled eggs and gherkins that AW's sells. The kinds of food AW's sells also appeals to kids since it involves the kinds of combinations of fat, sugar and salt that all children's favourites contain. This means that for parents fish and chips represents a relatively cheap treat that is also a solid and filling meal that the whole family can enjoy.

The demand for AW's output also relates to the fact that the shop is conveniently situated in the middle of town, and is near the pubs. There are also no direct substitutes in the town as there is no other take-away food outlet of any sort. The pubs do pub-grub that is not very different from AW's, but it is considerably more expensive. Consequently, many pub customers wait until closing time and go to AW's. There may also be a social element to the demand for AW's products; the Friday night rush, for example, has traditional religious roots that encourage the eating of fish on Friday. Also, many of AW's customers come direct from the pub, and going to pubs is a social activity broadly approved of within our society.

(iii) ## What complements and facilitators are there for the firm's products and who supplies them?

AW's sells many foods that complement each other, as well as drinks that complement the food. Salt and vinegar are also complementary products provided free at the point of sale. The importance of different complements varies person by person as it depends on individual preferences. There are, however, some patterns; the midday mainly young clientele have a slightly different demand profile in that they mainly buy just chips and fizzy drinks. The (mostly male) late-night customers seem to like spicier complements (gherkins, pickled eggs and so on) than the daytime customers. As discussed above, this may be due to the alcohol, so booze can be seen as a complement to some of the foods that AW's sells too, while the bus stop (just outside) and even the school can be seen as facilitators to the demand for the food AW's sells because if either of these were removed, demand would be less. Fortunately, Alan's brother is on the district council so he is well placed to find out about any changes to this part of the business environment for Alan. Indeed, he may even be able to block changes that would damage AW's trade. A rise in the price (or a reduction in the availability) of any complement, from salt and vinegar to beer in the pub, could reduce demand for AW's products. Many of these are provided by other firms and are thus a part of the business environment insofar as the supplying firms will act in their own interest with little regard to the effects on AW's.

(iv) ## What substitutes are there for the firm's products and who supplies them?

Some substitutes to fish and chips are sold by AW's, such as pies, but some substitutes that require a different production process, such as Indian and Chinese foods, are not. However, there is no Indian or Chinese take-away in town, therefore anyone wishing to avail themselves of such substitutes will have to travel to the next town, so these are not particularly close substitutes. Another substitute is to stay at home and cook a meal; to assist in this, supermarkets offer a range of convenience meals. Some of these are aimed at families, others are more specialised; however, all exhibit an increasing range of choice for customers, with the number and range of Indian convenience foods, for example, expanding rapidly. Another alternative available to the people of Mytown is a McDonald's situated on the outskirts of a nearby town. Many families from Mytown regard a trip to McDonald's as a reasonably inexpensive treat for the kids as McDonald's cater well for children, with a games area, complementary toys and the like, whereas AW's does nothing to cater for children specifically. There is also a growing use of direct substitutes for fish and chips for cooking at home that do not involve the time and effort of frying, such as microwavable chips and oven-bake fish. These have the added advantage that they are healthier than fried food because they have a lower fat content. These are, however, not perfect substitutes for AW's fish and chips, as they seldom taste quite the same, although some are getting close.

A fall in the price of a substitute (or an increase in its availability) will reduce the demand for AW's products. Given that other firms provide most substitutes, this is a part of AW's business environment. This matters because the suppliers of substitutes will act in their own best interest rather than that of AW's. Generally, we have seen a decline in demand for the products of fish and chip shops over the past few decades. This is largely due to the increase in the number of pubs offering food, the rise of McDonalds, the increasing variety in take-aways (Indian and Chinese cuisine, for example), and the growing range of convenient substitutes from supermarkets. These combine to shift supply in the 'takeaway food market' rightward, as shown on the left of Figure A1.1. This has put a squeeze on fish and chip shops, by reducing demand, as Figure A1.1 (right) shows, since the market demand is not elastic enough to allow more competition without hitting fish and chip shops' total revenue.

Figure A1.1

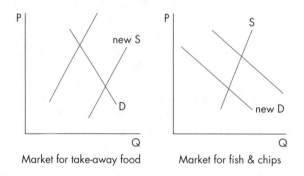

Market for take-away food   Market for fish & chips

(v) What factors are likely to cause shifts in the demand curves facing the firm?

We have already discussed some of the main factors that could shift the demand curve. A rise in the price of a substitute or a fall in the price of a complement, or an increase in the popularity of this type of food, and the weekend will all lead to a rightward shift in the demand curve. In addition, there are other factors in the business environment that can shift demand, such as the state of the economy, demographic trends, the social acceptability of fried foods and so on. There is, however, according to Mr Williams, no real difference between summer and winter sales levels; in other words, in his opinion, seasonality is not a demand curve shifter in this cafe.

I decided to find the demand curve for AW's by asking people what they would do if prices went up or down by 50p from the current average (according to the survey) of about £2. The resulting changes in weekly sales implied by their responses are shown in Figure A1.2.

Figure A1.2

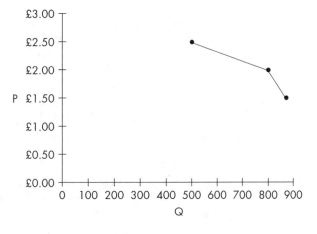

The shape of this demand curve is caused by a saturation effect, as people will buy more fish and chips at lower prices but not a lot more: people seem to have an upper limit on the amount of fish and chips they want that is not much greater than their current consumption levels. In other words, there is not much of a repressed demand for this product. Perhaps people are worried about consuming fish and chips too often because of the high fat content. The result is that demand for a price fall is inelastic. On the other hand, demand is elastic for a price rise; perhaps because 50p is such an obviously big rise, people may feel in answering this question that such a price hike would represent a rip-off. If so, then a more gradual price rise over time may not have such a bad effect on demand. However, although I think there is scope for raising prices by a small amount, I decided to look at the effect of a big price increase for the discussion (later in this report) of what will happen when the son, David, leaves the firm.

Table A.1 shows the revenue figures that can be calculated from the sales and price figures in the graph above.

Table A.1

Price	Sales	Total revenue	PeD
£2.50: Price rise	500	£1,250	Elastic
£2.00: Current price	800	£1,600	
£1.50: Price fall	870	£1,305	Inelastic

(vi)   What inputs does the firm use?

The costs AW's incurs in producing its output can be thought of as either fixed costs or variable costs. The amount of fixed costs does not depend on the amount of output the firm produces; variable costs, on the other hand, go up (or down) when the output of the firm goes up (or down). This means that although fixed costs affect the level of profits, only variable costs affect at what output level the firm maximises profits.

AW's inputs and costs can be broken down into:

1. Capital and land: The shop and adjoining residence are covered by one mortgage; the payments for this encompass the land it stands on but is mainly for the bricks and mortar. This is a 'fixed cost', as it does not change if AW's sells more food. It does change, however, when the building society changes its mortgage rate. Economists like to look at opportunity costs in their calculations as this gives a better idea of the real costs involved. The opportunity cost in this case is equal to the mortgage payments as this mortgage money could be spent on something else. Currently the weekly payment is £200. Therefore, economic costs (including opportunity costs) are £200. Other capital used by this firm are the various machines used in the shop; the bigger ones include the fryer, a fridge, a microwave oven and a potato chipper. These are all owned so the opportunity cost is implicit only; it is how much these machines could earn in some alternative use. In this case, there is, perhaps, not much else that can be done with this equipment, so I shall assume the opportunity cost is zero, giving us economic costs = £0. This might look odd, since these machines did cost money to buy, but that money has gone; it is a 'sunk cost' and as such should play no part in considering the firm's costs of production. There are also inputs like electricity, water and rates that are mainly fixed costs. All together, I estimate these at £300 per week. This gives total economic fixed costs of £500 per week. There are also some other inputs into the production process, raw materials that have been purchased to sell on, or are used to help create the finished product, including potatoes, fish, pickles and so on; these constitute the variable costs. The opportunity cost of these is simply what they cost to buy, as there is no alternative use. I calculate that this amounts to about £1 per £2 meal, giving £500 a week for sales of 500, £800 for sales of 800 and £870 for sales of 870. However, Mr Williams did expect that at higher levels of sales than the current 800, unit costs would rise, as they would be pushing the equipment. In other words, he anticipated that the law of diminishing returns would come into play. Therefore, for the sake of completeness, I have added 10% to variable costs on the 870 figure.

2. Labour: There is no labour cost for this firm because the family (mum, dad and one son, David) do all the work. It is unclear to me what the opportunity cost is in this case. If Mr Williams could earn more than £300 a week elsewhere, he should consider it, as this is what the profits are. However, the opportunity cost may be zero, as there are not many jobs

in the area. There is another issue regarding labour, and that is that the family is currently fully stretched meeting 800 orders per week. Even at 870 a week, I think they would have to employ someone. Therefore, I have included an extra £300 on sales of 870, to cover the gross costs of a wage, National Insurance and so on, as shown in Table A.2.

Table A.2 Summary of AW's costs per week.

	Fixed cost	**Variable cost**	**Total cost**
Sales of 500 per week	£500	£500	£1,000
Sales of 800 per week	£500	£800	£1,300
Sales of 870 per week	£500	£1,257 (870 + 10% + 300)	£1,757

We can also include knowledge as a resource that a firm uses, and certainly considerable experience about what the customers want, how to deal with local suppliers, and the mechanics of the business has been accumulated by Mr. Williams. However, very little of it has been codified (or indeed opened to question by others), so while Mr Williams has learnt a lot, the organisation, as it were, has not.

(vii) What market structure is the firm in?

This firm is in a situation best described as 'monopolistic (imperfect) competition' as there are a lot of fish and chip shops in Wales but only one in Mytown. Therefore, although there are many similar firms, AW's has a monopoly over a very small part of the market. Firms that find themselves in monopolistic competition do not have to engage in price competition in the same way that firms do under perfect competition. With monopolistic competition, firms are able to differentiate their products by being slightly different; the pubs in Mytown, for example, have slightly different clientele, and they target slightly different parts of the market. AW's position is more straightforward; it is different by virtue of being the only one in the town. In other words, it is differentiated by location, its goods have no perfect substitutes, so its demand curve is not perfectly elastic, and so despite the apparently large numbers of similar firms it has some power to set its own price. However, unlike a monopoly it cannot set any price, as it is not a 'price maker'; it is best described therefore as a 'price shaper'. This means that it can make some super normal profits in the short run and the long run as long as competition in Mytown does not increase. The danger in this position is that another take-away firm could open in Mytown at very little cost. There are, however, other barriers to both entry and exit. The barriers to entry are that planning permission would be needed and it may spark a price war with AW's which would result in lower profits all round. The threat of retaliation is therefore also a barrier. There are also barriers to exit; if it did not work out the newcomer would be stuck with equipment that would be difficult to get rid of which means their investment could rapidly become one big sunk cost. This market is, therefore, not very 'contestable' and is unlikely to be subject to much entry, but of course one rival would be bad enough for AW's. Indeed, in recent years the pubs have started doing good (but relatively expensive) pub-grub, which is largely chip based, and this must have had some effect on AW's.

(viii) What factors are likely to cause shifts in its supply curve and those of its rivals?

A change in costs would affect supply (unless the change was small and AW has decided to absorb it directly in lower profits). The main change to costs that I foresee is the result of the son's plan to go to university next year. The result of this is that AW's may have to hire someone to cover for his absence. David's desire to quit results not from anything the firm has done, but rather because of changes in the external environment. The changes are that more people are going to university these days, so competition in terms of qualifications is escalating, and the recent announcement of tuition fees for next year has made David think that if he does not enrol this year then maybe he never will. Hiring someone to replace him would increase AW's costs considerably, so much so that I think they would be forced to put prices up (Figure A1.3).

Figure A1.3

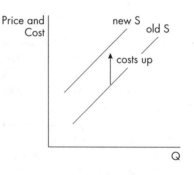

(ix) Why did the firm make a profit (or loss) last year?

The firm made a profit by virtue of the fact that its revenues exceeded its costs. The reason that it makes a profit above normal profits is that it does not face perfect competition because its product is differentiated by virtue of being the only fish and chip shop in Mytown. People need to eat and AW's sells some of the things they like to eat. It manages to supply food at a price that customers find acceptable by keeping costs down, largely by employing the family without paying wages (or tax). The figures in Table A.3 show the current situation based on my analysis above (the firm does not publish its accounts).

	Av. price (AR)	Total rev.	Total cost	Total profit (TR–TC)
Sales of 500 per week	£2.50	£1,250	£1,000	£250
Sales of 800 per week	£2.00	£1,600	£1,300	£300
Sales of 870 per week	£1.50	£1,305	£1,757	£–452

Table A.3

This shows that AW's output is around about the level needed to maximise profits, which can also be seen by looking at Figure A1.4. I have already discussed one factor that could change this situation, and more are discussed below.

Figure A1.4

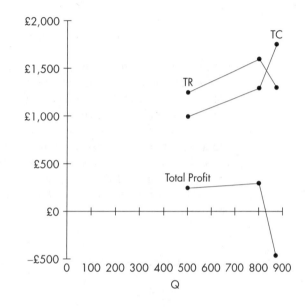

(x) **What developments in the business environment (trends or changes) could affect the firm over the next five years?**

The following factors are elements of the environment that might create opportunities or threats for AW's over the next five years:

1. The economy slows down. As we are nearing the peak of the current business cycle, the next five years may see a downturn.
2. The trend towards healthy eating continues.
3. Business taxes rise sharply due to entry, or preparation for entry, into the EMU.
4. Potato prices go up.
5. Opening of more McDonalds stores in the area.
6. The local pubs become more aggressive in competing for take-away food custom.
7. A major employer comes to Mytown.

In order to assess what factors in the business environment are important, we can use an impact assessment grid, since in deciding what to focus on there are two main considerations:

1. Will it happen?

2. Will it affect our firm?

		Will it happen?	
		Yes	*No*
Will it affect AW's?	*Yes*	*A*	*B*
	No	*C*	*D*

Of all the factors listed above, I would advise AW to make contingency plans for those labelled A which I believe covers numbers 1 to 4 in my list of possible changes. I would advise keeping an eye on those labelled B, in case the likelihood of their occurring goes up; from my list I have put numbers 5 and 6 in this category. For those falling into category C, the firm is advised to have a think about them in case I am wrong and they do come into effect. From my list, number 7 falls into this category. We can ignore contingencies that fall into the D category. I do not think any of my list can be put in this category. As A is the important box, it is those that fall into that category that I shall concentrate on.

(xi) Analyse the impact of these developments on the firm

1. The economy may be at the peak of the current business cycle, as Figure A1.5 shows.

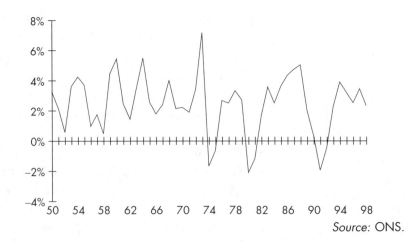

Figure A1.5 UK real growth rates 1950–98.

Source: ONS.

If a slowdown, or even perhaps a recession, occurs then demand for AW's output is likely to go down as in Figure A1.6.

Figure A1.6

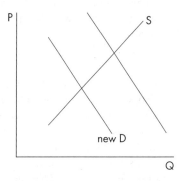

Many people, Mr Williams amongst them, assume that fish and chips are an inferior product, but I do not believe that in Mytown they are. The alternative of home-prepared food, in particular, is cheaper. In Mytown, because it is a relatively run-down town, a fish and chip supper is something of a treat, if not exactly a luxury. I could, of course, be wrong but since my advice on this differs from Mr Williams, I think it is worth him considering his options on this one.

2. Continued trend towards healthy eating. This is likely to continue and it will affect fish and chip shops because it is hard to see how they can produce a healthier output. Their main product is based on frying, so quite what can be done about this is difficult to say.

3. Business taxes are lower in the UK than in the rest of Europe and it is thought likely that such taxes will have to rise when (and if) we enter EMU. This could have a crippling effect on a marginal firm like AW's and I think it warrants some thought. Rather than make suggestions on this, I think it would be instructive to look at what happened the last time AW's was faced with a tax rise, which I shall do below in section xii).

4. Potato prices go up. At the moment the price for a 56 lb bag has fallen below £2, but next year they will go up again as farmers will plant fewer seed potatoes for the next season because of the poor prices now. Presently Mr Williams is taking the opportunity to buy potatoes from whoever is offering them cheapest, even from roadside vendors. Instead, I think he should be alert to the possibility of significant price rises next year and form a contract for potatoes with a local farmer for a period of years. The current situation will enable him to get a good price, and in return the farmer will benefit from knowing that he has a market for some of his crop. For AW's this will help to keep costs down for the next five years, even if it means paying a bit more now.

On balance, I think it may be hard for AW's to maintain profitability over the next five years. There is little that AW's can do about the macroeconomy, as it is very much external to this firm. AW's can, however, prepare for this more threatening environment by considering the possibility of special offers of some sort if demand falls and investigating the possibility of offering Chinese food (or pizzas). Many chip shops do this; as it is mainly fried food it is similar in terms of production to the firm's current output, and although for customers it may be a substitute, it is a relatively high priced one. It should, therefore, add more to revenues than it does to costs. All that is required is a few cheap utensils and a set of recipes.

In addition to the factors considered above I would like to consider the son David's plan to go to university (see viii) here too, since in a sense this could be seen as reflecting a change in the external environment – the introduction of tuition fees for university students. This is important, as this change is both likely to happen and when it does it will have a big effect on the firm.
    As stated in part viii), the effect of David leaving is likely to be that some-one has to be hired (in addition to the person who is employed when output reaches 870). In what follows I shall treat David's replacement as a variable cost on the assumption that they are paid according to the level of output, so that when it is quiet they are sent home, which is often the way it works in this kind of case. To keep it simple I assume that employing them adds an extra 50p to the cost of each meal. On current sales of 800 additional costs would be £400 (more than the person employed when output reaches 870 because of the extra workload and responsibility involved in being David's replacement). This means costs rise to £1,700; without passing the costs on, revenue would remain at £1,600 and AW's would make a loss of £100 per week. The alternative is to pass the cost rise on, as in Figure A1.7, and live with the consequences for sales (the supply curves are perfectly elastic over this range since we now have some spare capacity with the new employee).

Figure A1.7

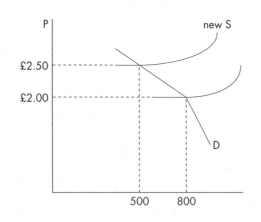

Demand will then fall to 500, costs will be £1,250 (other variable costs fall to £500 because sales are only 500. Fixed costs are still £500, but we now have an extra £250 to pay in wages). At the same time, the reduced sales means revenue falls to £1,250. Consequently the firm breaks even and stays in business, as shown in Figure A1.8.

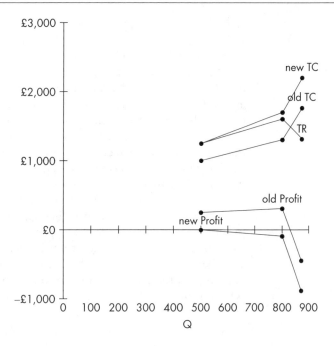

So cutting production, and thereby shifting the supply curve to the left, is the profit-maximising thing to do in this case. If we had treated David's replacement as a fixed cost, the profit maximising output would not move left and the supply curve would therefore not shift. However, the level of profits would still fall so, the prospect is bleak either way. This result leads me to the conclusion that this firm is paying too little attention to the problem of David leaving. In practice, they may hire someone on a very limited part-time basis and so perhaps the rise in costs will not be as significant as I suggest; perhaps therefore, this should be viewed as 'a worse case scenario'. On the other hand, David does do most of the work, a lot of hours at very inconvenient times, and it is difficult to see how AW's can replace him without putting its costs up significantly. I have therefore two recommendations to make:

1. Persuade David to go to his local university so that he can help out some evenings.

2. Get a member of the extended family to help out. If Mr Williams has a relative who can work cheaply then the problem will be reduced. In this case, the problem will have been dealt with by using the resources of the social environment.

(xii) **What changes in the external environment in the past have been of particular importance to the firm? Evaluate the reactions of the firm to these changes**

European rates of VAT on take-away food are similar to ours so I do not think it is particularly likely that VAT will go up. Nonetheless, I would like to look at the introduction of VAT in 1984 as a case study into how this firm deals with its environment.

The introduction of VAT in 1984 was well anticipated and its likely effect on AW's could have been predicted. There was a clear difference in the effect that the introduction of VAT had on different types of take-away outlets. Chinese and Indian restaurants suffered little, neither did McDonald's or Wimpy. However, traditional fish and chip shops were badly affected and newspapers at the time reported the closure of many establishments, although the effect is difficult to quantify exactly. Mr Williams himself remembers it as a very bad period. The bad effect was predictable, however, since for fish and chip shops it seems likely that the demand is elastic for a price rise, which means that any rise in costs will reduce firms' revenues: The burden of the tax cannot be passed on to the customers, and so it falls on to the firm, which experiences lower profits as a result, as on the left in Figure A1.9. On the other hand, the demand for Chinese and Indian take-aways is likely to be less elastic and this explains why they suffered little from the introduction of VAT. In effect, they were more able to pass the paying of the tax on to their customers, as shown in Figure A1.9 on the right.

Figure A1.9

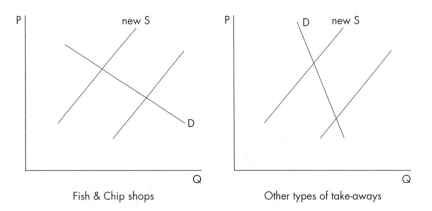

Fish & Chip shops   Other types of take-aways

Mr Williams could have foreseen this and could have built in some contingency plans; one such would have been to do Chinese food, which I have discussed already. He could also have thought about ways to reduce costs during this period. A better understanding of the problem would have alerted him to the need for the consideration of some options in advance; some planning, in other words. The conclusion that I draw from this is that this firm could improve its environmental analysis. I hope that my report will help convince them of this.

ASSIGNMENT, EXAMPLE 2

The model answer above shows that this approach can be used even for the analysis of small local firms. It is, however, more tricky to apply to the public sector. But it can be done, and the widespread acceptance of the need to encourage efficiency and entrepeneurship in the public sector means that the approach used in this assignment is increasingly relevant for all organisations regardless of which sector they are in. To illustrate this, a quick report on the police service is provided below.

(i) Who are the firm's stakeholders?

The general public, particularly those who are victims of crime. Within this, there are a number of patterns, with particular groups suffering more of particular types of crime than others do. The government is also an important stakeholder since its political fortunes can be affected by the performance of the police service, as can that of local government. People who are arrested by the police can also be thought of as stakeholders since they rely on the police for fair treatment.

(ii) Why do customers buy this firm's products?

The output of the police can be divided into the catching of criminals and the prevention of crime. People pay for these not at the point of contact with the police but through their taxes. The catching of a perpetrator affords the victim the opportunity to seek redress or revenge, or possibly just an understanding of why they did it. Prevention is desirable since being a victim can, even for petty crime, be extremely distressing, so in this case rather than desiring a good we are avoiding a bad. The reason that people generally expect the police to do this is that they have already paid for the service in their taxes.

(iii) What complements and facilitators are there for the firm's products and who supplies them?

There are lots of facilitators for the prevention of crime, such as good street lighting, a neighbourhood watch scheme, and so on, and for catching criminals, computers, video cameras and so on. More specifically, complements such as door locks, personal alarms and home burglar alarm systems are widely available from a number of suppliers.

(iv) What substitutes are there for the firm's products and who supplies them?

Although I would describe a neighbourhood watch scheme as complementary to what the police do, it can also act as a substitute, so that areas covered by effective schemes of this sort are patrolled less often by the police. Also, some of the home security devices on the market are increasingly seen as an essential replacement for the 'bobby on the beat', which is a relatively expensive form of crime prevention. Private security firms have in turn taken advantage of the lack of local police presence by providing low-cost protection by having personnel located near factories, warehouses or other likely commercial targets.

Even in the catching of criminals an increasing number of transgressors are not actively pursued, with the burden of pursuit being taken by private investigators, or simply written off.

(v) What things are likely to cause shifts in the demand curves facing the firm?

The demand for police services is a 'derived demand' since nobody wants it as a thing in itself but because of crime. So, changes in the nature of crime, or even in the amount of crime in society in total, will have an effect. A rise in the number of crimes committed will increase demand for police services, while a greater fear of crime will increase demand for more crime prevention regardless of whether crime has risen or not. A rise in price and less use of the home security, commercial security guards and other substitutes discussed above will also increase demand. In addition, increased use of complements such as security cameras and the like will also increase demand. There have also been changes in the nature of demand. Advances in technology such as computerised banking, for example, mean that the opportunities for computer-related frauds are increased, while use of roads has increased demand for traffic policing, and so on.

(vi) What supplies does the firm use?

The police use land, buildings and car parks. They also use all manner of capital machines, including cars, computers and communications technology. The labour they use can be divided into members of the police force, and support staff who are not members of the force. They also have extensive accumulated knowledge in staff, since many employees are in the force for all their working lives although there is a question about how well this experience is codified. In addition, they have extensive databases to assist in their detection work, again, however, there are questions regarding this, particularly about how well information is shared between forces because of the long-standing separation of the national force into regional units and specialist departments. There is often, for example, a gap between CID and the rest of the force even within a single police station. There have, however, been attempts of late to improve the use of their knowledge assets through the combining, examination and codification of what has been learnt across departmental and geographical regions, as in the widely publicised Operation 'Bumblebee'.

(vii) What market structure is the firm in?

Competitors do spring up; a central London borough has, for example, used a private 'police force' to patrol its parks, and some vigilante groups have been known to 'take the law into their own hands' as the saying goes. In addition, there are flourishing private investigation and home security industries in the

UK. Nonetheless, much of the service provided by the police is only effectively provided by them, which means that they do have some monopoly power. By law they cannot charge for what they do, but in this instance monopoly power could come out in other ways; an inefficient service, for example, would amount to overcharging taxpayers. A force could use its power to pick and choose which crimes to pursue and thereby in a sense act as a discriminating monopoly. To attenuate any tendency towards either of these or indeed any other way of exploiting customers, there is an extensive political involvement in the police force, from local council level up to cabinet level.

(viii) What things are likely to cause shifts in its supply curve and those of its rivals?

Advances in the use of information and communication technology have enabled the police to supply more of certain services for less. Changes in the price of the technologies that they use can also have an impact, since we expect the police to keep up with the latest advances. Labour costs may also change. Increasing use of support staff who are not members of the force has proved to be one way of keeping wage costs down. On the other hand, there is a widespread recognition of the difficulties of the job and a powerful 'trade union' both acting to increase police pay.

(ix) Why did the firm make a profit (or loss) last year?

Because this organisation is in the public sector it receives its revenue from taxation rather than being a function of the price paid for the good. In Figure A2.1, this budget is depicted as independent of the output of the police although in practice bigger forces will get more. The aim of the organisation is then to solve and prevent as much crime as possible, that is, to deliver as much output as it can within its budget, point 'x' on the graph.

Figure A2.1

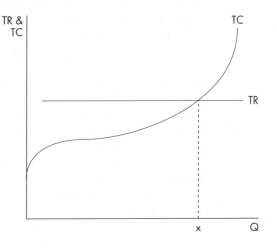

The aim is not therefore to maximise profits but to maximise output. For example, the police force can, by lowering its cost structure, move 'x' to the right as shown in Figure A2.2, which we would describe as an improvement in the efficiency of the police and might be revealed in such things as better clear-up rates and the like.

Figure A2.2

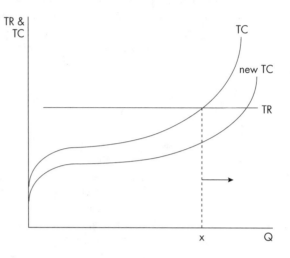

(x) What developments in the business environment (trends or changes) could affect the firm over the next five years?

One change that has been implemented by some police forces is the policy of 'zero tolerance'. The impetus to this change is largely a political and social one, since it stems from the widespread public concern over crime rates that has been taken up as a major issue by politicians. The idea behind zero tolerance is to discourage any crime, however petty, as a signal to the perpetrator of the seriousness of breaking the law, rather than as an indication of the scale of the offence. This is important since most criminals begin with petty crime, and it creates a culture in which potential criminals see risks in embarking on even the pettiest of criminal acts.

(xi) Analyse the impact of these developments on the firm

There are two main effects of this. Firstly, there is the direct effect on those forces that adopt this policy, and secondly there is the indirect effect on those that do not, since all forces' performances are compared.

The first effect is that those forces adopting this strategy will at least initially have higher costs than previously since there will be more crimes to process. In effect, this policy recognises the excess demand for the services provided by the police, 'a' to 'b' in Figure A2.3, and responds to this by supplying 'c', which will tend to raise costs.

Figure A2.3

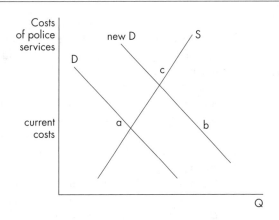

The second effect is that at 'c' in the diagram more demand is being met and more crimes solved, so that police forces who do not adopt this approach will look like under-performers at least in total, if not for the serious crimes. In addition, if the policy works, serious crime will be reduced as well. There may also be a displacement effect, however, for if some forces are spending more then some criminal activity will divert out of the higher-spending areas and into the lower-spending ones. In addition, if those that spend more in this way get more money from the government, and the Home Secretary has in supporting zero tolerance effectively underwritten the extra expenditure, then there is an incentive for all of them to adopt it. This would mean that it amounts to a rise in total spending on police services overall. If not, then there will be pressure to spend less elsewhere, in which case a zero tolerance area might also be an area of low spending on crime prevention, and the net effect of the policy on the organisation will be unclear.

(xii) **What changes in the external environment in the past have been of particular importance to the firm? Evaluate the reactions of the firm to these changes**

One environmental change that is beginning to have a belated impact on the police is the recognition and rejection of discrimination within and by organisations. This reflects changes in the social and demographic environment in the UK over the past few decades. In particular, it reflects a decline in overt racism and sexism, and the monitoring and airing of these issues in the media and though such bodies as the Commission for Racial Equality. Although discrimination continues, there is evidence that the changes in the employment policies of most firms are ahead of that of the police in reflecting these changes. The police have failed to respond to this change in a number of ways. Firstly, there is evidence of racism and sexism within the force, which discourages recruitment and the progress of discriminated staff. Not only does this raise ethical issues, it also impacts on the traditional concerns of economists such as productivity, for as Becker (1957) showed, discrimination reduces efficiency. Secondly, there is evidence of discrimination against other stakeholders too, in particular of treating the ethnic minority population in a different way than the rest of the population. For example, there are recorded instances of crimes against ethnic minorities being treated as in principle less serious than other crimes. In addition, there is evidence of a tendency within the force to 'stop and search' members of ethnic minorities more than anyone else. Indeed, matters have come to a head with a recent enquiry into the Metropolitan Police finding that racism may have played a part in the failure to both find and convict the murderers of Stephen Lawrence. This is not to suggest that every police officer is racist or sexist, or that these are not still facets of the broader social environment in the UK today. However, to the extent that these facets of discrimination are not evaluated and checked to the same extent as in other organisations, it exposes a failure within the force to deal with a change in its environment that is clearly having an impact on operational effectiveness.

ASSIGNMENT, EXAMPLE 3

Finally, a quick example from a large well-known firm on which information is freely available, Cadbury Schweppes plc.

(i) Who are the firm's stakeholders?

As a plc, Cadbury has shareholders, as well as workers, customers, suppliers and benefactors, including some national charities, sports events, and of course, the TV programme Coronation Street.

(ii) Why do customers buy this firm's products?

People enjoy the taste of chocolate and the other types of confectionery and drinks that Cadbury sells. Many of its products, such as its Milk Tray boxed chocolate and the loose Roses selection boxes for example. In addition, cocoa, which is a main ingredient of many of its products, including all those labelled chocolate, contain phenylethylamine, which by boosting the levels of seratonin in the brain triggers sensations of pleasure. People therefore can develop an attachment to the pleasure that chocolate brings above that of many other types of food. In addition, people buy Cadbury's because the range of products it supplies, each with slightly different characteristics, means that nearly everyone has a favourite. It also advertises heavily, with particular emphasis on the purple colour that is a consistent theme across many of their brands; indeed, it has attempted to copyright the colour itself.

(iii) What complements and facilitators are there for the firm's products and who supplies them?

Cadbury does not generally sell direct to the public, but through all manner of shops, from corner shops to supermarkets. Things that facilitate the sale of these can therefore include all the things that make corner shop or supermarket shopping convenient. In addition, many of the things sold within a shop will complement Cadbury products, such as tea and coffee. Indeed, think of the circumstance of giving a box of chocolates to someone and all manner of complements spring to mind: a card, flowers, champagne and so on.

(iv) What substitutes are there for the firm's products and who supplies them?

Mars and Nestlé are Cadbury's main direct competitors providing many similar sorts of products, and there is also a growing supermarket own-brand threat. In addition, there are types of drinks, such as alcoholic drinks, and other types of foods and snacks, such as crisps and nuts, that are not supplied by Cadbury but which can act as substitutes to Cadbury's output.

(v) What things are likely to cause shifts in the demand curves facing the firm?

A rise in the price of the substitutes listed above will shift the demand curve for Cadbury's goods to the right. So, for example, if Nestlé raises the price of its confectionery products, fewer people will buy them and more people will buy Cadbury's instead; as shown in Figure A3.1 this will shift the demand for Cadbury's products to the right.

Figure A3.1

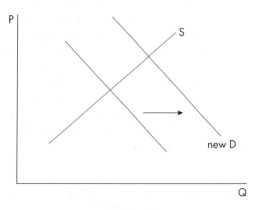

A similar thing would happen if the price of complements fell. If, for example, coffee prices fell and people who are in the habit of having some chocolate with it drink more of it, then the more chocolate they will eat. People may also eat more confectionery if the eating of it is made easier in some way. For example, installing more chocolate-vending machines in public places would facilitate more sales. A change in tastes favouring the good, or an improvement in the qualities of the good would also shift demand to the right, as would more advertising, or even a run of improved Coronation Street scripts. In addition, we may tend to see a rise in the sales of confectionery simply from rising incomes and population growth.

(vi) What supplies does the firm use?

Cadbury uses a range of edible materials such as cocoa, milk and sugar to make its confectionery and drinks. It also uses water which it takes from national supplies but which it further purifies before use. It also use plastics and boxes to wrap its products. In addition to these, the firm uses capital, packaging machines, computers and so on. Indeed, its factories are amongst the most technologically advanced in the world. In the 'Wispa' factory, for example, temperature is monitored at 1000 different points and is computer regulated, as is the size of the bubbles in the chocolate (to an accuracy of a third of a millimetre). Cadbury also employs over 41,000 people worldwide and over 10,000 in the UK.

(vii) What market structure is the firm in?

The firm is in an oligopolistic market, with the biggest three firms accounting for 70% of confectionery sales in the UK in 1997. Cadbury itself is the largest player, taking 30% of the total market, followed by Mars which takes 20% which is closely followed by Nestlé which takes 19%. Cadbury also has a sizeable chunk of the world confectionery and soft drinks markets. This means that profits are high and prices are sticky; indeed Cadbury publishes a list of recommended prices that can be compared with that of its rivals. The main forms of competition are branding, advertising and product differentiation, which in this case amounts to the floating of several new products each year. In this business this can, for example, amount to no more than making something smaller; indeed, 'bite size' bars were considered something of an innovation in the 1980s, while in the 1990s we saw the advent of ice-cream bars of favourite brands of confectionery. Generally, however, product innovation in this industry means simply mixing different amounts of nuts, biscuits, bubbles, flavours and textures to create a new bar.

(viii) What things are likely to cause shifts in its supply curve and those of its rivals?

A change in availability and price of any of the inputs listed above could shift supply curves in this industry. Over the past few years, some firms have managed to increase supply and lower costs by investing in improved capital equipment and factories, which is what Cadbury has being doing for some years. Many, including Cadbury, have also improved their training facilities and have adopted more flexible working patterns and arrangements. They are still none-theless subject to environmental changes such as changes in the cocoa and sugar crops as well as in milk production. They are also having to adjust their produc-tion methods and the extent of wrappings and such things in light of increased social concern for pollution and litter.

(ix) Why did the firm make a profit (or loss) last year?

Cadbury made nearly a billion pounds in profits before tax last year. It managed this by keeping its costs down through a slight reduction in staffing, but mainly due to a significant rise in productivity over the past few years. This is largely due to substantial investment in new and improved plant and machinery as well as a host of associated training schemes. On the revenue side, it continues to benefit from its oligopolistic position and has kept ahead of the competi-tion by continued heavy advertising, including a tie-up with the popular soap Coronation Street. Continued product innovation and good distribution channels have also played a part in this.

(x) What developments in the business environment (trends or changes) could affect the firm over the next five years?

One important change in this firm's environment would be the acceptance of the proposal that has been floated within the EU's corridors of power, namely to classify as chocolate only those products conforming to the European style. This could have a devastating effect on Cadbury as it would mean that most of the chocolate products it now makes would have to be called something else.

(xi) Analyse the impact of these developments on the firm

The effect of such a change, were it to happen, could be to reduce demand if people began to feel that it was inferior to 'real' chocolate. Cadbury could respond to this in a number of ways, but one obvious long-term solution is to start to replace its products with the continental-style chocolate. However, this is likely to put its costs up, as it would mean using more chocolate and less vegetable fat. This would mean either a reduction in margins or a reduc-tion in supply and higher prices being charged to the customer as shown in Figure A3.2.

Figure A3.2

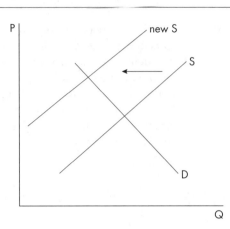

Costs will also tend to rise even if they do not, as the packaging would have to be redesigned, although most products, including its biggest selling chocolate-only product 'Dairy Milk', do not feature the word chocolate that strongly.

(xii) **What changes in the external environment in the past have been of particular importance to the firm? Evaluate the reactions of the firm to these changes**

One change in the environment that has been particularly important is that of the rise of consumer awareness and the proliferation of consumer programmes on TV. These developments mean that any lack of quality control in this industry, such as the finding of insect or animal parts in confectionery, can make the firm concerned a laughing stock. There has always been a problem of quality control in this industry since it involves the factory production of huge quantities of individually wrapped edible products. Even in the 1990s some of the French bottled water suppliers came to grief on this issue when their inability to stop unwanted elements contaminating their product became front page news. Cadbury, despite having a good record in this respect, has nonetheless been at the forefront of tackling this issue, and it is another environmental change, technological advance, that has allowed them to do it. Computer technology in particular has allowed the automation of production to such an extent that unwanted extraneous elements have few opportunities to get into the product. The scale of its investment in this can be gauged by the fact that it spent £40m constructing 10 processing plants across Europe to purify mains water before it is used in the production of any of its soft drink products.

PART 3

The role of environmental analysis

In this last part we look at how firms analyse their environments and discuss how this should be done in light of what we have learned in the first two parts. In other words, we will be looking at the role of environmental analysis.

Learning and quantification

After studying this chapter, you should be able to:

- distinguish between a reactive and a proactive approach to dealing with the business environment;

- be aware that learning is driven by our assumptions rather than independent of them and that different assumptions and indeed different strategies to learning will result in different things being learnt;

- understand that learning is costly both financially and in terms of time, which means there is a supply of it in respect of those costs as well as a demand for it for the benefits that it brings;

- appreciate how a firm might quantify the likely effects of future trends or changes in the business environment upon it;

- understand how supply and demand analysis can be quantified in order to provide both a prediction of the future and an explanation of the past;

- appreciate the role of scenarios based on the quantification of a range of possibilities in the formulation of firms' strategies;

- be aware of the limitations of quantification techniques and the importance of uncertainty;

- be aware of the limitations that organisational processes and contexts place on both learning and forecasting.

15.1   THE LEARNING ORGANISATION

Environmental complexity and turbulence mean that environmental understanding itself has become a source of competitive advantage, with many people now envisaging the successful firms of the future being those who can learn most about their environment and their scope for action within it. Alongside those who have a practical concern for the management of this and other kinds of knowledge within the organisation, such as information technology specialists and corporate planners, are academics looking at how this learning takes place. The concern is to discover how it happens and the factors that promote it or militate against it, which may be organisational, behavioural or indeed environmental. For example, as we shall see later in this chapter, turbulence increases the rewards for environmental learning but makes it harder to do. In looking at the acquisition of such knowledge a distinction can be drawn between what individuals in an organisation learn and what can be seen as having been learnt by the organisation itself in terms of its stock of codified information, procedures, common practices, and rules. References to this 'organisational learning' can be confusing, however, since what some people mean by this is the processes involved in acquiring the knowledge, while others refer to the outcome, that is, what has been learnt. For our purposes it is enough to note the importance of acquiring a stock of knowledge about the environment, and the firm's relationship to it, while recognising that only a subset of that learning will be encoded within the organisation itself. We will not concern ourselves here with the determinants of the size of that subset, even though the business environment may have an influence on that too.

15.1.1 Reactive and proactive approaches

The assumptions that are made by decision makers within the firm about the relationship between the firm and its environment will determine how they approach learning about it. We can identify two main contrasting approaches to this: reactive and proactive.

- The **reactive approach** is to wait and see what happens; the advantage of this is that what is being reacted to becomes clearer as it unfolds, and therefore the possibility of erroneous responses is reduced. It also allows time for everyone in the firm to be clear about the nature of the threat, or opportunity, so that the firm is more likely to move in unison and with a shared sense of purpose than if a more proactive approach is used. There may also be 'last-mover advantages', such as those that accrue, for example, to the last firm to use a new technology as they are able to learn from the mistakes of earlier movers. The disadvantages are that there may be bigger first-mover advantages and moving after the event may be too late; both of these are likely to be less of a problem in simple, stable environments. The requirement of this approach in terms of environmental information gathering is that the firm knows what is currently happening, which means that it must correctly interpret the signals from the environment.

- The alternative to this approach is the **proactive approach** in which the firm anticipates and acts in advance of events. The requirement for this is, again, that the environment is understood, but in this case, the emphasis is on prediction as well as on appreciating what is currently happening.

The disadvantages are, firstly, that the predictions might be wrong and any changes introduced will need to be reversed. Secondly, that it might not be clear what the best course of action is even if the prediction is correct, and thirdly, that the firm may not act in unison if the vision of what needs to be done is not shared. The advantages are that the firm moves early and is likely to be able to gain first-mover advantages and to be able to exert more control over events. This is probably of most value in turbulent and complex environments.

Which approach is used will depend on the culture of the firm, the experiences of decision makers within it, where it is on the environmental learning curve, what its goals are, and whether its environment tends to be turbulent or stable. With both approaches, environment information is required. However, gaining knowledge is not just a case of getting more information, since facts do not speak for themselves; the ability to use information effectively to deepen or broaden understanding means that interpretation is required. This implies that some modelling process of either a formal or informal nature is required to make sense of the data, which means that in looking at how firms come to deal with their environments we are dealing with a learning process rather than a data collection exercise.

15.1.2 How firms learn

People approach the analysis of events with certain assumptions in mind, formed from the stock of knowledge that they have accumulated about similar events in the past. They also approach learning itself with certain assumptions about how it is best done, so they have both ideas about what has occurred and ideas about how to find out about it. Given that firms are made up of people, we can refer to learning by firms in a comparable manner. This means that assumptions about what the firm does, what its place in the environment is, and how environmental analysis should be done are needed in order for decision-makers to decide what data is important in the first place. They might then conduct a search for such information, perhaps they write this process down in some way, in an impact assessment grid, for example, or perhaps they decide on what is important in a meeting or through discussions over lunch. But however, or wherever it is done, it is never done in a vacuum; within firms it is inevitably a collective process, so that where they look, how they look and what they do with the information are driven by their assumptions and the assumptions of those around them. Having searched in what they consider to be the right directions, the firm's decision makers might then begin to form some tentative explanations (hypotheses) by seeing patterns and connections in and amongst the data. This will then be cross-referenced with their existing knowledge and their approach to learning that actually led them in that direction in the first place. This means that in looking at how firms learn we are dealing with a reciprocal process, as shown in Figure 15.1.

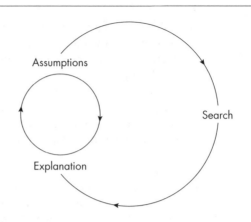

Figure 15.1 How firms learn.

15.1.3 The equilibrium amount of learning

The explanations in sum total constitute the firm's model of its environment and its relationship to it. This will enable it to react to, or even anticipate the effect of, events in the environment on it. If it does not, then the firm will be buffeted and surprised by events, its hypotheses will be falsified (proved wrong), and it will have an incentive to revise its explanations and interpretations (its 'model'). There is an incentive to do this since if others have a better model and are able therefore to make better decisions, a relatively poor model may be correlated with business failure. However, this does not mean that businesses close inexorably on the truth, since there are limits to what can be known; even with full information, certain patterns are unknowable except after the event, in cases where chaos rules, for example. In addition, events cannot be predicted if they are unique and unprecedented. Firms may also face limited competition, which reduces the pressures to perform optimally in everything they do, including their learning, so we may see more 'satisficing' than 'maximising' behaviour in this respect. Also, even if firms aim to maximise their environmental learning, they do so within the constraints of limited time and information. Moreover, the costs of gathering information are likely to rise the more of it is done, which means that there is an upward-sloping supply curve of information in respect of this search, as shown in Figure 15.2. On the other side of the equation the demand is a derived demand, since the information is of little interest in itself; it is desired only if it imparts power – if, for example, it leads to strategic advantages over rivals. Despite the constraints and limitations, there is evidence that firms' learning can be approached in this way, since, for example, they tend to review their assumptions in times of great upheaval when the gains for correct interpretations are likely to be at their highest. Similarly, firms in turbulent environments seem to expend more effort and have wider search patterns than those in stable ones, since a firm facing only a few possible sources of change is likely to have fewer benefits in widening its search. Its demand for information is likely to be less, therefore, than that of a firm in a complex and turbulent environment, as shown in Figure 15.2.

Figure 15.2 The optimal amount of information when there is a cost to gathering it.

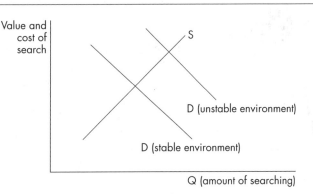

Firms in turbulent environments are therefore more likely to adopt a pro-active approach to learning and to do more searching and learning about that environment than other firms do. In other words, how firms approach learning about their environments, and how much of it they do, depends on the environment too.

15.2 QUANTIFYING THE RELATIONSHIP BETWEEN FIRMS AND THEIR ENVIRONMENTS

15.2.1 Scenarios

The economic approach that we have adopted in this text allows us to limit our search and conceptualise our firm's relationship with its environment in a relatively simple way. However, you will have noticed that the discussions thus far have focused on the directions of changes and the types of impacts they will have rather than the exact magnitudes of each. It is to the magnitudes that we now turn: If we can establish the magnitude of the relationship between a quantifiable factor in the environment and its effect on the firm, then we can see what will happen when we change the factor. By doing this we can predict the effects on a firm of any environmental events, be they classified as a change or as a trend. In fact, since perfect foresight is rare, we might decide in practice to look at several different scenarios based on a range of possible environmental outcomes, as in Figure 15.3. The diagram shows three scenarios for different levels of ice-cream sales for a small manufacturer in Cornwall based on how hot the summer is going to be.

The firm cannot predict how hot the summer is going to be, but it can develop some scenarios since the temperature in summer is likely to be within certain limits. At best, the summer will be a bit hotter than ever before and at worst as bad as it was two summers ago. This gives us two outer limits labelled 'hot summer' and 'cool summer'. The firm thinks sales will be somewhere between the two (although with so few years' data it may be failing to spot the upward trend in temperatures associated with global warming). From this the

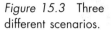

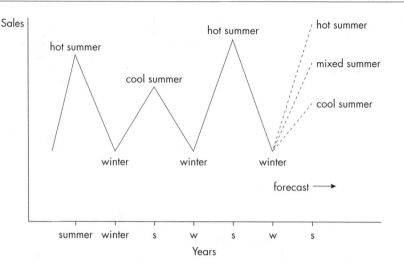

Figure 15.3 Three different scenarios.

firm might develop three scenarios and associated contingency plans for what happens in either extreme case, and for its central forecast between the two. In doing this the firm can ensure that it is not caught out by buying too much milk (or whatever), if it turns out to be a cool summer, or by hiring too few workers (or whatever), if it turns out to be a scorcher.

15.2.2 Quantification of effects

In the case above, the firm can establish the strength of the relationship between summer temperatures and ice-cream sales simply by looking at the graph and extrapolating. However, if there are two things that are likely to affect sales, graphical interpretation of this sort becomes tricky, and with three things almost impossible. Instead, we have to use statistical methods, in particular a set of techniques called **multiple regression analysis**. This works by identifying cause and effect relationships from multiple data, by isolating the effect on one variable, such as the demand for a firm's products, of changes in another variable, such as people's incomes, in the presence of lots of other things that are changing too. This is in the same spirit as the approach we have taken throughout this book except that in the diagrams we assume the absence of other factors. In, for example, explaining shifts in supply or demand we look at the thing that caused it to happen, assuming everything else remains equal. With diagrams we have to assume that other things remain equal otherwise we get a visual mess; with regression analysis, however, we are not constrained in this way.

In this text we do not cover how to do regression analysis; interested readers are referred to any introductory 'econometrics' text. We can, however, get a feel for how this analysis works. To do this we begin by looking at a simple supply and demand diagram (Figure 15.4), but in this case we will add in the numbers.

Figure 15.4 Supply and demand with numbers attached.

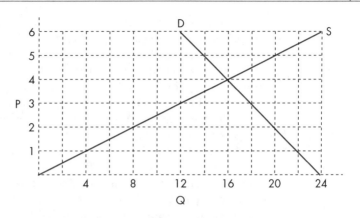

The diagram shows that there is a relationship between price and supply, specifically that supply goes up when price goes up. The behaviour is captured in the following 'behavioural' equation:

$$Qs = 0 + 4P$$

This says that quantity supplied is zero when price is zero and when price goes up supply goes up by four times as much. In other words, the relationship is a positive one and the strength of the relationship is four.

Demand, on the other hand, is inversely related to price, in this case:

$$Qd = 24 - 2P$$

In this case 24 will be demanded when price is zero, and each increase in price reduces demand by two.

15.2.3 Simultaneous equilibrium

The price and quantity that will be settled on in this market is simultaneously determined by the interaction of supply and demand. We can, as usual, simplify matters by just looking at equilibria; in this way we can develop a simplification of reality that covers its main features, which is to say that we can 'model' it. In this case the equilibrium where the lines cross and market demand = market supply is when the price is four and the quantity sold is 16. We can find this algebraically too:

$$
\begin{aligned}
Qd &= Qs \\
24 - 2P &= 0 + 4P \\
24 - 0 &= 4P + 2P \\
24 &= 6P \\
24/6 &= P \\
4 &= P
\end{aligned}
$$

We can use this to find the equilibrium quantity, since if $Qd = 24 - 2P$ then in equilibrium when $P = 4$, Qd must be $24 - 2 \times 4 = 24 - 8 = 16$.

Learning how to solve simultaneous equations is not our purpose here. It is simply that to quantify the things that affect prices and sales we have to start from the knowledge that these are determined simultaneously by two largely separate things: supply and demand. This in turn means that to explain P and Q and therefore revenues, costs and profits too, we need to quantify the things that affect supply and demand. We can do this, since any factor that we think could shift demand or supply, including any environmental ones, can be added and the model solved with their influence included, as long as we can quantify them in some way and if the regression analysis confirms that they are important. Even such things as political and social change can be quantified, at worst simply by giving events on a particular date a value of one and letting the regression quantify the effects associated with that date. More typically, firms will include easily quantifiable factors, such as, on the demand side, the price of substitutes (PS) and consumers' incomes (Y), for example. We can then add these shifters to our equation for demand, as shown below:

$$Qd = 24 - 2P + PS + Y$$

Since these factors are the causal ones, and can vary independently of our model, we refer to them as the independent variables. In contrast, P and Q are the dependent variables in this model since they are determined within it by the interaction of supply and demand, with what happens to them being dependent on what happens to the independent variables. Often the only way of measuring these effects is over time. But when we look at something over time, we know that any number of things will be happening as we go along. The art of econometrics in general and regression analysis in particular is therefore to untangle these effects so that a unique summary average value can be attached to the effect of each independent variable on the dependent ones. However, even with the aid of advanced statistical packages, once we have calculated these 'coefficients', denoted 'a', 'b', 'c' and 'd' below, we will generally find that we have not explained everything that has happened to the dependent variables, that something (denoted 'u' below) has been left out. This does not mean that we have made a mistake, as some residual error will remain for as long as the model is a simplification, since by definition simplifying means leaving something out.

Effect (dependent variable)	*Causes (independent variables)*
Qd	$= a - bP + cPS + dY + u$
	$a = intercept \quad u = unexplained, \ model \ 'error'$

However, it is essential not to leave anything important out. Whether you have or not can be difficult to assess, but one thing that can be used to check for this is the error term 'u', since if a graph or statistical tests on 'u' reveal a pattern then that suggests that something important has been left out. This is because a pattern in 'u' means that there is a pattern in the data of the dependent variable that we have failed to explain with the independent ones. On the other hand, simply adding more causal factors is not an option, since what we include must be important and there are a number of statistical tests of this, and there is a limit to how many variables we can have in each model. Good econometrics is therefore a balancing act with no automatic procedure for getting the right answer, which is why I have referred to it as an art even though it is based on a lot of science. Although we are not going to cover the maths involved in regression analysis, it is worth noting that the natural logarithms of variables are often used. This is done for a number of reasons but the main one is convenience, since doing this to both dependent and independent variables makes the coefficient that expresses the relationship between the two a measure of elasticity. In the model of demand above, we can simply, by using logarithms of our data, estimate 'b', 'c' and 'd' as the PeD, XeD and YeD. If, for example, the data for the model is converted into logs and the regression analysis produces an estimate of −1.5 for the 'own price' (coefficient b), then −1.5 is the PeD, with every 1% rise (or fall) in P causing a 1.5% fall (or rise) in Qd. This is very convenient but it means that we are assuming that the PeD is always −1.5 when, as we have seen, it is likely to vary along the demand curve, so that in fact price falls and price rises produce different figures. Ideally, the econometrician should test which form the variables should be calculated in to produce the best model, but it is very tempting to stick with the log form.

For supply, we could add in supply shifters in a similar manner. The two equations would then constitute our model of the determinants of P and Q in this market. In practice, we can add all manner of additional links; advertising, for example, could be included in our demand equation for although it is not an environmental factor and is decided upon by the firm, it nonetheless shifts demand. We could even predict it too, by including it as a dependent variable by modelling it. However, if we do, we are making things more complex, since advertising not only affects demand but is affected by demand, because firms with more sales can afford more advertising. In other words, we have a simultaneously determined feedback loop between advertising and sales, and sales and advertising, which means that in adding an equation for advertising, we will have to simultaneously solve three equations, not two. We might also want to consider the effect of sales on costs, since costs of production rise as sales increase (one of these costs being the costs of advertising), which would give us four equations to solve simultaneously. We can picture these links more clearly in a diagram (Figure 15.5).

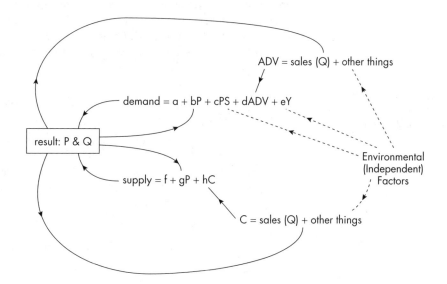

Figure 15.5 A system of equations based on supply and demand.

15.2.4 Using the model

By solving this model we can both explain the past pattern and predict the future path of sales (Q), prices (P), total revenue (P × Q), costs, and advertising spend that are all consistent with each other. By subtracting costs from revenues, we can also produce a profit forecast in which the constituent numbers are again all logically consistent with each other. If, therefore, a firm has the resources to do this kind of formal modelling, the benefits can be divided into those arising from both better explanation and from improved forecasting.

15.2.5 Explanation

Figure 15.6 A turbulent market.

Figure 15.6 shows a market with large swings in sales and prices on the left, and the associated time series graph showing the resulting pattern of sales on the right.

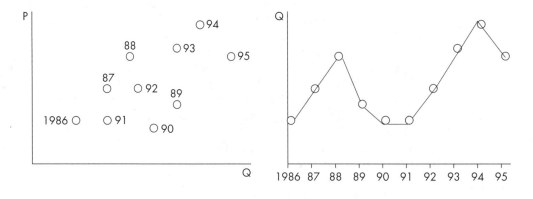

Using supply and demand equations we can undo the simultaneity and get at the separate causes, as shown in Figure 15.7. The advantage of quantification is simply that it can confirm which of the shifters was responsible for any given shift and how big the effect of each is. In the case above, we find that:

Figure 15.7 The explanation for the observed pattern.

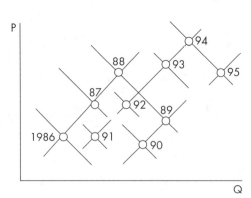

1. demand shifted right due largely to rising incomes: 1986–8;
2. the entry of new firms shifted supply to the right: 1988–9;
3. the boom ended and demand shifted left: 1990;
4. recession began with demand continuing to fall and some firms leaving the industry, so both demand and supply fell: 1991;
5. demand rose steadily as the economy began to recover: 1992–4;
6. a large Japanese supplier entered the industry, increasing supply: 1995.

15.2.6 Forecasting

Forecasts from these kinds of econometric models are created by putting in future values for the independent variables and seeing what they imply for the future of the dependent ones on the basis that the coefficients do not change. The future of the dependent variables is then simply the new data for the independent ones multiplied by the old coefficients that link the two. If, for example, we expect nothing to happen next year except that incomes rise by 2%, and the model shows that sales rise by 1% for every 1% rise in incomes, then sales will rise by 2% next year. The accuracy of our forecast depends on three things: firstly, that the model is a good representation of reality, secondly, that the co-efficients do not change in the future, and thirdly, that we get the right forecasts for the independent variables. For the first two, we have a plethora of statistical tests that help us to identify the underlying long-run relationships. However, the reliability of these will vary as both the reliability of the data and the volatility of relationships differ. On the third, we can search for the most reliable sources of forecast for these. We might use the government's own forecasts, or perhaps pay for some more detailed ones from an independent source such as the London Business School Centre for Economic Forecasting. In addition, we can put in different numbers in case things do not pan out as expected; in other words, we can investigate some different scenarios. We could, for example, have a central forecast based on incomes rising 2% and two alternatives based on what happens if we have 4% and 0% growth in incomes.

15.2.7 Scenarios and strategies

Considering the implications for the firm of a range of possible futures should help decision makers prepare for the future in two respects. Firstly, preparing for an anticipated change is easier than preparing for an unanticipated one, and secondly, they can determine which future is best for them and can work towards it, in effect to steer their environment in the direction that suits them. Firms, for example, envisaging a future threat may be able to eliminate it through lobbying parliament. The firm can also build different scenarios based on different things the firm might do. So, for example, although we have put advertising in the model as a function of past sales or profits, we can use it as a 'decision variable' and change it deliberately to see what happens, because we know that the firm can do that. Similarly, we might consider what happens if the firm lowers or raises its prices by some amount. A firm might do this to investigate a number of strategic options, particularly if it feels confident that its model captures rivals' likely reactions in some way, as this will allow them to establish the pay-offs and thus the best strategies in the 'games' they play. To assist firms with some forms of 'what if' analysis by showing what strategies work in different situations and environments, the Strategic Planning Institute set up a database in which this kind of information was collected, known as PIMS.

15.2.8 The PIMS model

The PIMS (Profit Impact of Market Strategy) model was designed to determine what strategies work best and in what circumstances (which means there is an environmental element). Data is collected on over 1000 businesses and over 2000 SBUs. Regression equations have been estimated using performance indicators of such things as profitability and cash flow, as the dependent variables. The independent variables used to explain these include things such as rate of growth, market share, degree of market concentration, product quality, labour productivity, spending on R&D, spending on marketing, investment spending, and so on. There are, however, a number of criticisms of the PIMS model. It is criticised by econometricians on the basis that it is not well constructed, and that it contains so many similar independent variables that causality is often difficult to determine, as the closeness of each makes separating out their individual effects hard. Finally, it is criticised by strategists on the basis that it does not tell firms how to get from one situation to another, which is what most strategists spend their time thinking about. As an example of the problems, we can consider perhaps the most important finding of this research, that a large market share and vertical integration are associated with high profitability and high cash flow. This might seem rather obvious and uncontroversial; however, while we would expect them to be related to each other, large market share may in part be the result of, as well as resulting in, high profitability. To investigate such issues of causality a more refined approach than that found in the PIMS model is needed. In addition, knowing that there is an association, a correlation in other words, between vertical integration, market share and profitability does not tell a firm how to become a vertically integrated market leader. What the PIMS model does provide, however, is a set of benchmark coefficients for firms to score their products against. So it can help answer questions like whether, given their market share and product quality, a firm is making as much profit as firms in other industries with similar market shares and similar quality products do. It can also help with 'what if' questions. So, for example, in launching a new product it is useful to know that high marketing expenditure coupled with a poor-quality product is associated with poor cash flow. That, in other words, a poor-quality new product does not fool people. This is a common-sense example but the scale and breadth of the PIMS database make it a useful check on a number of portfolio-planning issues for firms.

15.2.9   Limitations of environmental analysis

Econometric analysis does not contain an automatic truth search procedure; the econometrician has to make judgements about what to include, what to leave out, how to formulate the relationships and so on, which means that econometrics does not solve the searching and learning problem. It is helpful in determining what data to search for (insofar as the model shows what data is important and what can be ignored), and it helps us to learn about the environment (since the model's hypotheses are subject to standard statistical tests as well as judgement). But as there remains an interplay of facts, assumptions and interpretations even in the most formal search, learning and modelling procedures, then who does them, why, and in what context will remain crucial, as indicated in Figure 15.8.

Figure 15.8
Environmental analysis in theory and practice.

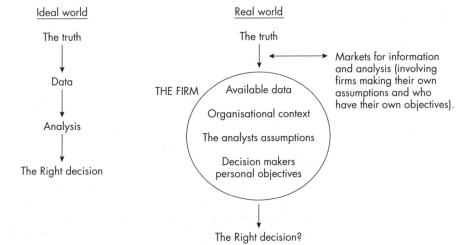

Even if we de-contextualise the process of learning about the environment and assume that we can, by maximising our use of information, create the best possible model, our rationality will, nonetheless, be 'bounded'. It will be bounded by the fact that the costs of gathering information and learning make some knowledge unaffordable relative to the benefits that it brings, as discussed earlier. It is also bounded by the fact that the world has an element of uncertainty within it, which means that there will always be surprises. The problem is that econometrics relies on finding patterns, when sometimes there is no pattern and the future is therefore inherently uncertain and unpredictable. Indeed some events are unique and, having no precedent, have created no pattern for the econometrician to find. In addition, recent research shows that even often-repeated events can be unpredictable in their details, so that even if we know what causes what, and how, there is a level of detail that we cannot get at: a level of unknowability and therefore of unpredictability. When this is encountered, systems exhibit a pattern that is governed by the laws of chaos, which are as yet largely unknown. To see an example of chaos in action, consider a model of house prices in which there are only two influences:

1. House prices go up because house prices went up last month because everyone wants to get on the bandwagon. There is, in other words, a positive feedback loop between last month's price and this month's.

2. House prices go down because people feel that at some point house prices will stop rising. There is, in other words, a negative feedback loop between last month's price and this month's.

Assuming that by econometric analysis we establish that the two coefficients that attach to this behaviour are 1.1 and 1.8 respectively, then we get an equilibrating system in which these two forces balance out. This means we can predict the evolution of a stable future for house prices over time, in the absence of anything else happening, as shown in Figure 15.9.

Figure 15.9 An equilibrating system.

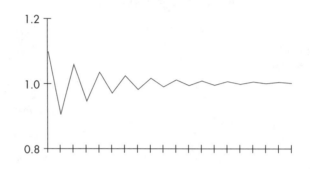

On the other hand, if we put in 1.33333334 and 3 respectively, we get explosive instability in which house prices go on falling continuously, which just shows that it is too simple a model, since in reality that cannot happen. However, what is interesting is that if we just change the first number fractionally to 1.3333333 we get a chaotic pattern, with at one point one type of feedback dominating and then the other in a random and unpredictable manner. If 1.3333333 is the coefficient in our model then, although the model may be right, the most that we can learn from it is that house prices will go up and down in an entirely unpredictable manner over time, as shown in Figure 15.10.

Figure 15.10 A chaotic pattern.

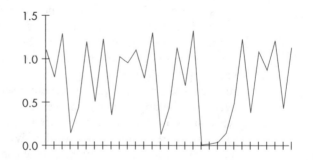

This does not of course mean that we should abandon modelling, since while chaos may be everywhere it is generally in the detail.

We also need to acknowledge that it is difficult to encapsulate in an econometric model the fact that the way something happens can affect the ultimate outcome, that how something gets to its destination can affect its destination, that, in short, history matters. As David's explanation of the continued use of the QWERTY keyboard discussed in Chapter 14 shows, sub-optimality is the inevitable result of the unfolding of history and how this leads to products, processes and indeed modes of thought that become locked in. We also saw a similar sub-optimal outcome resulting from the path of choices made in describing Arrow's impossibility theory. Indeed there is a growing body of research across a number to fields testifying to the fact that final outcomes depend on how you get there and that outcomes are 'path dependent', and which therefore puts the history of events at the heart of the analysis. This approach recognises that disequilibrium may not be a temporary state on the way to equilibrium but the only state there is. Perhaps the most colourful exposition of this different way of looking at the world is to be found in the work of G.L.S. Shackle (1949). He did a lot of work in the 1940s on how choices made in the face of uncertainty constrain the chooser's future options, although he is best remembered for his description of the economy as kaleidoscopic (after the toy), with small changes able to produce entirely new patterns. This ties in with a body of work on macro-economics by a group labelled 'Post-Keynesian' economists, who pick up on the theme of uncertainty, and the unknowability that it results in, mentioned in Chapter 12 of Keynes' General Theory.

15.3 ECONOMICS AND STRATEGY

Economists have tended to view strategy as some form of optimisation subject to the resource constraints of the environment and the opportunities and threats therein, so that ultimately the numbers can be plugged in and the problems solved. Indeed, some strides have been made in providing management with the tools to do this; computers certainly help and there is an analysis industry that includes all sorts, from astrologers who see clues to a firm's future in the stars, to management consultants who have plenty to say if the listener is paying and academics who have plenty to say even if no one is paying (or indeed listening). However, there is a fundamental limit to what can be known as our rationality is bounded, chaos is a feature of turbulent environments, and firms play games with indeterminate outcomes. In short, firms live in an uncertain world. So, in practice, there is no model that will tell a firm exactly what to do, and some kind of planning system, or process, is therefore required to establish the firm's position and options, and to decide on the best courses of action. A strategic planning algorithm can take many forms; what follows is a suggestion to show where environmental analysis comes in rather than any attempt to depict a typical one:

1. Specify objectives.
    In an owner-managed firm the emphasis may tend to be on profits; in a firm with a significant separation of ownership from control, then what managers want will have a high priority too. In a cooperative and in organisations

dominated by professional workers, what the workers want may have more priority than it does in other forms of organisations.

2. Conduct a PEST analysis and investigate implications either by using supply and demand diagrams or by employing econometric modelling techniques.

3. Conduct a SWOT analysis.

4. Evaluate strategic options. Conduct some 'what if' tests using scenarios based on the contingencies thrown up by the environment and simulate likely consequences of different courses of action by the firm.

In this process we bring together what we have learnt about the environment with what we know about the firm, as shown in Figure 15.11.

Figure 15.11 A planning process.

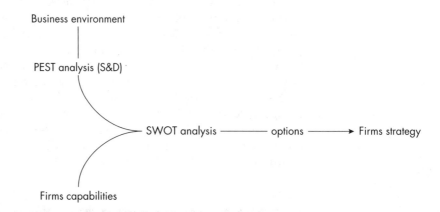

Having considered its options, the firm will then formulate its strategy, so now we shall turn to the link between strategy and environment. Unfortunately, there is no agreed link, and as the information firms seek (and what they end up doing with it when they get it) depends on this link we must consider a number of different approaches as outlined in the next chapter. Each of these has different implications about the role of environmental analysis, for although there is widespread agreement that the environment does matter, there is widespread disagreement on why it matters. But before we look at these differences we need to acknowledge that there are different approaches to strategy too.

15.4 STRATEGY

In formulating their strategies, firms may focus on shaping the company to meet environmental opportunities; this is the 'outside-in' approach. This is also sometimes called the market-led approach as the firm is looking at where the market is going as a cue to what it should do. Alternatively, the firm might use an 'inside-out' approach, in which the firm searches for opportunities to exploit its strengths. In this approach, as Clemens (1950, p. 2) points out, 'Any market reasonably accessible to the firm in which price is greater than marginal cost constitutes an invitation to invade.' The target market need not be related to the firm's existing markets in any way – all that is required is that the firm's competitive advantages (its strengths) can be utilised in it. In both approaches, the firm needs to understand its environment. For the outside-in approach it is rather obvious, as in this approach the success of the firm is seen as depending on its ability to fit its environment. However, it is also true, although less obviously so, for the inside-out approach. It is necessary in this case for three reasons. Firstly, a firm does not know what its strengths and weaknesses are except by comparison to other firms in its current, or target, market. Secondly, as previously mentioned in a different context, deciding whether some beneficial outcome results from one of the firm's strengths, or simply from an easily exploitable environmental opportunity, is not always easy. For example, a well-known British car manufacturer used to boast about the length of its waiting lists, as if that were a service to customers, and as it very rarely had any complaints about this it concluded that its customer relations were one of its strengths. However, although being in some queues has a certain kudos, in this case it was just a shabby neglect of its customers that it could get away with because it had a dominant position in a profitable niche. It began to realise the difference when the Japanese and German car manufacturers came and pushed it out of that cosy niche. Thirdly, environmental analysis is necessary in the inside-out approach to spot which markets have low entry and exit barriers and which can be profitably entered.

15.5 SUMMARY

- We can distinguish between a reactive and a proactive approach to dealing with the business environment.

- Learning does not occur in a vacuum; it is conditional upon our assumptions and the organisational context in which it takes place.

- Learning is also costly both financially and in terms of time. This means that not only is there a demand for it to reflect the benefits that it brings, but also a supply of it to reflect these costs.

- The equilibrium amount of learning is likely to be sensitive to the business environment itself. Historically, it certainly seems to be the case that firms have demanded more environmental analysis as environments have become more turbulent. We can picture this as a rightward shift in the demand for learning in turbulent environments compared to non-turbulent ones.

- Firms can quantify the likely effects of future trends or changes in the business environment upon it in a number of ways, including the attachment of numbers, by statistical means, to supply and demand curves. This enables the analyst to provide both a prediction of the future and an explanation of the past.

- In recognition that no forecasts are perfect, a range of scenarios based on the quantification of a range of possibilities can be used in the formulation of a firm's strategies.

- There are limits to how accurate forecasts of environmental changes are likely to be, since there is an element of uncertainty and chaos in the environment. We also have to be aware of the constraints involved; the previously mentioned costs suggest that learning will always be less than optimal, and we should add that organisational processes and contexts place limitations on the process too.

15.6 QUESTIONS

1. Present data on the main external influences acting on a firm of your choice, in what you consider to be an effective manner, and discuss how you would predict the future path of one of these using:
   (a) managers' views;
   (b) time series graphs;
   (c) analytical graphs (comparative static supply and demand diagrams, for example);
   (d) a monologue (in effect, you can tell the 'story' behind the data in words);
   (e) equations.

Figure 15.12

2. The figures shown in Figure 15.12 relate to the revenue for a hotel in Blackpool.

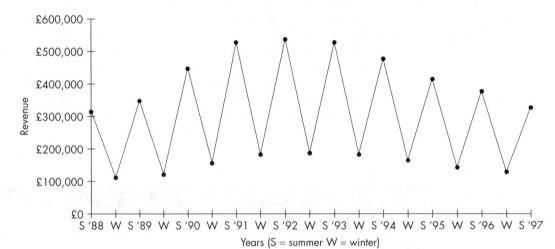

(a) Discuss what factors might have influenced these figures.
   (b) Offer some tentative explanations of the patterns in the data using supply and demand analysis.

3. (a) What are the costs and benefits of an organisation learning about its environment?
   (b) What are the barriers to organisational learning?
   (c) Outline a plan for the introduction of an environmental scanning and interpretation system for a small hotel chain. The plan should include a statement of:
      (i) the objectives of the implementation;
      (ii) capital requirements;
      (iii) labour requirements;
      (iv) the mechanisms to be employed for the dissemination of findings to organisational decision makers;
      (v) the type of information to be provided and the kind of feedback sought from decision makers;
      (vi) an assessment of any risks involved in introducing such a system, and a discussion of the opportunity cost of introduction.

CHAPTER 16

Different approaches

After studying this chapter, you should be able to:

- appreciate that there are a number of different approaches to analysing the relationship between the business environment and organisations;

- appreciate the historical background to these approaches;

- understand the difference between the looking-in approaches and the looking-out approaches;

- appreciate the difference between those approaches that look predominantly at strategic implications and those that look predominately at structural implications;

- be aware that the approaches are also differentiated by the degree of environmental determinism they assume;

- understand the key elements of the following approaches:
  population ecology
  neo-classical economics
  contingency theory
  strategic choice theory
  enactment
  social economics and economic sociology
  Institutional economics;

- appreciate the strategic implications for firms of adopting each of the approaches listed above.

16.1 DIFFERENT WAYS OF LOOKING AT THE RELATIONSHIP BETWEEN A FIRM AND ITS ENVIRONMENT

Assessing the assumptions (the theories) behind the tools that are used in environmental analysis is necessary since any advice an analyst may give could damage, rather than help, a firm if the assumptions of the advisor are untested; if, in other words, they uncritically follow the line of analysis that they were taught in their youth in business school. You may claim that this does not apply to you, that your views are always your own, but as the famous economist John Maynard Keynes argued, 'Practical men, who believe themselves to be quite exempt from any intellectual influences, are usually the slaves of some defunct economist' (1936, p. 383). Today we might replace the word 'economist' in this quote with the term 'economist or management guru', but as long as there remains some truth in this, you owe it to yourselves, as practical men and women, to avoid falling into this trap.

16.2 WHERE DO THE THEORIES COME FROM?

Rather than arising as an area of study in itself, the study of the relationship between organisations and their environments has developed out of two different disciplines. On the one hand, we have those concerned with management and organisations who have cast their gaze outwards, from the organisation towards the business environment, to help explain why management and organisations behave as they do. On the other hand, we have economists and social scientists that have begun to move on from studying the business environment as a topic in itself, to considering its effect on firms.

In both cases, the study of the relationship between the firm and its environment have been late developments, but there is now a growing interest in this topic not only within academia but also in the 'real world'. In particular, business people have demanded more tools with which to analyse their environments as a response to the rise in environmental uncertainty since the 1970s. Prior to this period, firms could afford to be oblivious to the business environment. The oil price hikes of the 1970s put paid to that, however, with for example, the US car giant Chrysler facing bankruptcy in the mid-1970s because its senior managers took too long to be convinced that the oil price rises would lead to a decline in demand for large cars. The stagflation period of the 1970s was a salutary lesson for all firms, since in the West everyone had become used to a stable macroeconomic environment. The return to turbulence and the powerful effect this had on firms, even giant ones, led therefore, somewhat inevitably, to a rise in interest in corporate modelling and forecasting. Moreover, in the 1970s not only did the Keynesian era of economic stability end, but global competition increased dramatically too, and new computer-assisted production started. The combined effect had a devastating effect on British industry. To get an idea of the scale of the change, consider two years, 1969 and 1980. In 1969, inflation in the UK was still below 5% (as it had been since the war). Unemployment in total did not exceed 500,000 (nor had it since before the war), and during this year no major employer went out of business (which was also typical of the post-war period). In 1980, in contrast, inflation was at 20% per annum and unemployment went up by over 500,000 in a single year. Moreover, in that single year nearly one-third of British manufacturing firms went bust. Clearly, the fact that the business environment had become such a problem meant that business people's attention shifted towards it. Another reason for the increased demand for environmental analysis since the 1970s was that it had become easier insofar as the use of computers meant that firms could access, tabulate and analyse data on their customers, suppliers and competitors as never before.

16.3 THE LOOKING-IN PERSPECTIVE

In this section we look at the 'neo-classical economic' approach to be found in most economics textbooks, and the 'population ecology' approach. These two approaches use different terms but come to a similar conclusion: that the environment determines who will succeed, that in other words markets, not managers, decide what works.

Although economics as a subject can be traced back to Adam Smith (1723–90) and beyond, many of the key assumptions of the economics found in textbooks is much more recent and follows a pattern established by the influential Victorian economist Alfred Marshall. In 1890 Marshall wrote that 'the struggle for survival tends to make those methods of organisation prevail, which are best fitted to thrive in their environment' (1961, p. 495). These sentiments reflect the ideas of Charles Darwin (1809–82) who in his book *On the Origin of Species* (1859) argued that a process of environmental selection, or 'natural selection' as he termed it, could explain the diversity of biological forms in the natural world. In this approach, the nature of the environment explains the forms (species) of the organisms that occupy it because organisms that survive do so because they fit the various slots, or 'niches', in that environment, better than those that do not. Like a jelly-mould, it is the shape of the niche that determines the shape of the thing that fits it, since what fits best wins, 'survival of the fittest' as the famous saying goes. (Be careful about the use of the word fit; in this context it does not mean fit like a Gladiator, but fit as in 'this suit fits'.)

In the Darwinian account, the process of filling the slots, of 'evolution' as it is called, occurs simply because genetic information is not replicated perfectly. This means that every now and again offspring are born that just happen to fit some niche or other better than any other organism and therefore survive to breed offspring that have the same advantage. As an example, consider the 28 different varieties (species) of honeycreeper birds on the Pacific Island of Hawaii, amongst whom the main difference is the shape of their beaks. It is believed that these all evolved from one species of honeycreeper. Over millennia this one type became many, since every so often, simply by chance, birds were born that had slightly different-shaped beaks. In some cases they turned out to be better at chiselling insects out of trees, in other cases for breaking nuts open, or for getting deep into flowers to sip the nectar therein. Any advantageous changes tended to be passed on, since these birds survived better than their cousins, and bred offspring with similar advantageous characteristics. Eventually one of the descendants would have offspring in which another advantageous mutation occurred and the process repeated itself so that advantageous features accumulated, creating offspring with even better shaped beaks for chiselling, breaking or sipping. So today on Hawaii we see the Maui bird which has an excellent beak for chiselling, the Kona which has a stumpy strong beak ideal for cracking nuts and seeds, and the Liwi bird which has a long thin beak for sipping nectar. The environment determines the variety of honeycreepers on Hawaii, since it was the existence of tubular flowers with sweet nectar in them, a hard coating that protects seeds and nuts, and the insects hiding in tree bark that gave rise to these different types of bird. The differences in the sources of food in the environment led to variety in birds, and by the same token the lack of variety in the consistency of sea water means that most sea animals are streamlined. But whether it leads to variety or 'one best way', it is the environment that accounts for the forms and behaviour we observe in nature. The animals themselves play no part in this; they cannot choose their genes and usually cannot choose their environment. This evolutionary process continues all around us, but it is usually so slow that we do not notice it. If, however, we were to visit Hawaii in a million years' time, we would find birds with even better shaped beaks for chiselling, breaking and sipping, unless, of course, the environment changes, in which cases the beak features discussed here may have become redundant.

We can divide Darwinian evolutionary theory into three parts: variation, selection and retention. In the case of moths, for example, genetic variation will occasionally produce a brown moth from a population of white moths. Environmental selection then occurs. If the habitat of these moths is light-coloured tree trunks and branches (where they rest during the day), because they stand out birds will eat them. If, on the other hand, the trees are dark brown then brown moths will survive; retention then occurs since the surviving moths breed and pass on the successful brown gene. We only need to understand the environment to know what will and will not work. In fact, biologists predicted the rise of new darker species of tree insects simply from observing the change in the shade of tree trunks resulting from airborne pollutants. In other words, simply by observing a change in the environment, biologists were able to predict certain changes in the animal world. If Darwinian evolution applies to the relationship between firms and their environments it would mean, that we need only study the business environment to know everything we need to know about what strategies and organisational forms will and will not work.

Although Marshall was both very influential and keen to develop an economics based on a dynamic evolutionary analogy, the tools he bequeathed economics actually led to the dominance of the comparative static approach. This meant that rather than investigate the evolutionary mechanism, mainstream economists simply accepted on trust that environments determine organisational forms, so that understanding firms meant no more than looking at the comparative statics of industries and markets. Hence, although textbook neo-classical microeconomics cannot be seen to be an evolutionary-based study, it is nonetheless an environmentally determinist one. However, before we review this approach we will look briefly at a relatively recent development called population ecology, which is more Darwinian than neo-classical economics both in terms of its recognition of the Darwinian legacy and in the degree of environmental determinism assumed.

16.3.1 Population ecology

Relatively recently, we have seen a development of ideas by those unconvinced by the neo-classical static approach to analysing the firm's relationship with its environment, but who accept the idea of environmental selection. The result is an environmental determinist approach that emphasises dynamics rather than comparative statics. We can divide these dynamic approaches into the 'population ecology' of Hannan and Freeman (1977) and Aldrich (1979), and the 'evolutionary economics' of Nelson and Winter (1982). The approaches are similar but not identical. The kind of evolutionary theory employed by Nelson and Winter pays more attention to firms' ability to influence environments than population ecologists do, but retains the idea that the limits for this are still given by the structure of the environment. Since they share the basic assumption of environmental determinism we include them here, but we will, in what follows, focus on population ecology.

Population ecologists apply the three essential processes of Darwinian evolutionary theory of variation, selection and retention to the survival of firms. Hannan and Freeman (1977) argue that variation is seldom the result of adaptation to environmental changes or planning by existing firms. Aldrich (1979) supports this view, seeing firms as floundering in the grip of environmental forces beyond their control, with self-conscious deliberate planned change being a rarity. Even luck, he argues, is a more likely explanation of successful adaptation than conscious action. If the new variant fits the environment better than its rivals, it will be selected and retained until superseded, regardless of how the fit was achieved.

There are two observations that population ecologists make, having studied some complete populations of organisations over time, such as the newspaper industry over 100 years in San Francisco (Hannan and Freeman 1989, p. 239), in their search for the ecological laws that govern the outcome of business decisions. Firstly, that new niches tend to be occupied by new firms, and secondly, that firms are slow to respond to changes in their niche. For example, it is hard for a company like Laura Ashley, which is so good at making flowery feminine dresses, to move into producing the androgynous casual wear now favoured by today's youth. Firms find it hard to adapt since technology, culture and attitudes that are geared to one environment may act as a brake on their ability to adapt. So, for example, having machines that embroider flowery patterns on linen is a liability rather than an asset if no one wants flowery patterns, or indeed linen. A new firm would invest in a different machine and would therefore, in this one obvious respect, fit the new niche better. Indeed any incumbent firm will have a problem if its assets are specific to what it currently does and what it needs to do changes. As well as asset specificity, more subtle barriers to adaptation might hinder a firm. The mere fact that its culture and attitudes are geared towards fulfilling the exigencies of one niche means that it will have a significant reorientation problem if its niche vanishes. Indeed, according to Nelson and Winter, firms largely remember by doing, therefore expertise in one niche is no guarantee of success in another, and since 'the routines of the organisation as a whole are confined to extremely narrow channels' (1982, p. 111), breaking free of them can be difficult. If we add these observations together, we might conclude, as many population ecologists do, that if a firm's environment changes significantly then it will have difficulty changing sufficiently to regain fit. As Hannan and Freeman put it, 'inertial pressures prevent most organisations from radically changing strategies and structures' (1989, p. 22). The result is that environmental change leads to new organisations, not transformed ones. (The biological parallel is that no organism can evolve in its own lifetime.) This is not to say that population ecologists see no role for managers, as they have to understand the environment they are in to benefit fully from the niche, in the same way that a leopard cub must learn the herding habits of its prey to fully exploit its niche. Indeed, Argyris (1987) argues that managers' inability to understand their niche is a primary reason for business failure. So understanding is important, but for population ecologists it is not enough to guarantee survival, since what is possible is determined by the niche and if it changes there is little that firms can do about it. As Hannan and Freeman put it, there is little evidence that the 'major features of the world of organisations arise through learning or adaptation' (1977, p. 957), and, if therefore the business environment no longer favours a firm the chances are that it will die, however well it understands its environment.

Criticism of population ecology

The main criticism of this approach is its degree of environmental determinism as in this approach the environment is treated as standing apart from the action of firms, in the same way that the natural world is separate from the biological organisms that occupy it. But in the case of firms, this implies a standing apart; a 'reification' of the environment that denies the importance of firms, as it dismisses their power to influence events or shape their environments, and underplays the role of people in the intermediation of these forces. In such a world, as Perrow (1979) argues, all sacked workers would have been fired by the environment, and this is not how it is currently perceived, and proving that it is like this will require more evidence than has so far been provided by the proponents of population ecology.

Case study of new niches being dominated by new firms

MOBILE PHONES

The network operators have invested huge amounts in erecting masts up and down the country to ensure that they can claim the most coverage. Indeed, network operators provide us with a lesson in managing the political environment, since they have arranged a deal with successive governments that allows them to by-pass planning regulations that apply to everyone else. As a result, their masts can spring up anywhere, spoiling the view even in national parks and areas designated as being of outstanding natural beauty. There is an onus on planners to accept at least one mast as long as the telecom providers can demonstrate a need, that is, as long as they can show that there is a part of the country, in particular roads, that their current signals do not reach. In addition, the planners and councils know that if they reject a proposal, any appeal over their heads by the telecom providers to the ministry is likely to be accepted. This favourable treatment reflects the view in government that mobile phones are now a business necessity and as such should be seen as crucial to our overall economic success. There is perhaps also not as much concern for visual intrusion as there once was. In addition, as the pollution these masts emit is invisible waves of 'extremely low frequency electromagnetic radiation' rather than visible pollution, they do not cause public concern, despite evidence of the possibility of harmful effects being regularly cited in the *Cancer Journal*. Orange, a subsidiary of Hutchison, has been most successful in providing uninterrupted signals throughout the UK although it has yet to make a profit from this; analysts predict that it may do so in 1999. However, the intense competition in the industry means that the profits made on each subscriber have fallen so much that analysts are also predicting that 1999 may also be the last year in which Orange makes a profit in the UK. Some, however, have made huge profits almost from day one, in a different part of this market. In the manufacturing of the handsets, for example, firms such as Nokia and Motorola have made huge profits, while in the retailing of the handsets entirely new firms have emerged since, unlike in manufacturing, there was no competitive advantage for established firms. In short, as no experience was required, those that won were simply those that turned out to be good at selling phones. In this instance then, the rewards have gone to those who happened to be in the better of the two niches, the retail rather than the telecom provision market, rather than the best at managing their environment. Also, in this instance the more profitable of the two niches is a new one with no advantages to existing firms and therefore it is newcomers who have exploited it.

16.3.2 Neo-classical economics

If we can establish what a firm needs to do to survive, then we can use this as a way of deciding what it needs to know about its environment. In the case of firms, one of the main determinants of survival is profit, since this is what is paid to the owners and most owners are not in it for charity. Profits are simply the difference between earnings and costs. This is where textbook economics comes in, since the main link to firms' profits is the price it pays for its inputs and the price it gets for its outputs. The markets for goods and services (outputs) determine the firm's revenue and the markets for factors of production (inputs) determine the firm's costs. Therefore, in Figure 16.1, to cut a long story short as long as the price of inputs 'a' needed to create the output is no greater than the price at which it is sold, 'b', then the firm makes normal profit and survives. If 'b' exceeds 'a', super normal profits are made; on the other hand, if 'a' is above 'b' then cost exceed sales revenue and a loss is made.

Figure 16.1 The neo-classical economics approach.

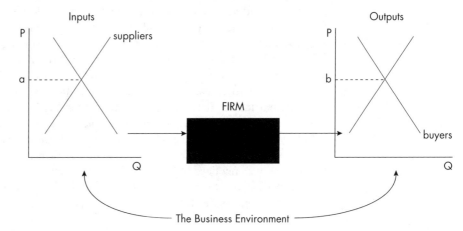

The firm in the diagram is just covering its costs; it is making normal profits. The main determinant of prices in the neo-classical tradition is the amount of competition. Consider, for example, what has happened in the UK since the 1970s when the UK manufacturing sector began to face intense global competition for home markets, in the production of cars, electronics, motorbikes and so on (Figure 16.2).

Figure 16.2 Decline in demand for UK goods.

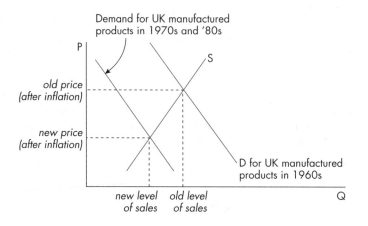

Note that because we are dealing with a long time scale here, during which we have had inflation, the price figures are in real terms.

The decline in sales means that the main way for UK firms to regain their competitiveness is to be more efficient and thereby cut costs and lower prices. Indeed, rationalisation and efficiency drives were the dominant strategic response of those UK manufacturers that managed to survive this period. So for neo-classical economics the level of competition is the crucial dimension of the environment, and it is largely the number of firms, and the ease of entry and exit of firms to an industry, that determines this. What happens within the firm is of secondary importance since firms must bow to the dictates of the environment to survive. Hence in this approach we are 'concerned with the environmental setting within which enterprises operate' and so we 'do not take an internal approach, more appropriate to the field of management science, such as could inquire how enterprises do and should behave' (Bain, 1959, p. 7). Using economic jargon, we only need to know what market structure a firm is in to know what it can and cannot do. This is termed the structure–conduct–performance, or simply S-C-P, paradigm; it is the main conclusion of a school of thought developed by economists such as Mason (1939) and Bain (1959) that is sometimes called industrial organisation theory. In this approach the market structure dictates what strategy (conduct) must be pursued to reach an acceptable performance. For example, in a perfectly competitive market, firms must minimise costs if they are to match their rivals and provide a sufficient return on capital for owners to keep the firm in existence. Since with this approach we only need to know the market structure to predict a firm's behaviour, we can treat the firm as a 'black box', as in Figure 16.1. It does not matter what goes on inside this box; those that survive will be those that 'somehow managed to maximise profit' as Milton Friedman (1953) put it. It does not matter how managers think they did it, since it is markets, not managers, that decide what will work. Today, there is more interest amongst economists in how firms tick. However, it is still the case that in the mainstream economics literature and textbooks the environmental determinism is retained and firms are modelled largely in terms of a production function, in which outputs are related to inputs by means of a line, as in Chapter 3, which represents only a very small step up from ignoring the organisation of the firm altogether.

Porter's version of Neo-classical economics

The aim of the neo-classical economic analysis of industry was not to inform firms of their position so much as to discuss policy issues like whether more competition is a good thing or not. It is largely in the work of Michael Porter that neo-classical economics has been used as a tool of environmental analysis to help firms in formulating their strategies. The main device for this is his 'five forces' analysis, discussed in Chapter 5, since 'the five forces determine industry profitability because they influence the prices, costs and required investments of firms in an industry' (1985, p. 4). For Porter the main flow of causality remains from the environment to the firm. 'The strength of the five competitive forces is a function of *industry structure*, or the underlying economic and technical characteristics of an industry' which he argues is relatively stable. This environmental determinism is not absolute, however, for although using the five forces to pick the attractive industry and understand the nature of the niche are 'important tasks for any firm, and are the essence of competitive strategy in some industries, a firm is usually not a prisoner of its industry structure. Firms, through their strategies, can influence the five forces' (1985, p. 7).

Criticisms of the neo-classical approach

This approach gives firms a starting point for collecting information about the environment since at a minimum it suggests the need to understand how the markets for its inputs and outputs work. On the basis of this, we might advise the firm to scan the markets where they get their inputs to see what their options are and where the bargaining power lies. In addition, we might advise them to do some scanning of their customer base to establish the nature of the demand for their output. However, as they dig deeper they will find that the influence of backgrounds, culture, perceptions and attitudes, of what in short we call society, plays a part. Similarly, they will find that what supplies they can use and how they can use them are prescribed by laws and regulations and ultimately political attitudes, indeed the very existence of the firm is determined in this way. In other words, before long we need to consider a host of environmental factors in order to explain the firm's profits. Therefore, while an emphasis on inputs and outputs is a good starting point for deciding what information to scan the environment for, it does not tell us which part of the business environment is important in the way that neo-classical economists like Porter, have assumed.[1] So that, for example, a change in attitudes about what a firm does can be more important than a change in the number of competitors, and a change in regulations can have more effect than any possible price change. Take chocolate, for example. One of the biggest changes on the horizon for UK chocolate manufacturers is rising competition from Europe, but more significant is the prospect that UK chocolate may not be defined as chocolate at all under proposed European regulations.

16.3.3 Classical economics

An alternative within the economics tradition which predates neo-classical economics but nonetheless still has adherents is classical, and radical, economics, or 'political economy' as it was termed by its exponents. Classical economists like David Ricardo (1772–1823) reintroduced class relations and power into consideration, in response to the interpretation of Adam Smith who saw markets as arenas in which more or less equal parties exercise their free will to the benefit of all. For Ricardo the overriding feature of economic relationships was power and control by unequal parties; in particular, he argued that the class who owned capital, the capitalists, had power over labour in the production process. This idea was developed by Karl Marx (1818–83), who emphasised the exploitative nature of this relationship for those who did not own capital or land and therefore had to make a living by working. However, although in these approaches firms are seen as powerful, their actions are nonetheless predetermined by the capitalist system as they are agents of capital. This need not even be a conscious compliance by them and need not involve the coercion of labour because, as Marx argued, 'the ruling ideas in any epoch are the ideas of the ruling class'. So, for example, the logic of industry and our own consumerism combine to tie us to the production process but are accepted by most of us as givens; for most of us they do not feel as if they are imposed at all. This means that, although providing us with a broader conception of the business environment, this approach gives little scope for firms to act independently of the dictates of capitalists. Therefore, although the route is different, the destination is the same as neo-classical economists – environmental determinism.

16.4   THE LOOKING-OUT PERSPECTIVE

We now turn to the views of those who began by looking at how organisations work and have started to look outward to investigate the effect of the environment on organisations. This second group, being initially and primarily concerned with how organisations work, tend to concentrate on the effects of environments on 'structure' rather than 'strategy'. In other words, on decisions about how firms are organised; the arrangement of tasks, and the control, com-

---

1   This is why in this book I have broadened the scope of neo-classical economics to cover the social, political and other aspects of the business environment, in a manner that would not be found in a standard economics text.

munications and reporting structures, and suchlike, rather than on decisions about pricing, marketing and product portfolios.

16.4.1 Classical organisation theory

The history of organisation theories can be thought of as beginning around the turn of the twentieth century with the work of Max Weber (1922) and Frederick Taylor (1911). Their work is characterised as seeking the 'one best way' to organise, which is now labelled 'classical organisation theory'.

Weber observed the rise of formally organised firms with highly specialised management functions that exhibit rule-governed behaviour within hierarchical structures. He thought this form of organisation had evolved to deal with the technology of mass production since this requires a large division of labour into specialist, routinised tasks, which can be most easily managed and controlled through formal organisation and hierarchical chains of command, responsibility and communication. In other words, in his view, formal, rule-governed, inflexible hierarchies fit the mass production environment (Figure 16.3).

Figure 16.3
Organisational
hierarchy.

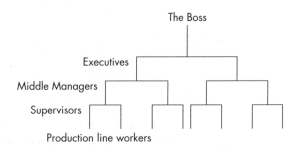

For Weber this represented the most efficient form of organisation thus far encountered, and he termed this type of organisation 'bureaucracy'. Since then the word bureaucracy has collected a lot of baggage; it is now used as a pejorative term implying excessive routinisation, red tape, and a robotic mindset. Weber was not blind to these shortcomings, which even in his day were becoming apparent; however, he also recognised the great increase in productivity and efficiency that this kind of organisation heralded over previous forms of organisation. Taylor was less circumspect than Weber and actively encouraged firms to become more formal. He advised them to increase the routinisation of jobs using what he termed 'Scientific Management'. This became popular in both the West and in the newly established USSR. Scientific Management involved 'time and motion' studies in which workers' activities were studied in minute detail to see if the way they worked could be rationalised and improved. By the 1930s many scholars were beginning to pursue a different line of thought, feeling that the search for the 'one best way' to organise was leaving people out of the equation. Writers such as Abraham Maslow (1943) and George Elton Mayo (1949) emphasised the importance of people within the organisation; how they feel, how they behave, and how they relate to each other. Their 'Human Relations' approach drew on a number of studies of a large factory in Chicago.

The Hawthorne studies

Studies at the Hawthorne factory of the Western Electric Company, Chicago, between 1924 and 1932 showed that any change to working conditions, regardless of whether it made things easier or not, could lead to an increase in productivity, particularly if the workers wanted it to. Indeed, people today warn that in studying how beneficial an organisational change has been it is necessary to wait a while for the 'Hawthorne effect' – the short-term beneficial effect however daft the change – to wear off.

The Hawthorne studies identified five important factors about people in organisations:

1. People's motivations matter.
2. People have a need for recognition and like to feel a sense of belonging within an organisation.
3. People are not just motivated by money, but by recognition, responsibility and a sense of belonging.
4. People's attitudes to work are shaped by the attitudes of others: their peers at work and their families and other groups outside of work (in the business environment).
5. People form cliques (little groups of friends at work) and these are particularly important in motivating people in particular directions.

Although Weber saw bureaucracy as resulting in response to the environmental contingency of mass production and the division of labour, it is fair to say that organisation theorists as a group have only relatively recently begun to 'look out' at the relationship between firms and their environments. It was not until the 1950s that attention within organisation studies turned to the nature of the firm's environment and the firm's relationship to it. This was spurred mainly by Talcott Parsons' (1956) attempt to conceive of the firm as a system within a larger system. This led away from the search for the 'one best way' towards a 'horses for courses' approach in which the organisational form is seen as contingent upon the exact mix of external forces to which the organisation is subject. As Donaldson puts it: 'The structure which is most appropriate for an organisation depends on the situational contingencies' (1985, p. 172). This approach is termed Contingency Theory.

16.4.2   Contingency theory

In this, the contingencies (including the environmental context) are assumed to determine the structure of the organisation. We can therefore adopt an 'if-then' approach that would ultimately tell firms which structures fit which environments. For example: *If* the firm is in a turbulent (changing) environment *then* it will need a flexible organisational form. If we are just looking at survival then all we need to prove that turbulence and flexibility go together is to look at how many firms in turbulent environments have flexible forms. If we find that 80% do, then this correlation suggests that flexibility is an important prerequisite of survival in a turbulent environment. If we want to measure success in terms of profitability or growth then we would have to see if firms in a turbulent environment that adopt a flexible form are more profitable than those that do not. Whatever the measure of success used, the primary concern is with correlations between structures (and to a lesser extent strategy) and contingencies. The size of a correlation may be used to gauge how powerful the equilibrating force is. If the correlation between a contingency variable and a structural one is 1, it means that there is no alternative structure to be found in respect of this contingency. This suggests that there is likely to be a strong force pushing firms towards the right structure. However, even the biggest correlations in this literature seldom exceed 0.6, and most are considerably smaller.

In general, the contingency 'causes' used in this approach include such environmentally related factors as the ownership pattern of the firm, what technology is available, where the firm is located, resources available in the environment, and in particular the degree of turbulence of the environment. The contingencies do not have to relate directly to the environment; size, for example, is categorised as a contingency, because in a sense it is part of the firm's context as it is hard to change, but we would not include it as an environmental factor. The contingencies are held to determine the structure of firms in terms of such things as the degree of standardisation, centralisation, specialisation, formality, and the configuration of authority within the firm. Some examples of the approach are shown below.

Examples of contingency theory research

Burns and Stalker (1961)

Burns and Stalker in a study of 20 firms found that those operating in stable environments developed bureaucratic, 'mechanistic' forms with clear hierarchies, task specialisation and vertical communication structures. In contrast, those in less stable, more turbulent, environments where more innovation and change are required developed less formal, more 'organic' organisational forms with more lateral communication and more flexible rules and tasks for employees. In effect, Burns and Stalker identified two different niches. Lawrence and Lorsch (1967) extended the work of Burns and Stalker to consider the different levels of turbulence facing different parts of the same organisation. Further work focusing on turbulence includes that of Emery and Trist (1965).

Emery and Trist (1965)

Emery and Trist used two dimensions of the environment to investigate the sources of competitive advantage: the distribution of resources in the environment (which can vary between totally concentrated and totally randomised), and the volatility of the environment (which can vary between completely stable and completely unstable). With these dimensions in mind, they drew up a list of the types of environments that they found, which they lumped into four categories:

1. Placid randomised environment: In this case, resources are randomly distributed and the environment is stable. In this case, they concluded that no

competitive advantages seem to exist. This is similar to perfect competition since no firm can put a barrier around some resources in the environment (either customers or suppliers). This means that anything one firm does can be copied, and so the only way to win is to be more efficient and thus cheaper.

2. Placid clustered environment: This is a stable environment but there is an unequal spread of resources within it. In this case proximity to, and knowledge of, the dispersal of resources gives competitive advantage (again this parallels the ideas on market structure of economists; in this case we have monopolistic competition).

3. Disturbed reactive environment: In this case, resources are concentrated and the environment is unstable. Survival then becomes based on matching rivals' moves. This category is similar to economists' oligopoly type of market structure in which strategy revolves around move and countermove.

4. Turbulent environment: In this case, there is a high rate of change in the environment, as well as increased interconnectedness and thus complexity, which leads to pervasive uncertainty. The key to survival is then to understand the business environment to reduce the uncertainty. This last one is important since for Emery and Trist there is a tendency for all environments to become turbulent and therefore for environmental analysis to become increasingly important for firms. Ansoff (1981), who argues that firms need to develop business environmental analysis as a response to the increasing turbulence that they face, takes up this point.

Ansoff (1981)

Ansoff produces a typology of possible environments based on the degree of turbulence firms face and brings out the implications for environmental analysis of each:

1. Stable: In this case, environmental change is infrequent and can be predicted from what happened in the past, which gives firms time to react. In such circumstances, environmental analysis is easy, and any inaccuracies and misperceptions that occur in it do not matter much since there is time for the firm to realise its mistakes and change tack.

2. Reactive: Change that is more frequent is experienced in this case but it is predictable, so that incremental adjustment (reaction) is sufficient to maintain the competitive position of the firm.

3. Anticipatory: In this case, the environment is less predictable and the firm has to extrapolate trends and anticipate changes.

4. Exploring: In this case, the level of uncertainty about changes means that extrapolation will not do. Instead, firms must 'analyse' and search for 'weak signals' (the first signs of changes). In this context, firms need to explore rather than rely on anticipation or their ability to react.

5. Creative: In this extreme case, the firm faces frequent surprises and there is a high degree of uncertainty and chaos. In response, the firm must be innovative, must search for weak signals and must constantly analyse the environment for clues. It must become a learning organisation that can respond quickly and flexibly to the changing needs of the environment.

Ansoff argues that all environments are tending towards more turbulence, complexity and uncertainty and hence towards a greater need to be a responsive learning type of organisation. In addition, where Emery and Trist suggest a gradual drift towards turbulence, Ansoff argues that environments become turbulent at different rates. It can be gradual, but it can also be very rapid and when it is large adjustments are required of firms if they are to remain in fit with their environments.

Although organisation theorists tend to focus on the degree of turbulence of an environment as the key environmental influence, there have been those who have focused on other facets of the environment. In particular, Joan Woodward (1965) suggested that the technology used by manufacturing firms is of prime importance in determining the authority structure of the firm. Mintzberg has also done a considerable amount of work on identifying the relationship between organisational structure and a number of environmental contingencies, as we shall see by looking at an example of his work.

Mintzberg (1979)

We will now briefly examine a simplified version of a representative contingency approach developed by Mintzberg in which he identifies five important niches. Although he has since come up with some variants we shall look at this older version, because it encapsulates in less detail much of what has come since and because it has been so influential with managers. The reason for its popularity is that it appears to provide a simple guide to organisational design, as for each case a summary of the organisational structure of what Mintzberg believes are the five most significant environmental niches is provided.

- Type 1 – Simple structure (Table 16.1). This environment contains many threats, for example, from established firms trying to protect their niches. In such a hostile environment a firm needs to focus on its core competencies, which can most easily be achieved by centralised control. Many small firms are likely to fall into this category.

Table 16.1
Simple structure.

Cause	Effect
(Contingency)	(Structure)
Age of firm = young	Standardisation = low
Size = small	Centralisation = high
Technology = simple	Specialisation = low
Environment = hostile	Formalisation = low
	Configuration = hierarchical, direct supervision

- Type 2 – Machine bureaucracy (Table 16.2). The stability of this environment allows a formalised control structure and centralised decision making since few decisions have to be made and there is no rush. The automation of the technology allows a great division of labour, which is very efficient but needs formalisation of duties and standardisation of procedures. Most car manufacturers in the 1950s and 1960s would fall into this category.

Cause	Effect
(Contingency)	(Structure)
Age of firm = old	Standardisation = high
Size = large	Centralisation = high
Technology = part-automated	Specialisation = high
mass production	Formalisation = high
Environment = simple and stable	Configuration = hierarchical, long command chains (i.e. formalised control)

- Type 3 – Professional bureaucracy (Table 16.3). The complexity of this environment requires decentralisation, but its stability allows standardised skills to be applied with a large degree of autonomy. Most universities still fall into this category.

Cause	Effect
(Contingency)	(Structure)
Age of firm = varies	Standardisation = standardised by skill (profession)
Size = varies	Centralisation = low
Technology = simple, but requires complex knowledge	Specialisation = high
Environment = complex but stable	Formalisation = high
	Configuration = decentralised

- Type 4 – Divisionalised (Table 16.4). Because it is diversified the environment of this kind of firm covers several markets, which means that decisions are best made in separate divisions covering the necessary functional areas – marketing, accounts and so on, despite the fact that this means duplication of functions. Most modern ('post-Ford') multinationals fall into this category with separate divisions in separate countries, and even separate divisions for separate markets within each country too.

Cause	Effect
(Contingency)	(Structure)
Age of firm = mature	Standardisation = high
Size = very large	Centralisation = low
Technology = divisible	Specialisation = high
Environment = diversified – firm operates in several markets which individually are simple and stable	Formalisation = high
	Configuration = decentralised

- Type 5 – Adhocracy (Table 16.5). A complex turbulent environment requires innovation and the cooperative efforts of various types of experts, so decision making is spread with teams coordinating laterally. The Sony Corporation is one of many Far Eastern firms that fall into this category.

Table 16.5 Adhocracy.

Cause	Effect
(Contingency)	(Structure)
Age of firm = varies	Standardisation = high
Size = large	Centralisation = low, team based
Technology = sophisticated and automated	Specialisation = high
	Formalisation = high
Environment = complex and dynamic	Configuration = organic decentralised matrix, team based

In Mintzberg's view, as environments become more complex and turbulent we get a general tendency of firms to become more 'organic'. As Mintzberg put it, 'simple structure and machine bureaucracy were yesterday's structures . . . professional bureaucracy and the divisionalised form is today's' . . . Adhocracy is tomorrow's' (1979, p. 459). It is, however, important to realise that these are simplified, stylised, ideal types with limited empirical support. This means that assumptions and common sense play a major part in constructing these kinds of typologies. Mintzberg, for example, admits that he proceeds 'on the assumption that a limited number of configurations can help explain much of what is observed in organisations' (1995, p. 346). Most subsequent contingency theory continues in this vein with even the most complex covering a few environmental dimensions only, such as resource availability and turbulence, and resulting in a limited number of significant niches and their associated organisational forms.

The 'SARFIT' model

We can divide contingency theory into two types: 'static' contingency theory in which limited numbers of contingencies are associated with a limited number of ideal structures, and 'dynamic' contingency theory in which we look at the process of adaptation to regain fit. If, for example, there is a change in a contingency then a structure–contingency misfit (disequilibrium) will occur. This results in a decline in performance to which firms need to respond by changing their structures to regain fit.

Change in contingency (a change in the business environment for example)

> → *structure–contingency misfit (disequilibrium)*

>> → *poor performance*

>>> → *change structure to regain fit (equilibrium regained)*

This is the approach embedded in Aston University's SARFIT model (structural adjustment to regain fit). Those working in the Aston tradition include

Blau (1970) and Donaldson (1985). We can contrast their approach based on careful investigation of correlations with the American 'management guru' tradition of lumping firms into five- or seven-fold categories. Practising managers often prefer quick fixes based on 5's and 7's rather than tentative conclusions based on masses of correlations, which is why every year a new book comes out with the latest five or seven 'best ways' to organise.

Summary of results from contingency theory research

We can summarise the findings of contingency research on the influence of the environment on organisational structures as follows:

1. The more complex the environment, the more decentralised the structure needs to be, as decentralisation enables the firm to cope with the complex information decision-making that this environment requires.

2. The more turbulent the environment, the more organic the structure needs to be. In a stable environment, firms can predict the future and rely on standardisation for coordination but dynamic environments demand flexibility.

3. The greater the degree of separation of the firm's markets, the greater the need to divisionalise as each market requires its own division responsible for marketing, accounts and other functional areas. Diversified firms need therefore a multidivisional form rather than a unitary organisational form as shown in Figure 16.4. This enables 'interfunctional co-ordination for numerous unrelated product market activities, each requiring distinct knowledge and expertise which would overload central management' (Donaldson, 1987, p. 5).

Figure 16.4 M-form and U-form organisational structures.

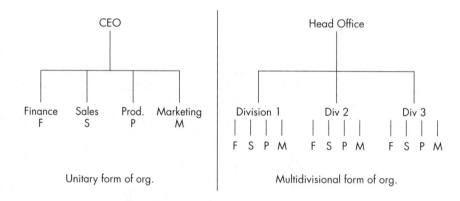

We can also add a fourth, non-environmental-related conclusion, that is nonetheless worth pointing out since it is often assumed that the opposite is true, which is that bigger firms have relatively few managers compared to their output. In other words, managerial economies of scale are confirmed in Contingency Theory research.

Contingency theory and economics

You may think that contingency theory is the same as neo-classical economics and population ecology. Certainly they share an element of environmental determinism, but contingency theory has a number of distinguishing features:

1. Contingency theory is mainly about organisational 'structure'; it largely ignores other facets of firms' strategic options such as pricing and marketing.

2. Contingency theory involves looking for cross-sectional correlations. For example, if today we find that 70% of firms that are diversified have a divisionalised structure, this would suggest that if a firm operates in several separate niches it should divisionalise. In contrast, economists and population ecologists tend to look at several factors in one go in order to explain causality rather than to assume it. For example, an economist would attempt to explain why firms divisionalise using several causal factors to build a model. They might include the degree of concentration in the industry, the pattern of demand in the industry, and so on. Doing this usually reduces the apparent strength of simple correlations, so we might find, in the case of diversification and divisionalisation, that our figure falls from 70% to 30%, possibly even to a negligible amount! This is an essential difference between the 'multiple regression' techniques of econometrics and the correlations approach of contingency theorists. This is why many economists take the correlations produced by contingency theorists with a pinch of salt and explains why I have not bombarded you with correlation numbers derived from contingency research. As an example of the difference, consider the correlation between people going skiing and winter. Most people go skiing in winter so there is a strong correlation between the two; common sense fills in the causality – winter causes skiing. Economists would instead ask what causes people to go skiing and would include such things as incomes, the popularity of the sport, the cost of skiing holidays, exchange rates and snow conditions. In doing this the correlation between winter and skiing would be reduced as some of the correlation is explained not by the fact that it is winter but by the fact that there is more snow in winter, and so on. In other words, in reality, other factors are involved and the term winter can act as a proxy for all those things if we do not include them in our statistical analysis.

3. Economists and population ecologists tend to look at things over time, to learn from the past, whereas contingency theorists tend to focus on one period in time (cross-sectional analysis). So although nearly all of the examples of static contingency theory above mention the way the authors think things are going, they are seldom based upon looking at how things have gone. The problem is that with so many possible dimensions to look at it is a big job, especially as the amount of reliable time series data on firms is not great.

Criticisms of the contingency theory approach

Measurement problems

Whilst acknowledging the importance of the contingencies mentioned above, we have to recognise the problems of measuring both contingencies and structural factors. Consider, for example, factors like 'the degree of turbulence'. This is impossible to measure with any accuracy; not only is there no agreed measure of turbulence, it is in fact a largely constructed variable. Yet the results obtained regarding the fit between structures and this contingency depends on how it is measured (or indeed constructed). This is a major problem as the dominant characteristic of the business environment within contingency theory is its degree of turbulence.

Correlations do not prove causality

There are two problems here. Firstly, two things can be correlated because they have a similar cause but are otherwise unconnected. Hair growth is faster in summer and more cricket is played so there is a correlation between hair growth and cricket, but no causality. Secondly, we have to decide what causes what. The categorisation of causes and effects within contingency theory seems open to question; mostly it is left to common sense when looking at a correlation to conclude what is causing what. However, some of the causal variables selected by contingency theorists are subject to choices made by the firm and could equally be seen as effects with the decision to label them as causes reflecting the assumption of environmental determinism rather than empirical research. The fact that, for example, large hierarchical firms dominate stable environments is taken by such environmental determinists as proof that this organisational form fits that kind of environment: Hierarchy is efficient in many ways, its weakness is its inflexibility. This means that the usefulness of hierarchy is less in turbulent environments where decentralised decision making and flexibility become more important. However, the correlation between hierarchy and stable environments may also reflect the fact that big firms are able to stabilise their environments, or at least its effect on them. We have therefore an observational equivalence between things that are environmentally determined and those that are not, which no amount of cross-sectional contingency–structure correlations can clarify, as it is unclear what is adjusting to what. The problem for contingency theorists is that the causality cannot be deduced from looking at the correlations. If we cannot identify the underlying processes from looking at scales of association then as contingency theory is an empiricist approach concerned to show what associations exist, the causality behind observed correlations has to be assumed. Moreover as the data categorisations are based on the assumed causality, we also find that the data is constructed to fit the theory, making the correlation results themselves unreliable. If we adopt a more dynamic approach and try to see what is adapting to what, we find the causality can run in both or either direction. There is, for example, a long tradition, typified by Chandler (1962), based on looking at business histories that document how changes in contingencies like size, technology and location often follow changes in strategy rather than vice versa. In a similar vein, Khandwalla (1977) shows that the poor performance associated with centralisation that contingency theorists have found can result from poorly performing firms centralising in order to tighten controls, reduce costs, and regain a unified sense of purpose. A debate on causality might seem a very dry topic but it is important for decision-makers. If, for example, we look at centralisation it is vital to establish whether centralisation is a problem or the answer to a problem. If it is the latter then advice to avoid it based on observing the correlation between concentration and poor performance would be duff advice.

Problems of regaining fit

Contingency theory is popular as it purports to show managers how to adapt the design of their organisation to regain fit. However, the degree of adaptability assumed within the theory may be overstated. Hannan and Freeman (1989) point out that in fact there is considerable inertia within organisations and the actual act of changing is likely to involve costs as well as benefits. In Donaldson's own reckoning, getting back into the right shape 'may take a considerable period of time and frequently spans decades'. Moreover, the penalties for being out of the equilibrium are often weak, so that the benefits of adopting the 'right' form may not exceed the costs of getting there.

Contingency theory uses a narrow definition of the business environment

Another problem with contingency theory is that it only looks at the immediate 'task' environment, involving a firm's day-to-day operations. Taking some of the concepts employed in contingency theory and applying them to the broader business environment may prove difficult. Consider, for example, how hard it would be to distinguish between firms in the UK suffering different amounts of 'political', 'social' or 'technological' turbulence. By ignoring the wider context, contingency theory also downplays the kinds of political and cultural differences between regions, nations and religions that can cut across general universal principles of organisation. This is not to deny that some correlations are generalisable. The question is whether it is reasonable to assume 'that organisations may be sufficiently alike across institutional settings and national boundaries to make such enquiries sensible' (Donaldson, 1985, p. 117). For Donaldson it is an empirical issue; if the contingency–structure relationships are themselves contingent on contexts then we can add these in or dismiss them depending on the weight of evidence. Indeed, Donaldson refers to this as hyper-contingency theory but it is more a criticism than a refinement, since it suggest that these relationships are human constructs rather than given by general laws of efficiency. Consider, for example, the convergence thesis of Kerr et al. (1973) that there is increasing global homogenisation of organisational forms and practices that comes from the observation that: 'The industrial society is world wide. The science and technology on which it is based speak in a universal language . . . (so that) . . . discrepancies in the methods of production which now exist . . . will tend to decrease over time' (1973, p. 55). This harks back to Weber's view that industry has its own logic. But there is a wide literature regarding the cultural differences between firms, even those operating in global markets that suggests that the language business is (hyper) contingent upon culture and continues to have many dialects. The Japanese, for example, have a level of collaboration amongst their big firms exceeding those in the West, made possible by long-standing family arrangements that can be traced back to the Shogunate. The Koreans, in contrast, tend to subdivide their firms into little units. Although rationalised in many a management textbook on the basis of the benefits of devolved decision making and so forth, if you ask the Koreans, it seems to have more to do with their family business traditions than any business logic. In both cases industrial logic gives way to cultural tradition; moreover, despite their geographical proximity the different traditions have given rise to different ways of organising their production that have both resulted in world-beating firms.

16.5 ENVIRONMENTAL DETERMINISM

The assumption of environmental determinism within economics and organisational theory is a difficult one to test, although some have tried. For example, Schmalensee (1985), an economist, argues that three-quarters of the profit performance differences between firms can be attributed to industry (environmental) factors. On the other hand, Rumelt (1991), a management scientist, puts it lower at a still nonetheless significant 50%. However, even if we take such all-encompassing statistical averages at face value, we would be forced to conclude that, although there are gains to be made from firms fitting their environments, there is nonetheless scope for firms to act independently of their environments too. In addition, these figures hide rather than reveal the extent to which firms control their environment, as the direction of causality is assumed rather than proved. In light of this we will now look at the views of those who recognise the scope for firms to act independently of their environments, and those who emphasise the power of firms to control, rather than be controlled by, their environments.

16.5.1 Strategic choice

So far, we have looked at theories in which the assumption of environmental determinism dominates, so that as Thompson (1967, p. 1) put it, 'organisations do some of the basic things they do because they must – or else!'. We are now going to look at an approach that, in contrast, emphasises the scope firms have for free choice.

John Child (1972) criticises contingency theory on the basis that correlations do not speak for themselves, and that the causality inferred within contingency theory that context determines structure may be wrong. Causation might run the other way and, if it does, the advice to firms will be different. We have already discussed the issue of centralisation – is it the problem or the solution? However, Child takes this one step further by considering whether in general our advice should be 'change the structure' or 'change the contingency'? If, for example, a machine bureaucracy's environment becomes complex then its centralised decision making no longer fits it, the centre cannot effectively deal with the complexity, decision making deteriorates, miscommunication occurs, and performance deteriorates until the firm decentralises. However, the firm might instead choose to diversify and thereby change the contingency; this is the alternative 'strategic choice' formulation presented by Child – the last step in the regaining fit sequence becomes change the structure *or* change the contingency.

In general, firms have choices over:

1. Which environments to operate in: Firms can choose which markets to enter by changing their location, using different inputs, producing different outputs, targeting a particular market segment of the business environment, and so on.

2. The standards by which they are judged: Firms have some choice about how they will be judged as the rules applied to some firms are looser than those applied to others. Shareholders can, for example, be persuaded to accept low dividends if they trust the managers, or if the managers can persuade them that things will get better.

3. The boundaries between organisations and their environments: These are partly defined by the kinds of relationships the firm's decision makers choose to make. Therefore, for example, if a firm chooses to make a product that has no negative health implications, they are thereby also choosing to remove health legislation from their business environment.

Child also notes that despite a lot of effort, contingency theory does not provide a blueprint for organisational design as: 'In practice there does appear to be some variation in the structures of otherwise comparable organisations, a variation which is sustained over periods of time without much apparent effect on success or failure' (Child, 1972, p. 12). Child concludes from this that firms are strong rather than weak in respect of environmental forces; what firms end up doing is the result of the choices they make, not environmental dictate. Hence, rather than look outside at the pressure for survival in the environment to explain what firms do, Child argues that we need to look inside. Decisions are the result of some strategic choice process, and it is this that we need to look at in explaining the relationship between firms and their environments.

The strategic choice approach also has an implication for the nature of environmental analysis. If we take the determinist view, it is how the environment really is that matters and the role of strategic managers is to find out how it really works or suffer the consequences. In that case, how the environment is perceived is only important insofar as if the perception is wrong it needs to be changed (Argyris (1987) outlines the kinds of 'errors' managers make in respect of this). On the other hand, the strategic choice approach would put less emphasis on the importance of correcting such errors and more on the way the perceptions are formed and the power plays within organisations that lead, ultimately, to the decisions we observe. This interest in perceptions leads on to the enactment theory approach to the business environment.

16.5.2 Enactment theory

Look at the picture in Figure 16.5. What do you see? Most people perceive either the shape of a vase or two people in silhouette facing each other, and often our perception switches between the two views.

Figure 16.5
Perception and reality.

So, perception clearly has an existence that is partly independent of the object-ive reality (the objective reality in this case being a few lines and some shading). In general, the reality we deal with every day, at home and at work, depends on our perception of it. It is a part of 'us' as well as 'it'. This is not to say that our perceptions are 'wrong' necessarily, it is simply to acknowledge that it does not have the objective existence that we ascribe to it. This has implications for our study of the business environment. It means that people's perceptions of it matter, right or wrong, since what people do depends on their percep-tions. It also means that different people can interpret the same events in differ-ent ways and therefore seek different courses of action in response to the same stimuli. For a discussion of the effects of perception in determining what hap-pens within firms, see Weick (1969 or any of his later work). Enactment theory takes these ideas one step further; look at the picture above, think 'vase with flowers on', and look at Figure 16.6.

Figure 16.6 A flowery vase.

You did it! By perceiving the picture as a vase you made reality make up its mind. Well, no, of course not, but this is what enactment theory suggests happens when we look at the business environment. It is not as daft as it may seem, for the difference between the drawing and the business environment is that the drawing has a degree of objective reality that much of the business environment does not. Some things in the business environment seem very concrete; interest rates at my bank are 7%, there are about 59 million people in the UK, but what goes on out there if you take people out of the business environment? The answer is, of course, nothing. People are the business environment in their roles as consumers, suppliers, regulators, politicians and so on. If people constitute the business environment and re-create the reality of it by the actions they take every day, then, since what people do depends on their perceptions, perceptions help create that reality. In other words, people, including crucially the firms decision-makers create the business environment on the basis of how they perceive it. As in this approach the environment is seen to be created by the actions of people, we use the term 'enacted'.

The idea that we create the reality around us can be applied to the physical environment since we work in the buildings we create and live in the houses we build, and tarmac the roads that we drive across. However, this idea extends beyond what we physically construct to encompass all the institutions of society, because unlike roads (except perhaps the M25) these have to be rebuilt every day. This idea of people re-creating society daily stems from the work of the sociologists George Mead (1863–1931) and one of his students, Herbert Blumer (1962). The two key elements of their approach are, firstly, that people act on the basis of the meaning that they give to things. This means that we cannot see people as simply reacting to external stimuli, and we cannot therefore see firms (which are simply organised groups of people) as simply reacting to their environments either. Secondly, meanings are not fixed because events are reinterpreted in response to what happens when people interact. This means that meanings are modified and created every day, by what people do and as what people do is shaped by meanings, there is a continuous reciprocity between actions and interpretations. These ideas were developed upon by Berger and Luckmann (1967), and taken to their limit by Garfinkel (1967) who argues that society only exists insofar as people perceive it to exist. This idea is based on research that Garfinkel conducted on his own students. They were asked to take part in a new form of psychotherapy in which their problems would be dealt with by an expert counsellor. However, they would only be given yes or no answers. The students found the answers they received helpful, sensible and of practical use, and some of the students said they would deal with their problems on the advice they were given. However, in fact the answers were determined in advance of the counselling sessions in an entirely random manner. Garfinkel concluded from this that the students had constructed the reality from assumptions about the context (that it was a counselling session in the department of psychiatry). It seems likely therefore that, to some degree at least, decision makers within the organisational context construct their environment too by perceiving patterns and acting on those perceptions.

We can compare the enactment approach with other approaches by looking at the three main ways of perceiving the environment as categorised by Smircich and Stubbart (1985):

1. The objective environment: In this view the environment exists 'out there' as a thing in itself. Whether we look at it or not it is there. If so, then environments constitute a set of forces to be adapted to, or at least taken account of. For some, the firm is weak relative to these forces, as population ecologists and Porter argue; for others, the firm is strong relative to these forces, as Child argues. But as Smircich and Stubbart put it, neither group 'question the pivotal notion of environments as independent, external, and tangible entities' (1985, p. 725).

2. The perceived environment: The environment is still objective but strategists are not all-knowing rational maximisers, but have 'bounded rationality' (Simon, 1957). The role of environmental analysis is then to bridge the gap between the reality and strategists' flawed perceptions.

3. The enacted environment: In this approach the environment is seen as a product of the actions of people and what is produced depends on how people look at it. Therefore, unlike the preceding approaches, the business environment is not seen as independent of observers' theories, tastes and experiences and therefore has no objective existence. In this approach environmental determinism and the treatment of the business environment as a reified thing in itself independent of the actions of the people that constitute it are rejected. In this view 'the environment is a phenomenon tied to processes of attention and . . . unless someone is attending to it does not exist' (Weick, 1969, p. 28). This means that in fact 'the human actor does not react to an environment: he enacts it' (ibid., p. 64). In other words, the environment is what we perceive it to be.

The implications of enactment theory are that:

1. firms do not need to adapt to the environment;
2. the facts can be interpreted in a multitude of ways that suggest different courses of action;
3. what is possible depends on what you believe and do;
4. managers must look to their own perceptions in explaining environments.

The important message of enactment theory is that to understand the environment we need to stop treating it as if it were real and look instead at how we perceive it. Take, for example, the observation that most novel and successful new strategies come from newcomers to an industry: For population ecologists, this proves that incumbent firms are locked into their niche and cannot change when it does. In contrast, for enactment theorists it may prove that set patterns of thought pervade an industry and it is these that constitute the constraint rather than any objective 'environment'. This is important insofar as it underlines the role firms have in selecting and defining the threats and opportunities to which they will respond. This is a useful caution to bear in mind when considering what we take as proof of environmental trends or changes, and an invitation to get away from thinking that all responses to environmental contingencies can be categorised into right ones and wrong ones.

Criticism of the enactment approach

The common criticism of enactment theory is simply that the business environment does have an objective reality beyond people's perception of it. This means that by emphasising the flexibility and freedom of people to act in different ways, enactment theorists ignore the constraints on such action that laws, norms of acceptable behaviour, and power impose. For although we create the world we do not create it just as we please, since past actions become enshrined and embedded in the norms, laws and institutions of society – a process that Giddens (1979) describes as 'structuration' since it imposes a structure that enables us to do some things and stops us from doing others. For example, the norms that guide strategy come not from any limited perception but from shared social rules, as culture defines what is appropriate and reasonable behaviour. Similarly, the existence of differences in the distribution of power means that a large firm can enact its environment in a way that a small firm cannot. Moreover, since in reality firms are owned in law by their shareholders, they cannot forever choose to make no profits. These laws, the available technology, social structures and power relationships are all sources of empowerment and constraint, which means that the facility to enact the environment is partly determined by objective factors in that environment and that it does have a reality that is separate from us. In failing to recognise that, enactment theory means that a firm's environment 'takes on a fantastic quality. It has no objective existence, it does not exist in laws, institutions, or material reality' (Clegg and Dunkerley, 1980, p. 272).

16.6 SOCIAL ECONOMICS AND ECONOMIC SOCIOLOGY

J. Schumpeter (1883–1950) described the neo-classical economics approach as 'methodological individualism', because the method they employ is to reduce all economic and business activity to individual psychological givens. This approach dominates textbook economics: open any economics textbook and chances are you will not find words like society, families, kinship, religion and so on. Instead, what you will find is social activities, such as market exchange, being explained as a product of individuals' desire to maximise their own welfare; in this view the fundamental driver of markets is self-interest. As Adam Smith put it, 'It is not from the benevolence of the butcher, the brewer, or the baker, that we expect our dinner, but from their regard to their own interest' (1776, p. 26). A neo-classical economist can stop there; there is nothing further to explain since self-interest is a psychological trait that we are born with. However, others argue that all human traits are modified by our societal tendency because since prehistoric times we have relied on mutual support in families, clans and tribes to assist our own survival. Indeed, the process of socialisation of learning to live in society means that it is impossible to know what traits are learnt and what traits are genetic. Marx, for example, argued that the trait of self-interest was in fact a product of capitalism, and clearly any system that depends on a particular attitude to maintain itself, in the way that capitalism requires production, is likely to develop mechanisms to inculcate that attitude. To ignore this kind of reciprocity is to fail to treat people as a social product, to ignore their socialisation into the norms and values of the society in which they live. Therefore, as Granovetter (1982) and others adopting an 'economic sociology' approach argue, methodological individualism means treating people as 'under-socialised'. On the other hand, the Marxist alternative to neo-classical economics does take society seriously. However, for Granovetter, Marxists tend to adopt an equally incorrect but opposite 'over-socialised' approach in which all people and all firms are seen as acting slavishly on behalf of capitalists, so that instead of behaviour being entirely explained by individual traits, it is entirely explained by context. Either way, free choice is denied.

There is, however, an alternative approach encompassing both those with a background in economics and those with a background in sociology that recognises that people and firms are 'embedded in society' (as K. Polanyi (1886–1964) put it), and thus not under-socialised. But this approach also recognises that firms have genuine choice because decision-makers are not over-socialised to such an extent that their decisions simply reflect the norms of society and their background, since each individual's socialisation is imperfect. Those with an economics background tend to label their approach 'social economics' while those with a sociology background describe their work as 'economic sociology'. They are separate traditions but they share the common theme that people and thus firms are embedded in a network of kinship, state, professional, educational, religious and ethnic ties.

Embeddedness has certain implications for our study:

1. Environmental analysis by firms: We should recognise that the production of information is embedded in society, it is a social product, and often involves firms selling their interpretations. Even hard news has gone through a social and political filtration process, so that, as the saying goes: 'News is old'. Furthermore, the interpretation that is then placed on information by the firm depends on the dominant ideas within the firm. Most firms, for example, adopt a patriarchal outlook as men dominate most organisations; a different view often emerges when we look at the interpretation of events in women-dominated firms. Finally, how individuals then respond to the information depends on their personal ambitions, their backgrounds, how they learnt to learn, their class, sex, ethnicity, and so on.

2. The environment is not only a constraint on firms, it also empowers them: Traditionally the environment is seen as a constraint on the actions of firms but the social and cultural resources of society are used by firms every day to legitimate what they do. So, for example, when firms close a factory, even the workers involved accept it as a legitimate act if the factory is not making 'enough' profits.

3. When studying firms we need to consider society: You might think that you will; after all, its one of the four PEST factors. The problem is that society is not one factor, it encompasses all the factors; our culture defines the forms of economic activity that are allowed, the technology that is available, and the kind of politics that are permitted. As an example of how easy it is to ignore society, Whittington (1989) argues that even the work of the self-styled 'contextualists', whose detailed case study work on firms can run into many hundreds of pages, 'define their contexts too narrowly' as they 'leave unexamined the social sources of their actors powers and motivations'.

Case study in the process of legitimating firm's actions

BRITAIN'S LAZY WORKERS?

BMW has recently acquired Rover. The workers at Rover's manufacturing base at Longbridge have been told to improve productivity or face redundancy (unless the Germans can persuade the government to subsidise production there). Output per worker at Longbridge is over 30% below that of BMW's German operations. This has been met in the media by a host of references to the relatively poor productivity of our workforce, and it seems quite likely that we will again accept that it is our 'own fault' that we are losing jobs. So, once again, the power of a firm to close a community will be seen to be a legitimate response to that community's own shortcomings. However, the UK also boasts the most productive workforce in Europe at the Nissan plant in Sunderland, where average output per worker at almost 100 cars per year is nearly 30% above that achieved in Germany. The difference, of course, is not the workers at all, but the amount of capital used, the efficiency of the organisation of production and so on. In Sunderland, Nissan started from scratch with new buildings, new machines, new contracts with suppliers and workers and an extensive and ongoing training programme for all staff.

16.7   INSTITUTIONAL ECONOMICS

Many of the insights of social economics draws upon the work of a broad tradition of economists unhappy with the textbook approach, but unwilling to adopt the 'over-socialised' approach of Marx. This approach builds on the idea that studying social, political and economic institutions can form the basis of analysis, rather than the individual or the system taken as a whole. In this 'institutionalist' approach, both environmental determinism and methodological individualism are rejected. Key figures in this tradition are T. Veblen (1857–1929), J. Commons (1862–1945), G. Myrdal (1898–1987) and J.K. Galbraith (1908–).

If we adopt this approach to our topic then before we can answer the question of how much scope for free choice firms have, we need to look at the institutional arrangements in the UK which might act to limit that choice. In other words, we need to investigate the mechanisms by which the business environment might be able to force firms to follow its dictates.

- Competition: If there is an environmentally determined optimal path then firms that do not follow it will have lower value for money products than those that do. That is, they will produce goods that offer either lower quality for the same price, or offer the same quality at a higher price than the firms they are in competition with. Either way, customers will drift away from them, and their rivals on the right path will emerge as outright winners. The question then is: how much drift of this sort is there in practice in the UK today? This depends on three things:
    - Can consumers compare products accurately? If they can then the sub-optimal firms will be found out and punished by losing sales, until they get back in line with the dictates of the environment. Under perfect competition this is what we assume, but in reality people are unaware of all the alternatives. Indeed, firms differentiate their products so that fewer direct comparisons can be made, and substitutability is thereby reduced. Take cars, for example; if all cars were identical except for the fact that cars produced by sub-optimal firms were slower, then these firms would be found out and forced to improve or be squeezed out. Whereas, in reality there are so many types of cars that a whole industry exists to tell us about them, and despite all their efforts a definitive guide to the best car at each price does not exist.
    - Can consumers switch? If the switching costs are high then even if consumers become aware of differences in value for money, they will tend to stick with their current choices. To encourage loyalty, firms offer loyalty inducements that add value to their products. Firms also collaborate to reduce the possibility of price wars that could destroy firms, since every firm knows that even a firm with lower costs than its rivals cannot guarantee to win a price war. In a fair fight maybe, but in reality all kinds of backers will support either side to share the rewards of destroying a competitor since their removal will allow the winner to push prices back up above pre-fight levels. The result is that firms put a lot of strategic effort into avoiding price competition, and focus instead on non-price competition, such as branding and styling, which again makes it harder to see who is best. Finally, firms can side-step comparisons, and make switching harder, by creating new products and thus invent new markets to operate in through research and development activities or by focusing products on particular segments of the market.
    - Do consumers want to switch? Firms can encourage loyalty so that regardless of whether it offers the best value for money, consumers may want to stick with a brand. Indeed, the manipulation of demand may go beyond keeping what the firm already has to actually creating additional demand. Marketing, for example, might be seen as simply providing information;

on the other hand, marketing might be seen as an attempt to get people to buy something they would not otherwise have bought. If so, then the firm is manipulating the demand for their products. Indeed, image can become one of the characteristics that count when considering value for money. So, even if a product is apparently offering less value for money than its rivals, the firm can change that without changing the product one iota.

- Capital market control: If the owners of capital can compare the performance of firms accurately then they will switch their funding away from duff firms towards the best performers. There is clearly a tendency for this to happen; however, direct control from shareholders on firms has been reduced by the rise of the joint stock company in which ownership is greatly dispersed. So, for most big plc's there is a separation of ownership from control, so that relatively poor performance is tolerated, which, as Holl (1977) found, means that there can be very large differences in profit levels even within a single industry. There is also some element of indirect control of firms by banks; certainly many small firms are scrutinised by their local bank managers. However, most big firms are largely self-financing through plough-back of profits and can again avoid such scrutiny.

- Market for corporate control: Although the owners of capital may have diminishing scope for punishing poor performance, the threat of a 'take-over' by a firm doing a better job can act as an incentive to pursue optimal strategies. This in effect would mean that corporate control (the running of firms) is open to market forces; however, so numerous are the defences against take-overs that a hostile take-over rarely works. In fact, there is evidence that, rather than weed out bad management, the market for corporate control works to absorb good management, as Herman (1981) found, since it is often the least profitable big firms that take over the more profitable smaller ones! There is also the question of the extent to which firms want to do battle in this way. It is often very damaging for both firms and the managers, since it entails the replacement of one team of managers by another. In addition, even if one management team did feel inclined to run the risk of failure, they may lack the killer instinct insofar as they have friendship and kinship ties with their rivals. Scott (1985), for example, found that 49 of the UK's top 250 firms were controlled by one extended family. There are also a number of other studies showing the extent of interlocking directorships, which means that the people at the top sit on each other's boards and are therefore often friends, if not actually related.

In conclusion, analysis of the specific institutional arrangements suggests that firms have scope for different strategies when confronted with the same environmental contingencies. This is because the mechanisms by which we can compare different strategies and punish those who do not obey the dictates of the environment are incomplete, as:

1. sub-optimality does not come out in product failure;
2. sub-optimality does not result in shareholder revolt or bank intervention;
3. good management does not drive out bad management, so again sub-optimal firms nonetheless survive.

This means that even if the environment does dictate that some strategies are better than others, we are going to have a job spotting them, since firms pursuing the sub-optimal strategies will survive alongside the optimal ones. Indeed, they may take them over. So, what really matters is power, and although the environment may exert a powerful force on firms, the reverse is also true. For institutionalists there are therefore two sides to the equation; the other side being the power of firms to control their environments, and in light of this a number of ways of managing and controlling the environment have been researched.

16.7.1 Managing the business environment

Galbraith (1967) found that many firms were not so much adapting to their environment, as actively adapting it to suit them by means of the following:

1. Eliminating markets: By internalising part of the environment, for example, by vertical integration through taking over other firms, a firm is able to make what was a part of its environment into a part of the firm. In this way firms eliminate the countervailing power of their suppliers or buyers.
2. Controlling markets: Short of eliminating a market, firms can exert powerful control over a market by getting bigger by horizontal integration, or by advertising, or by effective branding and product differentiation.
3. Suspending markets: By removing a part of the environment or by 'capturing' a part of it, the effect of a part of the environment on the firms is suspended. For example, when firms make agreements with their 'rivals' that reduce competition, or with their suppliers, they are effectively suspending any threats that might come from those parts of the business environment. At the board level, firms are constantly trying to form a link with those outside of the organisation to exert some influence over them. I have myself experienced this kind of thing when a cartel broke up and senior managers went on what I can only describe as a 'lunch'-based strategy to re-establish links with their erstwhile partners in the cartel. Today, many industries are subject to regulation by government-appointed bodies; however, those in the industry 'wine and dine' the regulators in order to get members of such bodies begin to identify with the industry and develop friendships within it. They may also be offered lucrative positions within the industry when they leave their regulatory job. In such a case, the regulation may be less stringent than it should be, and although it is difficult to prove, there is a widespread concern about such 'regulatory capture'. At a broader level, firms employ lobbyists to influence parliament and academics to help get their 'concerns' across to the public, all in the hope of influencing legislators.

Case study in trying to get control of a market

MERGER MANIA IN THE OIL INDUSTRY

Although experts regularly predict that oil reserves will run out one day, today supply is rising faster than demand; as a result, in 1998 oil prices fell by nearly 50% to less than $6 a barrel. In real terms this puts today's price below that of the 1970s. In response to the decline in prices and margins, merger mania has begun, with BP paying $33bn to merge with Amoco and Exxon (Esso) paying $82bn to merge with Mobil. In both cases, massive economies of scale are anticipated which will allow for considerable job cuts. This has led Shell, who cannot find a suitable partner, to slash jobs in an attempt to remain cost competitive too. However, without the benefits of the economies of scale of its rivals, Shell has to look at different ways of ensuring that such cuts do not damage its business. One solution that it is pursuing is to reorganise and de-layer, that is, to remove all manner of middle management jobs that make up the layers of management in the Shell bureaucracy, including the complete dismantling of some regional centres. In addition, continued asset sales are likely, particularly in the weakest non-core activities. Unable to find a merger partner, Shell had made arrangements to combine certain operations with Texaco and benefit from economies of scale in that way. However, this fell apart when agreement on the division of the spoils could not be reached. The merger between Exxon and Mobil is the biggest in history, forming a company valued at around $250bn (or in other words a quarter of a trillion dollars), with 123,000 employees producing around 2.5 million barrels of oil a day. The low price of oil is also likely to have an effect on investment by this industry. The problem is that for many firms $12 dollars a barrel is the minimum price below which further exploration in the North Sea becomes unjustifiable, since it costs about $11 to get the stuff out of the ground. Oil prices are not, however, determined entirely by how much is dug up; indeed, you will have found little change in the price you pay for petrol in 1998 despite the massive price falls, since over 80% of the price in the UK is tax. In addition, as oligopolists the big suppliers are reluctant to cut retail prices. Also, demand is not static. A cold winter will alleviate the problems, while a mild one will exacerbate them. But most of all it depends on what the members of the Organisation of Petroleum Exporting Countries (OPEC) cartel do, for in recent years there has been little cooperation amongst oil-exporting nations. However, since ultimately the economic fate of whole nations depends on it, price falls are likely to concentrate minds considerably.

16.7.2   How firms manage their environments

How exactly each firm goes about managing its environments depends on the 'boundary-spanning activities' of the firm, since which jobs within a firm form the main links to the environment, which in other words span the boundary between the two, will affect how the management of the environment occurs. For Virgin, for example, the main link is a public relations and political one formed by Richard Branson, since he is both a great self-publicist and a friend of Tony Blair. Generally, the main boundary-spanning activities involve top management (in their family and social networks). In addition, different parts of the organisation deal with specific elements of the environment, so that, for example, marketers and public relations people form links to buyers, human resources specialists form links to labour markets, and IT specialists link with the technological environment.

Firms also have options in terms of what they can do. We are all familiar with attempts to influence consumers by marketers. However, what about attempts to control regulators, politicians, suppliers, the competition, social acceptability and so on? These may be equally important; indeed, in looking at successful firms' integration (take-overs), collusion, gaining community support and legislative backing are often the secrets of their success. We remember those that have apparently got there by great marketing because that is what we are exposed to in our daily lives as consumers, but many of the biggest got there by other means. So we need to consider dimensions of strategy beyond pricing and advertising, such as:

1. Political strategy: Occasionally, firms' strategies to influence political processes and people are exposed in the media. We have, for example, recently seen controversy regarding donations to the Labour Party in connection with the exclusion of Formula 1 racing from the tobacco advertising ban which was interpreted as part of a strategy by tobacco firms to limit further restrictions on their activities. But what we see in the media is the tip of an iceberg in which all kinds of legitimate lobbying, persuasion and back-scratching go on (and no doubt some illegitimate kinds too). In addition, many firms fund pressure groups; FOREST (pro-smoking) is a rather transparent one being entirely funded by the tobacco industry. Firms also form associations such as the Confederation of British Industry and Institute of Directors to influence the economic strategies of governments. But even acting alone, some individual firms are able to influence governments throughout the world simply because of their size and importance; this is particularly so for some multinationals in Third World countries who virtually run the economy and set the national political agenda.

2. Social strategy: There are firms who seem to be 'in the right place at the right time' to benefit from changes in their environments. However, often when we look deeper we see that they were in some way involved in creating those changes. One way in which they do this is to influence the attitudes and norms of society. Today, for example, nearly all 'young' couples want to own their own homes. In Holland they do not; most people rent, and the houses they occupy are bigger (by nearly a third on average), so it is not inevitable that we should want our own homes. Indeed, in the UK it was not until comparatively recently that we put a priority on home ownership; in fact it was in the 1980s that it rocketed up the political agenda and became almost overnight a cornerstone of Conservative ideology. This, of course, was a fortuitous change in the business environment for 'starter home' house builders. However, one of the reasons that Conservative governments began to place such emphasis on home ownership was surveys that showed that if people owned their own homes they would become more likely to vote Conservative and these surveys were originally commissioned, and the questions set, by house builders.

16.7.3 Implications of institutionalism

If firms can be either fitting their environments or shaping their environments to suit them, then we cannot use cross-sectional correlation-based analysis, such as that typical of contingency theory. When causality is open to question then we have to resort to historical analysis, and if we want empirical support, we will need regression analysis of time series data. Consider, for example, the case mentioned in Chapter 4, of the massive decline in sales of denim jeans in the early 1980s that resulted from a change in the environment favouring lightweight cotton trousers (chinos). This was largely due to the fact that at the time chinos were fashionable and acceptable in discos too, whereas jeans were not. This resulted in lower revenues and profits for firms specialising in denim jeans. Most of the firms affected that nonetheless survived were those who regained fit with their changed environment by lowering their prices and by switching production to trousers rather than jeans, which is consistent with the new equilibrium as shown in Figure 16.7.

Figure 16.7 The fall in demand for denim jeans in the early 1980s.

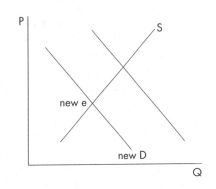

However, when we look at this industry with hindsight we can see that the main change has been in the environment, with the decline in the popularity of jeans having been entirely reversed. This was not, however, an entirely spontaneous environmental change. It was largely the result of the actions of one firm: Levi-Strauss. The Levi Corporation did not accept the dictates of the environment, since the prospects of lower prices and diversification did not bode well for them. Instead they sought to re-establish jeans in the minds of the public through unprecedented levels of advertising. In effect, Levi's enacted their environment, but it was institutional power that enabled them to do it. Therefore, in the long run we observe causality running both ways, with, in this case, one firm shaping its environment while the others adapted to it. The timings and balance of power involved are likely to vary case by case, but in carrying out such research, we are likely to observe that, in general, one or more of the following apply:

1. Some level of simultaneous causality between firms and their environment is common. This, of course, makes understanding the relationship

between firms and their environments more complicated than we would like. However, if you have difficulty envisaging causality in this way, then try using the analogy of a river. The river and the land determine where the banks of the river will be and where the bends in the river will be. The river carves out a path but the land resists depending on the types of rocks and soil therein. The combined effect is a twisting river created by the action of both the water and the land.

2. The greater the amount of competition, the smaller the degree of organisational slack and the greater the need to obey the immediate dictates of the environment. This is not to say that big companies can ignore the environment; the econometric evidence of individual cases is that failure to fit the environment is important even in oligopolistic industries. The poor performance, for example of the computer giant IBM is largely due to a rise in competition, which IBM has been unable to destroy, and it has instead been forced to respond by reorganising to increase efficiency. Also even when firms have been able to exert some power over their environments, the result is not a foregone conclusion. Returning to the Levi case above, it is worth noting that there was a period between the fall in revenues for Levi and their re-establishing the demand for their jeans when the future of the company was in doubt. Nonetheless, we would expect that under perfect competition the firm's strategic options are zero, its room for movement independently of the environment is minimal, and unlike IBM or Levi, it has to regain its fit as a matter of urgency. This is borne out empirically; the more competition there is, the faster the adjustment to environmental change and the less re-engineering of the environment is possible.

3. The fact that some firms have re-engineered their environments while others have adapted to them does not imply that in any situation all choices are equally likely to lead to success; this is the 'equifinality fallacy'. This arises when we look at the final result and find that firms have followed a number of routes that have all led to success; we conclude incorrectly that all routes are – in the end – equal.

4. The fact that firms can affect their environment does not mean that they are free of its influence; a firm can exert power over its environment in one direction and yet be constrained in another.

5. What choices firms make depend on a number of things: firstly, how managers perceive or model the change itself. Secondly, how they perceive or model their firm's relationship to the environment, as the effect of any change will impact upon different firms in slightly different ways. Thirdly they will reflect the values, preferences and power of managers, which reflect environmental social norms, and values that can be related to managers' backgrounds and personal motivations. However, as Whittington (1989) argues, these are not wholly reducible to managers' social and cultural backgrounds; an element of genuinely free choice remains. Either way, the effect of individual personalities can be found in the choices made by many firms, except for some of the largest – where decision making tends to be more dispersed, as Miller and Droge (1986) found.

Case study on different perspectives

THE LAURA ASHLEY COMPANY FROM DIFFERENT PERSPECTIVES

Laura and Bernard Ashley formed the Laura Ashley company in 1954. The firm was established to produce textiles, clothes and furnishings. The traditional style of the products is based on small floral patterns and muted colours. It is often described as 'English country rose' style (although originally partly inspired from patterns found in mid-Wales). Today the firm is international and sells a diverse range of garments, home furnishings and related products such as perfume and tableware. It is highly vertically integrated, designing, manufacturing and retailing almost everything it sells. It can be described as up-market insofar as its products are not cheap and the ambience of its stores and the style of its adverts suggest refined quality. Its market segment, to put it crudely, is middle-aged, middle class, women. It has for a number of years found making profit difficult however, as Figure 16.8 shows. Indeed, during the recession in the early 1990s it made losses. Like many firms, it chose to deal with recession by having more special-offer 'sales' rather than taking the full effect in lower output. In this way, it sacrificed some profit to keep output up. The 1995 figures were particularly affected by the costs of continued and wide-ranging restructuring of the firm.

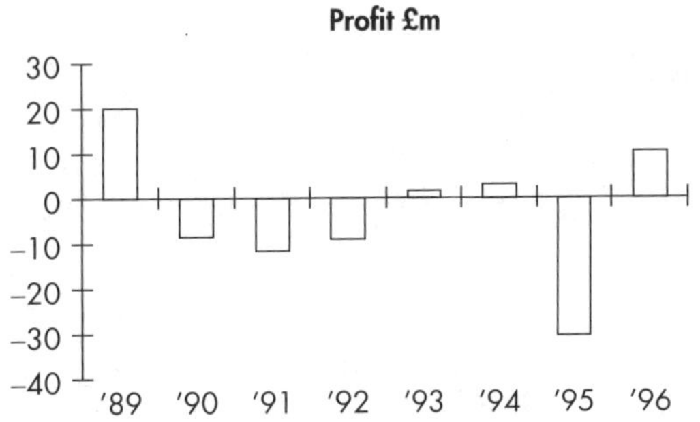

Figure 16.8 Profits of Laura Ashley.

Below is a discussion of Laura Ashley, taking ideas from the different perspectives outlined in the last section.

Population ecology

The niche for Laura Ashley (LA) was very clearly defined by the vision of Laura herself. The vertical integration of the firm and its small size allowed her to produce the kinds of 'feminine' designs that she liked and, for a time, it coincided with what the public wanted. The social environment was ripe for a change in the late 1960s and 1970s from the androgynous fashions of the early 1960s, and again in the 1980s there was something of a revival in interest in the firm's products. However, the niche has shrunk; today, fewer people wear the kinds of clothes or use the kinds of furnishings that we would identify as traditional Laura Ashley. In response, the firm has changed its style in an attempt to revamp, and migrate to another niche. From a population ecology point of view we should point out that there are considerable barriers and costs involved in the type of change envisaged at Laura Ashley. So even if staying put means occupying a shrunken niche, it may be better than the alternative and it should be remembered that many profitable firms occupy relatively small niches: The car market is a very big market and Porsche occupy only a small part of it, but they have done so, profitably, for many decades. Pointing out that a niche has shrunk and that it is hard for firms to change niche might seem to be bad news for Laura Ashley. However, all it really means is that the firm should appreciate that there are costs as well as benefits in changing and that these have to be set against the costs and benefits of staying put. This means assessing what level of profit their traditional niche can generate. Their traditional niche has certainly shrunk; few young women wear milkmaid dresses today. However, the conclusion that this niche cannot support a firm of Laura Ashley's size cannot be taken as proven by the fact that the firm is in difficulty. Its difficulties do not prove that the problem is the niche since poor management and poor organisation have played a part. It may still be that the firm's best chance of survival is to remain within its established niche. Figures on the size of this niche are not easy to come by since it involves looking at the demand for an indefinable style. However, what is clear is that some women, at least, continue to wear the LA style of clothing, and several new firms have sprung up to supply the kinds of things that LA used to supply but is now shunning. Moreover, top designers still create fashions that bear some resemblance to the 'English country rose' style. The company has under the direction of Chief Executive Officer Ann Iverson revamped its products and introduced a large new portfolio. Since from the population ecology viewpoint we must emphasise the barriers involved in changing niche we should point out that in this case one of the main ones will be overcoming people's preconceptions about Laura Ashley products. A massive advertising campaign might change this and the costs of it should be included as part of the costs of the strategy, as it is difficult to see how perception can be changed without this. As yet, no such advertising campaign has emerged.

Neo-classical economics

The main problem for LA can be gauged by looking at a simple supply and demand diagram (Figure 16.9); it is, in short, that they have become unfashionable and demand for their products has fallen, pushing the firm towards somewhere like 'b', with some combination of price cuts and reduced sales.

Figure 16.9 The Laura Ashley business environment.

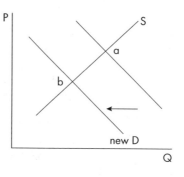

The five-forces approach, applied to LA, suggests that as a vertically integrated firm it can push its costs down. However, relative to its rivals, it pays high wages, by virtue of manufacturing in Wales and other parts of Northern Europe rather than in the Far East or Third World. It is also relatively small and thus benefits little from economies of scale. In addition, its production techniques and technology are relatively primitive so that the productivity of its workers is not much greater than those working (for far less), in the Far East. This is a problem if the reduced demand is, as suspected, likely to be permanent. One long-run solution to this would be to lower costs by shifting production abroad as in Figure 16.10, to move from 'b' to 'c'.

Figure 16.10 Producing in the Far East option for LA.

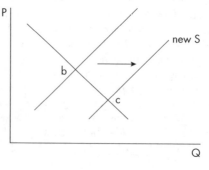

On the other hand, it has considerable power over its remaining loyal customers insofar as it offers a well-differentiated product in the 'English country rose' style and thus can face inelastic demands for the right products: The products are not a necessity and plenty of other clothes and home furnishing shops exist, so LA would not expect to face an inelastic demand unless its products are very well branded and occupy a distinctive style niche.

The niche may have shrunk, but the inelastic demands and consequent high margins are enough to overcome the relatively high costs of production, as long as products can be kept off the sale rail. This suggests that the low cost-strategy is not a viable option unless the firm moves production abroad, which it could do although it would be costly. It may also entail hidden risks for top of the range firms, as Marks & Spencer have found out: Although M&S has only dipped its toe, as it were, in Far Eastern production and buying clothes on the open market, its reputation for being British made and of top quality has come under attack as a result, and a similar problem could face LA if it chooses to move its manufacturing out. This is not to say that such problems are insurmountable, but it does mean that the alternative option of differentiation across a small product range, in other words having a 'focus' strategy, should be seriously considered. This puts the onus on identifying the right products, which in turn suggests the need to understand its current customers' requirements before identifying new ones. As it turns out, the company seem to have opted for what it describes as a 'differentiation' strategy which means creating a product that is different from its rivals then if it is popular it will have a relatively low elasticity and will be able to charge relatively high prices as a result. If a firm creates a product that is different to what it has ever produced but is very much like the products of its rivals, then this is not a differentiation strategy. It may or may not work depending on the quality of the goods, but the overall advantages of fewer substitutes does not apply and a rival producing the same products at lower costs will win. This is what appears to be happening with LA; a lot of its new range does not have the traditional LA feel but is rather similar to the products of Next, Richards, M&S, and a host of other large-scale retailers. The question then is whether LA can compete on a like-for-like basis with them; the answer is that it seems unlikely since many of them are bigger than LA and have lower costs. Therefore, they can offer essentially the same product at lower prices. In these circumstances customers might then question why they should pay more for something that they can get cheaper elsewhere. Increasing

stocks, and a burgeoning sale-rail at LA, suggest that this is indeed happening, which means that LA is inadvertently choosing a 'getting stuck in the middle' rather than a differentiation strategy.

Contingency theory

The success of the firm meant that the organisation had grown like topsy; in the late 1980s the organisational map looked like spaghetti, and there were 22 SBUs. These operated as stand-alone businesses, with no integration of essential functions such as distribution, personnel, marketing or finance. Indeed, their management information computer systems differed so much that central management often did not know what was going on within them. The centre had, in short, lost control. One solution would have been to set overarching targets based on an integrative plan for the whole business that would have ensured that the SBUs worked for the benefit of the parent company; in other words, that would have ensured the agents did what the principal wanted. However, in fact they were set independent targets that collectively could be met, while adding up to losses for the parent company rather than profits. The independence of the SBUs allowed managers to pursue their own objectives, and this could be seen by the proliferation within the SBUs of layer upon layer of management. On top of this, the firm's level of vertical integration meant that, without clear leadership from the centre, the different parts of the supply chain were often in conflict. This organisational disharmony results from a failure to identify core activities within an overall vision as the question of whether LA was primarily a design house, a retailer or a manufacturer remained unanswered.

The previous CEO, Dr Jim Maxmin, and the current one, Ann Iverson, introduced measures to cut costs and reduce complexity, including the elimination of most of the SBUs, and a considerable number of senior and middle managers. However, there remains considerable work still to do on eliminating duplication of effort and in simplifying and updating production, planning and control mechanisms. All of these are aimed at dealing with what has, in short, become a more 'turbulent' environment, with considerable new entry by fashion houses into retailing and by general retailers into selling clothes. In addition, there has been a proliferation of catalogue-based retailers as well as the globalisation of production to areas of cheaper labour. One response to this globalisation has been an increasing use by Laura Ashley of products manufactured outside of the firm. It has also responded to increasing turbulence by focusing attention on its environment by beginning to do market research on its customers. The general thrust of these measures is consistent with the findings of contingency theory, but there are problems:

1. The firm has centralised; centralisation in turbulent markets is correlated with failure. However, it is not clear whether centralisation is the problem or the solution; in this case centralisation is a response to the coordination problems facing the firm. The danger that the centre becomes overloaded should not be ignored, however, as it seems Ann Iverson is adopting a very hands-on approach and does seem to want to make the decisions on absolutely everything.

2. Contingency theory research suggests that a more turbulent environment requires more environmental analysis. This kind of analysis is poorly developed at LA. Some starts have been made in terms of research, but little and late. It was, for example, not until 1992 that the firm began to develop a system for profiling its customers, and it was also in the 1990s that it employed its first marketing specialists. Before this, it relied on its designers to come up with something that its customers would like. This had worked for Laura herself but the burgeoning level of unsold stocks suggests that those that came after her (she died in 1985) by and large failed to do this. There is also evidence of failure to do the environmental research that entering new markets requires. For example, the recent aggressive expansion into the USA focusing on wallpaper, curtains and other home furnishings was done on the back of a very narrow type of research and, to an outsider at least, looks decidedly unconvincing.

3. While recognising that firms do have strategic choice, policy reversals are a sign of poor choices and at Laura Ashley several policy reversals are evident: Australia was targeted and then abandoned. A decision to subcontract to Federal Express to solve distributional problems was subsequently reversed in 1996. Profit sharing schemes for staff to encourage loyalty and shared sense of purpose were also introduced and then dropped, and further shake-ups in manufacturing activities, including the undoing of previous fixes, were initiated in 1996.

Enactment theory

The latest CEO, Ann Iverson, has addressed the issue of organisational chaos by centralising everything around herself. Complementary to this, she has articulated a set of core values and a clear vision. Given that the firm is very vertically integrated, she is in a strong position to enact her vision in the same way that Laura Ashley herself did. However, if we accept that enactment has its limits, we have to consider whether her vision is the right one, and whether (in light of the size of the firm) it is within one person's ability to oversee the details of every part of it in the way she intends. When Laura Ashley first decided to produce long floral dresses, there was an element of creating the demand. However, there was also a backlash against the androgynous fashions of the late 1960s, so that magazines and the media latched onto the Ashley style and it became very fashionable. The vision therefore has to be set in context. Ann Iverson's vision seems to be that the traditional styles are 'dated' and that the future for the firm lies in diversification, in terms of both products and regions. She has embarked on a massive expansion in the USA and a revamping of product lines. It is important, however, to appreciate that entering a new market is costly (particularly when one feature of the current business environment is a high cost of borrowing), as is increasing the range of products offered, and this expansion does seem to be causing problems. These problems have resulted from the perception that LA's traditional niche is untenable. From the enactment perspective it is instructive to note how much damage this has caused the firm, since the problem may be as much to do with that perception as any objective reality.

Institutional economics

The rapid growth of this company was largely due to an increase in demand and the way the firm's vertical integrated structure was able to handle this. By controlling the product from design, through manufacture to retailing and marketing, the Ashleys were able to give customers very clearly branded products. Laura knew what she wanted to make and the vertical integration allowed her to produce exactly what was in her mind. As the firm grew, the pressures on the centre increased and the firm fragmented; the power that it had over its suppliers, being its own supplier, became irrelevant since all parts of the firm began to pull in different directions. The firm's desire to control its buyer environment seems also to be marred, in this case simply by a level of disinterest, insofar as it makes few adverts, seldom utilises product placement, and conducts too little market research. It does get involved in take-overs and collaborative arrangements but rarely, and without reference to anything that we could reasonably call a strategy. On the political side, the firm does no lobbying and when jobs are threatened it makes no political capital from it, even if these jobs are lost in areas of already high unemployment, such as Wales. It also makes little attempt to utilise the talents of the local environment, despite being located in and around some of the most fertile parts of the world for design talent.

16.8 **CONCLUSION ON DIFFERENT PERSPECTIVES**

1. Environments affect firms and vice versa.
2. Firms differ in the power they have over the environment but it is not just a matter of market structure.
3. Different ways of dealing with environmental contingencies exist. Firms can adapt to it, sometimes they can ignore it and focus on what they are good at (as Prahalad and Hamel (1990) found), or they can change it.
4. Strategically speaking, we cannot divorce the environment from firms and we have to consider this in formulating our strategies. This means that we need to look at tools that encourage us to think of firms and environments in an integrative way, such as SWOT analysis or simultaneous equation econometric modelling.

There are ways of picturing a firm's environment to see how the firm should adapt to it (neo-classical economics, and contingency theory). Although, for some, adaptation is not easy (population ecology), for the rest it is up to you to learn the stuff and get your firm to fit. On the other hand, do not forget that your firm will have choices (strategic choice) and how you approach the problem matters (enactment). Remember also that many firms are powerful and can manage their environment using strategies that encompass integration, political and social actions and not just marketing (institutionalism).

Case study in the determinants of small business success

THE TEN PERCENTERS

Since the early 1990s, David Storey and colleagues at Warwick University and at management consultants Deloitte & Touche have been studying the fastest-growing 10% of small and medium-sized firms in the UK in an attempt to identify the factors that contribute to their success. Nearly all are found to be in fast-growing niches that have benefited from some environmental change. Very few are cases of excellent performance of firms in established niches winning at the expense of relatively badly run rivals. This seems to support the idea that it is not what you do as managers that leads to success but being in the right niche at the right time, although those who benefit thus attribute it to spotting opportunities rather than good fortune. It seems to be therefore that entrepreneurial insight in spotting fast-growing niches is more important in becoming a fast-growing firm than being a good manager in a slow-growing niche. Indeed, many of the firms admit to having poorly organised and ill-defined management functions and procedures, although this may reflect the fit between environmental turbulence and adhocracy rather than weak management as such.

The other major finding of this research that is of interest to us, is that the ten percenters are very outward looking. We could summarise their approach as being more concerned with what their customers want, for example, than with how the firm is run. There is, however, a twist to this tale for it is also found that each year around a quarter of these high flyers have crashed. Some have been taken over, so although they no longer exist as a firm they cannot be classed as failed. Some, however, appear to have found that their niches have collapsed. Others have simply failed to make the transition to being a big stable firm, and this may be because of a lack of organisation and formalisation. Indeed, some of the ten percenters certainly seem to think that consolidating their position does depend on traditional good management as well as entrepreneurial insight. To clarify whether this is indeed so, the link between long-run success and good management practice will be the focus of more detailed investigation in a future 'ten percenters' report.

16.9 SUMMARY

- There are a number of different approaches to analysing the relationship between firms and the business environment.

- Springing from different sources, these have recognisable differences in the approach they take and the assumptions they make. This means that each has different strategic implications for firms for reacting to or managing their environments.

- We can differentiate the approaches by their backgrounds, with some showing a clear bias towards the tools of economists and others the tools of sociologists, and we can differentiate them by the degree of environmental determinism they assume.

- Although stylistically very different, population ecology and neo-classical economics approaches share a high degree of environmental determinism, and their strategic implications reflect their pessimism regarding the ability of firms to manage their environments.

- Contingency theory contrasts with classical organisation theory, since while the focus is still on the effect of the environment on organisational structures, it adopts a 'horse for courses' rather than a 'one best way' approach. It, however, shares an attachment to environmental determinism, which is attacked by those studying organisations from a strategic choice perspective.

- Enactment theory contrasts with other approaches in the degree to which environmental determinism is rejected. In this approach, the emphasis is on the extent to which the environment's existence is entirely conditional upon the interpretation of firms. This approach is, however, criticised for taking the rejection of environmental determinism too far by ignoring the real constraints that environments put upon firms.

- Social economic, economic sociology and institutional economics, although reflecting different traditions, all recognise the reciprocity of the relationship between firms and environments, seeing them as both constrained by the business environment and empowered by it too. In the institutional approach this empowerment is interpreted in terms of the power of many firms to manage their environments, and a number of ways of doing this have been discovered.

16.10 QUESTIONS

1. Outline plans for the introduction of an environmental scanning and interpretation system for:
    (a) a pub;
    (b) Everton Football Club;
    (c) Microsoft Corporation;
    (d) Marks & Spencer plc.
    The plan should include a statement of:
    (i)   the objectives of the implementation;
    (ii) capital requirements (equipment and so on);
    (iii) labour requirements (staff needed for setting the system up and for operating it);
    (iv) the mechanisms to be employed for the dissemination of findings to organisational decision makers;
    (v)   feedback;
    (vi) risks.

2. Compare and contrast the national cultural influences on the types of cars produced by the following firms:
   (a) Honda
   (b) Morgan cars
   (c) Ford
   (d) Mercedes
   (e) Citroen 2CV

3. Outline the boundary-spanning activities of the following organisations:
   (a) Nike
   (b) Virgin
   (c) An NHS trust

4. Scan the media to find an organisation that is in some form of 'trouble' (of any description) and devise:
   (a) a political strategy to deal with the problem;
   (b) a marketing strategy to deal with the problem;
   (c) a public relations strategy to deal with the problem.
   In each case, you must consider a strategy with at least four options. These should be substantive differences rather than the same strategy in different forms (so presenting the same public relations argument to four different newspapers, or indeed four different forms of media, would not count).

5. Analyse the strategic implications for a named company of adopting an approach to the analysis of the relationship between the firm and its environment based on one of the following:
   (a) population ecology (and evolutionary economics);
   (b) neo-classical economics;
   (c) enactment theory;
   (d) contingency theory;
   (e) strategic choice theory;
   (f) institutional economics.

6. (i) Discuss the types of organisational designs that Mintzberg's static contingency theory research suggests might fit the environments listed below.
   (ii) Discuss the limitations of this type of contingency approach.

   • The corner café. Established earlier this year, this is a small café on the corner of two streets in south London. It comprises little more than a few tables and chairs, a cooker, tea-maker and microwave. The owner/manager and her assistant have (so far) managed to meet demand without too many mishaps, but they are worried about the hostile reception from their nearest rival a short distance along one of the adjoining streets. They are also aware that the area is an 'up and coming' one and that as a result new rivals are likely to spring up around them in future.
   • The sock manufacturer. This firm supplies hundreds of thousands of socks each year to some of the biggest retailers in the UK. The socks are made using a largely automated production process that has changed little in recent years, with few advances since the basic weaving process was automated some time ago. In addition, the types of socks demanded have changed little over the years.
   • The legal firm. This firm operates from a set of offices near the Inns of Court in central London. The lawyers use very little technology and although the laws that they interpret are undeniably complex, the mode of operation of this firm has changed little since it was established over 200 years ago.
   • The bottle manufacturer. This firm has production facilities in several countries, so although generally the demand for bottles is stable, the types of bottles required in

each country vary considerably. Wine-producing countries tend to require a lot of wine bottles, while the UK is unique in requiring 1 pint milk bottles.

- The electrical components firm. This firm supplies a wide range of electrical components that are used in a number of types of domestic appliance and a range of industrial equipment. This year alone, there have been five directives from the European Union that affect the appliances and equipment that this firm's components are used in, as well as two directives that relate directly to the way this firm operates. There have also been a number of technological advances over the past few years that have had immediate and far-reaching consequences for this firm. In addition, a new and innovative rival has recently entered into direct competition with this firm. Everyone in this firm agrees, therefore, that they are in a complex and dynamic environment.

7. (a) Discuss the effects on UK hotels of the following:
   (i) A rise in the exchange rate of the pound
   (ii) A rise in health awareness within the population
   (iii) An ageing population
   (iv) A recession

(b) How might the owner of a chain of hotels attempt to manage her environment in respect of the changes listed above?

APPENDIX A

THE FIRM IN ENVIRONMENTAL CONTEXT; CASE STUDY

Below I have included a summary example of how you might depict the relationship between one firm and its environment.

AN ANALYSIS OF BRITISH AEROSPACE'S BUSINESS ENVIRONMENT

1. Background to the firm:
   History
   Objectives
   Stakeholders
   People
   Products
   Places
   Market segments

2. The internal environment:
   Company structure
   Internal control structure
   Culture
   Human resources
   Physical resources
   Core competencies

3. Recent performance:
   Organisational and cultural changes
   Financial performance
4. The external environment:
   The competitive framework: five-forces analysis
       Buyers
       Suppliers
       Substitutes
       New entry
       Competitive rivalry
       Generic strategies
5. Future prospects:
   PEST analysis
   Impact assessment
   SWOT analysis
   Conclusion

A report on the firm's business environment will inevitably have strategic implications; it is, however, anticipated that the reader will go on to do a course in strategy and so no attempt to follow the implications is made here. There is, however, one respect in which such a report does need more work, and that is in terms of the quantification of the factors and impacts discussed. This is not always easy from the outside, but within the firm, particularly within a large successful firm like BAe, it is likely to be practised as part of their planning process.

1   BACKGROUND TO THE FIRM

BAe's core business is the manufacture of civil and military aircraft, including the famous Harrier Jump Jet, as well as guided weapons systems, guns and ammunition. It is currently Europe's largest defence contractor, and defence remains its largest and most profitable business. It is also involved in a number of other manufacturing activities and related services, as well as being a shareholder in a broad range of other firms. Its main competitors include Boeing, MacDonnell Douglas, GEC, Aerospaciale, Saab and Mitsubishi. BAe is involved in a number of joint ventures with erstwhile competitors with-in Europe, and it owns 20% of Airbus Industrie, the European aerospace consortium. Its total revenue in 1996 exceeded £7.4 billion, with an order book of over £19 billion, of which nearly 90% are exports. It directly employed over 47,000 people in 1996, although this figure is considerably less than in the past. For example, at the start of the 1990s it employed well over 100,000 people.

History

BAe was formed as a nationalised corporation in 1977 by combining a number of UK-based firms that individually were finding it hard to compete on the world stage. These companies could trace their own family trees back to the makers of such famous planes as the Hurricane, Spitfire and Lancaster. In 1981, it became a plc, but the government retained a special stake that ensured that the company remained in British control. In 1989, the firm increased the autonomy of separate subsidiaries by making them responsible for marketing their own products under their own names. In 1992, it restructured to reduce investment in non-core activities, which had over the years become quite extensive and not entirely complementary. BAe has established relationships over the years, through partnership and collaboration, with a number of foreign governments and in particular has developed a close working relationship with the British authorities.

Objectives and stakeholders

As a plc British Aerospace has a commitment to its shareholders; it also, however, expresses a commitment to its collaborative partners too (whose stakeholding is the success of the collaborative venture). In addition, the British government is a stakeholder that acts as a major customer and as a provider of support in securing contracts from overseas governments. It also provides a highly trained pool of labour and scientific expertise through the university system. It even, on occasion, provides financial aid for BAe projects. BAe also emphasises the importance of its customers, who it depicts as 'deserving of through-life support' which is to be achieved by ensuring the quality and reliability of its products and by after sales support. BAe also stresses the importance of its suppliers, and is, for example, supporting training programmes in a number of less developed countries to help develop their indigenous industrial capabilities in engineering. This also fosters good relations with the communities in which it operates. Generally, BAe has been keen to involve staff in decision making at shop-floor level, and to get staff to buy shares in the firm. There was, however, a clash of stakeholder interests between workers and shareholders in the recession in the early 1990s which initially led to a squeeze on profits but which was dealt with in the end in large part by shedding staff. Staffing levels are now less than half what they were before the recession.

People

The main focus of strategic direction within the firm is believed to be Sir Richard Evans CBE, the current Chief Executive Officer (CEO).

Products

The current core activities of BAe can be divided into two, military and civilian. The military side encompasses military aircraft, guided weapons, guns and ammunition, and support services such as training and consultancy. The civilian side of the business is largely involved in the production of different types of passenger aircraft. It also encompasses several other outputs including flight simulators, motion sensors, and the like. In addition, BAe is involved in airport development and property services. Although currently small, the firm is developing the space flight support side of its business too.

Places

BAe has partnership deals that cover 28 countries in Europe, North and South America, Africa, the Middle East, Australasia and the Pacific Rim. In addition, it currently exports to 72 countries.

Market segments

Despite its geographical diversity and wide product range, two key features of the market segment stand out. Firstly, the main customers are governments and large firms. Secondly, most of the output can be described as 'high tech', since it employs both considerable amounts of technology, has generally taken years to develop, and requires specialist training to use.

2 THE INTERNAL ENVIRONMENT

Company structure

BAe is a holding company owning subsidiary companies that are independent profit centres. Day-to-day control of each company is in the hands of its managers and only general strategy is dictated from the centre. In other words, the firm has an M-form structure that probably has advantages in this case since it is diversified both geographically and in terms of products.

Internal control structure

The directors of each subsidiary are responsible for internal control but the holding company has clearly defined reporting and authorisation procedures covering sales, investment and treasury activities. In addition, it has an integrated strategic planning system based on business plans derived from rolling five-year forecasts of key targets for each subsidiary. Annual budgets and monthly reporting of performance against forecasts act as a check and control mechanism on progress towards these targets. Recent reorganisations have been undertaken to reduce costs and improve efficiency throughout the group. A thorough review of all essential processes was undertaken and resulted in the elimination of significant duplication within the various production processes and an improved exploitation of economies of scale. This was largely achieved by focusing on core activities, even to the extent of selling off non-core subsidiaries, such as the Rover car group. As Dick Evans put it in the Chief Executive's review in the 1994 report and accounts, 'The disposal of business has resulted in a change in the nature of British Aerospace from a conglomerate to a focused company structure.'

Culture

The large-scale review mentioned above helped to focus minds on what the core activities of the firm are and where the future of the company lay. In addition, BAe has adopted a range of modern techniques such as just-in-time (JIT) production and an emphasis on total quality control which, in combination with a new emphasis on communication and consultations with the workforce, are likely to have encouraged a shared sense of purpose within the group. Employees are now actively encouraged to take part in the decision-making process by becoming shareholders in the company and by adopting a flexible approach to using their skills with an emphasis on skill rotation and investment in learning. These measures should encourage an attachment to the firm's culture by the workforce, although since many of them will remember the big loss of jobs in recent years, an element of scepticism about the unified purpose of the firm may remain.

Human resources

Considerable investment has been made in developing a flexible, multi-skilled workforce in recent years. Lines of communication have been improved and a learning culture encouraged. There has also been an emphasis on cross-fertilisation of ideas and skills across the subsidiaries. There are, for example, exchange mechanisms for young engineers to broaden their experience and allow different parts of the firms to draw on their expertise.

Physical resources

An important feature of BAe's physical resources is its investment in highly capital-intensive, high-technology production processes. It owns considerable productive capacity and land, particularly in the UK. It is investing in production facilities to deal with new components, such as ceramics, as well as future products such as ultra high capacity civilian aircraft and variable geometry fighters.

Core competencies

The core competencies of the firm are its ability to deliver high-technology products with the kind of extremely high reliability that is essential in the aircraft industry.

3   RECENT PERFORMANCE

Organisational and cultural change

The firm has introduced a number of changes to improve communications and enhance decision making, and it has also reduced the costs of production by shedding staff and improving production techniques.

Financial performance

Profitability

Profits and profitability declined in the early 1990s, largely because of recession and fluctuations in exchange rates. As Bob Bauman put it in the Chairman's statement in the 1994 reports and accounts, 'this company has moved forward from very severe difficulties that resulted from the recession in many of its markets'. The firm was unable to stop changes in the business environment hitting its profit, despite being a large oligopoly with influence within the political establishment. It did, however, continue to pay its shareholders a dividend.

Figure A1.1 shows profits in the early 1990s. Note that these profit figures are not adjusted for inflation on the assumption that inflation hit revenues and costs equally.

Figure A1.1

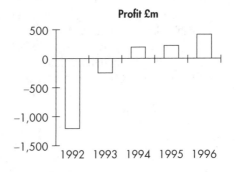

Another way of looking at profit is in terms of profit margins and returns on capital employed, which show a similar picture (Figure A1.2).

Figure A1.2

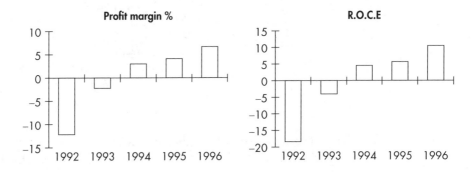

Revenues, costs and efficiency

The effect of the recession of the early 1990s on BAe was negative, but to some extent ameliorated by the fall in the pound, which helped exporters, BAe included. The main problem was the costs of meeting that demand since the fall in the pound put costs up and there was an outstanding issue of the efficiency of the firm that had not been addressed, which the rise in costs brought to the top of the firm's agenda. In response, it restructured and improved efficiency, as indicated in Figure A1.3.

Overall the firm has improved its efficiency more than many of its rivals, but a few have greater economies of scale that BAe cannot match at present. The efficiency gains at BAe are the result of concerted management action to improve productivity, including the shedding of staff (Figure A1.4). The favourable industrial relations climate in the UK that has resulted from trade union reform and high unemployment in the 1980s have also no doubt played a part in this. There have also been helpful falls in world prices for some metals and other commodities used by BAe. Also, while the fall in the pound in the early 1990s tended to put costs up, the subsequent rise in the pound has tended to keep them down in recent years.

Figure A1.4

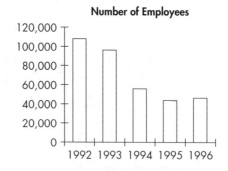

Liquidity

The firm's short-term financial position is not a major concern as the graph for the current ratio shows (Figure A1.5), although the firm is highly geared.

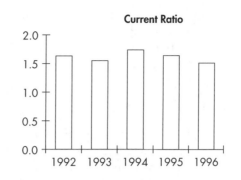

Current Ratio

4 THE EXTERNAL ENVIRONMENT

The competitive framework: five-forces analysis

Buyers

Buyers are major airlines on the civilian side and governments on the defence side. Often for government contracts the government, as a monopsonist, can exert considerable downward pressure on prices. However, the products are not perfect substitutes so buyers will have preferences, and if these can be identified, that is, if BAe is sure that its product fits the bill better than any-one else's, then it will have some bargaining power too.

Suppliers

BAe has established a 'preferred supplier' strategy where it has reduced the number of suppliers it uses but has sought to establish longer-term relation-ships with those that remain. This involves partnership agreements, and other means of locking suppliers in so that they share some of the risks. This is par-ticularly important to ensure flows of supplies when using a JIT system.

Substitutes

There are always alternatives offered within the industry, except that no competitor offers a vertical take-off fighter plane. Broadening our discussion, we should note that other forms of transport such as boats are a substitute on the civil aircraft side of the business. However, there are no close substitutes since the characteristics of other modes of transport are very different. On the defence side there is the possibility of substitution of some ground combat capability rather than air combat capability, but again they are different and are normally seen as complements rather than substitutes. One clear substitute is weapons of mass destruction such as atomic weapons, which BAe is not involved in; however, such alternatives are becoming generally less popular with governments.

New entry

There are significant barriers to new entry in both the civil and military sectors, including high set-up costs and legal restrictions, particularly in connection with the production of weapons. In addition, major technological investment is generally required and considerable learning may be necessary before a new entrant, even a large one, can match an incumbent firm. Finally, there is considerable value in reputation in this industry given the nature of the products involved. This means that a newcomer would have to invest heavily to establish the kind of reputation that incumbent firms have taken decades to acquire.

Competitive rivalry

Many firms in the aviation business are realising the benefits of collaboration, particularly as a means of countering the strength of American rivals. The main source of profit for BAe is the defence side of the business. However, defence spending is unlikely to return to Cold War levels although further reductions are unlikely. Figure A1.6 gives a forecast of this market currently taken as the most likely outcome within the industry. It shows the market stabilising at around $700 billion, with little future growth in nominal terms and no growth in real terms.

Figure A1.6

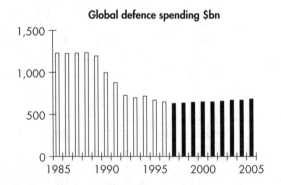

The main area of growth is likely to be on the civilian side, and given the decline in world defence spending, we are already seeing the civilian side matching the defence side in terms of orders if not yet in terms of profit. Figure A1.7 shows the trends.

Figure A1.7

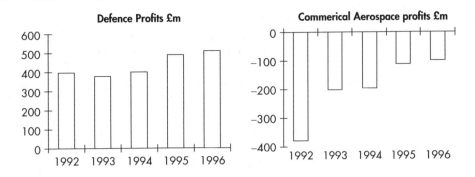

Generic strategy

For some SBUs, where elasticities are relatively high, competition can be based on price. Indeed, governments support the collaborative arrangements within Europe to enable European firms to produce on a sufficient scale to compete on price with American giants Boeing and MacDonnell Douglas. However, for many SBUs, particularly in the defence sector, competition is based on differentiation rather than price, (although it depends on the contract). In addition, because in this industry sales are driven by a few major contracts with foreign governments, competitive strategies may be adjusted for each bid.

5   FUTURE PROSPECTS

PEST analysis

We can collect our thoughts on likely PEST influences by constructing an impact assessment grid for BAe focusing on the next five years.

Impact Assessment Grid

Impact on firm

HIGH   Medium   LOW

| *Likelihood of change occurring or trend continuing* | HIGH | 1. Economic slowdown |

2. Continued increase in world spending on civil aviation

3. Decline in world defence spending

4. Change in government policy

LOW

The first factor listed is the economic cycle, as despite successive governments' best efforts a boom–slump cycle persists. The effect of a downturn on BAe will form the focus of the discussion below, but it is worth mentioning the other factors identified too. A change of government is likely to herald a change in defence spending priorities; however, the Labour government plans to maintain overall spending at current levels and to maintain support of this industry. Some changes are nonetheless likely; Labour has, for example, made a commitment to introduce certain ethical limitations on what can be sold and to whom. However, if it is likely to mean job losses the differences between this government and the last one may be minor, and so my forecast is that the change in government will not represent a major threat to BAe in the next five years. Consequently, I have placed it in the middle rather than in the 'high impact on firm' box. The increase in spending on civil aviation is a trend that forecasters in this industry see as continuing, which means that one part of BAe's core business is growing. However, spending on defence is forecast to level out because of the ending of the Cold War, although further reductions are thought unlikely, as conflict and uncertainty remain a feature of the world.

Four factors may not seem like many, but for four factors we actually have 16 different combined outcomes, which could mean 16 different contingency plans. In addition, of course, if we add quantitative differences between these cases the number of outcomes would multiply further. If, for example, instead of having one plan based on economic slowdown and one based on continued growth, we used percentage figures for growth of −2, −1, 0, 1, 2, 3, we would end up with a corresponding increase in the number of scenarios. It is important therefore to limit our ambitions, and in this case, for illustrative purposes I shall keep it as simple as possible and look at only one scenario in isolation. The contingency I have chosen is that the rate of growth in the UK economy slows in the late 1990s. The main weapon used to slow the economy down is a combination of fiscal 'prudence' and higher interest rates. We shall look at the firm's strengths and weaknesses in connection with this contingency rather than in general, again in order to keep things short.

SWOT analysis

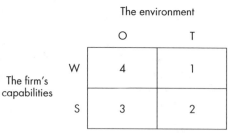

Taking each in turn:

1. The expected slowdown is a threat even though most of BAe's sales do not occur within the UK, since higher interest rates will push sterling up and will hit exporters of manufactured goods, of which BAe is one. Its

weakness here is that many of its competitors are based in countries at different stages of their economic cycles. This means that BAe's relative competitiveness will be affected.

2. The firm's strength in respect of this threat is that in being big BAe can hedge against the rise in sterling more than many small manufacturers. Clearly, BAe should be investigating ways of minimising this in terms of the contracts it signs now. This may continue to have an impact on the firm even after the UK enters EMU, since most deals are likely to continue to be done in American dollars. Another strength is that BAe's links to the political establishment and the Ministry of Defence in particular may ensure that it has government support. However, while this might extend to support to stop significant job losses it is unlikely to extend to keeping interest rates down just to help BAe. Another strength is that it is more efficient now than it has been for some time and more so than many of its major rivals.

3. The opportunity that the rise in sterling will bring is a reduction in the cost of imported raw materials. The slowdown will itself herald several additional opportunities; insofar as it may propel the UK to become a part of the single currency, options for further expansion across Europe will be enhanced. Furthermore, the single currency as a powerful currency bloc could mean that it faces fewer exchange rate problems in the future and that more of the contracts that BAe bids for will be denominated in the Eurocurrency. BAe is well placed to take advantage of this opportunity, as it is now relatively efficient compared to its European rivals and has the ability to collaborate successfully with them.

4. The prospect of expansion across Europe could encourage some European countries to increase support for their own firms in competition with BAe, particularly since BAe's underlying efficiency is better than some of its European counterparts.

Conclusion

Although a powerful oligopoly with government support, this firm was hit by the recession in the early 1990s, and could be adversely affected, despite significant increases in its efficiency, by an economic slowdown over the next five years. Its main options are to merge with a European partner and work on its relationship with the new Labour government.

APPENDIX B   TYPES OF FIRMS IN THE UK

1. Self-employed (also called a sole trader): This is where an individual carries on a business in their own name. About 80% of all firms in the UK are of this type but they tend to be very small, usually employing less than five

people. Examples include window cleaners, electricians, plumbers and so on. The advantages of this type of business arrangement are that it is easy to set up and the amount of information about the firm's accounts required by the authorities is limited. Because of this, many sole traders can avoid paying the full tax on their activities. The main disadvantage is that the individual has unlimited personal liability for the debts incurred by the business. Therefore, for example, if someone sues the business the individual has to pay up, even if this means selling their house or other assets.

2. Partnership: This is where two or more people get together to pool their resources. The disadvantages of doing this are that each partner has unlimited personal liability for the debts of the business regardless of whether those debts were incurred by the recklessness of the other partner. The main advantage of this type of arrangement is that resources are pooled. For many professions this is a popular option because they face few risks in running the business and are subject to codes of conduct that limit the types of arrangements they can choose.

3. Limited company: The idea behind this is to limit the liability of the individuals who set up the firm, to encourage risk taking which is an important element in the wealth creation process. With limited liability the firm has its own legal identity separate from the owners so that if the firm fails the owners can lose what they put in, their investment in time and money, but not their personal assets.

    There are two types of limited company
    (i)   Private limited companies: The advantage of this arrangement is that it is cheap to set up, with a minimum share capital of £100 and a few hundred for registration. The disadvantage is that, relative to sole trading, it is more complicated to set up and annual accounts have to be produced, which reduces the scope for tax avoidance.
    (ii) Public limited companies (plc): The advantage of this arrangement is that the firm can offer shares in the ownership of the company to the public and thereby raise additional funds. These shares can be sold repeatedly, which means that investors can withdraw their loan by selling the shares to someone else, but as far as the firm is concerned, the loan continues. The price of the shares of different companies are shown in most newspapers; these indicate the success of the company as successful companies' shares are likely to be in demand and rising in price. The price of the shares indicates the value placed on the company. Extra shares are issued to raise more funds if investors think it is a good bet. In this case, existing shareholders will need to be compensated or appeased in some way if share prices are not to fall. The disadvantages of this arrangement are that the firm needs a minimum 'share capital' (invested cash) of at least £50,000 and there are more legal hurdles to be jumped before the firm is approved than for a private limited company.

4. Co-ops: There are hundreds of co-operative societies in the UK, where groups of people get together to form a company that has its own legal

identity and confers limited liability on the owners. Ownership is conferred by buying a single share in the company, which entitles the shareholder to one shareholder vote on the future of the company. This 'industrial democracy' extends further in some cases, with workers directly represented at board level and involved in the day-to-day policy of the company. Generally, co-ops are set up to provide a service to the community of shareholders. Although co-ops can be organised in a variety of ways, there is a basic common theme of eliminating the need for capitalists, with workers providing the capital and enterprise, and in return sharing the rewards. The largest co-operative movement in the UK is known as 'The Co-op' and is one of the biggest companies in the country, with interests in a variety of areas including food, retailing and banking.

5. Mutuals: This is similar to a co-operative but control of the company by shareholders is relatively limited and all customers become shareholders. All building societies and many insurance companies are 'mutuals' with all profits being ultimately returned to customers. Customers automatically become shareholders entitled to one vote and no more when they open an account, take out a mortgage or enter an insurance contract with this type of company.

6. Not for profit organisations: If a company fulfils certain criteria it can be registered as a charity, which has certain tax advantages; generally these types of arrangements have a charitable objective in mind beyond maximising the wealth of the owners by maximising profit.

7. Public organisations: These are 'companies' run by, or on behalf of, the government; generally these are allocated a budget and expected to perform certain functions, that is, to supply goods or services as well as they can within that budget.

GLOSSARY OF TERMS

A

Aggregate demand   The total of all planned expenditure in an economy (such as Wales, the UK or Europe) in a given period of time. If we look at what people plan to spend at different prices then we have the aggregate demand curve for the economy.

Appreciation of a currency   A rise in the value of a currency relative to other currencies.

Assets   Something that can provide a flow of benefits in the future. A distinction can be drawn between financial assets, such as money, bonds and shares, and physical assets such as machines, buildings and land.

B

Balance of payments account   The accounting record of a country's financial transactions with the rest of the world.

Bi-lateral exchange rate   The value of a currency with respect to one other currency.

Business cycle (trade cycle)   The observed tendency of economies' outputs (and thus employment and prices) to go up and down over time with a periodicity of 7–10 years.

C

Capital   This term is used to mean two things:

1. As a factor of production, this encompasses the stock of physical assets that has been created over the years by investment and which can now be used to produce more goods and services.

2. Financial assets.

Cartel   A group of suppliers who have a formal arrangement to fix prices or other aspects of a market.

Central bank Responsible for regulating the banking sector of an economy. Often also responsible for setting interest rates and other aspects of monetary policy.

Centrally planned economy An economy in which planning by government agencies or departments determines what to produce, how to produce it and who to produce it for.

Ceteris paribus Latin term meaning 'other things remaining constant'. It is necessary to employ this assumption to isolate the effect of one thing on one other thing in a world in which in truth everything affects everything else. The effect of the other things can then be dealt with in a similar manner one at a time.

Chaos theory It has been found that the behaviour of systems, be they biological, physical or organisational systems, are not always determinate or indeterminate, but that there is a region in between in which behaviour is unpredictable but structured. Chaos theory relates to the investigation of this phenomenon.

Commercial banks Financial firms that are allowed to make loans and accept deposits from the general public against which the issuing of cheques is permitted. Also referred to as deposit banks.

Comparative advantage Having a lower opportunity cost in producing something compared to somebody else. First discussed in detail by Ricardo to show why specialisation in the production of some things and trading to get the rest is best, even for a country that is a world beater in everything.

Complementary goods and services Goods or services that are consumed together so that if the price of one falls the demand for the other will rise, such as fish and chips.

Conglomerate integration When firms producing completely different goods or services are joined through a merger or a take-over.

Consumption function The mathematical or graphical form of the relationship between planned consumption and the things that affect it.

Contestable market A market in which there are few barriers to entry or exit. Firms in such a market are likely to be under constant attack from new entrants if they believe that the niche is likely to be a profitable one for them.

Cross-price elasticity of demand (XeD) Calculated by dividing the percentage change in the quantity demanded of one good by the percentage change in price of some other good, this is an indicator of the relationship between different goods or services. A positive number indicates that the goods are complements, a negative number indicates that they are substitutes. A high number indicates a strong relationship.

D

Darwinism The belief that variety of forms can be explained by the process of competition to fill environmental niches.

Deflation The act of lowering aggregate demand to slow an economy down. Or sometimes used to mean a fall in the average level of prices in an economy (disinflation).

Depreciation of a currency The fall in value of a currency relative to other currencies.

Deregulation Reduction or complete removal of rules imposed on business that limits the free play of market forces.

Dirty floating   A floating exchange rate in which there is significant central bank intervention to keep the exchange rate within the range that the government decides is sensible.

Disinflation   A fall in the average price level in an economy.

Division of labour   Where the production process is broken up into parts so that different people can specialise in the different parts.

E

Economic and monetary union   The coming together of previously separate economies into one region in which there is free trade and one overarching monetary policy.

Economic rent   The surplus that a factor of production receives above the minimum necessary to keep it in that use.

Economies of scale   Factors that raise average productivity and therefore lower average cost as the scale of a firm is increased.

Econometrics   The statistical examination of economic hypotheses.

Entrepreneur   Person who organises economic activity in new ways.

Entry barriers   Obstacles that stop firms entering a market and competing profits down.

Equilibrium price   The price at which the quantity of goods supplied at a price is the same as the quantity of goods demanded.

Equilibrium national income   The level of national income that equates to the level of planned spending.

Exchange rate   The value of a currency relative to other currencies.

Exit barriers   Obstacles, such as high unrecoverable 'sunk' costs that make it expensive for a firm to leave an industry once entered and which will therefore make entry less likely in the first place.

Externality   The effect of an economic activity on parties not directly involved in that activity.

F

Factors of production   The resources that can be used to produce goods and services; these can be grouped under four main headings: land, labour, capital and knowledge.

Fiscal policy   Government policy that relates to its spending and taxation role in the macroeconomy.

Fixed costs   Costs that do not change because the firm has changed the level of its output.

Floating exchange rate   An exchange rate that is determined without government intervention in the currency market.

Free market economy   An economy in which markets determine what to produce, how to produce it and who to produce it for.

G

Game theory   A way of looking at strategic behaviour by limiting the scope of the interactions considered.

General equilibrium analysis   Looking at the points of rest in all markets taken together. See also *Partial equilibrium analysis*.

General training   Training that transfers across jobs and firms. This kind of training makes an employee more productive for a number of firms, not just the firm that provides the training, and may therefore be under-provided unless government shares some of the costs of its provision. Schooling is, as far as firms are concerned, a form of general training. See also *Job-specific training*.

Giffen good   Goods for which a rise in price leads to an increase in demand because of the low incomes of the consumers and the lack of substitutes for the good.

H

Horizontal integration   When firms producing similar goods or services are joined through a merger or a take-over.

Human capital   A person's stock of skills and knowledge that are accumulated by investment in education and training, or through experience.

Hyperinflation   A very high rate of inflation may be referred to as hyperinflation despite the fact that there is no generally recognised figure at which inflation ends and hyperinflation begins.

I

Imperfect (or monopolistic) competition   A market in which there are a large numbers of firms selling products that are different in terms of some characteristics only, such as location. For example, all pubs in a town may be classed as being in the beer-selling market, but they may sell different ranges of beers, be in different parts of the town and have different 'atmospheres'.

Income effect   A fall (or rise) in the price of a good or service means that the purchaser has more (or less) income remaining after the purchase and thus is effectively made richer or poorer by the price change. Since a change in income can induce either more or less consumption of a good, this effect means that in some cases a price rise can lead to more demand rather than less.

Income elasticity of demand (YeD)   Calculated by dividing the percentage change in the quantity demanded of a good, or service, by the percentage change in income, this is an indicator of the effect of income changes on demand. If the calculated figure is negative we are dealing with an inferior good since this indicates that a rise in incomes reduces demand. If the figure is positive then we are dealing with a normal good. If the figure is less than 1 it may be thought of as a 'necessity', if greater than 1 a 'luxury' or 'superior' good.

Indirect tax   A tax on the sale of goods or services which can be either a 'specific tax' or an '*ad valorem* tax'. A specific tax is levied as a fixed amount in pence per unit on the price, such as 90p on the price of a packet of cigarettes. An *ad valorem* tax is levied as a percentage of the sale price of a good, such as VAT in the UK, which in buying a computer, for example, adds 17.5% to the price.

Inferior goods   Goods or services for which a rise in income results in a decrease in demand, and for which a fall in income raises demand.

Inflation   A rise in the average level of prices in an economy.

Injection   An addition to spending within the circular flow of income.

Invisible trade   Exports and imports of services.

Investment   Using current resources to create assets (or, in other words, more or better resources) rather than to meet the needs of current consumption.

J

J-curve   A graph that shows how, in many cases, the balance of trade deteriorates before it improves when a currency depreciates or is devalued.

Job-specific training   Training that involves learning tasks that are only applicable to the individual's current job. This type of learning adds to the individual's human capital but only in respect of his or her current job, which means that the benefits are kept within the firm that provided the training. See also *General training*.

K

Kinked demand curve   In oligopolistic markets a firm may face an elastic demand if it raises its prices, and an inelastic demand if it lowers them. This discourages it from changing prices and means that when depicting its demand curve we need to draw a kink to indicate the difference in elasticity between price rises and price cuts.

Keynesian   A school of thought that, following J.M. Keynes, believes that because aggregate demand is inherently unstable, keeping output up and unemployment down means that the macroeconomy needs to be actively managed mainly through fiscal policy.

L

Labour   As a factor of production this encompasses any physical or mental activity done by people that contributes to the production process.

Laissez faire   French for 'let it be', used to signify the approach that believes that governments should reduce their 'interference' in the economy.

Land   As a factor of production this encompasses all natural resources both in and on the land, sea, air and cosmos that contribute to the production process.

Law of demand   The commonly observed inverse relationship between the quantity demanded of some good, service or factor of production and its price.

Law of diminishing marginal returns   The tendency for the marginal product of a variable factor to eventually decline as more of it is applied to a fixed factor.

Leakage   A withdrawal of potential spending from the circular flow of income.

Long run   When all factors of production are variable.

M

Macroeconomics   The study of the economy taken as a whole.

Marginal cost   The change to total cost that results from producing one more unit of output.

Marginal physical product of a factor of production   The change to total output that results from using one more unit of a factor of production.

Marginal propensity to consume   The fraction of an extra unit of income that is spent on consumption.

Marginal revenue   The change to a firm's total revenues that results from selling one more unit of output.

Marginal revenue product of a factor of production   The change to a firm's total revenue that results from using one more unit of a factor of production.

Market   Any arrangement by which trade occurs. The trade might be of a good, service, factor of production or financial commitment.

Market for corporate control   The control of firms constitutes a market insofar as this control can be changed through the buying of shares, by take-overs, and by wielding influence over existing shareholders.

Merit good   A good or service that the government is willing to subsidise because it feels that the merits of it are greater than people might at first think, and which might therefore be under-provided by the private sector.

Methodological holism   The method of some Keynesian and Marxian analysis that seeks the explanation for economic behaviour in the arrangements that define whole economic systems, such as the arrangement between workers and capitalists that define capitalism, or between consumers, firms and governments that define the macroeconomic arrangements of society.

Methodological individualism   The method of traditional neo-classical economics that is based on seeking the explanation for economic behaviour in the motivations of individuals.

Methodological institutionalism   The method of institutionalists that is based on seeking explanations for economic behaviour in the particular arrangements that characterise the main institutions of a society at a particular point in time.

Mixed economy   An economy in which both planning by government and free market forces determine what to produce, how to produce it and who to produce it for.

Monetary policy   Government policy that relates to its ability to control the amount of money in the economy.

Monetarists   A school of thought that, following Milton Friedman, believes that the macroeconomy is inherently stable and that fluctuations in it are largely due to the profligate monetary policy that is the side effect of Keynesian demand management.

Money   Any generally acceptable means of payment.

Money multiplier   The ratio of the change in the size of the money supply that results from a change in the monetary base to the size of the change in the monetary base.

Money supply   The amount of money and thus spending power in an economy.

Monopolistic competition   see *Imperfect competition*.

Monopoly   A market dominated by one supplier.

Monopsony   A market dominated by one buyer.

Multiplier   Calculated by dividing the size of a change in national income that results from a change in an injection by the size of the change in the injection. This is a measure of the scale of extra output that an injection generates.

N

National income   The sum of all incomes generated in an economy in a given period of time, such as a year.

Normal good   A good or service for which an increase in income leads to an increase in demand and a decrease in income to a fall in demand.

Normal profits   The minimum return necessary to keep a firm in its current business. This must be equal to the opportunity cost of risk capital since, if it is not, funds will go elsewhere.

O

Oligopoly   A market dominated by a few sellers.

Opportunity cost   The value of the next best alternative use for the resources that are used up in the production of any good or service.

Organisational learning   The knowledge that is embodied within an organisation or the process that the organisation uses to accumulate such knowledge. Related to but separable from the learning and knowledge of the individuals in the organisation.

P

Partial equilibrium analysis   Looking at the point of rest in individual markets rather than all markets taken together. See also *General equilibrium*.

Perfect competition   A market that has an infinite number of sellers selling exactly the same (homogenous) products.

Phillips curve   A curve first envisaged by A.W.H. Phillips that shows an inverse relationship between inflation and unemployment.

Price discrimination   Charging different prices to different consumers for the same product, or charging the same consumer different prices for the same product depending on how much he or she buys.

Price elasticity of demand (PeD)   Calculated by dividing the percentage change in quantity demanded by the percentage change in price, this is an indicator of the sensitivity of demand to price.

Price elasticity of supply (PeS)   Calculated by dividing the percentage change in quantity supplied by the percentage change in price, this is an indicator of the sensitivity of supply to price.

Privatisation   The act of selling the public sector to the private sector.

Profit   Calculated by subtracting costs from revenues, this surplus is paid to the owners of the firm as payment for the use of their capital.

Public goods   Goods or services which have the characteristics of 'non-excludability' and 'non-rivalness'. That is, they provide benefits that are not exclusive to the purchaser but accrue to others too (non-excludability), but which are also not diminished by being shared (non-rival consumption). Examples include the light from a lighthouse, signposts and national defence.

Q

Quasi (internal) market   An arrangement, often in the public sector, that has some of the features of a market but not all.

R

Real terms   The value of something after inflation is stripped out of the figures.

Rent   Payment for the use of land or buildings. See also *Economic rent.*

S

Short run   Period in which at least one factor of production is fixed.

Social capital   The stock of goodwill within and amongst the members of an organisation.

Substitution effect   When the price of a good changes demand will change for two reasons. Firstly, because the change in price means that the good has become cheaper (or dearer) relative to other goods, people will switch to it (or away from it). This is the substitution effect. Secondly, the price change effectively makes consumers richer (or poorer) since when they buy it more (or less) is left over for other things. See also *Income effect.*

Sunk costs   Costs that cannot be recovered if a firm decides to exit from a market. The higher this and other exit barriers are, the more firms have to risk in entering a market. This means that firms planning to enter a market have to consider exit as well as entry barriers. See also *Contestable market.*

Super normal profits   Profits in excess of normal profits. See *Normal profits.*

Supply   Amount made available at different prices.

Supply curve   A graph of the amount that would be made available at different prices assuming other things remain constant. See also *Ceteris paribus.*

Supply-side economics   A school of macroeconomists who believe that the manipulation of aggregate demand is an ineffective way of improving output and that therefore more emphasis should be given by governments to encouraging the supply side of the economy.

T

Transfer earnings The minimum payment necessary to attract and keep the services of a factor of production.

Transfer payments Payments made by governments to people that do not involve an exchange for productive effort, such as pensions and social security payments.

U

Unemployment In theory, the number of people who would work at the prevailing wage if they could find a job. In practice official definitions vary.

Utility The satisfaction a buyer gets from a good or service.

V

Variable costs Costs which are affected by the level of output of a firm.

VAT (Value Added Tax) An indirect *ad valorem* tax levied in the UK on the sale of many goods and services.

Veblen good (conspicuous consumption good) A good for which a price fall will lead to less demand because a part of the reason for buying the good is because it was expensive. This is likely where the good can be seen to confer high status to the buyer (even if only in the minds of the buyers themselves), although examples are rare.

Vertical integration The joining, through merger or take-over, of firms at different stages of production. For example, a clothes manufacturer may move upstream into the production of cloth or downstream into clothes retailing.

Visible trade Exports and imports of tangible goods.

W

Wages The price of labour.

Wage–price spiral Since workers' real incomes are reduced if their pay increase does not match an increase in inflation, a rise in inflation can lead to higher wage claims. Higher wages will put firms' costs up which will mean that their profits fall unless they pass this on in terms of higher prices, and so a vicious circle can be formed in which wages and prices spiral higher and higher. The fundamental problem is that neither workers nor firms are willing to accept a cut in their real incomes.

World Trade Organisation (WTO) The framework that ensures regular agreements are signed to keep countries open to international trade.

X

X-inefficiency Failure to produce at minimum costs.

REFERENCES

Adler, N.J. (1991) *International dimensions of organizational behaviour*, 2nd edn. Kent: PWS

Alchian, A.A. and Demsetz, H. (1972) Production, information costs and economic organization. *American Economic Review*, **62**(Dec.), 777–95

Aldrich, H.E. (1979) *Organisations and Environments*. Englewood Cliffs: Prentice Hall

Ansoff, I. (1981) *Strategic Management*. New York: Halstead Press

Argyris, C. (1987) Review essay; first and second order errors in managing strategic change; the role of organisational defensive routines. In *The Management of Strategic Change* (Pettigrew, A.M., ed.). Oxford: Blackwell

Arrow, K.J. (1950) A difficulty in the concept of social welfare. *Journal of Political Economy*, 58

Arthur, W.B. (1996) Increasing returns and the new world of business. *Harvard Business Review*, July–August

Bacon, R. and Eltis, W. (1976) *Britain's Economic Problem – too few producers*. London: Macmillan

Bain, J.S. (1959) *Industrial Organisation*. New York: Wiley

Bank of England (1996) How do companies set prices'. *Bank of England Quarterly Bulletin*, **36**(2)

Baumol, W.J. (1959) *Business Behaviour, Value and Growth*. New York: Macmillan

Baumol, W.J., Panzar, J.C. and Willig, R.D. (1982) *Contestable Markets and the Theory of Industry Structure*. New York: Harcourt Brace Jovanovich

Becker, G.S. (1957) *The Economics of Discrimination*. Chicago: University of Chicago Press

Becker, G.S. (1975) *Human Capital*. New York: Columbia University Press

Berger, P.L. and Luckmann, T. (1967) *The Social Construction of Reality*. Garden City, NY: Anchor Books

Blau, P.M. (1970) A formal theory of differentiation in organisations. *American Sociological Review*, **35**(2), 201–18

Blumer, H. (1962) Society as symbolic interaction. In Rose, A.M. (1969) *Symbolic Interactionism*. Englewood Cliffs, NJ: Prentice Hall

Burns, T. and Stalker, G.M. (1961) *The Management of Innovation*. London: Tavistock

Cadbury, Sir A. (1992) *Report of the committee on the financial aspects of corporate governance*. London: Gee

Chandler, A.D. Jr. (1962) *Strategy and Structure: Chapters in the History of American Industrial Enterprise*. Cambridge, MA: MIT Press

403

Child, J. (1972) Organisational structure, environment and performance; the role of strategic choice. *Sociology*, **6**(1), 1–22

Clegg, S. and Dunkerley, D. (1980) *Organisations, Class and Control*. London: Routledge & Kegan Paul

Clemens, E.W. (1950) Price discrimination and the multiple product firm. *Review of Economic Studies*, **17**(1), 2

Coase, R.H. (1937) The nature of the firm. *Economica*, **4**(Nov.), 386–405

Coase, R.H. (1960) The problem of social cost. *Journal of Law and Economics*, **2**(Oct.), 1–40.

Cyert, R.M. and March, J.G. (1963) *A Behavioural Theory of the Firm*. Englewood Cliffs, NJ: Prentice Hall

Darwin, C. (1859) *The Origin of Species by Means of National Selection, or the Preservation of Favoured Races in the Struggle for Life*. London

David, P.A. (1985) Clio and the economics of QWERTY. *American Economic Review (Papers and Proceedings)*, **75**(2), 332–7

Donaldson, L. (1985) *In Defense of Organisation Theory; a Reply to the Critics*. Cambridge: Cambridge University Press

Donaldson, L. (1987) Strategy and structural adjustment to regain fit and performance; in defense of contingency theory. *Journal of Management Studies*, **24**(1), 1–24

Emery, F.E. and Trist, E.L. (1965) The causal texture of organisational environments. *Human Relations*, **18**, 21–31

Fama, E.F. (1980) Agency problem and the theory of the firm. *Journal of Political Economy*, **88**(6)

Friedman, M. (1953) *Essays in Positive Economics*. Chicago: University of Chicago Press

Friedman, M. (1962) *Capitalism and Freedom*. Chicago: University of Chicago Press

Galbraith, J.K. (1967) *The New Industrial State*. London: Hamish Hamilton

Garfinkel, H. (1967) *Studies in Ethnomethodology*. Englewood Cliffs, NJ: Prentice Hall

Giddens, A. (1979) *Central Problems in Social Theory: Action, Structure, and Contradictions in Social Analysis*. London: Macmillan

Granovetter, M. (1982) Problems of explanation in economic sociology. In *Networks and Organisations: Structure, Form and Action* (Nohria, N. and Eccles, R.G. (eds)). Boston: Harvard Business School Press

Hall, R.L. and Hitch, C.J. (1939) Price theory and business behaviour. *Oxford Economic Papers*, **2**, May

Hannan, M.T. and Freeman, J. (1977) The population ecology of organisations. *American Journal of Sociology*, **82**(5), 929–64

Hannan, M.T. and Freeman, J. (1989) *Organisational Ecology*. Cambridge, MA: Harvard University Press

Herman, E.S. (1981) *Corporate Control, Corporate Power*. Cambridge: Cambridge University Press

Hofstede, G. (1983) Dimensions of national culture in fifty countries and three regions. In *Expiscations in Cross-Cultural Psychology* (Deregowski, J., Dziurawiec, S. and Hunis, R.C. (eds), Lise, Netherlands: Swets and Zeitlinger.

Holl, P. (1977) Control types and the market for corporate control in large US corporations. *Journal of Industrial Economics*, **25**(4), 259–73

Hughes, A. (1993) Mergers and economic performance in the UK: a survey of the empirical evidence, 1950–90. In *European Mergers and Merger Policy* (Bishop and Kay, eds). Oxford: Oxford University Press

Jensen, M.C. and Murphy, K.J. (1990) CEO incentives – its not how much you pay. *Harvard Business Review*, **68**(3), 138–53

Jobber, D. and Hooley, G. (1987) Pricing behaviour in UK manufacturing and service industries. *Managerial and Decision Economics*, **8**, 167–77

Kerr, C., Dunlop, J.T., Harbison, F. and Myers, C.A. (1960) *Industrialism and Industrial Man*. Cambridge, MA: Harvard University Press

Keynes, J.M. (1936) *The General Theory of Employment, Interest and Money*. London: Macmillan

Khandwalla, P.N. (1977) *The Design of Organisations*. New York: Harcourt Brace Jovanovich

Kondratieff, N.D. (1922) *The world economy and its cycles during and after the war*. Vologda: Oblasture Otdelenie Gosudartsvennogo Izdatelstva

Lancaster, K. (1971) *Consumer Demand: A New Approach*. New York: Columbia University Press

Lawrence, P.R. and Lorsch, J.W. (1967) *Organisation and Environment: Managing Differentiation and Integration*. Boston: Division of Research, Graduate School of Business Administration

Layard, R. and Nichell, S. (1985) The causes of British unemployment. *National Institute Economic Review*, No. 111, February

Leibenstein, H. (1966) Allocative efficiency versus x-efficiency. *American Economic Review*, 56(3)

Levitt, T. (1983) The globalisation of markets. *Harvard Business Review*, May–June

Manne, H.M. (1965) Mergers and the market for corporate control. *Journal of Political Economy*, 71

Marris, R. (1964) *The Economic Theory of Managerial Capitalism*. New York: Free Press

Marshall, A. (1890) *Principles of Economics; an introductory text*. London: Macmillan (1956)

Maslow, A. (1943) A theory of human motivation. *Psychological Review*, 50(4), 370–96

Mason, E.S. (1939) Price and production policies of large-scale enterprise. *American Economic Review*, supplement 29, 61–74

Mayo, G.E. (1949) *The Social Problems of an Industrial Civilisation*. London: Routledge & Keegan Paul

Miller, D. and Droge, C. (1986) 'Psychological and traditional determinants of structure'. *Administrative Science Quarterly*, 31(4), 539–60

Mintzberg, H. (1979) *The Structuring of Organisations; A Synthesis of the Research*. Englewood Cliffs, NJ: Prentice Hall

Mintzberg, H. (1995) The structuring of organisations. In Mintzberg, H., Quinn, J.B. and Ghoshal, S., *The Strategy Process*, pp. 332–53. London: Prentice Hall

Nelson, R.R. and Winter, S.G. (1982) *An Evolutionary Theory of Economic Change*. Cambridge, MA: Harvard University Press

Nordhaus, W. and Tobin, J. (1972) Is growth obsolete? In *Economic Growth*, National Bureau of Economic Research 50th Anniversary Colloquium, New York: Columbia University Press

Nyman, S. and Silberston, Z.A. (1978) The ownership and control of industry. *Oxford Economics Papers*, 30(1)

Parsons, T. (1956) A sociological approach to the theory of organisations. *Administrative Science Quarterly*, 1, 63–85

Penrose, E.T. (1958) *The Theory of the Growth of the Firm*. Oxford: Basil Blackwell

Perrow, C. (1979) *Complex Organisations: A Critical Essay*. Dallas: Scott Foresman

Phillips, A.W. (1958) The relationship between unemployment and the rate of change of money wage rates in the United Kingdom, 1861–1957. *Economica*, 55(Nov.)

Porter, M.E. (1980) *Competitive Strategy: Techniques for Analysing Industries and Competitors*. New York: The Free Press

Porter, M.E. (1985) *Competitive Advantage: Creating and Sustaining Superior Performance*. New York: The Free Press

Porter, M.E. (1990) *The Competitive Advantage of Nations*. New York: Macmillan

Prahalad, C.K. and Hamel, G. (1990) The core competencies of the corporation. *Harvard Business Review*, **66**, 79–91

Pratten, C.F. (1988) A survey of the economies of scale. In *Research on the Costs of Non-Europe*, Vol. 2 (CE Commission). Office for Official Publications of the European Communities

Prowse, S.D. (1992) The structure of corporate ownership in Japan. *The Journal of Finance*, **47**(3), 1121–40

Rumelt, R.P. (1991) How Much Does Industry Matter? *Strategic Management Journal*, **12**(3)

Scott, J. (1985) The British upper class. In *A Socialist Anatomy of Britain* (Coates, D., Johnson, G. and Bush, R. eds). Oxford: Polity Press

Schmalensee, R. (1985) Do markets differ much? *American Economic Review*, **75**(3)

Schumacher, E.F. (1973) *Small is Beautiful: A reconsideration of Economics as if people mattered*. London: Blond & Briggs

Shackle, G.L.S. (1949) *Expectation in Economics*. Cambridge: Cambridge University Press

Shipley, D.D. (1981) Primary objectives in British manufacturing industry. *Journal of Industrial Economics*, **29**(4)

Simon, H.A. (1957) *Models of Man*. New York: John Wiley & Sons

Simon, H.A. (1959) Theories of decision making in economics and behavioural science. *American Economic Review*, **69**(3)

Smircich, L. and Stubbart, C. (1985) Strategic management in an enacted world. *Academy of Management Review*, **10**(4), 724–36

Smith, A. (1759) *The Theory of Moral Sentiments*. New York: A.M. Kelly (1966)

Smith, A. (1776) *An Enquiry into the Nature and Causes of the Wealth of Nations*.

Stinchcombe, A.L. (1965) Social structure and organisations. In *Handbook of Organisations* (J.G. March, ed.). Chicago: Rand McNally

Taylor, F.W. (1911) *Scientific Management*. London: Harper & Row (1964)

Thompson, J.D. (1967) J.D. *Organisations in Action*. New York: McGraw Hill

Tinbergen, J. (1952) *On the Theory of Economic Policy*. Amsterdam: North–Holland

Von Neuman, J. and Morgenstern, O. (1944) *Theory of Games and Economic Behaviour*. Princeton, NJ: Princeton University Press

Weber, M. (1922) *Economy and Society*. New York: Bedminster Press (1968)

Weick, K. (1969) *The Social Psychology of Organizing*. Reading, MA: Addison-Wesley

Whittington, R. (1989) *Corporate Strategies in Recession and Recovery*. London: Unwin Hyman

Williamson, O.E. (1963) Managerial Discretion and Business Behaviour. *American Economic Review*, **53**(5).

Woodward, J. (1965) *Industrial Organisation: Theory and Practice*. London: Oxford University Press

INDEX